# THE COMPLETE URBAN GARDENER

# THE COMPLETE URBAN GARDENER

## by Joan Puma

*Drawings by Jeryl English*

*A Harper Colophon Book*

1817

Harper & Row, Publishers

*New York, Cambridge, Philadelphia, San Francisco*
*London, Mexico City, São Paulo, Singapore, Sydney*

FIRST EDITION

*Designer: Nancy Sugihara*

Library of Congress Cataloging in Publication Data

Puma, Joan.
  The complete urban gardener.

  Includes index.
  1. Gardening. I. Title. II. Title: Urban gardener.
SB453.P77 1985     635.9′86     83-48376
ISBN 0-06-015402-0                    85 86 87 88 89 10 9 8 7 6 5 4 3 2 1
ISBN 0-06-091106-9 (pbk.)             85 86 87 88 89 10 9 8 7 6 5 4 3 2 1

*This book is dedicated to Kenny and Jesse*

# Contents

# Part Two
## The Plants  175

# Part Three
## Special Gardens  317

*Color illustrations follow page 210.*

*I'd like to thank the following people without whose help this book would not have been possible: Susan Cohen, Steve Wylie, Gary Cohen, Mindi Auten, Paul Blutter, and Nancy Bruning.*

# Introduction: Why Urban Gardening?

*On the well worn stone*
*Garlanded with*
*Pinks of spring . . .*
*Oh to drink and doze!*
  *—Basho*

BLARING HORNS, filthy streets, hot, crowded subways and stifling apartments are all conditions we have reluctantly accepted as a natural function of urban living. We need to live here and we enjoy living here, but cities are artificial environments that breed tension and frustration. We need the balance of a more natural surrounding to relax and find renewal in the basics of life. A few creative individuals have found a way to achieve that balance and enrich their lives in a unique way: They have brought nature to the city through rooftop or terrace gardening.

To them, gardening has become a necessity, an essential part of their urban environment. High above the city streets they enjoy the evening twilight with friends, or the Sunday paper in solitude. They can experience the exquisite pleasure of the first warm spring day when the air is clear and light filters through young green leaves, creating the transparent quality of stained glass. Flowers never seem quite so beautiful and the taste of fresh home-grown fruits and vegetables can't compare with the puny store-bought varieties. Roof or terrace gardens simultaneously represent an inexpensive substitute for a country home, a much-needed vacation, a new form of entertainment, and a challenging pastime. These tiny patches of green that are found throughout our cities do more than help freshen our air and reduce our noise; they help attract the last remaining wildlife that inhabit our concrete desert. High above the street-level confusion, a giant dragonfly with delicate transparent wings perches on a brick wall. Birds come to feed, filling our heads with delicate melodies. A praying mantis snaps into action. Few city dwellers are aware that such things exist in an urban environment. There are quite a few surprises in store for a novice gardener.

In a sense, roof and terrace gardening is the creation of mini-ecosystems —environments where even the soil must be supplied. But this also has its advantages. You control and manipulate most aspects of your garden. Plants that could never normally grow side by side can do so in containers. Whether your fantasy is a casual English cottage garden or a Japanese garden complete with goldfish pond for quiet contemplation, you can realize your dream—even if you have no prior knowledge of gardening. *The Complete Urban Gardener* makes it possible for you to succeed. It is broken down into easily assimilated chapters that both the beginner and advanced gardener will find interesting and informative. This book will give you more than a general understanding of the different forces that affect your plants; it also tells you how to manipulate these forces and apply them to rooftop gardening. It offers solutions to those problems that are most often encountered, with special emphasis on the ones most responsible for failure. At the end of many chapters are easy reference charts to put pertinent information at your fingertips quickly.

*The Complete Urban Gardener* is the result of years of experience and study. It is the only book of its kind available today, and it will make your gardening experience a much more enjoyable and rewarding one.

# PART ONE

# Gardening Techniques

# ❧ 1 ❧
# Before You Begin

BEFORE CREATING YOUR HIDEAWAY PARADISE IN THE SKY, you'll need to do a little homework, to make sure all your efforts don't backfire.

( ) 1. Check the building codes in your area, making sure there are no local ordinances prohibiting roof gardening. Also check the fire codes, which should be listed in the Department of Housing in your municipality. Follow any regulations pertaining to roof gardening, or the use of the roof, to the letter.

( ) 2. Get written permission from your landlord or co-op association. If he refuses to grant you permission, it is because he fears damage to the building. Agree to be responsible for any repairs that you may incur. Follow his wishes precisely. Roof gardening takes time and work; make sure you don't have to dismantle it a month later.

( ) 3. Once your landlord does agree, you should discuss who has right of access. The fire codes in most cities stipulate that any doors to the roof must be capable of being opened from the inside. This means that you cannot lock the door to keep your neighbors out. One of them may decide to spend a great deal of time there enjoying your hard work. This can result in a difficult situation which can be settled before the matter arises if you attach a rider to your lease giving you sole right of access to the roof except in case of emergency.

( ) 4. Check the roof's structure for soundness, and if you need it, get expert advice from an architect or building contractor. They can tell you how much weight your roof can comfortably hold, as well as where to place any large containers for the best weight distribution. Depending on its size, a container of wet earth can weigh several hundred pounds. Also ask them if the roof appears to be draining sufficiently and quickly.

( ) 5. Consult a roofing contractor on the nature of the surface material. Make sure it is in good condition to begin with. You certainly don't want to pay for any damages you didn't cause. Make sure it can take the weight of heavy containers (especially after the surface has been softened by the sun's heat) and the constant contact with moisture. Also ask if a deck is needed to save wear and tear on the roof.

( ) 6. Last but not least, decide on the amount of money you can afford to spend—and stick with it. Projects of this magnitude have a way of escalating. Remember a garden is a long-term project and need not be built in one season. Now is the time to find out if friends living in the country can give you some free plants or gardening supplies.

# ❧ 2 ❧

# The Design

YOUR GARDEN CAN BE AS SMALL AS ONE CHAIR surrounded by a few flowerpots or it can be as elaborate as any estate, complete with flowering trees and a grape arbor. Whatever you desire, the best designs begin with a sound budget and a good plan. Knowing what you can afford to spend allows you to establish your priorities and a timetable for major projects. Planning can also cut down on unnecessary work over the years.

It is possible to spend almost any amount of money on the design of a beautiful garden, but it can be just as rewarding to produce the same results inexpensively. If this is your first attempt at roof gardening, begin with a limited number of containers. Supplement these with your houseplants, which will respond with lush growth in exchange for their "summer vacation." A garden in artificial surroundings depends on you for its very existence. It takes a great deal of effort, and, if done on a large scale, can be a costly experiment.

## *The Overview*

The best way to begin your design is with a thorough evaluation of your roof or terrace. Using graph paper, draw an accurate floor plan including the dimensions and indicating compass points. Later on when you are actually working out the garden design you can do so with tracing paper laid over the detailed plan. Spend time in the garden space just sitting and looking. One of the first things you'll notice will be its shape, whether it is square or rectangular, whether there are any large structures such as skylights, a water tower, or elevator housing. You'll also notice whether your space affords any privacy, or whether it is relatively open. The more time you spend the more details you'll observe. You'll begin to get a feeling for the good points, such as a great view, and the bad points that you'll want to disguise completely. Jot these down on paper and begin thinking of them in terms of features or problems.

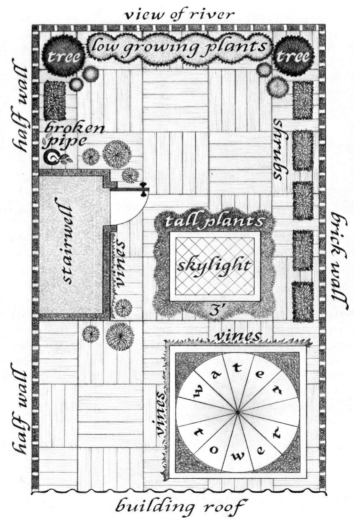

Fig. 1   *A good floor plan of a rooftop garden*

Next, consider how you intend to use your garden. Do you want a quiet corner to sit and read, or a place to entertain friends? Decisions like these can make a major difference in the design. The best gardens are those that are based on the uniqueness of each situation. Slowly you'll begin to have a pretty good idea of what you want and the problems you'll need to solve.

## Balcony and Terrace Design

If you are planning a balcony or terrace garden, don't forget to spend time studying the views of your garden that can be seen from inside your apartment. These little scenes will be viewed all year long, so remember to choose plants that will have interesting forms in December. Include some evergreens for winter cheer.

If you have a roof over your balcony don't forget about it when designing your garden. If you think the roof is unattractive then consider covering or painting it. You can also use it to hang baskets of flowers or string wire from floor to ceiling for permanent vine support.

## The Basic Elements

There are several basic elements that go into every design: the surface, lighting and electricity, the plants, color, plant containers, and garden furniture. Each element is treated separately but all combine to produce an easily maintained garden that has a feeling of unity.

## The Surface

A balcony is made to be walked upon and support weight, so surface is not a critical issue. For a roof garden, the surface is the single most important element that you will have to deal with while designing your garden. It determines whether you need to build a deck, the type of furniture to use, and even the type of footwear to be worn. It must be handled in a way that causes the least amount of stress to the building below.

No matter what your surface is made of, both your roof and your plants will fare better if your containers are raised. The roof will not be in constant contact with moisture and the plants will benefit from better air circulation and cooler temperatures by not being in constant contact with the roof's broiling surface. A concrete or tile surface can take the constant abuse of heavy traffic and furniture legs. Concrete, however, is hot and may become uncomfortable to walk on. You may decide to build a wooden deck for needed relief.

If your roof is covered with tar paper, you will have to build a deck to protect it. The paper is a soft material that can tear easily. Bricks or cinder blocks should not be used to raise plants since they can puncture the tar paper once it has been softened by the heat of the sun. They also retain moisture for long periods, which is damaging. Furniture legs or high heels can also damage the surface. Limit your guests to flat, soft-soled shoes. If someone should forget, I keep an assortment of Chinese thongs on hand and ask them to change into these. My concern is not only for the surface but also for the safety of my guests.

A custom-made deck may not be for everyone, but it certainly goes a long way toward creating a good design. Try using a triangular or circular motif to counterbalance the feeling of a bowling alley. Also consider building a multilevel deck to create a more interesting visual space. The best woods to use in terms of long life are redwood, cedar, teak, and cypress, but these are more expensive than pine. In any event, all wood needs to be treated to prevent rotting.

Even if you rent, you may wish to build a custom deck. A deck need not be permanent. It can be designed in modular units for easy removal and transport (3' × 3' units are a good versatile size). There are other advantages to these modular units. If a problem develops with the roof's surface, you can get to it easily without ripping up the whole deck. It's also easier to clean up plant debris. If you don't have the money to build a custom deck, don't despair. They are nice, but not necessary. If you live near an industrial area, keep an eye out for the skids or pallets used to load or unload merchandise from trucks. Very often perfectly good ones are thrown away, and these can make an adequate deck. You can preserve them with a coat of polyurethane, but because of the nature of the wood they're made of, they won't last for more than a few seasons. Still, considering the price, this isn't a bad deal.

## Garden Lighting

If you plan to use your garden at night, now is the time to incorporate some form of lighting for safety reasons. This need not be elaborate or even permanent. An extension cord made for outdoor use can run from your apartment to the roof. (Be careful not to use it if the plug or outlet gets wet.) One or two flood lamps in most cases will do the trick. If you wish for more moody lighting, try hiding a few low-watt bulbs behind plant containers.

## Using Plants Effectively

No matter what design problem you need to solve, there is a plant that can do it. Plants vary in size and shape, texture and color. Some are tall, others short, some cascade or climb. Any area, no matter how unattractive, can be beautified with the well-thought-out addition of a few plants.

Liabilities can be turned into assets, and assets into star attractions. An old pipe or broken wall can become a place of interest with the addition of a surprise or two. Of course, make sure that pipe you plan to use is not a vent line.

In order to use plants effectively there are a few basic rules you should follow. A good design incorporates the principles of balance, proportion, and visual unity to achieve impact. Plants are much more effective when massed together in asymmetrical groupings to act as a focal point. Balance and proportion can be achieved by using mass, form, and color to create visual weight. When creating a border of plants, don't stretch out the containers into a thin, straight, single-file line. The individual plants will look lost on a roof. Instead, create curved borders, especially around corners, to soften the hard geometric lines. Use a double or triple row of closely spaced plants, with the taller ones in large containers at the rear and shorter or cascading plants in small containers in the foreground. If you have a large specimen such as a tree or shrub, surround it with smaller containers filled with colorful flowers. As they grow, the foreground plants will mask the larger containers behind them.

*Fig. 2   Softening a corner*

Visual unity is an important element in any design, and in a garden where there are so many diverse elements it becomes all the more important. Pick a couple of plant motifs and repeat them throughout the garden. This can take the form of repeating certain species such as petunias, and by choosing a color scheme and sticking to it. Your containers should be limited to one type of material, such as wood, or one color, such as all green containers. The same goes for garden furniture.

Visual unity does not rule out variety but rather acts as a means of taming it. Variety in a garden is important and necessary, but it doesn't necessarily mean a wide assortment of plants and colors. It also means a diversification of forms and textures. Plants come in all sizes and shapes from the tall and narrow to the short and creeping. Leaves can be soft and feathery, swordlike, or deeply lobed and shiny. Green also comes in many shades, from dark forest green to silver gray. Plants grown for their foliage are a wonderful contrast to those grown strictly for their flowers.

Remember that plants can be grown vertically as well as horizontally. Make use of vines and hanging baskets or containers to accent and decorate walls. Place some above eye level. In nature you are completely surrounded by greenery; try to continue this feeling in the garden. Also remember that the shortest distance between two points is not always the most interesting. Create a little mystery by hiding certain areas from view and connect them with a meandering path to explore. Experiment a little. If you make a mistake, there is no need to worry. Plants in containers can be moved at will to create a new look.

# Color

While you're deciding what plants to use, another factor to consider is the use of color to create visual effects. Color in any garden is important, but in a roof garden flowers are concentrated in a small area and make a greater impact than in normal gardening situations.

Once you understand the theory of color you can begin to use it to your advantage to create the effect you want. For example, color can effectively frame a lovely view or draw your attention to a distant spot. It can make your garden seem larger, longer, or wider. It can calm, cool, or excite the viewer. Artists and designers have been using these principles ever since they were discovered. Gardeners, working with plants as their palette, can use them too.

*The Color Wheel.* The easiest way to begin to learn about the theory of color is by using an artist's color wheel. This simple device makes it much easier to understand. In nature it may be impossible to find colors that directly match the true colors of the wheel; nevertheless, the device will enable you to visualize what colors will harmonize or serve as dramatic complements to each other.

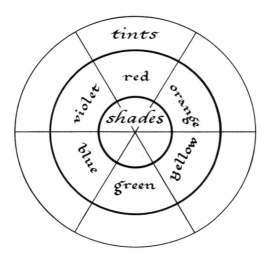

*Fig. 3    The color wheel*

There are six basic colors of the rainbow—red, orange, yellow, green, blue, and violet. These are arranged in a circle like the spokes of a wheel. Each color has another one directly opposite. When these opposite colors are placed side by side they enhance or complement each other, creating an explosion of color. Thus they are called *complementary colors.* No other combination of colors will grab the attention more than a pair of complementary colors. For a more restful approach substitute the pastel tints of the same colors. This will give you a similar effect but in a much softer, more subtle way.

Bright colors such as red and yellow hold the attention better than pastels or blues. To draw attention to a particular spot or view, plant bright red or yellow clumps of flowers as illustrated in the color insert following page 212. These same colors planted on the outside of a window will make the room appear larger. But take these same colors and plant them in multitudes along the edge of your roof and they will confine the attention of the viewer to the roof. Blues and violets give a feeling of coolness and quiet. Planted at the far end of a garden, they will give the impression of greater depth and will make a small terrace appear less claustrophobic.

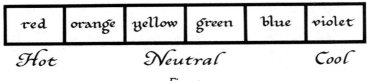

*Fig. 4*

Whatever colors you choose, they are as much a reflection of you as the clothes you wear. Some people feel a small splash goes a long way, while others enjoy color in bold strokes. While some gardeners approach color with a sense of precision, choosing flowers to achieve various degrees of subtlety, others seek to make the biggest splash possible.

Whatever you decide your design should look like, trust your own instinct. A beautiful garden can be created with a color wheel, but a gardener who stands back and surveys his empty space will create just as beautiful an effect. And just in case, Mother Nature will be there to smooth out rough edges.

## Choosing Containers

A good plant container does more than just hold soil, and its size and shape should conform to the needs of the plant it holds. Just as plants vary, so do their root systems. Some have shallow fibrous roots, while others have longer tap roots. The same container would not be right for both. A good plant container should have ample room for good healthy root growth, yet it cannot be so large that it dwarfs the plant it contains. A 6-inch flowerpot will not hold a 3-foot plant and a 6-inch plant will not be noticed in a 3-foot container.

A container must provide good drainage, yet it should help hold moisture for a reasonable period of time. If the container is too small, water will quickly evaporate on a hot roof, robbing the plant of much-needed moisture. At the same time, excess moisture must drain quickly or plant roots will be robbed of much-needed air and suffocate. A container should hold at least a gallon of soil—about as much as a standard 8-inch flowerpot. Any plants that are rootbound, (whose roots have outgrown

Fig. 5  Found objects as containers

*Fig. 6    A custom-made wooden container*

their containers and have become entangled) should be repotted before being placed on a hot roof.

One of the easiest ways to have your garden look good is by keeping all the containers uniform. They can vary in size, but should be made of the same material. They should also be unobtrusive, bringing out rather than diminishing the character of the plants they contain. Stay away from containers that are elaborately decorated or brightly colored.

Found objects can make excellent containers and add a whimsical touch. An old john, a chest, or even that old bathtub you were going to discard, can be pressed into service. Wooden packing crates and bushel baskets make wonderful containers even though they only last a few seasons. If you're an apartment dweller, that may be all that is necessary. Wonderful containers can be obtained from building sites. Plastic five-gallon cans used to hold jointing compound are perfect once you remove the label, and old terracotta chimney pots can make lovely additions to any garden.

*Wood Containers.* Wood containers give a pleasing natural look to an otherwise unnatural environment. Against the brown and gray tones of wood, plants stand out beautifully. Wood is also a good insulator, holding in heat at night and protecting roots against sudden changes in temperature. Because it is also porous it allows for good ventilation, but at the same time it can also mean a quicker loss of moisture and the need for more frequent watering. This is especially true of small containers. It is a good idea to line all small wooden containers with plastic garbage bags. Remember to poke drainage holes in the plastic. Whiskey barrels sold in garden centers will not need to be lined, but a few holes must be drilled in the bottom with a ½-inch bit for drainage.

Because wood is a natural substance, it goes the way of all natural substances eventually. In the face of constant weathering and the onslaught of various microbial organisms, it begins to break down. You can help wood last longer by preserving it. A word of caution here: Petroleum-based preservatives such as creosote or pentachlorophenol are toxic to plants. Instead, try polyurethane or a preservative based on copper naphthenate (Cuprinol for Florists No. 14, or Salignum), which are totally safe for plants.

Whether you use packing crates or have your containers custom made, reinforce the corners. Just because water is mixed in with a little soil doesn't prevent the old rule from applying, namely that water expands when frozen. Unfortunately, so will your container.

*Terracotta and Clay.* Terracotta flowerpots are the old standard of the gardening world, coming in many sizes and shapes, glazed and unglazed, from the tiniest thumb pot to those large enough to hold small trees.

Pot size, whether terracotta or plastic, is always referred to by the diameter of the top inside wall. All terracotta pots fall into three categories according to the depth of the pot. A standard pot is as tall as it is wide. An azalea pot (so called because it is traditionally used to pot azaleas) is three quarters as tall as it is wide, and a *pan,* usually used for planting bulbs or small groupings of plants, is half as high as it is wide.

Tall plants that have a tendency to get knocked over in a strong wind are best potted in a terracotta azalea pot. The heavy weight of terracotta and the squat shape of an azalea pot combine to act as a firm anchor to keep plants upright. This is important to prevent serious plant damage.

Of course terracotta, like wood, is porous unless it is glazed. It is also a thirsty material, absorbing moisture in large amounts. It can actually pull moisture from the soil, making small terracotta containers impractical on a hot roof. You will be better off with plastic containers. Terracotta pots must also be emptied and turned over every fall to prevent breakage from freezing.

*Plastic.* Plastic is a lightweight, durable, nonporous material with tremendous insulating properties. It comes in an array of textures and colors, suitable to any decor, and it is extremely inexpensive. Plastic requires no maintenance and, unlike terracotta, it is fairly unbreakable.

Plastic containers don't have to be limited to those bought in plant stores. There are many kitchen pails and basins that are attractive and inexpensive. A toddler's wading pool can also be pressed into service to house an array of small low-growing species. Since plastic is nonporous, all plastic containers will need an adequate number of drainage holes (the easiest way to make them is with a poker or a screwdriver heated over a kitchen stove). Be sure to place a generous layer of drainage material in the bottom of each container as well. Taller plants tend to be top heavy and can blow over. For this reason it is best to reserve the use of terracotta for larger plants and use plastic containers for small ones.

*Styrofoam.* Styrofoam has many qualities that make it an ideal container material. It is porous, allowing air circulation to the roots, lightweight, durable, and a good insulator. It will keep roots cool in summer and warm in winter. Many plants that will not survive in other kinds of containers will make it when planted in styrofoam.

Small styrofoam pots can be found in most dime stores, as can styrofoam ice chests. Try purchasing these at the end of the summer when they are on sale. Remember to punch holes in the bottom for drainage.

*Metal.* Like plastic, metal containers are nonporous, but unlike plastic they are poor insulators. On hot days they will absorb heat quickly and burn plant roots, while on cool nights they will not hold soil warmth. Plants in metal containers are much more prone to frost damage, and rusting metal is damaging to plants. Unlike plastic, metal is not an inert substance. As it oxidizes, it combines with other elements in the soil, locking up nutrients.

Enamel bowls that are found in variety stores fall under this category but have somewhat better properties. The metal is enclosed and cannot oxidize as quickly, and white enamel will reflect more heat than it will absorb; but it still is a poor insulator.

*Concrete.* Concrete containers are extremely heavy and are not recommended for a roof. They are also alkaline and will change the pH of your soil unless properly conditioned. Conditioning can be accomplished by leaving them outside to weather for a season, or by treating them with a solution of potassium permanganate. To do this, fill the container with water and add a sufficient amount of potassium permanganate grains to turn the water the color of port wine. Leave it for two or three days and then empty. Scrub the walls and base well with a yard broom and rinse with fresh water.

## Choosing Garden Furniture

A major concern of all gardeners is choosing furniture to make your experience more enjoyable. The choice of designs is wide enough to suit any taste or price range, but no matter what way your desires run there are two points that you should be aware of before choosing garden furniture. The first concerns the surface of your garden space. A furniture design incorporating four narrow postlike legs can puncture a tar-paper surface. They can also fall through widely spaced slats, taking their occupants for a tumble. If this describes your situation, choose furniture with bent-pole construction, which is not as likely to result in these types of problems. Redwood furniture, with its large 2 × 4 frames, will not usually cause any damage either.

The second point involves the weight of the furniture and the wind. If you suddenly find a favorite chair missing, don't blame your neighbor. Instead, look in the street below and pray that no one was hurt. It is amazing how much stronger a simple summer breeze at street level becomes on a roof. Up that high there are few obstacles to slow it down, and it can pick up a chair and carry it away easily. Unless you have wrought-iron or redwood furniture you should be concerned. Fold all chairs flat to the ground when not in use. An umbrella can become a giant sail and pull a table right over. Make sure they are closed when not in use. If a storm threatens, take all lightweight furniture inside for the duration and lay wrought iron and redwood chairs and benches on their sides. Chain all tables to a wall to ensure that they are not capable of being carried away. This is not an idle warning; the safety of others is at stake here.

# Commonly Encountered Design Problems

Here is a list of the most commonly encountered trouble situations found in roof and terrace gardens with suggestions on how to deal with them. Use these as a basis for solving your own unique situations.

## Severe Geometric Shape

The straight boxlike quality of most roofs can be softened by allowing the flower border to form curves, especially at corners. Varying degrees of plant height will also break up a linear feel. Include a tree and some shrubs as well as low-growing or cascading plants in the foreground.

## Bowling Alley or Tunnel Shape

You can break up the long narrow feeling of a roof by cutting it in half with a curved flower border. Leave room for a path to other areas of the roof. Group plants along the sides in a zigzag pattern to break up any long straight lines.

*Fig. 7  Avoiding a bowling-alley effect*

## Limited Space

Use vertical gardening to add a new dimension to a limited space. Walls are empty canvases waiting to be decorated with hanging plants and vines. Most garden centers carry containers made expressly for that purpose, or you can easily construct your own from a multitude of materials including wood, chickenwire, or plastic bags. Many garden plants including vegetables can be grown in this manner.

*Fig. 8    This grape arbor underplanted with ivy and bulbs breaks up a wide expanse of wall.*
*Landscape designer:* Nadine C. Zamichow *Photo:* Gene Klavan

# Unsightly Structures

Is that elevator housing or stairway housing an eyesore? Then cover it! Structures like these are waiting to be decorated with plants. This is a perfect opportunity for vertical gardening. To soften the corners place a tall plant at the center of the corner and gradually decrease the size of the plants as you move further away (see Fig. 2).

# A Water Tower

If you have a water tower on your roof, count yourself very lucky. The support structure is extremely sturdy and quite capable of supporting a woody vine such as a wisteria. With a minimum of effort, you can also convert that structure into a wonderful shady retreat or even a rainproof dining area.

# No Privacy, or Terrible View

To create privacy or block out a terrible view, construct a fence. Fences can be custom-built to conform to a wide variety of design styles. If you

*Fig. 9 This trellis not only masks an unsightly view but creates privacy also.*

*Landscape designer:* Nadine C. Zamichow *Photo:* Gene Klavan

cannot afford this approach or want something less permanent, you can construct an inexpensive fence from plastic garden netting or chicken-wire. Plastic netting that measures 6′ × 18′ can be purchased at garden centers. Place a few upright 2′×4′s across the roof at 4-foot intervals for support and attach the netting. Fast-growing vines will cover the netting in no time.

## A Crumbling Wall or a Broken Pipe

Don't fret. A crumbling wall can make a fine home for a rock garden. Plant succulents such as sedum or sempervivum (hens and chickens, house leeks). Include some phlox or miniature bulbs. A broken pipe makes a fine support for a climbing plant.

# ❧ 3 ❧

# Your Growing Environment

ROOF AND TERRACE GARDENING IS VERY DIFFERENT FROM IN-GROUND GARDENING. It is not subject to the same climatic conditions of an in-ground garden that exists a block away. The biggest difference involves temperature. The primary reason for this is that concrete absorbs and radiates more heat than soil, which tends to act as a buffer, insulating plants from fluctuating temperatures. What this means is that on a hot summer day plants that are grown in a sunny location are subject to more heat stress. This stress becomes far greater when the size of the container is very small. That is why container size is so important (see Chapter 2). Certain plants that do not tolerate intense heat will not do well on a roof even though they may thrive just a block away when planted in the ground. In winter, heat radiating up from the building below can also make it possible to grow certain marginal plants in a sunny, sheltered spot next to a wall. Certain plants normally grown as annuals and even certain houseplants have been known to survive these conditions in New York City during a mild year. The problems often associated with plant loss take place in the spring and fall. At these times temperature fluctuation is greatest. Plants grown in containers are not as well insulated. A severe early frost can damage plants before they are fully prepared for winter. A late winter thaw can warm up the soil too soon, tricking plants into their growth cycle early. Because of these factors, which can result in both dieback and root damage, certain plants that grow quite well in the ground nearby may not prove hardy on a roof or terrace. Temperature fluctuation in winter can also make it impossible to grow those plants that require an extended period of cold weather in more moderate areas. Plants grown in shady locations may on the other hand suffer damage from the lack of insulation around the roots during cold periods.

These higher temperatures will also affect the amount of light a plant may tolerate, since temperature and light are closely linked in their effect on plant metabolism. The more heat a plant is subject to, the less light it will tolerate. You may find that certain plants that require full sun elsewhere will only tolerate partial shade on a roof or terrace.

Drying winds are also a factor to contend with. High above the street there is nothing to break the force of the wind, and our urban canyons create strong updrafts. Wind, like water, follows the path of least resistance. If your building is shorter than the surrounding ones, you may find yourself in the middle of a wind tunnel. Topheavy plants will be knocked over. It is important to plant these in heavy, squat containers. A windy location will require more water, and winter damage may be more severe. Wind also has one big advantage: It keeps you and your plants cooler, making the summer season more tolerable and even pleasant.

One decidedly big difference in container culture is the soil. Although it is true that you will have to haul all of it to the garden, the advantage is that you can begin with the very best instead of having to contend with what is already there. This in turn allows you to space plants much closer together than is usually recommended unless you live in a particularly humid area such as the Pacific Northwest. Containers do limit the spread of plant roots, and it becomes doubly important to fertilize on a regular basis. Most large plants such as trees will eventually outgrow their containers and will need more permanent homes in the ground somewhere, but if you choose smaller, slower-growing specimens they can be enjoyed for many years. Container gardening will allow you to grow plants that have entirely different soil requirements side by side—an advantage not normally available to in-ground gardeners.

## Water in the Garden

Hotter temperatures, drying winds, and confinement in containers all add up to a tremendous need for water. Unlike in-ground plants, container-grown plants have no underground water deposits to draw on. The little bit of soil they are grown in dries out quickly. Instead of a deep once-a-week watering, your plants will probably have to be watered every day. This isn't such a terrible disadvantage, really. It gives you the opportunity to observe and enjoy your garden more closely and helps you to spot trouble before it gets out of hand.

Watering is a simple task but one that gives the novice a great deal of trouble. The difficulty arises when one does not know the difference between the terms soggy, wet, and moist. Soggy soil drips when you squeeze it and is used by children to form mud pies. Wet soil is just short of being soggy, while moist soil will not drip when squeezed but will form a ball in your hand. Soil should never be permitted to get soggy except for bog plants, even after the most intense storm. With proper drainage excess water should run out of the bottom of your containers. When watering you want to saturate the soil until it is *wet.* This includes large tubs, which tend to be underwatered. Remember that soil can hold one quarter of its volume in water. There is no need to worry about overwatering if the proper number of drainage holes have been drilled.

The problem of overwatering may occur if you water too frequently. You should always let the soil dry out until it is barely moist to the touch one inch *below* the surface before watering again. For most roof and terrace situations this means once a day in summer. To check, poke your finger into the soil before watering and then just after. Sometimes it may seem to you that you have watered enough because water is coming out the bottom of the container, but this can be deceiving. Your soil may have compacted, making it difficult for the water to penetrate. Instead it is running down the sides and out of the bottom without wetting the soil at all. Your plants will still suffer from lack of water. To remedy the problem cultivate the soil and then water again.

In the event of a good rain, you will not need to water your plants, but just because it rains doesn't mean your plants have received enough water. Very often what appears like a deluge to you doesn't last long enough to do the job. The way to tell is by installing a rain gauge. This is a simple plastic tube with gradations to show exactly how much rain has fallen. Rain gauges are sold in most garden centers and mail order catalogues.

Plants need moisture all year, not just during the growing season. They need it in autumn when they are preparing for the cold months ahead as well as in winter when they are in a dormant state. Lack of water at these times weakens them, making them susceptible to disease and frost damage, and this, not freezing temperatures, is one of the biggest causes of plant failure in winter. This is especially true of evergreens, which do not have a dormant period, and spring bulbs, which make most of their root growth in the fall. Very often the top inch or two is moist but the the area below, where important roots are located, is bone dry. Check your soil periodically to make sure there is enough moisture. A good watering once a month may be necessary. The best time of the day for watering in cold weather is in the morning when the air temperature is above freezing and is expected to remain so for most of the day. If the water freezes too quickly, plants won't have enough time to absorb the necessary moisture and root damage may occur.

In early spring, before there is any real outward sign of life, deciduous trees are already awake and their need for water increases. This is often a very dry time of the year and it is important to see to it that your plants are watered. As the season progresses from spring into summer, their need for water increases gradually. With the onset of the spring rains, there usually is no need for a full-blown watering program until late May or June. Once the hot weather hits, you will have to water every day. As long as the nighttime temperature remains cool, it is best to water in the morning before ten o'clock. In this way you avoid any trouble from funguses, which favor moist, cool conditions. Once the nighttime temperature remains high, I begin watering my plants in the evening between four and six o'clock. Strong winds and warm temperatures tend to dry off plant foliage before sunset, hindering any infectious diseases. Plants watered in the morning don't have enough time to replace the necessary moisture lost through transpiration and evaporation. They can, like people, become dehydrated from too much sun exposure, wilting in the afternoon. They will often require a second watering later in the day.

As autumn approaches and temperatures cool down, I switch back to a morning watering schedule (usually by the end of August in the Northeast). As the days become cooler, trees and shrubs need less and less water, and only an occasional watering becomes necessary. In fact, overwatering at this time of the year may signal plants to keep growing and result in frost damage.

## Watering Covered Terraces

Many terrace gardens have roofs and receive almost no rainfall. They must rely solely on you for all their watering needs throughout the year. Care must be taken in setting up a seasonal watering system that conforms to nature and to the needs of your plants. Study the principles laid out in this chapter and set up a system accordingly. True, some rainfall will be received, but to determine if it is enough, attach a rain gauge to the wall that receives the least amount of precipitation before judging if your garden needs more water.

## Watering Systems

If all you have is one or two plants on a terrace, then all you will need is a watering can and a trip to the sink. But as your garden grows, all those trips to the sink become tiring, not to mention messy. It is now time to invest in a garden hose and an adapter. You can transport water easily to the garden even if your apartment is a few floors below. Garden hoses come in both 25- and 50-foot lengths and are available in most hardware stores or garden centers. What is important is choosing the right adapter. Check the size and threading of your faucet, then take a trip to your local hardware store. It is best if you can find an adapter that screws onto your faucet, but if you can't find one then you can purchase a snap coupler that will attach to any faucet and any standard garden hose.

With just a hose, you can walk around watering each container. It takes quite a bit of time to soak each plant properly but the time can be well spent taking care of such garden chores as pruning, weeding, and checking for bugs. You can really get to know your plants while watering them, but if you are the impatient type, you may not take enough time to soak your plants thoroughly and they may begin to exhibit signs of shallow watering. This is especially true in older buildings where the water pressure is very low. If this is the case, then the holding-tank method may be for you. This requires a large container such as a 25-gallon plastic garbage can. Use a hose to fill the container before you begin to water your plants. Then simply dip a watering can into the holding tank and water each plant. It takes much less time and you can actually measure the amount of water each plant is receiving. This is great if you plan to go away and have a friend look after the garden. You can then leave specific instructions on how much water to give each plant.

## Drip Irrigation Systems

Much has been written recently about drip irrigation systems and their advantages. The major drawback is expense. It takes an outlay of a few hundred dollars to set up a system that will really do what you want it to do. The small inexpensive kits advertised in mail order catalogues unfortunately are not worth the money. The advantage of the system is first and foremost a saving of up to 60 percent in water usage, making it a great conservation tool. Most water supplied to plants is lost through evaporation and runoff. Drip irrigation is a slow, even watering method that allows time for the water to soak in and as a result promotes better overall growth. It is also a great time saver. Gone are the days when there was no time to water the plants. All you have to do is turn on the faucet. If you go away on vacation, the system can be hooked up to an automatic timer and will not require the services of a well-meaning friend. You'll never have to come home to dead plants again. By adding a fertilizer injector you will also have the most efficient method of fertilizing your plants, for the system will measure and deliver the right amount to each plant. Unfortunately it will require the use of highly soluble chemical fertilizers.

Drip irrigation works by using piping or tubing or both to deliver water to the root zone of each plant. The main supply line is usually ½-inch polyurethane tubing that is connected to the main water source. Connected to the main supply line by a series of tee connectors are smaller water lines known as laterals. These run along the plants being watered and have emittors placed at intervals to deliver water to the root zone.

The most important fittings in the system are the emittors. There are several different types and sizes for different situations. They can deliver anywhere from ½ to 4 gallons of water per hour depending on the type used. The determination of which type and how many to use depends on the plants being watered, the size of the container, and the water pressure present at different points along the lines.

The biggest problem that usually arises with the system is uneven water pressure which results in improper distribution of water to the plants. This is usually the result of poor installation, and the use of wrong emittors. Most plumbers don't understand the way the system is supposed to work and few country landscape contractors are familiar with the problems inherent in urban roof and terrace situations. Locate an urban landscape designer or an architect who has designed such a system or contact the manufacturing company of the system you wish to use. Many have consultants willing to help or even to design a system for you.

In a small urban roof or terrace garden most people would find the sight of the tubing offensive. In this case the lateral lines can be placed behind the containers with the water being delivered by spaghetti tubing to the plants. Among the most widely used systems of this sort is the Chapin Watermatic, which incorporates the spaghetti tubing.

Drip irrigation systems have to be flushed out from time to time to prevent algae buildup and clogging. Using a chlorinated city water supply will keep this from becoming much of a problem. The tubing should also be protected from ultraviolet rays of the sun, which will eventually cause the material to break down. Protecting the tubing is easily done by covering it with mulching material, which is a good horticultural practice anyway. Once assembled properly, a good system should give you very few problems.

## Water Conservation

Using water efficiently should be a goal that we all try to achieve at all times, not just during a water emergency. Water is one of our most precious assets and should be treated as such. Normal gardening practices such as cultivation, mulching, and weeding faithfully carried out weekly will not only make your garden look and grow better but will actually help to conserve water. A soil that contains much organic material and is cultivated regularly to keep it loose and well aerated will hold more water and allow quicker penetration. This means less work for you by cutting down your time spent in watering. Mulching cuts down on surface evaporation, helps keep the soil loose, and maintains a more even soil temperature, all factors that minimize water loss. By pulling weeds regularly, you will prevent them from competing for the light, nutrients, and water your plants need to survive. Water each plant in spurts, giving the soil a chance to absorb it and prevent runoff. Check each plant before and after to make sure none are being overwatered. Grouping plants close together and placing them where they will receive some shade during the day will also cut down on water loss through surface evaporation. In a water emergency reduce the amount of fertilizer by one half. This will help slow growth without hindering health or attractiveness. Less growth means less water use. Try choosing plants and varieties that tolerate dry conditions. There are many lovely plants and vegetables too that do not need tremendous amounts of water. Read garden catalogues carefully. Lastly, use a broom instead of your garden hose to clean up plant debris.

## Setting Up a Graywater System

During times of drought many cities declare a water emergency and outlaw the use of water for gardening purposes. If this happens to you it doesn't have to mean the end of your garden for the year. You can still water your plants by collecting graywater. Graywater is water that has already been used once to wash dishes, rinse clothes, or take a bath as opposed to blackwater, which has been used to flush your toilet. Graywater is perfectly safe to use on your plants as long as harsh detergents or chemicals such as chlorine bleach have not been added to the water. Depending on the size of your garden, your basic water usage (without waste!), and the conservation practices just outlined, you may be able to collect enough water to take care of all your horticultural needs. To protect your investment, any water you collect should first be used on trees, shrubs, and perennials, since annuals will be replaced next year anyway. If you still cannot collect enough to take care of all your plants, then a decision must be made to sacrifice some plants to save the rest. A plant weakened by drought will have a hard time staving off insect attack or frost damage.

A graywater system can be set up in one of two ways. The first simply involves siphoning the water from a bathtub or sink into a bucket and transporting it to the garden where it may be stored in a holding tank for later use. This practice works well when only a small number of plants are involved—few people could do it for very long for a large garden.

The second system is for larger gardens and will involve a small initial investment and possibly the services of a plumber. Underneath every sink and bathtub is an S-shaped trap to collect objects accidentally washed down the drain. At the base of the trap is a screw-in plug to make the trap easy to clean. Just unscrew the plug, add the proper-sized adapter, a cutoff valve, and a rubber hose to transport the water. The rubber hose is connected to a main line (another rubber hose) via a tee connector that carries all the graywater collected from various sources to a holding tank in the garden. Since the hose is flexible it can run discreetly along the baseboards and should not be too unsightly. When the emergency is over the entire system disassembles easily for storage. You may also need a small marine pump to transport water to a roof garden, but all this including the pump shouldn't cost more than two hundred dollars. This is a small price to pay to protect the investment you have already made.

## Light in the Garden

Because you can't control the amount of light you receive, you should choose plants that can adapt to the amount of light present. You've heard this a hundred times before and it seems easy enough but the hard part is to determine exactly how much light you are receiving. Theoretically a terrace that faces south receives the most light, followed by one that faces east, then west, and last by one that faces north, which receives no

*Fig. 10   This lighting floor plan illustrates the number of hours of direct sun each area receives.*

direct sun. In practice a terrace facing south can actually receive less light than one that faces west if the sun is blocked by some tall buildings. If it is covered by a roof, it will receive even less light. This holds true for roof gardens also. City gardens may also receive light from an unexpected source. It may be reflected off other buildings, making it possible to grow plants that need some direct sun on a terrace facing north.

All of this can be rather confusing, but what is important to know is the amount of hours of direct sun or bright light received at different spots in your garden. A lighting diagram can help, as shown on page 27. By noting what areas of your garden are in shadow at different times of the day you can determine the amount of light you are receiving. Vegetables and sun-loving plants need at least six hours of direct sun each day. Plants that tolerate partial shade will do well with less.

To determine if a plant is receiving enough light, just look at the plant. If it is receiving too much, the leaves will have a dull, bleached color, the edges will turn brown and feel like paper, or they may curl under away from the sun. New growth may be small and too compact, with little room between leaf axils. A plant that is not receiving enough light will be long and leggy with a dull, light-green color. Older growth will begin to turn yellow from the bottom up, sacrificed in favor of younger growth in the competition for the little food present. Few blooms or fruits will form. The remedy in either case is to move the plant to a new location. Your lighting diagram will help you to choose the right spot. Remember that the light recommendations for plants are only a guide. You should use your own powers of observation to determine what works for you. Many plants that will tolerate full sun elsewhere will only tolerate partial shade. If you live in a cool climate, the reverse may be true.

# *Your County Agent*

Each county across the country, regardless of the extent of urban development, has a county agricultural agent. Most gardeners are not aware of the services they offer or the vast amounts of knowledge to which they have access. This includes everything from insect control and air pollution, to nutrition and health and safety programs. All of these agents operate under the Cooperative Extension Service System which is financed by combined funding of the federal, state, and county governments, and is administered by a university designated by each state's legislature. Anyone is entitled to the services they offer. If your agent doesn't have the specific information you need, he can consult a vast network of researchers. If you are confused about what varieties are suitable for your area, or the effects of pollution, contact him. He's there to help.

## Drought Resisting Plants

| | | |
|---|---|---|
| Achillea | Dianthus | Phacelia |
| Arctotis | Euphorbia | Poppy |
| Armeria | Gaillardia | Portulaca |
| Brachycome | Gypsophila | Rudbeckia |
| Cactus | Helianthus | Scabiosa |
| Calandrinia | Iris, Bearded | Sedum |
| Calliopsis | Mesembryanthemum | Sempervivum |
| Catananche | Nasturtium | Yucca |
| Centaurea | Oenothera | |
| Coreopsis | Penstemon | |

## Plants For Partial Shade

| | | |
|---|---|---|
| Achillea | Clematis | Lobelia |
| Aconitum | Coleus | Mignonette (Reseda |
| Adlumia | Coreopsis | odorata) |
| Alyssum | Cyclamen | Myosotis |
| Anchusa | Digitalis | Physostegia |
| Anemone | Doronicum | Hardy primrose |
| Aquilegia | Hardy ferns | Rhododendron |
| Astilbe | Helleborus | Saxifraga |
| Azalea | Hemerocallis | Thalictrum |
| Balsam | Hosta | Torenia |
| Begonia | Hypericum | Viola |
| Campanula | Ilex spp. | |
| Centaurea | Impatiens | |

---

## Close Plant Spacing for Containers
### (in inches)

| | | | |
|---|---|---|---|
| Antirrhinum (dwarf) | 6 | Eggplant | 18 |
| Beans (bush) | 4 | Impatiens | 6 |
| Beans (pole) | 8 | Kale | 15 |
| Begonia (fibrous) | 6 | Lantana | 8 |
| Cabbage | 12 | Lettuce (head) | 10 |
| Callistephus | 8 | Lettuce (leaf) | 7 |
| Carrots | 2 | Lobelia | 6 |
| Coleus | 6 | Lobularia | 4 |
| Corn | 12 | Marigold | 8 |

| | | | |
|---|---|---|---|
| Marigold (dwarf) | 6 | Petunia | 8 |
| Mustard greens | 4 | Radishes | 1 |
| Nicotiana | 8 | Salvia (dwarf) | 6 |
| Onions | 3 | Spinach | 4 |
| Peas (bush) | 3 | Squash (bush) | 18 |
| Peas (pole) | 6 | Tomatoes | 18 |
| Pelargonium | 8 | Verbena | 8 |
| Peppers | 12 | Zinnia (tall) | 12 |

# ❧ 4 ❧

# Understanding Your Soil

ONE OF THE MOST IMPORTANT, yet least understood, factors governing plant growth is the soil plants are grown in. Just as a bad foundation will make for a structurally weak house, poor soil structure will produce weak plants. To be fertile your soil must have a physical structure that allows good air circulation and drainage, a large proportion of organic matter to nourish both plants and soil bacteria, and a nearly neutral pH to support a wide range of plants. Fertile soil must be able to hold enough moisture to sustain plants for a reasonable period of time without being soggy. It must also remain loose enough to be easily penetrated by plant roots. By taking the time to really take care of your soil you will be providing your plants with the proper environment to grow strong and healthy, enabling them to withstand heat, drought, disease, and even insect attack. Tend the soil and the plants will take care of themselves.

## The Physical Structure of Soil

Everyone knows that plants need moisture, but it is not widely known that plant roots also need oxygen. A healthy soil is made up of 50 percent air to support both plant and bacterial respiration. Oxygen is needed to absorb nutrients, build cell walls, and produce the proteins, starches, sugars, and fats necessary for life. In order to have this volume of air, the soil structure must be open and loose, and it must have a good mixture of both sand and clay particles.

Sand particles are large and irregular in size. They rest against each other in a haphazard fashion, creating large air pockets. Soil with a high sand content drains very quickly, leaving very little moisture or nutrients behind. Clay soil is quite the opposite. Each clay particle is very small and shaped like a flat plate. These fit so closely together there is little room for the air or water plants need. Water forms puddles on the surface of clay soil and penetrates slowly; when wet, clay soil feels slick and sticky and remains soggy too long. As it dries, it becomes a hard mass that plant roots cannot penetrate. Clay soil is a rich source of nutrients, but unfortunately its physical properties make it impossible for plants to use them.

For both sandy and clay soils the remedy is the same—add a soil amendment. A soil amendment is any substance that is in itself a good growing medium when water and fertilizers are added. Soil amendments are spongy materials with large and irregular particles that hold tremendous amounts of moisture without being soggy and at the same time allow good aeration. They are basically divided into two groups, organic and mineral substances.

Organic substances such as peat moss, leafmold, and compost not only improve the crumb structure of bad soils, but as they break down they provide nutrients for plants and bacteria. But organic substances are not inert; they will also alter the chemical composition of your soil by making it more acidic. The addition of lime becomes necessary to maintain the correct pH balance. Perlite, pumice, and vermiculite are all inert mineral amendments that remain unaltered in the soil except for the gradual effects of weathering. Although they don't alter the chemical composition, neither do they have any nutritive value. What makes them so valuable to container gardeners is that they are extremely lightweight and do not compact easily—all very important considerations when you are placing large quantities on your roof.

How do you determine the kind of soil you have? A simple test will tell you the basic structure and properties of your soil. Squeeze a slightly moist lump of soil in your hand. If it will not form a ball, your soil is too sandy. Clay soil will form a ball that is somewhat hard and some pressure will be needed to crumble it. Soil that will form a ball but crumbles easily is said to be friable, allowing the adequate passage of both air and water.

## Organic Matter

Organic matter has aptly been called the storehouse of the soil's nutrients. It consists of residues from decomposed plant and animal materials that are broken down into finer particles by soil bacteria and fungi and then combined with clay particles to form a soil colloid known as humus. This substance is extremely valuable in proper plant development. It forms its acids slowly, releasing nutrients to plants as they need them, not in one massive dose like most highly soluble chemical fertilizers. Its presence is a vital factor in building and maintaining soil fertility.

Because it is continually being broken down and used by plants and bacteria, organic matter must be reintroduced into the soil twice a year, in spring and fall, if fertility is to be maintained. This can take the form of any organic soil amendment or mulching material (see Chapter 6) that is applied at least two inches thick (you cannot apply too much) and then dug deeply into the soil. At this point, I must stress the word *deep* in order to encourage proper root growth. Shallow root systems leave plants vulnerable to drought, sunburn, windburn, heaving, and frost damage.

Certain substances such as sawdust or bark chips do not contain enough nitrogen to take care of their own decomposition (any material with at least 1.5 percent has enough) and a nitrogen fertilizer must be included to make up the difference. For every cubic foot of these materials added to your soil you must add three ounces of blood meal, hoof and horn meal, or one ounce of ammonium nitrate. Plants should be watched closely for any yellowing of the leaves, and if any is noted, a second application should be made.

## Soil Microorganisms

Plants and soil microorganisms live together in a symbiotic relationship, the one not existing without the other. In nature plants cannot draw their nutrients directly from the soil. They don't exist in a form that plants can use. Rather, they live on the by-products of soil microorganisms. It is the bacteria and fungi that break down organic and mineral matter, releasing nutrients. For example, soil microorganisms convert the nitrogen that is present in organic matter into ammonia and release it to plants in the form of nitrates. In another example, fungi can form structures known as mycorrhizae on the roots of plants by inserting their hyphae (threads) directly into the plants' feeder rootlets. These fungi convert nutrients, especially phosphorus, into a form plants can assimilate while conveying the food directly. At the same time the plant produces enzymes and waste products that are needed by the fungi. In order to maintain the proper levels of bacteria and fungi (each gram of good garden soil can contain up to a billion individual organisms), the level of organic material must remain high. The use of harsh chemical fertilizers and pesticides can actually reduce the number of bacteria in the soil and should be kept at a minimum.

# Acidity and Alkalinity

Have you ever had a plant that was suffering from a nutrient deficiency, but when you applied fertilizer it didn't do any better? The problem may be not the lack of fertilizer, but rather a soil that is either too acidic or too alkaline. Acidity and alkalinity exert a great influence on the availability of essential nutrients to plants.

Acid soil is most common in areas that receive abundant rainfall. Most woodland soil, especially in the northeast, is slightly acidic from the amount of leafmold and pine found in the humus material. Garden soils containing large amounts of peat moss, sawdust, or bark chips are also acidic.

Another more disturbing cause of acid soils is spawned in our own midwestern industrial centers. Factories spew out contaminants such as nitrogen and sulfur oxides, hydrocarbons, carbon monoxide, and many others. These, along with emissions from millions of automobiles, are picked up by global wind currents and carried for thousands of miles following the major weather patterns of the world. Within two to four days the nitrogen and sulfur oxides present in the atmosphere change to nitric and sulfuric acid. Rain and snow falling east of Indiana and north of Florida contain up to fifty times more dilute sulfuric and nitric acids than in the past. In rare cases an isolated storm may actually contain as much acid as white vinegar. The areas that receive most of this contaminated rainfall are in the northeastern mountain regions. Since these are also the primary watershed areas for the eastern states, the tap water we use to water our plants may also be affected.

There is a broad spectrum of plant disorders associated with acidic soil. The level of acid present can change the rate of the decomposition of organic matter and alter the metabolism of soil microorganisms that fix nitrogen in the soil, making them almost totally inoperative. In soils low in organic matter with a pH of 5 or less, phosphorus locks up with iron and becomes unusable. Acid soils can cause trace elements to leach away and aluminum and manganese to be released in such large amounts that they poison plants. Some other disorders associated with acidic soils are reduced germination of seeds, a decrease in the number of seedlings successfully established, interference with photosynthesis, lower resistance to plant disease, and needle stunting on evergreens.

Fortunately, the situation is easily corrected with the addition of lime. Some plants actually prefer an acid soil but most enjoy one that is nearly neutral or only slightly acidic. Lime comes in several basic forms, both organic and chemical. Carbonate of lime is ground chalk or limestone. It doesn't burn foliage and is completely safe to use. When dosages are given for the application of lime it is usually for carbonate of lime. Dolomite is a limestone-like rock containing 52 percent calcium carbonate and 45 percent magnesium, thus supplying plants with these two essential nutrients. It is widely used in soilless mixes and is the most advantageous form of lime to use if you can find it. The recommended dosage corresponds to that for carbonate of lime. Hydrated lime comes from quicklime, which has been treated with water and is known chemically as calcium hydroxide. It is a much stronger compound than the natural forms of lime and should not be spread during windy weather. It is capable of irritating the skin and burning foliage. When used, cut the recommended dosage for natural lime in half.

Lime can be applied at any time, although the best time is in the fall so it has a few months to work before planting. Approximately one cup of carbonate of lime per square yard of surface area is enough to raise the pH about one point and should last for about three years.

Alkaline soils have much the same effect on plants as acid soils but for different reasons. Nutrient ions take up most of the space in soil particles, crowding out hydrogen ions. This causes the nutrients to become insoluble or, worse, to be leached from the soil. When the pH reaches 7.3 phosphorus locks up with calcium to form an insoluble calcium phosphate. Too much lime can also make iron unavailable, causing a condition known as chlorosis. The spaces between the veins of leaves turn yellow while the veins remain green. Eventually the leaf dies and so does the plant.

Alkaline soil is common in areas of light rainfall such as the southwest and southern California, and in areas where the water has been chemically softened (although it is great for dishes it is horrible for plants). If you live in such soil-type areas, the best thing to do is to buy good-grade topsoil with a neutral pH. You have a certain advantage when gardening in containers in that your soil will remain neutral longer because of its isolation. If you live in a soft-water area take frequent pH readings (about every three months) to make sure the problem doesn't build up from the use of tap water. By adding generous amounts of an acid soil amendment such a sphagnum peat or leafmold the problem can be neutralized. Another way to deal with the problem is to grow plants that prefer alkaline conditions.

## *Testing Your Soil's pH*

Studying the effects of acids and alkalines on the solubility of plant foods makes it easier to see why it is important to determine the pH of the soil.

No knowledge of chemistry or ability with numbers is required, but you will need a soil testing kit or an electronic soil tester to check acidity. If you use the kit, take care to use digging tools and containers that will not contaminate the test and affect the accuracy of the reading. Don't touch the soil sample with your hands. The procedure is simple: Just mix some dry soil with the solution provided and compare the sample to the color chart. An electronic soil tester is the quickest and easiest method to use but the initial expense is greater. It will give you an accurate reading instantly when pushed into moist soil. The plates must be kept clean and should be wiped between each test with fiberglass or fine sandpaper to ensure good contact with the soil.

## Adjusting Your pH

Most plants prefer a pH level between 6.5 and 7.0. The essential elements necessary for plant growth are most readily available between 6.0 and 6.9. Some plants prefer a reading below 6.0 while others prefer a pH over 7.0. A list of pH requirements of some popular plants appears on page 39.

To adjust a soil that is too alkaline, try adding generous amounts of coffee grounds or cottonseed meal and retest in a few days. If a more radical adjustment is needed, water your soil with a solution of ½ cup of superphosphate dissolved in a gallon of water and wait a day or two before retesting. For a soil that is too acidic use a solution of ½ cup of lime dissolved in a gallon of water and treat as above. The organic matter in the soil will act as a buffer.

## *Salinity*

Salinity is a common soil problem in areas where excessive chemical fertilizers have been used. You've probably seen it on your houseplants. Its presence can be detected by a white crust on the surface of the soil. It is also a sign of shallow watering. Salinity can prevent seed germination and damage plant roots. Plants become stunted and foliage burned. The best remedy is to remove the top few inches of soil and replace it with fresh soil mix. To prevent this condition try using organic fertilizers. If you really do prefer chemical fertilizers, once a month water your containers deeply, allowing the water to drain from the bottom for several minutes. This will leach most of the salts out.

# Basic Soil Mix for Container Gardening

Now that we have completed our discussion of what makes up a fertile soil, we are ready to discuss a basic soil mix for container gardens. It is not advisable to use straight garden topsoil in your containers for three good reasons. The first is that container gardens are not part of a complete ecosystem. Although many organisms that live in normal garden soil will appear in your garden, many more will not. Such insects as earthworms with their constant tunneling create passageways for air and water to enter, playing a major role in keeping garden soil loose and well aerated. Without their presence soil in containers quickly becomes compacted. The second reason is that soil in containers is more exposed to the elements and dries out more quickly. We need to add a soil amendment to retain moisture. The third is that straight topsoil is quite heavy, putting great stress on the building below. The addition of a lightweight soil amendment that adds volume without weight can reduce the strain considerably. Gardening in containers also means starting from scratch, so it is easier to create the optimum conditions for plant growth. The following soil mix will promote good soil structure and fertility as well as create an environment where soil bacteria can flourish.

Combine the following:

* *1 cubic foot garden-grade topsoil
* *1 cubic foot vermiculite
* *1 cubic foot peat moss
* 1 quart packaged dried cow manure
* ¾ cup ground limestone
* 1 cup blood meal or dried blood
* 2 cups bone meal
* 3 cups greensand marl or granite dust

This mixture has high water retention properties and good aeration as well as an abundance of organic matter. Substitutions for the nutritional ingredients can be made if you can't find the ones listed. In the next chapter on fertilizers you can find out more about this, or you can ask your nurseryman. If you have access to compost, you can change the proportions to equal parts of topsoil, vermiculite, peat moss, and compost for an even better garden mix.

Garden-grade topsoil can be purchased inexpensively at any plant store specializing in landscape or terrace design; it will be of high quality, free from disease and plant pests. Sandiness will vary a little from bag to bag

---

*Approximately 2 gallons.

but it will have a neutral pH. Don't use potting soil meant for house-plants. It is much too costly and unnecessary. Some of you may wish to take a trip to the country to dig up your own in hopes of saving some money, but without extensive testing you won't be sure of what you have and you may be introducing some serious plant pests and diseases into your garden.

Never substitute sand or gravel for vermiculite. Although it will pro-mote good drainage it is much too heavy and will not contribute to the water-retentive quality of your soil. You may substitute perlite but I prefer the moisture-holding capacity of vermiculite.

Dried cow manure as sold in most garden centers has been treated with a deodorant and is quite pleasant to use. Never use fresh manure that has not been composted for a sufficient period of time or it will burn plant roots.

If you wish to grow plants that prefer more alkaline conditions, add more lime using the chart below. On the other hand, if you want to grow plants that prefer acid soil, leave out the lime altogether. In both cases be sure to test your soil's pH and adjust accordingly.

Choose a day that is not too windy and make sure you have everything on hand before mixing your soil. Containers that hold more than five gallons of soil should be placed where they are to remain permanently before filling. Mix your soil next to them. If you find later that you want to move a container, wait for it to dry out and it will weigh considerably less. Before filling, make sure all your containers have the proper drainage holes. Line all porous containers such as packing crates with plastic gar-bage bags. Once filled these bags can be trimmed to the surface of the soil for a neat appearance. Remember to punch drainage holes in the plastic. Fill the bottom of each container with drainage material. Perlite does well and is much lighter than gravel. Broken pot shards are also good. Use a large bucket to mix your soil in small amounts. It will be much easier to

### Amount of Lime Needed to Sweeten Soil

| TO RAISE THE pH OF YOUR SOIL | LBS. PER SQ. YARD (9 SQ. FEET) OF LIME | PER 100 SQ. FEET |
|---|---|---|
| ½ point | 1 | 9 lbs. |
| 1 point | 1½ | 13½ lbs. |
| 1½ points | 2 | 18 lbs. |
| 2 points | 2½ | 27 lbs. |

The above figures relate to ground chalk or limestone. If hydrated lime is used, the dressing should be half the above recommended amount.

handle this way and you will get a more evenly mixed finished product. Add your soil mix to within 2 or 3 inches of the top of the container and then water. Wait a day or two before planting to let the material settle and add more soil if needed. Now add your plants. Congratulations—you are now the proud owner of a new urban garden!

---

## pH Requirements for Various Plants

### Plants preferring a very acid soil (pH 4.5)

| | | |
|---|---|---|
| Azalea | Gardenia | Lady slipper |
| Blueberry | Holly | Rhododendron |
| Cranberry (bog) | Hydrangea (blue) | Trailing arbutus |

### Plants preferring moderately acid soil (pH 5.5)

| | | |
|---|---|---|
| Bayberry | Grape | Potato |
| Blackberry | Laurel | Pumpkin |
| Fern | Lily of the valley | Spruce |
| Heather | Plum | Yew |

### Plants preferring a slightly acid soil (pH 6.5)

| | | |
|---|---|---|
| Anemone | Hyacinth | Radish |
| Aster | Candytuft | Centaurea |
| Bean | Canna | Chrysanthemum |
| Columbine | Iris | Chives |
| Corn | Kale | Raspberry |
| Cosmos | Larkspur | Rhubarb |
| Crocus | Marigold | Snapdragon |
| Cucumber | Narcissus | Spinach |
| Dahlia | Onion | Spruce |
| Eggplant | Pansy | Stocks |
| Endive | Pea | Violet |
| Feverfew | Phlox | Watermelon |
| Fuchsia | Poppy | Wisteria |
| Gladiolus | Primula | Zinnia |

### Plants preferring an alkaline soil (pH 7.1 to 7.5)

| | | |
|---|---|---|
| Bluegrass | Dogwood | Parsley |
| Carnation | Geranium | Petunia |
| Carrot | Heliotrope | Pink |
| Deutzia | Nasturtium | Sweet pea |

# ✤ 5 ✤

# Fertilizers and Plant Nutrition

EVERY SPRING MILLIONS OF GARDENERS all across the country determine that this year they will have the best garden ever. They rake and hoe and run down to their local garden center to purchase their yearly supply of peat moss and fertilizers. Finding themselves standing in front of a rack of various garden products at their favorite plant store, they become confused. How do they choose which fertilizer is best for their needs? There are so many different substances to choose from. There are formulas for flower and fruit production, those for promoting leaf growth, some for specific plants such as roses, and still others containing only one compound. The gardeners go home and add a handful of this and a cupful of that and plant their seeds. All goes well for a while but then things seem to peter out. Here and there deficiencies seem to arise and plants begin to turn yellow.

Unless they are fed regularly, plants must ration whatever they can pull from the soil. Photosynthesis is slowed, no new chlorophyll is manufactured, sugars can't be used properly, and cells can't divide normally. If the problem isn't corrected quickly, they will shed their lower leaves in favor of their growing tips. Once this happens, it is very difficult, if not impossible, for them to regain their former vigor. Plants that are not properly fed have a hard time fighting disease, drought, insect attack and frost damage. They produce fewer, less flavorful fruits and fewer flowers.

Applying concentrated chemical fertilizers that raise the salinity of your soil and may ruin soil structure may not be the answer. What is more important is not the relative strength of each nutritional element but its availability in relation to other elements present. Too much is just as bad as too little. In fact an excess of one element can easily lead to a deficiency of another. This is often seen in apples and tomatoes, which display symptoms of magnesium deficiency when given too much potash.

It is known that plants absorb at least sixty different chemical elements. Out of these only thirteen are known to be essential for plant nutrition. Six elements are used in fairly large amounts and are classified as the major elements. These include nitrogen, phosphorus, potassium, magnesium, calcium, and sulfur. Of these, nitrogen, phosphorus, and potassium are used in the greatest quantities and are found in most fertilizer formulas. There are also seven elements, known as the trace elements, which plants use in minute quantities. These include iron, manganese, boron, chlorine, molybdenum (mol-LIB-den-um), copper, and zinc. Each of these thirteen elements has a particular job to do. One element cannot replace another. You can't have normal plants when nitrogen is in short supply even if there is plenty of phosphorus or potash.

To be able to determine what your plants do need you must know what each element is used for and what the symptoms of a deficiency look like. Very often, gardeners, rather than carefully observing their plants, give up, thinking the real cause is their own black thumb. Although the symptoms that plants display for many deficiencies often do resemble each other they are dissimilar. What is necessary to make an accurate diagnosis is a little knowledge, a lot of observation, and the power of deductive reasoning. Let's begin by discussing the various elements.

## *Nitrogen*

Nitrogen is needed by plants in larger amounts than any other nutrient and is frequently the first to become depleted from unreplenished soil. Nitrogen is present in hundreds of important chemical compounds such as proteins, and also in hormones that regulate vital chemical reactions. It is also needed in the manufacture of stems and leaves and to induce rapid green growth. Plants need nitrogen most in the spring when they are making early rapid growth. Fortunately this is also when it is present in the soil in the largest quantities. Though nitrogen makes up four-fifths of the earth's atmosphere, plants cannot absorb it directly. They must rely on microorganisms to convert the nitrogen found in plant and animal wastes into nitrates and ammonium compounds. As a result, nitrate production is greatest in the spring and early summer when the soil is warm (above 42°F.) and moist, both conditions that favor bacterial activity.

A nitrogen fertilizer should be applied in the spring, especially after cold, rainy weather, and as a side dressing during the growing season. It should not be applied late in the season to perennials, trees, or shrubs since it will promote late green growth that could be subject to frost damage. Good natural sources of nitrogen are dried blood, cottonseed meal, and dried manure.

# *Phosphorus*

Phosphorus is intimately associated with all life processes but is especially needed for root formation, as well as normal flowering, fruiting, and ripening. It is needed for the production of starches and plays a role in the division and growth of individual cells. Phosphorus is also necessary for food storage and the manufacturing of starches.

Phosphorus, like nitrogen, is never found in the soil in the free state since it oxidizes rapidly. Rather it is absorbed as phosphates, the salts of phosphoric acid. The most common form used by plants is calcium phosphate, which forms in soil water as a result of the decay of organic matter and the weathering of rock minerals.

Phosphorus can be added to your soil in the form of phosphate rock, bone meal, or superphosphate. Phosphate rock is best added in generous amounts in the fall. This will give it time to break down and begin working by early spring. Bone meal works much faster and is applied in the fall to spring-flowering bulbs to promote strong early root growth before the weather turns too cold and again in the spring and throughout the growing season to all plants. Superphosphate is an inorganic form of phosphorus that dissolves easily in water and acts quickly. It is not recommended for use as part of a regularly scheduled fertilizer application program because of its long-term effects on soil fertility, but it is recommended as an emergency application to correct a deficiency in midseason.

# *Potassium*

Potassium is a strange element. Although it's found in all parts of the plant and is extremely important in the manufacture of starches, sugars, and proteins, it is not actually a part of any of these vital plant constituents. Apparently it stays in the plant sap and moves around to wherever it is needed. We really don't know much about how it works, but it seems to be most important in the formation of flowers and fruit and plant parts such as leaves and growing tips. We know it plays a significant role in photosynthesis at low light levels and in internal water regulation. It also improves the flavor and color of fruits, vegetables, and flowers. Potassium balance may also be linked to all-round plant health and vitality. It has also been found that when the amount of potassium present equals the amount of nitrogen present, plants suffer less from insect attack, disease, and frost damage.

Natural sources of potassium are found in both mineral and vegetable form. Mineral sources include granite dust, greensand, glauconite, and basalt rock and take a very long time to dissolve into a form plants can use. They are excellant long-term fertilizers best applied in the fall. A faster-acting vegetable source such as wood ash, tobacco dust, or seaweed should be used to provide an immediate supply of potassium during the growing season alone or in conjunction with a mineral source. When using wood ash, which is an excellent source of potash, containing anywhere from 6 to 10 percent, be sure to test your soil's acid level. Wood ash is extremely alkaline and will raise the pH. Never use it on acid-loving plants and keep it away from seedlings.

There are also highly soluble chemical sources of potassium such as muriate of potash and potassium nitrate, but using these may cause the plant to take up an excess of the element that can block the uptake of magnesium, causing a deficiency of that essential element.

# Magnesium

Without magnesium there would be no photosynthesis, for at the center of every particle of chlorophyll is a molecule of magnesium. This fact alone is enough to make it essential, but magnesium is also necessary for a plant to properly use the elements nitrogen, phosphorus, and sulfur, and to cleanse the plant of toxins that arise as a by-product of its own metabolism. It is also needed in the formation of proteins.

The best cure for a magnesium deficiency is to add dolomitic limestone. This is a natural lime that contains magnesium. Another good source is Epsom salts, but very little is needed and overcompensation is quite possible. An excess of magnesium is rarely encountered, but it can cause a calcium deficiency.

# Calcium

When it occurs naturally, calcium is an abundant metal usually found in combination with other elements. Calcium adds strength to the plant structure much as it does in the human body. It is needed by roots and growing tips for the manufacture and growth of cells, and as a main constituent of cell walls, it prevents the leaching of vital elements and helps bind cells together to form complete plant structures. It also serves in the building of plant proteins. Another important function calcium performs is to prevent magnesium toxicity and to neutralize certain toxic acids that are a by-product of the plant's metabolism.

Although calcium is needed in fairly large amounts, there is very little need to worry about not having enough. Calcium gets into the soil in many garden products and is usually in abundant supply. Every time you add lime, you add calcium. Other sources are lime sulfur fungicides and soil conditioners such as gypsum, wood ashes, dolomite, bone meal, and oyster shells. A toxic excess of calcium can result if too much or too little of the elements magnesium, potassium, and boron are in the soil.

## Sulfur

Sulfur is a nonmetallic element which occurs naturally in several forms. When oxidized in well-aerated soils, sulfur combines with other ingredients to form sulfates. There is rarely a shortage of sulfur. It gets into soils in ways you'd never expect. For instance, in industrial areas rainwater washes sulfur dioxide out of polluted air and into the soil. Municipal water supplies also contain some sulfur and it is added through such garden products as lime-sulfur fungicide and gypsum.

Sulfur acts hand in hand with nitrogen in making new protoplasm for plant cells. It is used to build proteins and somehow is involved in chlorophyll production. In some plants, sulfur is found in the form of mustard oils, which is where radishes and watercress get their pungent taste.

Sulfur's availability decreases in direct proportion to the amount of nitrogen present and it leaches easily from sandy soils. It may also become unavailable by changing to sulfides, which is especially true in water-logged soils.

## The Trace Elements

The trace elements are primarily catalysts promoting important reactions and cannot be replaced or done without no matter how little is needed. Too much of a trace element can be as much of a problem as a deficiency. The analysis of either a lack or excess of a trace element is not always easy because it is often due to an imbalance of the nutritional components of the soil. For instance, overmanuring with phosphates may induce a lack of iron or zinc, while sometimes the addition of one nutrient can cause a deficiency of another, as in the case of manganese and iron respectively. If you suspect a deficiency of a trace element is the cause of your particular problem, the best course of action is to seek expert advice. Contact your local county agent and get your soil tested.

# Iron

Iron has long been recognized as playing a major role in the formation of chlorophyll, and as a result, iron deficiency can be confused with nitrogen or magnesium deficiency. However, there is a difference. Iron-deficiency chlorosis begins at the top of the plant and works its way down instead of the reverse. Besides chlorosis, other symptoms are the dying back of newer growth and the discoloration of fruit.

Iron deficiency is the most common problem associated with trace elements, but it is usually not caused by a lack of iron in the soil. The usual cause is that the iron present is locked up and unavailable for plant use. Very often this is a result of the soil having too high a pH level, making acid-loving plants such as azaleas and rhododendrons most susceptible. If the pH of your soil is already low and the deficiency still occurs, spraying your plants with a chelated iron compound will correct the problem. Iron sulfate, iron oxide, and iron chloride are all suitable and are not susceptible to the fixing or locking that has made the natural iron unavailable. Please note that these products can result in the formation of soluble salts, such as ferrous sulfate, which are toxic to plants. The best solution to the problem is to add organic matter to the soil.

# Manganese

Manganese serves as a catalyst in the process of plant nutrition and encourages the growth and maturation of plants. It is closely bound to iron, and an excess of one frequently leads to a shortage of the other, even though the deficient element may be in abundant supply. Manganese deficiency is very hard to diagnose since the visual symptoms resemble those of iron deficiency or damage from air pollution. It is treatable with manganese sulfate.

# Boron

Boron plays a part in fifteen different plant functions that we know of, including the movement of sugars within the plant, the regulation of water intake by individual cells, nitrogen and carbohydrate metabolism, and the germination of pollen grains. It is also necessary for proper cell division and allows the plant to use calcium in cell wall formation.

Few soils are boron deficient but too much calcium can hinder boron availability. Maintaining a high level of organic matter is the best method of ensuring the availability of boron and most trace elements. In a pinch, ¼ teaspoon of household borax mixed in a gallon of water is sufficient to treat 20 square feet of growing area. Don't overdo it—too much is just as bad as too little.

# Chlorine

The role chlorine plays in plant nutrition is not understood, but it is thought to be needed for nitrate and carbohydrate metabolism. A chlorine deficiency is not possible if you use a municipal water source.

# Molybdenum

Molybdenum deficiencies are rare but most often occur in soils that are highly acid (below pH 5.2). Taken up by plant roots in the smallest amounts, molybdenum is believed to be closely associated with the nitrogen cycle and is a catalyst in the reduction of nitrates to ammonia in nonlegumes. It is also needed by nitrogen-fixing bacteria or leguminous plants to reduce atmospheric nitrogen to ammonia. Molybdenum excesses are more often a problem. As a pollutant in industrial smoke, molybdenum is thought to be responsible for some animal and plant poisonings. Deficiencies can be treated by applying lime, or sodium molybdenum.

# Copper

Although copper's function is not completely understood, we know it is very important to photosynthesis. It is found in the tiny green lens-shaped bodies known as chloroplasts in which photosynthesis takes place and which are a component of every green plant cell. Copper is also a component of several enzymes and is thought to act as a catalyst in plant respiration and iron utilization.

Fertilizers such as copper sulfate and other copper salts are a traditional remedy. The problem can also be solved by digging sawdust, wood shavings, or grass clippings into your soil.

# Zinc

However uncommon it is for trace elements to be deficient, zinc will be more frequently deficient than most of the others. Scientists are just beginning to understand the vital role zinc plays in plant, animal, and human nutrition. Zinc, like copper, is a necessary component of several enzymes that regulate various metabolic activities. Zinc is also needed for the formation of auxins, the hormones that promote plant growth.

Zinc deficiency can be cured by applying zinc materials to the soil as a soluble salt (zinc sulfate) or in chelated form, as well as by applying phosphate rock, which does contain some zinc. Foliar sprays are also effective in curing the deficiency.

Excessive zinc can poison plants and can also cause chlorosis. Zinc contamination can occur when water is stored in a galvanized container as well as from some sewage sludges.

## *Identifying Nutritional Deficiencies*

| NUTRIENT | SYMPTOMS | SOIL TYPE |
|---|---|---|
| Nitrogen | Plant turns pale green, then yellow. Chlorosis begins at the tips of leaves at bottom of plant and works its way in the direction of the main stem. Yellowing gradually spreads up the plant to the top. Older leaves die. | Very sandy soils or soils low in organic material. Also excessively wet soil or soils with a high or low pH. |
| Phosphorus | Early in this deficiency, plants look almost too healthy. Growth is normal but undersized. Plants become dark green frequently changing to purple, especially the undersides of leaves. Sometimes stems also take on this color. Leaves then yellow in the final stages. | Very wet or very acid (below pH 5) soils. Soils high in peat or sand; also very alkaline (above pH 7.3) soils. |
| Potassium | Older leaves become mottled or spotted, leaf edges become dry and scorched. Dead spots begin to appear on leaves, stems are weak, root systems are poor, fruit ripens unevenly. | Sandy soils, soils with a high or low pH, soils high in peat. |
| Magnesium | Because it moves freely within the plant, the deficiency first shows up in the lower leaves. They first turn yellow, then orange and finally brown. Leaves sometimes cup upward. | Wet soils, acid soils, soils high in peat or sand. Also soils given a high concentration of potash fertilizers. |

## *Identifying Nutritional Deficiencies* (cont'd)

| NUTRIENT | SYMPTOMS | SOIL TYPE |
|---|---|---|
| Calcium | Since calcium doesn't move freely within the plant, the symptoms first appear in new growth. Chlorosis begins first at leaf edges then moves in. Terminal buds become distorted. Young leaves turn yellow, then brown. Tomatoes develop "blossom end rot." | Acid soils, sandy soils. Soils that contain an excess of magnesium. |
| Sulfur | Resembles nitrogen deficiency. Plants turn pale green. Effects show up first in young growth. Leaves turn yellow but don't dry out. Stems are weak. Legumes are most affected. | Sandy soils, very wet soils, soils containing excessive amounts of nitrogen. |
| Iron | Chlorosis begins at the top of the plant and works its way down. Leaves turn yellow but retain green veins. Shoots may die back and fruit may be discolored. | Alkaline soils. |
| Manganese | Very difficult to diagnose since it resembles iron deficiency. Chlorosis is most severe at the top of the plant. Yellowing of the leaves appears first near leaf margins and develops in a V-shaped pattern. Leaves then develop tan or gray spots that can easily be mistaken for air pollution damage. These spots are the major difference between manganese and iron deficiency. Lesions develop on pea and bean seeds. | Alkaline soils high in humus or peaty soils with a pH of 6.0 or over. |

## *Identifying Nutritional Deficiencies* (cont'd)

| NUTRIENT | SYMPTOMS | SOIL TYPE |
|---|---|---|
| Boron | Corky spots develop on fruit. Rust-colored cracks develop in stems and leaf-stalks, which later develop a corky edge. Leaves become thick, leathery, discolored. Plants fail to bloom. Growing tips die. | Any soil, especially those high in calcium. |
| Molybdenum | Growing points die, leaves of young plants are chloritic, leaf margins yellow and curl. Older leaves become abnormally large, while young leaves remain very small. Brassicas are most affected. | Acidic soils (soils with a pH of 5.2 and below). |
| Copper | Young leaves become chloritic in a very strange way. Leaf centers yellow while veins and leaf margins remain green for a while. Shoot tips die, terminal leaves brown, leaves may fail to develop. | Soils to which too much lime or phosphate has been applied. |
| Zinc | Chlorosis shows up first in young leaves, which are also reduced in size. Leaves are closely spaced, forming rosettes, and may be malformed. | Soils that are sandy and acidic or soils that are alkaline and rich in humus. Soils excessively high in phosphates. |

# *Choosing the Right Fertilizer*

Standing in front of all those shelves of fertilizers trying to choose the right one can make you wish you had paid more attention in chemistry class, but all those different names and substances shouldn't intimidate you. It's actually quite easy. All fertilizers are either straight fertilizers or complete fertilizers and are derived either from chemical sources, organic sources, or a combination of the two.

A straight fertilizer supplies one specific element such as nitrogen and nothing else, while a complete fertilizer supplies nitrogen, phosphorus, potash, and sometimes some trace elements in varying percentages. Complete fertilizers are usually balanced for a specific use. Some are high in phosphorus for flower and fruit production, while others are high-nitrogen formulas to promote green growth and still others are more specific, such as rose or azalea food.

Chemical fertilizers are either manufactured or are purified salts from natural underground deposits. They are fairly concentrated, highly soluble, and fast acting, supplying nutrients in a form plants can readily assimilate without waiting for the action of soil microbes. At the same time, chemical fertilizers also have serious side effects that include burned roots and soil structure problems. The giant boost they give all at once may be more than your plants can handle, and can be compared to a diabetic eating too much chocolate cake. At the same time, they are so soluble that most of the fertilizer leaches away before the plant has a chance to utilize it. With chemical fertilizers, your plants at first are served a big Thanksgiving dinner and then are starved until their next big overindulgence. The increased salinity and acidity also associated with chemical fertilizers may in time cause serious soil problems. Sodium, which is a component of most chemical fertilizers, tends to accumulate and combine with carbonic acid to form sodium carbonate. This causes the soil to assume a cement-like hardness, which affects drainage, friability, and aeration. Other chemicals such as chlorides and sulfates are poisonous to beneficial soil organisms, while such acids as sulfuric and hydrochloric acid tend to increase soil acidity. In the long run, chemical fertilizers represent short-term maintenance without regard for long-term effects, although they are beneficial in correcting a deficiency in midseason quickly. If you do plan to use chemical fertilizers, it is best to cut the recommended dosage in half and apply it twice as often.

Organic fertilizers are derived from plant and animal sources. Their nutrients are locked away inside a complex structure of proteins and other materials that the natural processes of the environment break down and release slowly over an extended period of time. Because the substances are natural, plants cannot be overfed or damaged. The use of organic fertilizers represents a long-range commitment to soil fertility by creating a beneficial environment for the soil bacteria that plants need, as well as actually improving soil structure.

Synthetic organics are chemical combinations of organic and inorganic substances but shouldn't be confused with organic fertilizers. Synthetic organics are much stronger than their organic counterparts and are much closer in character to chemical fertilizers regarding their effects on plant roots and the soil. Their only advantage is that they break down slowly, making one application enough for an entire growing season.

In order to know if in fact a fertilizer is really organic or chemical, read the label carefully. It should have a guaranteed analysis of the product that should tell you how much of each element the fertilizer contains as well as its origins. Many labels are misleading and use words like "natural" or "organic" when in fact they are not. The guaranteed analysis should also give you some indication of the product's acidity so that you can determine its long-range effects on your soil. Beware of "miracle" or "wonderworking" fertilizers that do not show this information.

Fertilizer labels all carry a series of three hyphenated numbers that are collectively known as the NPK number. This number tells you the proportion of available nitrogen (N), phosphorus (P), and potash (K) in any given fertilizer. The numbers are standardized, always appearing in the same order. A number that reads 0–10–0 means that the fertilizer is a straight phosphorus fertilizer that contains 10 percent available phosphorus. An NPK number that reads 10–5–5 represents a complete fertilizer which contains 10 percent nitrogen, 5 percent phosphorus, and 5 percent potash.

This does not tell you the entire story behind the NPK number. Using it alone without knowing what substances the fertilizer is derived from can be deceiving. If you were to compare a formula with an NPK number of 10–5–5 to a formula that reads 20–20–20, logic would dictate that the 10–5–5 formula is weaker and a less desirable product. This may not be so. The percentages are generally listed for the immediately available nutrients, not the total nutrient content of the product. That is why the NPK value of organic products is generally lower than chemical fertilizers. Organically derived nutrients are released over a longer period of time and are governed by soil type, bacterial conditions, and soil acidity. Phosphate rock, for example, provides only 1.5 percent available phosphorus the first year even though the percentage of total phosphorus is closer to 30 percent. The rest is released over three or four years. Superphosphate, on the other hand, has a rate of 19 to 21 percent and is only available briefly before being leached away, leaving behind salt concentrations.

The label will also tell you how much to use and when to use it, what plants it is best used for and any warnings concerning the product. Some strong chemical formulas are in granular form and may dissolve so slowly that one application is enough for an entire season. Other strong formulas are meant to be applied frequently in very diluted concentrations. This may not be practical because the amount of fertilizers it would take to feed your garden would make the cost astronomical.

## *Creating Your Own Fertilizer Formula*

We all know it is important that plants be fed on a regular schedule throughout the growing season, but what is not widely known is that the needs of our plants change throughout the year. Just as the diet of an athlete changes as he goes into training, the diet of a plant changes as the year progresses. In the spring when plants are making a lot of green growth, for instance, they need a fertilizer that is high in nitrogen. Plants that are grown for their foliage, such as herbs and certain vegetable crops, continue to need this kind of diet throughout the growing season. Others that are grown for their flowers or fruit need a fertilizer high in phosphorus. What is just as important as the necessary nutritional element is the ratio in which it is applied. A cupful of this and a handful of that may not be combining substances in correct ratios to work well. If you've just dug in some dried cow manure and then applied a fertilizer with an NPK number of 7–7–7, you have fed your plants a formula high in nitrogen. On the other hand, if you have added a fertilizer high in phosphorus you have wound up with a formula that has a nitrogen-to-phosphorus ratio that is much more equal.

It isn't very difficult to create an organic fertilizer tailored to your needs if you know the percentage of nutrients various substances contain. That is why the NPK number is so important. Let's say you had blood meal, bone meal, and greensand on hand and you wanted to combine them to form a complete fertilizer. How much of each would you need? You could combine a cup of each to form three cups of a complete fertilizer but you still wouldn't know exactly how much nitrogen, phosphorus, and potash your mixture contained. Blood meal contains 15 percent nitrogen, 1.3 percent phosphorus, and .70 percent potash. This means that out of every 100 parts of blood meal 15 parts equals nitrogen, 1.3 parts equals phosphorus and .70 parts equals potassium. Bone meal, on the other hand, contains 3.5 percent nitrogen while greensand contains none. If you add together the number of parts of nitrogen each substance contains and divide by three, you will know the exact percentage of nitrogen your mixture contains. For example:

    100 parts blood meal contains 15 parts nitrogen
    100 parts bone meal contains 3.5 parts nitrogen
    100 parts greensand contains .00 parts nitrogen.

The sum total equals:
    300 parts fertilizer which contains 18.5 parts nitrogen

We now divide the total volume of the fertilizer and the total volume of nitrogen by three. A hundred parts of our new mixture then contains 6.13 parts nitrogen or 6.13 percent nitrogen. We now have the first number of our new NPK number. The procedure is repeated for the other elements, then it is divided by three.

| | AMOUNT | SUBSTANCE | NITROGEN (PARTS PER 100) | PHOSPHORUS (PARTS PER 100) | POTASSIUM (PARTS PER 100) |
|---|---|---|---|---|---|
| | 1 cup | blood meal | 15.00 | 1.30 | .70 |
| | 1 cup | bone meal | 3.50 | 18.00 | .00 |
| | 1 cup | greensand | .00 | 1.50 | 5.00 |
| TOTAL | 3 cups | mixture | 18.50 | 20.80 | 5.70 |

1 cup mixture       6.16 percent N       6.93 percent P       1.90 percent K

The NPK number for our mixture then is 6–7–2. We now notice the amount of potash is seriously lacking. We must alter the original amount of greensand to come up with a more equitable formula. By combining 1 cup of bloodmeal, 1 cup of bone meal, and 3 cups of greensand, we come up with an NPK number of 6–8–5, a much more balanced formula.

Knowing what the NPK number represents and how to alter it has other uses as well. If you had some bone meal that contained 16 percent phosphorus and you wanted to substitute it for phosphate rock, which contains 30 percent phosphorus, the percentages would tell you that you need twice as much bone meal to supply the same amount of phosphorus to the soil. Or perhaps you have an azalea plant that needs a mixture that is more acidic. Knowing how to compute the NPK number also has another advantage. It saves you money. Complete fertilizers are expensive, and when you buy different formulas to take care of your different garden needs, the expense adds up. By purchasing only a few basic ingredients and creating your own complete formulas, you can easily take care of your entire garden.

## Composition of Common Fertilizers

| SUBSTANCE | SPEED OF ACTION | CHEMICAL REACTION | PERCENT OF | | | CONTAINS TRACE ELEMENTS |
|---|---|---|---|---|---|---|
| | | | N | P | K | |
| Activated sludge | slow | acid | 4 | 3 | 0 | |
| Ammonium nitrate | fast | acid | 35 | 0 | 0 | |
| Ammonium phosphate | fast | acid | 10 | 50 | 0 | |
| Ammonium sulfate | fast | acid | 20 | 0 | 0 | |
| Basic slag | fast | alkaline | 0 | 8 | 0 | x |

## *Composition of Common Fertilizers* (cont'd)

| SUBSTANCE | SPEED OF ACTION | CHEMICAL REACTION | PERCENT OF | | | CONTAINS TRACE ELEMENTS |
|---|---|---|---|---|---|---|
| | | | N | P | K | |
| Bone meal | fast | alkaline | 0 | 11 | 0 | |
| Calcium nitrate | fast | alkaline | 16 | 0 | 0 | |
| Coffee grounds | fast | acid | 0.2 | 0.4 | 0.7 | |
| Cottonseed meal | slow | acid | 7 | 3 | 1.5 | |
| Cow manure (dried) | slow | acid | 2 | 1 | 1 | x |
| Diammonium phosphate | fast | acid | 18 | 45 | 0 | |
| Dried blood | fast | acid | 13 | 3 | 0 | |
| Fish emulsion | fast | acid | | | | x |
| Granite dust | slow | neutral | 0 | 0 | 5 | x |
| Greensand (glauconite) | slow | neutral | 0 | 1 | 6 | x |
| Hoof and horn meal | slow | alkaline | 13 | 2 | 0 | |
| Horse manure | slow | acid | 1 | 0 | 1 | x |
| Incinerator ash | fast | alkaline | 0 | 5 | 2 | |
| Magnesium sulfate | fast | acid | 0 | 20 | 21 | |
| Muriate of potash | fast | acid | 0 | 1 | 6 | |
| Phosphate rock | slow | acid | 0 | 5 | 0 | |
| Potassium nitrate | fast | acid | 13 | 0 | 45 | |
| Potassium sulfate | fast | acid | 0 | 0 | 50 | |
| Poultry manure | slow | alkaline | 3.5 | 2.5 | 1 | x |
| Seaweed | slow | acid | 2 | 1 | 5 | x |
| Sodium nitrate | fast | acid | 16 | 0 | 0 | |
| 20 percent superphosphate | fast | acid | 0 | 20 | 0 | |
| Superphosphate (concentrate) | fast | acid | 0 | 45 | 0 | |
| Superphosphoric acid polyphosphate | fast | acid | 0 | 75 | 0 | |
| Urea | slow | acid | 45 | 0 | 0 | |
| Wood ashes | fast | alkaline | 0 | 2 | 7 | x |

## Common Organic Fertilizer Formulas

*6–8–5*
1 part dried blood
1 part bone meal
3 parts greensand

*4–5–4*
1 part dried blood
1 part cow manure
1 part bone meal
2 parts wood ash

*2–3–2*
3 parts coffee grounds
1 part bone meal
1 part greensand

*2–5–3*
3 parts cow manure
1 part phosphate rock
1 part wood ash

*4–5–5*
1 part dried blood
1 part bone meal
3 parts granite dust

*2–3–3*
3 parts cow manure
1 part phosphate rock
1 part granite dust

*4–6–5*
1 part dried blood
1 part bone meal
2 parts wood ash

*2–2.5–2*
1 part cottonseed meal
1 part phosphate rock
1 part granite dust

*2–3–2*
1 part cottonseed meal
1 part phosphate rock
1 part greensand

*4–6–5*
1 part hoof and horn meal
1 part bone meal
2 parts wood ash

*4–6–4*
6 parts cow manure
1 part bone meal
1 part greensand

# Foliar Feeding

Foliar feeding is the act of applying nutrients directly to the plant's foliage rather than the soil. Among the many uses foliar feeding has is to give a quick boost to plants that have been heavily taxed by flower or fruit production, or whose growth has been checked by rainy weather or cold temperatures. Certain nutrients that are "locked" and unavailable to plants due to an imbalance in the soil may be provided through foliar sprays, and plants whose roots are unable to absorb sufficient nutrients from the soil because of a restricted, injured, or diseased root system can receive the nutrients they need. At the first sign of a nutrient deficiency, a foliar spray can be applied to help diagnose and treat the problem quickly. If the plant shows signs of recovery, the soil can then be enriched for more permanent results and a second foliar spray should be applied in two or three weeks.

There must be sufficient leafy growth for foliar feeding to be successful. In order for plants to develop to this stage, the soil must be properly prepared before sowing or planting. Foliar feeding cannot take the place of the traditional methods of applying fertilizers and manures.

Foliar feeds can be administered as either a dust or a spray. Sprays are more effective since most of the material being applied sticks to the plant. For even greater adherence, a wetting agent can be added to the mixture. Consult your county agent on what is best to use with the fertilizer you wish to apply. Do not use soap, which is often recommended for use with pesticides. Dusts are most advantageous when applying trace elements that are poisonous in large quantities. Even on a calm day most of the material will fall off the leaves.

Foliar feeds are best applied on a calm, cloudy day, or late in the afternoon when the sun isn't as strong and the temperature has dropped. At these times there is very little chance of leaf scorch, and the slow drying time often associated with these conditions achieves the best results. Be sure to apply the material to both the upper and lower leaf surfaces. It is the lower leaf surface where most of the absorption will take place. A light, even coat is all that is needed—too much can result in leaf scorch and eventual defoliation.

## Suitable Fertilizers for Foliar Feeding

| NUTRIENT | FERTILIZER | OUNCES PER GALLON |
| --- | --- | --- |
| Nitrogen | Urea | $3/4$–$1\frac{1}{2}$ |
|  | Potassium nitrate | $\frac{1}{2}$ |
| Phosphorus | Triple superphosphate | $\frac{1}{2}$–$1$ |
| Potassium | Sulphate of potash | $1\frac{1}{2}$ |
| Magnesium | Magnesium sulphate | 3 |
|  | Epsom salts | 3 |
| Iron | Iron chelate | According to directions |
| Manganese | Manganese sulphate | $\frac{1}{2}$–$1$ |
| Copper | Copper sulphate | $\frac{1}{2}$ |
| Boron | Borax | $\frac{1}{12}$ |
| Complete foliar feeds |  | According to directions |

# Straight Fertilizers in General Use

*Ammonium chloride (nitrogen).* Used as a component of compound fertilizers, ammonium chloride yields 26 percent nitrogen and 66 percent chlorine. Seed germination is reduced as chlorine builds up in the soil with constant use. Watering with city tap water aggravates the condition.

*Ammonium nitrate (nitrogen).* This is a component of many complete fertilizers. It yields 32½ percent nitrogen and is manufactured by passing ammonia gas through nitric acid.

*Ammo-phos (nitrogen, phosphorus).* This is used as a source of both nitrogen and phosphorus in complete fertilizer formulas. Grade A breaks down into 11 percent nitrogen and 24 percent sulfur. It is strongly acid and deadly to certain beneficial bacteria.

*Basalt rock (phosphorus, potassium).* Widely distributed along the New England coast, basalt rock contains significant amounts of phosphorus, potassium, calcium, magnesium, and iron. It is applied directly to the soil at the rate of 2 cups per square yard.

*Basic slag (phosphorus).* This is a by-product of the smelting process for pig iron. It is a slow-acting, long-lasting, inorganic phosphate fertilizer that contains large amounts of trace elements. Its lime content makes it a good liming agent and fertilizer for acid soils. When used on light soils potash minerals should be applied with it. Apply it during the fall or winter at the rate of 8 ounces per square yard. Do not use it with lime.

*Blood meal, dried blood (nitrogen).* These are two of the most rapid organic fertilizers when used in warm, moist soils. They are mostly used in powder form, but there is a fully soluble form that can be used as a liquid feed. Use them as a top dressing throughout the growing season at a rate of 2 to 3 ounces per square yard. Eventually they will make your soil more acidic.

*Bone meal (phosphorus).* This is a good organic fertilizer for general use. It's made from waste bones from slaughterhouses that are steamed under pressure to remove fat, then dried at high temperatures to kill disease organisms. The nitrogen and phosphate content varies, depending on exactly what went into the mixture. All plants will benefit from its use and it is especially good for bulbs. Bone meal is usually spread at the rate of 4 ounces per square yard. Overfeeding will not harm your plants.

*Calcium nitrate (calcium, nitrogen).* This is an inorganic compound that can be used as a straight fertilizer or as a component of a complete formula.

It breaks down into 24 percent calcium and 15 percent nitrogen. Because of the high amount of calcium present, it will, with repeated use, make your soil more alkaline.

*Chelates.* These are organic compounds that attach to metal molecules such as iron, making them available to plants. Treated metals are said to be "chelated," such as chelated iron. Follow directions carefully when applying chelated compounds since overapplication may be poisonous to your plants. The best chelator of all is the organic matter in the soil, which should be increased whenever possible.

*Cottonseed meal (nitrogen).* Used chiefly as a rich source of nitrogen (7 percent) it contains about 2 to 3 percent phosphoric acid and 1.5 percent potash as well as trace elements. It is primarily used as a fertilizer for acid-loving plants, since it will lower the pH of the soil. Applying cotton-seed meal is a good way to compensate for a limited supply of organic matter, and helps to stretch the little that is present to its maximum benefit. It is a slow-acting fertilizer that is best applied twice a year, once in the late fall and again in the early spring just after the first flowers fade.

*Fish meal, fish emulsion (nitrogen).* High in nitrogen, products made from fish meals, fish emulsions, and seaweeds are high in trace elements as well.

*Green manure.* The true definition involves a cover crop such as clover that is grown and then turned under to enrich the soil. I use it in a much broader sense to mean any green plants or weeds that are cut up and dug into the soil in the fall after the season ends. This practice adds a variety of valuable nutrients to the soil. Every element that is present in plant tissues is returned to the soil to be reused. Be sure to dig in only disease-free plants.

*Greensand, glauconite (potash).* Rich in iron potassium silicate, greensand is a naturally occurring marine deposit that contains 7 percent potash, and being an undersea deposit, it contains most of the trace elements plants need. Greensand is an excellent soil builder and has the ability to absorb large amounts of water and to release it slowly over a long period of time. Superior deposits contain 18 to 23 percent iron oxide, 3 to 7 percent magnesium, and small amounts of lime or phosphorus. Combining green-sand with dried manure and phosphate rock should seriously be considered, since such a mixture seems to make all the nutrients more readily available. It should be applied at the rate of ¼ cup per square foot. Do not overapply, as it contains aluminum.

*Hoof and horn meal (nitrogen).* This is not generally available. It acts fairly quickly in warm, moist soils, and is long lasting. The finer the grade the faster it works. Apply at the rate of 4 to 6 ounces per square yard.

*Leafmold (potash).* An excellent soil builder, leafmold is a good quick source of potash. It is very acidic and a must for woodland plants such as ferns.

*Magnesium sulfate (magnesium, sulfur).* This is an inorganic, coarsely crystalline, soluble material that contains 20 percent magnesium and 26.5 percent sulfur. It is used only where magnesium is lacking and is applied at the rate of 1 to 2 ounces per square yard, or as a foliar spray at the rate of ¼ ounce per gallon of water.

*Manure.* This is the most common source of nitrogen fertilizer in use and contains all the nutrients plants need including trace elements. Its source (poultry, cow, horse, etc.) determines the percentage of nutrients available. It can be purchased dried and bagged and it can be used at any time during the growing season without harming your plants. Fresh manure should never be applied directly since it can burn tender roots. Instead, it should be composted until it is well broken down, or it can be applied in the fall and allowed to break down over the winter. Never use dog or cat manure, which contains pathogens that can be spread by its use.

*Muriate of potash (potash).* This contains 53 percent potash and 47 percent chlorine and is a fast-acting potash fertilizer. Its continued use lowers the protein content of certain food crops, particularly potatoes, and damages their quality.

*Nitrate of soda (nitrogen).* All the nitrogen is present as a soluble nitrate and is immediately available to plants. If watered in, its effects will be seen in a few days. Nitrate of soda is applied in the spring and during summer and is especially effective to boost growth checked by slow, wet weather. When applied in large dressings at too frequent intervals, it can destroy the crumb structure of your soil. It should be applied at the rate of ½ ounce per square yard at intervals of several weeks.

*Potassium sulfate (potassium, sulfur).* This is made up of 48 percent potash and 16 percent sulfur. Sulfur can build up with continued use and may become a problem.

*Seaweed (potassium, nitrogen, trace).* One of the best all-around fertilizers and soil builders you can find, seaweed has a composition similar to barnyard manure. While it contains only moderate amounts of nitrogen, it contains large amounts of potassium. Seaweed also supplies all the trace elements necessary for proper plant nutrition and acts as a natural chelator; only the amount of phosphorus is disappointing. Even the growth-producing hormones present in seaweed, gibberellins and auxins, can be passed on to your garden plants, increasing yields.

Fresh seaweed can either be spread directly in the garden as a mulch or dug into the soil around plants. It should not be left sitting in a pile since it decomposes quickly and loses its nutrients. You can also make a seaweed "tea" by soaking two pounds of chopped seaweed in a gallon of hot water overnight; water your plants with it the next day. The tea can also be used for foliar feeding, as can commercial seaweed extractions.

*Sludge.* Activated sludge is the end product of the waste treatment process and the use of sludge is currently under some controversy. Clean sludge, like barnyard manure, is beneficial to plants and is quite safe to use, but contaminated sludge can contain pathogens, heavy metals, or industrial chemicals. What must be remembered also is that both heavy metals and industrial chemicals have a cumulative effect on your soil.

In most cases the sludge you would be using has been analyzed. If it has not, or if you can't get hold of the analysis, don't use it. Raw, untreated sewage sludge should never be used under any circumstances.

Use activated sludge as you would any other manure. It is best applied in the fall and allowed to winter over, or in early spring, four to six weeks before planting.

*Sulphate of ammonia (nitrogen).* This is a good early spring fertilizer, especially for acid-loving plants. The ammonia is preserved from immediate loss during wet weather by clay particles and organic matter which hold it. When the soil warms up (above 42°F.) the ammonia is converted to nitrates that plants can absorb. Repeated use will lower the soil's pH. Apply at the rate of ½ to 1 ounce per square yard or dissolve 1 teaspoon in a gallon of water and apply.

*Sulphate of iron (iron).* This is useful for correcting iron deficiency in acid soils only.

*Sulphate of potash (potash).* This substance acts quickly and is held by the clay and humus in the soil until it is required by the plants to correct potash deficiency. Dissolve 1 ounce in a gallon of water and wet the soil thoroughly. Always use sulphate of potash on soft fruits such as currants and gooseberries instead of muriate of potash.

*Superphosphate of lime (phosphate).* Raw, ground phosphate rock is treated with sulfuric acid to form a highly soluble fertilizer. It does not supply lime to plants in spite of its name. It can be used at a rate of 1 to 2 ounces per square yard before sowing or planting.

*Tankage.* This is refuse from slaughterhouses and butchershops. Depending on the amount of bone present, the phosphorus content varies greatly. It is a good hurry-up fertilizer but has an alkaline effect on the soil.

*Urea-form (nitrogen).* This is a synthetic organic fertilizer and is a combination of urea and formaldehyde. In spite of its high analysis, it will not burn plants. Its nitrogen is gradually converted by soil bacteria into a form plants can use. One application will feed plants continuously for several months. Apply at the rate of 1 to 2 ounces per square yard.

*Wood ashes (potassium, calcium).* Wood ash is a fast-acting fertilizer which, depending on the temperature of combustion, can contain from 4 to 10 percent potash ar' ·naller amounts of phosphorus. Wood ash also contains many trace elements including copper, zinc, manganese, iron, and sodium sulfur. More important, wood ash is highly alkaline, containing about 45 percent calcium carbonate, a compound found in lime. It has a pH factor of 13 while most garden plants require a soil that is slightly acid (pH 6.5). Never use wood ashes on acid-loving plants or newly emerged seedlings. Wood ash can also destroy the tilth of clay soils if applied in too great a quantity. Four to 8 ounces per square yard is sufficient. Store wood ash in a dry place, as potassium carbonate quickly leaches away.

### How to Cure Deficiencies with Straight Fertilizers

| NUTRIENT | SUSCEPTIBLE PLANTS | FERTILIZERS |
| --- | --- | --- |
| Nitrogen | All plants, especially leafy plants | Dried blood, blood meal, hoof and horn meal, nitrate of soda, potash nitrate, sulphate of ammonia |
| Phosphorus | All plants, especially root crops and bulbs | Basic slag, bone meal, phosphate rock, superphosphate |
| Potassium | All plants, especially potatoes, beans, gooseberries, apples, currants | Fish meal, granite dust, greensand (glauconite), hybrolite, muriate of potash, potash nitrate, seaweed, sulphate of potash, wood ashes |
| Magnesium | All plants, especially potatoes, carrots, cabbages, apples, gooseberries, tomatoes | Dolomitic limestone, magnesium sulphate (Epsom salts) |

## How to Cure Deficiencies with Straight Fertilizers (cont'd)

| NUTRIENT | SUSCEPTIBLE PLANTS | FERTILIZERS |
|---|---|---|
| Calcium | All plants | Lime |
| Sulfur | Deficiency unlikely | Many garden products |
| Iron | Acid-loving plants, also apple, plum, pear, cherry, raspberry, currants, strawberry | Iron chelate |
| Manganese | Potatoes, brassicas (cauliflower, broccoli, etc.), peas, dwarf and runner beans, onions, carrots, celery, apple, plum, cherry, raspberry | Manganese sulphate |
| Boron | Brassicas (broccoli, cauliflower, etc.), celery, beets, carnations | Borax |
| Chlorine | Deficiency unlikely | |
| Molybdenum | Cauliflower | Usually cured with lime, sodium molybdenum |
| Copper | Vegetables, some fruits | Copper sulphate (bluestone), copper oxychloride, fungicide |
| Zinc | All plants | Zinc sulfate |

# Converting Amounts of Fertilizers

Many fertilizers come with directions based on "pounds per acre," which is a bit strange for a small urban garden. The following information should make computing proper dosages easier. Please note that the depth of your container is not a factor in computing fertilizer dosage. Bagged fertilizers may be heavier or lighter depending on bulk. The figures given are for the average.

1 pound = 1 pint, or 16 ounces
16 ounces or 1 pint = 2 cups, 32 tablespoons, 96 teaspoons, or slightly less than ½ liter

To compute the area:

the area of a square container = the length × the width
the area of a round container = 3.14 × $r^2$
1 acre = 43,560 square feet, or 4,047 square meters

Square feet can be rounded to 40,000; square meters can be rounded to 4,000.

## Using pounds per acre

For each 44 pounds per acre the rates for smaller amounts would be:

|  |  |
|---|---|
| 1000 square feet | = 7½ ounces or 1 cup |
| 100 square feet | = 1½ ounces or 3 tablespoons |
| 25 square feet | = ½ ounces or 1 tablespoon |
| 1 square yard (9 square feet) | = ¾ teaspoon |
| 2½ square feet | = ¼ teaspoon |

For each 100 pounds per acre the rates for smaller amounts would be:

|  |  |
|---|---|
| 1000 square feet | = 2½ pounds or 2½ pints |
| 100 square feet | = ½ pound or ½ cup |
| 25 square feet | = 1 ounce or 2 tablespoons |
| 1 square yard (9 square feet) | = ½ ounce or 2½ teaspoons |
| 2½ square feet | = ½ teaspoon |

For each 2000 pounds per acre (1 ton per acre) the rates for smaller amounts would be:

|  |  |
|---|---|
| 1000 square feet | = 50 pounds |
| 100 square feet | = 5 pounds or 5 pints |
| 25 square feet | = 1¼ pounds or 2½ cups |
| 1 square yard (9 square feet) | = ½ pound or 1 cup |
| 2½ square feet | = 2 ounces or 4 tablespoons |

# ❧ 6 ❧
# Mulching

A MULCH IS A LAYER OF MATERIAL that is placed on the soil around plants in order to conserve moisture, maintain a more even soil temperature, and smother weeds. It is man's version of a very natural occurrence that takes place every autumn when the trees shed their leaves. This natural winter blanket, when maintained year round, has many other benefits besides protecting plants from freezing temperatures. It adds organic matter to the soil, creating good soil structure and providing nutrients; it helps conserve soil moisture and cut down on competition from weeds. The soil beneath a mulch remains loose, in little need of cultivation. This all adds up to a lot less work and a lot more enjoyment for the gardener.

## Benefits of a Summer Mulch

The biggest advantage of a summer mulch is water conservation. A good mulch will reduce water loss through evaporation by one-half. A mulch places an insulating barrier between the soil and the warm air, creating a temperature difference. Moisture that would normally be lost through evaporation condenses and falls back onto the soil. Plants benefit by not drying out so quickly, a worthy point to be remembered by container gardeners. When watering, runoff is reduced because of the loose quality of the mulching material and the soil beneath it. It allows water to pass through easily while at the same time creating a physical barrier that allows the soil time to absorb it. The soil temperature remains 10 to 15° cooler during the hottest part of the day, an important consideration since plant growth slows and finally stops with excessive soil warmth (over 90°F). On cool nights, mulched soil remains warmer, which is especially important in spring and autumn, when an unexpected frost can damage or even kill plants. This stabilizing effect on temperature also favors the bacterial activity so important to growth.

Mulching cuts down on weeds in two ways. Every time you cultivate your soil you stir up seeds that have been buried too deeply to germinate. This means that every time you cultivate you are destroying one generation of weeds while planting another! Because you need to cultivate mulched soil less often you will find yourself with fewer weeds to pull. The second way mulching prevents weeds is this: Seeds only have enough stored nutrients to sustain them through their germination. They must reach the sunlight before their supply of food runs out. A thick mulch prevents all but the strongest perennial weeds from reaching the surface, and these are easily pulled by hand.

# A Winter Mulch

The primary function of a winter mulch is to maintain a stable soil temperature. It is not steady freezing temperatures that cause most plant damage but the alternate freezing and thawing of the soil. A late-winter thaw that lasts for several days can send the wrong signal to plants. They will begin to grow before they should and will be damaged by freezing temperatures that follow. Constant freezing and thawing can also heave plants right out of the ground and expose their roots. This is especially true of newly planted specimens that have not had time to make good root growth.

A winter mulch will also guard against the deep penetration of frost, especially when it occurs without the benefit of a snow covering (snow has been called the poor man's mulch). Shallow-rooted shrubs such as azaleas and rhododendrons can be severely damaged. Other tender perennials, such as strawberries, will not survive if their crowns freeze. Even English ivy *(Hedera helix)*, a hardy perennial, will benefit from a mulch in December to keep its leaves from turning brown.

A winter mulch will also help conserve moisture, keeping plants and bulbs from dehydrating, another major cause of winter plant failure.

Fig. 11    Pine roping, which is usually used for winter seasonal decorations, also makes a fine winter mulch.

## Mulching and Soil Fertility

Mulching improves soil structure as decaying organic matter works its way into the soil, stimulating root growth and biological activity. Some mulching materials, especially leguminous hays and grass clippings, can also add substantial amounts of nutrients to the soil. Potash, which tends to be fixed near the surface, penetrates much deeper in mulched soils. Whatever nutrients and trace elements are present in the mulching material will eventually be released into the soil to benefit your plants. There is a disadvantage to this if a leguminous or heavily fertilized material is laid down in the fall. It could stimulate excessive late growth that would subject the plant to winter injury. Materials high in nitrogen should be avoided at this time of the year.

Some materials which contain large amounts of cellulose, such as sawdust, corncobs, or bark chips, do not contain enough nitrogen to take care of their own decomposition and will deplete the supply present in the soil. This situation can easily be remedied by adding a nitrogen fertilizer such as dried blood to the mulch before spreading. Dampen the mulching material first so the fertilizer will stick to it and mix well. Watch your plants for signs of nitrogen deficiency and apply more fertilizer as a side dressing as needed. Do not scratch the fertilizer into the soil as this will only cause more of the mulching material to be mixed with the soil, compounding the problem. Instead, water the fertilizer in. A chemical fertilizer such as nitrate of soda or ammonium sulfate is the quickest acting.

Certain materials such as leafmold, oak leaves, or pine needles are acidic and make wonderful mulches for acid-loving plants. These will lower the pH of the soil slightly.

# Mulching and Disease

We have been told that it is good gardening practice to clean the garden of old plant debris because it is a home for disease. This is true, and it is also true that mulches can be a source of potential problems in this area. At the same time, mulching can help prevent the spread of disease, if handled properly. Disease is generally a reflection of unhealthy growing conditions and bad gardening practices. Harmful bacteria and fungi are constantly present around us and only need the proper conditions to gain a toehold. Poor air circulation, a soil that is too heavy or wet, a garden that is watered too late in the day and foliage that remains wet on a cool night are more usually the causes. Healthy plants properly cared for are usually not susceptible.

Mulching can help prevent such problems as blossom end rot on tomatoes, which is caused by a soil that is alternately too wet and too dry. Mulching will keep low-hanging or trailing fruits from rotting by coming into contact with wet soil. Most other fungus diseases are not spread by plants coming into contact with debris but rather by splashing water that spreads the spores from soil to stem to leaf. This is especially true of black spot on roses. A finely textured mulch such as buckwheat hulls can actually act as a barrier between the soil and infected leaves. Infected material falling on such a mulch can easily be spotted and removed before it infects the soil. When this does happen, the entire mulch should be discarded at the end of the season (do not compost!) and replaced with fresh material. Loose material such as bark chips, which can catch and hold infected material, should be discarded immediately. One material, tobacco stems, is a natural insecticide and repellent and can actually cut down on attack by insects and the diseases that they may carry.

Certain materials that retain moisture, such as grass clippings, leafmold, hops, or compost, should not be allowed to come into contact with plant trunks, especially during wet weather. They make a perfect place for disease to incubate and can cause stem and crown rot. Leave a few inches between the trunk and the mulch. Be sure not to mulch seedlings too early to help prevent damping off. In the fall, avoid using these same materials on roses as they can cause rose cankers on plants.

In areas where blights are prevalent, wait until after the spring rains have passed before mulching plants. This is especially true south of Washington, D.C., where camellia blight and azalea blight are quite common. If you find your plants affected, remove the mulch until the disease is eradicated.

# Year-Round Maintenance

Mulching is an advantageous year-round horticultural practice that is easy when done properly. There are only a few principles to keep in mind. Late spring, after your plants are well established, is the time to begin mulching. Be sure the ground is free of weeds and the soil moist. A minimum depth of 2 inches of most materials is required to be effective in both moisture conservation and weed control. Better results are possible with even deeper mulches but for container culture, when all the available depth is needed for soil, a deep mulch is not always possible. When applying the mulch, be sure to make it slightly deeper than 2 inches because the material will settle within a few weeks. To be sure it is deep enough, it should then be checked again.

For a summer mulch, I prefer a finely textured, attractive material such as buckwheat hulls or cocoa bean shells that lend a neat appearance to the garden. They are also best in conserving moisture. Never use peat moss as a mulching material. When dry it cakes and sheds water. Buckwheat hulls can be placed right up next to plant stems without fear of stem rot. The mulch should remain in place for the duration of the growing season and should be removed first from perennials, trees, and shrubs in September or early October, depending on the area of the country you live in. You want these plants to go dormant in time to prevent early frost damage. By maintaining a mulch under annuals they may make it through a couple of light frosts and give you a few extra weeks of color.

Dig the mulch into your soil to add vital nutrients and organic matter for next year and allow your perennials, trees, and shrubs to remain uncovered until after the ground freezes. In New York City, for example, this means waiting until mid- or even late December before applying a winter mulch. In other cities wait two to four weeks after the average frost date listed in the chart on pages 168–169. Then apply a deep (at least 4 inches) layer of a coarsely textured material such as straw, oak leaves, or pine needles. I prefer coarse materials because of their better insulating properties. The winter mulch should be left in place throughout the early spring. As the time for new growth nears, begin checking underneath the mulch for signs of life but do not remove it until growth appears. It should be removed first from early flowering spring bulbs and perennials. Keep plants that may be subject to frost damage covered until danger of frost is past. This will keep them from emerging too soon. What is left of the mulching material may then be dug into the soil or removed and composted. The soil should remain bare until early summer, giving it a chance to warm up. The exception to this is the use of black plastic as a mulch, which will warm the soil faster for earlier planting of warm-weather crops.

## Some Recommended Materials

*Bark chips.* These are sold in garden centers everywhere and are attractive and long lasting. They are best used as a permanent mulch around shrubs, especially acid lovers. They should not be dug into the soil since they contain a high percentage of cellulose and will rob the soil of nitrogen. Bark chips are wonderful for windy situations, since they will not blow away.

*Buckwheat hulls.* This material makes a near-perfect mulch for container gardens. Its dark color and fine, even texture make it an attractive mulch for the ornamental garden. It will not readily absorb water but at the same time allows water to pass through, creating little chance of stem rot even when placed up against stems. To add to the list of advantages, buckwheat hulls will not blow away in windy situations. They do take up to two years to decompose and should be composted rather than dug into the soil, unless the soil needs lightening.

*Cocoa bean shells.* This material is very attractive, turning from a dark brown to black within a few months. When first applied, it has a pleasant chocolate odor that disappears within a couple of weeks. Cocoa bean hulls perform best when mixed with sawdust at a ratio of 2 to 1, which keeps it from matting down. This material should be kept away from plant trunks because when fully saturated on a warm day, it will heat up and can cause some plant damage. It will also at times become moldy in warm weather, but this will not affect your plants or its performance.

*Corncobs.* Shredded corncobs are commonly found in the midwest and make an excellent mulch for roses. Some people, however, may object to its appearance in a small ornamental garden. This material will cause a nitrogen deficiency and should be mixed with a nitrogen fertilizer before applying. Be sure to remove it to the compost pile rather than digging it in.

*Hay, straw, salt marsh hay.* All of these materials make excellent winter mulches for perennials, bulbs, and shrubs. They have great insulating properties and will break down over the course of the winter, adding many needed nutrients. Straw should be combined with a nitrogen fertilizer since it can cause nitrogen deficiency. Salt marsh hay can be gathered at the shore in the fall for use.

*Lawn clippings.* Lawn clippings can be used in moderation and only when you are sure that they have not been treated with herbicides. If they have been treated, they can seriously damage or even kill your plants. When applied in too thick a layer, lawn clippings tend to form dense mats that will not decompose or let air penetrate. They will also become odorous. They are a great source of nitrogen and are best applied in the spring. Avoid applying them in late summer or fall as they can promote late green growth.

*Plastic film.* A fairly recent innovation in mulching is the use of black plastic sheeting as a mulching material. It has some interesting advantages. Plastic has a greenhouse effect on the soil, heating it up much faster in the spring. In clear weather, soil that is covered with black plastic will remain 10° to 15° hotter than uncovered soil, which means a longer season and earlier harvests as plants make strong early growth. At the same time, without proper precautions, your plants could suffer damage from an unexpected frost. Clear plastic heats the soil up even faster but weeds can germinate beneath it and even survive. Under black plastic they germinate but without the benefit of light they quickly die, making weed control nearly complete.

Plastic conserves moisture better than anything else and the soil beneath it remains loose, requiring no cultivation. An added benefit is that it may help with insect control in some cases. Some flying insects lay their eggs in the soil. These later hatch into larvae, which feed on the plant above. If the adult insect cannot lay her eggs in the soil, she will go elsewhere.

There are several disadvantages to plastic, but nothing that is not workable. Plastic adds no nutrients or matter to the soil, nor will it break down over time. Rain cannot penetrate so all watering must be done by hand through a slit in the plastic unless you have a drip irrigation system. It may not be easy to tell if you are overwatering or underwatering. When combined with a drip irrigation system plastic creates a nearly maintenance-free garden.

Black plastic is of course not very attractive and can blow or tear in the wind. These problems can all be solved by covering it with a more attractive material such as bark chips.

Plastic sheeting is generally laid down a week or two before planting, which is then done through a slit in the plastic. It is best to make only one cut instead of two at right angles so there is less chance of tearing and so less soil is exposed. For early spring crops the soil is worked and covered in the fall. Most weed seeds will sprout then and die and the soil will warm up much faster in the spring, allowing planting when bare soil is still frozen. In extremely cold climates, such as northern Canada and Alaska, black plastic has allowed gardeners to plant a wider variety of plants.

*Pine needles, pine boughs.* Don't throw away that Christmas tree! Cut off the branches and place them on your perennial beds. Remember that pine needles, although an excellent mulch, will acidify your soil. They are great for acid-loving shrubs. Remember to check the pH of your soil annually.

*Sawdust.* When using a sawdust mulch only a shallow 1-inch layer is necessary around most annuals, perennials, and vegetables, while a 2-inch layer will take care of most shrubs. A thicker mulch may mat down, limiting aeration and causing stem and crown rot. Sawdust makes a terrific winter mulch for strawberries by affording wonderful protection while not covering the plants. It is also good for spring-flowering bulbs, which are not as affected by a deficiency of nitrogen.

Try to get a supply from a sawmill since it is not as fine as that from a craftsman's shop and will not mat down as easily. If you find a mill that handles redwood or red cedar, the sawdust will be darker in color and not as objectionable in appearance. Always mix it with a nitrogen fertilizer before applying.

*Seaweed.* Seaweed makes a fine mulch and is rich in trace elements and minerals. It turns dark brown or black with time and its appearance is not offensive. There is no need to wash off any salt since there is too little to harm your plants.

## Recommended Mulches

| MATERIAL | SOURCES | DEPTH IN INCHES | BEST USE | COMMENTS |
|---|---|---|---|---|
| Bark chips | Garden centers, saw-mills | 2–4 for shrubs; 1 for vegetables and flowers | Permanent year-round | Extremely attractive. It may cause a nitrogen deficiency if dug into soil. Long-lasting. |

## *Recommended Mulches* (cont'd)

| MATERIAL | SOURCES | DEPTH IN INCHES | BEST USE | COMMENTS |
|---|---|---|---|---|
| Buck-wheat hulls | Garden centers | 1½ | Summer | Fine textured and attractive. Will not blow away. Will not promote stem or crown rot. Best to compost in the fall. |
| Cocoa bean shells | Garden centers | 2–4 | Summer | Best mixed with sawdust. Good color and appearance. Keep away from plant stems. |
| Compost | Home pro-duct, garden centers | 1 | Summer | Best for acid-loving plants. Can be used on all plants with the addition of lime. Improves soil structure and adds nutrients. Will absorb moisture. |
| Corncobs (crushed) | Garden centers (Mid-west) | 2–3 | Summer, year-round | Best for roses but not very attractive. Can cause nitrogen deficiency. |
| Mush-room com-post | Garden centers, mush-room farms | 2–4 | Summer | Dark color; will supply nutrients. |
| Peanut hulls | Garden centers (South) | 2–4 | Year-round | Not especially attractive. Do not dig in; compost instead. |

## Recommended Mulches (cont'd)

| MATERIAL | SOURCES | DEPTH IN INCHES | BEST USE | COMMENTS |
|---|---|---|---|---|
| Pecan hulls | Garden centers (South) | 2–4 | Year-round | Same as peanut hulls. |
| Plastic film | Garden centers | Surface | Summer | Good weed and moisture control. Soil remains warmer. May present watering problems. Unattractive. |
| Pine needles and boughs | Wherever conifers grow. Rarely sold | 2–4 | Year-round | Good for acid-loving plants and alpines. Will acidify soil. |
| Salt hay | Seashore | 4–6 | Winter | Not attractive; adds minerals. |
| Seaweed | Seashore | 2–4 | Winter | Not attractive for ornamentals but valuable for minerals and trace elements. Use as winter mulch; it will decompose by spring. |
| Hay | Garden centers | 4–6 | Winter | Good insulation properties. Provides nutrients, rots quickly. Turn under in spring, or compost. |
| Lawn clippings | Home product | 1 | Summer | Rich in nitrogen; do not use in the fall. Beware of herbicides. Do not apply thickly. Turn under in the fall. |

## *Recommended Mulches* (cont'd)

| MATERIAL | SOURCES | DEPTH IN INCHES | BEST USE | COMMENTS |
|---|---|---|---|---|
| Leaves | Home product | 2–4, 4–10 | Year-round | Better if composted first. Attractive when shredded. Will add nutrients. Rots quickly. May mat down. May be acidic. |
| Leafmold | Garden centers | 1 | Summer | Attractive; will add nutrients. Keep away from stems. Will acidify the soil as well as improve structure. Turn under. |
| Manure (cow or chick-en) | Garden centers, farms | 1–2 | Summer | Do not use fresh. Provides some nutrients. May have odor; can be expensive. Work into soil at end of season. |
| Sawdust | Sawmills, lumber-yards | 1, 2 for shrubs | Year-round | Good but not attractive. Will cause nitrogen deficiency. Do not apply thickly. |
| Straw | Garden centers, feed stores, farms | 4–6 | Winter | Coarser, more durable than hay. May contain seeds that sprout. Can cause nitrogen deficiency. |
| Tobacco stems | Garden centers (South), tobacco farms | 2 in sum-mer, 4 in winter | Summer, winter | Not attractive, but natural insecticide. Coarse textured. Turn under or compost. |

# ❧ 7 ☙

# Composting

A PROPERLY MANAGED COMPOST PILE can occupy less than 2 square feet of space and transform your garden soil into the stuff dreams are made of. Roof and terrace gardeners shouldn't dismiss the practice because of odors or appearance. The smelly eyesores of our childhood are a thing of the past. By using a good container and proper management techniques, composting can be a pleasant, rewarding experience. There is considerable satisfaction to be gained from recycling waste into a beneficial product that costs nothing.

The composting process changes waste materials, both chemically and physically, into a rich, almost black, crumbly material that is actually the product of billions of naturally occurring bacteria and fungi. By supplying soil microorganisms with the proper conditions of a varied diet, moisture, air and warmth, a compost pile creates an environment in which they can live and reproduce at the highest rate of activity. Each individual organism splits apart to become two every twenty minutes under optimum conditions. These bacteria and fungi digest organic wastes, absorb nourishment, and release important chemical compounds, including nutrients, growth-producing hormones and natural antibiotics, back into the soil. Plants rely on bacteria not only to extract nutrients they cannot do directly themselves but also to help fight disease.

The chemical changes that take place release so much heat that if the night temperature remains above 50°F., the compost pile will heat up to 160°F. within a few days. This is the first major indication that everything is going well. Dryness, wind, and temperature variations can slow the process down, reducing the temperature of the pile. Within a few weeks of building the pile, it will shrink to half its former size and turn almost black. When the material is ready to use the temperature will drop and the compost will be crumbly in texture, with a sweet, rich aroma, making it pleasant to handle.

Garden compost is a pure form of humus, with a multitude of applications. As a fertilizer, it's more valuable than its low chemical analysis would indicate. Its nutrients are released slowly in small amounts that plants can easily absorb. Very little is wasted and there is no danger of burning tender roots. At the same time, it is a natural soil conditioner, improving tilth,* a claim that no chemical fertilizer can make. It will break up sticky clay soil and improve the moisture capacity of sandy soil. The addition of compost to your soil can also extend your growing season, protecting your plants against light frosts. By darkening your garden soil, it will enable it to absorb more heat. Compost can also be used as a mulch, keeping roots cool and moist, while releasing a constant supply of nutrients.

All this from something you were going to discard! By following the few simple procedures outlined in this chapter you are only a few weeks away from better soil and healthier plants.

## *The Ideal Container*

An ideal container should be neat in appearance, conceal the compost materials from view, and at the same time allow proper air circulation. It should be equipped with a tight-fitting lid to keep out rain and retain the right amount of moisture. It should be made from a good insulating material such as plastic that will retain heat and can protect against weather fluctuations. And the ideal container should be round so heat can radiate evenly from the center and there are no corners to dry out.

There are many good compost containers on the commercial market but the most notable are those manufactured by the Rotocrop Company. These are neat in appearance even for the small-space gardener and come in several sizes. The design incorporates all the necessary features and easy access to the finished compost. The one drawback these have for the roof gardener is that they are designed to be set directly on the ground, and have no bottoms. If you opt for one of these it will have to be fitted with a very fine screen mesh and placed on a platform.

An excellent inexpensive container can be made from a plastic garbage

---

*The cultivation of land; tillage.

*Fig. 12   A compost bin*

can that comes with a lid. Use a hot knife or poker to make 1-inch holes at 6-inch intervals along the sides and bottom. These will provide proper ventilation and drainage. Near the bottom make an opening 12 × 12 inches to easily accommodate a trowel for removing the finished compost. No matter what kind of container you decide on, it should be placed on a raised platform so the compost doesn't come into contact with the surface of the roof. By placing it on a platform you will allow better air circulation around the pile.

## *The Ingredients*

Any healthy plant material that is free from infestation, disease, or impregnation with toxic materials such as pesticides or herbicides is suitable compost material. This includes leaves and clippings, old mulch materials, and weeds. Remember that whatever these plants took from the soil is present within the plant and can be returned to the soil. Kitchen scraps are also valuable additions to the compost pile, and are rich in nutrients and trace elements. Everything from eggshells to coffee grounds is suitable. What should be avoided, though, are meat scraps and bones, which smell badly and attract vermin. Pet droppings of any kind should not be included for the same reasons as well as the fact that they may harbor harmful pathogens.

What is important is that a large variation of materials be included. Various plants pull nutrients from the soil in different amounts and this is reflected in the plants themselves. By including a wide variety of ingredients, your finished compost will contain a more balanced proportion of nutrients. Materials need not be confined to fresh plant material either. Wood ashes are a fine source of potash and lime, and go a long way toward neutralizing the finished compost as well as acting as a natural deodorant. Remember that charcoal ashes are also a wood product as is sawdust. Seaweed is also a good addition and should be added at every opportunity. When you take a trip to the beach this summer, bring some back; it is a rich source of trace elements.

What is essential to the composting process is nitrogen. Weeds and young clippings contain plenty in the spring when they are still young and tender, but as the season progresses these plant materials become tougher and harder to break down. Certain materials such as sawdust contain less nitrogen than the bacteria needed to break them down, in which case they deplete the supply present in the pile. A pile that doesn't contain enough nitrogen will compost very slowly and may not heat up at all. An "activator" in the form of extra nitrogen becomes necessary. Wait until after the spring rains end and then apply a dusting of dried blood, hoof and horn meal, cottonseed meal, or a water-soluble high-nitrogen fertilizer. Granular fertilizers don't do the job properly, and lime, contrary to popular belief, is not an activator.

Adding nitrogen as an activator should not be confused with commercial activators sold on the market. These are meant to introduce certain strains of bacteria into the pile. Unfortunately, different strains of bacteria exist under different conditions. The conditions within individual compost piles are determined by a variety of factors and cannot be controlled; you can never predict which strains of bacteria will survive let alone operate most efficiently. Better to let nature take over and decide the issue for you. The best way to introduce the needed bacteria into the pile is to add some topsoil. This need not be your best topsoil but could be some discarded potting mix as long as it is not infested with soil-borne pests or disease.

The beauty about composting is that in a sense you are creating your own custom fertilizer. Each plant in your garden has removed nutrients from your soil in certain proportions. When these same plants are converted to compost and that compost is placed back into the soil, much of what has been removed will be returned. You'll also begin to notice that certain ingredients will be placed in the pile in greater proportions. If you keep a close eye on these, you can roughly predict the nature of the finished compost. If these ingredients are acidic, your finished product will be acidic; if they are rich in potash, your finished compost will be. By being able to predict the end result, you can begin to alter it a little. At the end of this chapter (see page 81) is a list of materials and how they break down nutritionally. If you wish to know the pH of a material which is not included, place a bit of the substance in a small amount of distilled water overnight and test the water in the morning.

# *Shredding, Mixing, and Building the Pile*

Various studies have shown that the best results are obtained when the organic materials in the pile are separated at 6-inch intervals by a 1-inch layer of soil which has been dusted with nitrogen, mineral powders, and lime. This practice is known as building the pile in layers. First a layer of vegetable material is laid down, then a layer of soil, then a layer of fertilizers, and so on. In this way microorganisms and all necessary raw materials are more evenly distributed and quick high-quality results are ensured. Older methods, which basically consisted of piling garden refuse in a haphazard manner, often resulted in an inferior product and a waiting time of one to two years before the finished compost was ready. By building the pile in a more methodical fashion, you can have completed compost in just a few short weeks.

Building a pile in layers, however, does not mean the addition of a large amount of a single substance at one time. This generally results in a mediocre compost with an uneven texture and poor nutritional content. Materials such as grass clippings, leaves, or sawdust also tend to become compressed into airtight, waterproof mats that slow the process down when added in bulk. Finer materials are best combined with coarser materials to ensure good air circulation and moisture distribution. A wide variety of materials, mixed well before being added, is most desirable.

It stands to reason that larger items that are tough, such as shrub prunings, take much longer to break down than something small such as a blade of grass. The same is true of kitchen wastes. The skin of half a grapefruit, left whole, takes much longer to decompose than one that has been cut into smaller pieces. Shredding and chopping your ingredients before adding them to the pile is well worth the extra effort. It reduces volume while exposing more surface area to bacteria, and the fluffy texture results in better air circulation and moisture distribution throughout the pile. The only time that shredding should be avoided is when adding the very first layer of material at the bottom of the pile. By keeping the pieces larger you ensure better air circulation and drainage.

Shredding can be a time-consuming process, but certain items can be cut up with a kitchen food processor or blender. If you keep up with your garden chores every week, the small amount of prunings and weeds that accumulate can be chopped up with pruning shears.

After the topsoil is applied, the addition of mineral powders, such as ground phosphate rock, bone meal, potash, or greensand, adds to the nutritional content of the finished product. These products are also a good way of altering the acid content. For more neutral results add bone meal and wood ashes, and of course a dusting of lime. This results in a product that is more desirable for normal garden conditions, but if you wish to use the compost for a wild flower garden, then you need a finished product that is more acidic and you should add ground phosphate rock and greensand instead.

Building a pile in this manner is not as much work as it seems and is well worth the effort for your finished compost will have a better texture with a better distribution of nutrients throughout. The compost placed on your roses will have the same nutritional value as that placed on your geraniums or tomatoes and will be achieved by taking a few minutes a day to shred and mix ingredients.

# Heating Up the Pile

During aerobic composting, microorganisms convert the carbon present in organic materials into energy, creating heat. The greater the bacterial activity, the more heat released. This heat means more rapid decomposition and kills weed seeds, roots and diseased plants. It is important that it be retained and intensified.

A well-made pile can heat up to 160° F. within a few days and can be checked with a kitchen meat thermometer. Many factors can result in a lowering of temperature, including a lack of volume, or a night temperature that is too low (below 50° F.). But if this is not the case, then the lack of heat buildup is your first indication that something is wrong. The problem may be a lack of air or moisture, or a lack of nitrogen, or a combination of these. Review the principles laid out in this chapter and adjust your pile accordingly.

A gradual drop in temperature over a period of several weeks is normal as the composting process nears completion. When ready the finished compost will be cool and damp.

# Proper Ventilation, Stirring the Pile

Ordinary soil contains two kinds of bacteria: aerobes and anerobes. Anerobes cannot survive in an oxygen environment and are responsible for the unpleasant odors associated with composting. Aerobes, which must have oxygen, are clean and sweet-smelling and more efficient, resulting in a shorter composting time.

The right container goes a long way toward creating the proper conditions for aerobes, as does shredding and pre-mixing all ingredients. Proper drainage is also important. A soggy pile leaves little room for air. Turning and/or stirring the pile every week is also important.

Before the pile gets too deep, turning the pile with a shovel is an easy task and takes only a few minutes. As the pile gets deeper, turning it becomes difficult and stirring is easier. Use a wooden stake long enough to reach the bottom and strong enough to move through the dense material without breaking. Move it in a circular motion, letting in air and breaking up clumps. If everything is going well, there should be no smell and the stick should come out hot and damp. If it is wet, there is too much water present; if it is dry there is not enough moisture. When the compost is ready, the stick will come out cool and damp, covered in a black crumbly residue.

## *Keep the Moisture In*

No living thing can survive without moisture, and that includes the bacteria found in a compost pile. The material held in your bin should be as damp as a well-squeezed sponge. A container with a tight-fitting lid will ensure protection from rapid evaporation as well too much moisture added by rain.

Your compost pile should be checked from time to time to ensure that the proper moisture level is being maintained. If it is dry you will have to water the pile. In the spring it will probably not require much added moisture but at the height of the summer it may require watering as often

### *Nutritional Value of Common Composting Ingredients*

| SUBSTANCE | N | P | K | TRACE |
|---|---|---|---|---|
| Apple skins | 0 | 3 | 13 | |
| Banana skins | 0 | 3 | 42 | |
| Cantaloupe rinds | 0 | 10 | 12 | |
| Cucumber skins | 0 | 12 | 27 | |
| Eggshells | 1 | 0 | 0 | |
| Grapefruit skins | 0 | 4 | 31 | |
| Lemon skins | 0 | 7 | 30 | |
| Orange skins | 0 | 3 | 27 | |
| Potato skins (raw) | 0 | 5 | 28 | x |
| Salt marsh hay | 1 | 0 | 1 | |
| Seaweed | 2 | 1 | 5 | x |
| Sweet potato skins (raw) | 0 | 3 | 14 | |
| Tea leaves | 4 | 1 | 0 | |

as twice a week. When you do add water, add very little. If your pile holds 25 gallons of material then add no more than the equivalent of 3 to 5 gallons of water.

# *Conclusion*

A well-run compost pile, managed according to some well-thought-out scientific principles, will improve your gardening pleasure for years. The effects are cumulative. Each year as you add more compost to your soil the improvements take a qualitative leap, with increased yields, better moisture retention, and stronger plant growth. It is a gardening practice not to be overlooked.

# ~ 8 ~

# Pests and
# Diseases

WHENEVER ONE FINDS A BIT OF SOIL and a plant one finds insects and microbes. Many of these are beneficials that man cannot garden without, but others are pests that destroy plants or cause disease. Man has been trying to control them, usually unsuccessfully, since ancient times and has come up with various substances that have proved to be poisonous to the pests in varying degrees. Modern pesticides were not discovered until World War II, and were developed for use in chemical warfare. They are extremely lethal, posing a serious health threat to anyone who handles them, and their use has raised some serious biological questions. At the same time, the insects they were meant to control have developed a higher tolerance to them, requiring larger and larger doses to keep them contained. As a result, horticulturists have begun to take a closer look at the importance of a natural biological balance and, consequently, some of the older organic-based compounds that were in use prior to the discovery of chemical pesticides. These seem to point a way to a safer means of control, especially for the home gardener. This is not to say that chemical pesticides still do not have their place. If handled in a mature, educated manner, their benefits are enormous and their risks can be minimized.

# Biological Control of Insects

The ideal form of insect management is to enlist nature's aid, which does not result in the severe side effects associated with synthetic chemicals— the poisoning of fish and birds and the buildup of harmful chemical residues. At the same time, you must understand and accept a certain amount of insect damage. You can't have an insect-free garden and encourage beneficial insects at the same time. As the population of a particular insect pest grows, so does the population of the predators that feed on it. The best course of action when an insect pest is discovered is to do nothing, thereby giving natural forces a chance to take over.

Among the beneficials that help control garden pests are birds, lizards, toads, many insects and spiders, and certain bacteria, fungi, and viruses. Those that attack, kill, and feed on a variety of insects, as opposed to monophagous feeders with highly specialized diets, are generally the most effective and should be encouraged. Insect-eating birds can be attracted by providing suet cakes and bird seed, as well as water and the shelter of

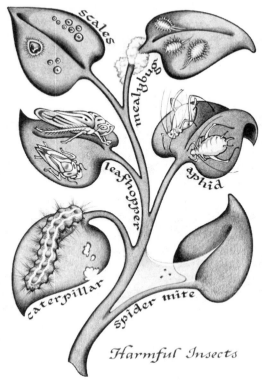

*Fig. 13*

a few trees and shrubs. Protection from cats will also be appreciated. Although chameleons are not naturally found inhabiting high rises, they can be purchased in pet shops and then turned loose in the garden. They will find plenty of food to sustain them, but they will need to be provided with water, shelter and, like birds, protection from cats.

Not all the insects that visit the garden are pests to be eliminated. Many are important predators and parasites that are not always easy to recognize since their appearance often belies their true nature. Some resemble close relatives that really are pests while others are so awful looking our first instinct is to eliminate them. Gardeners must learn to distinguish between friend and foe and should overcome the urge to squash an unfamiliar bug before learning exactly what it is. Some of the most important beneficial insects you may find include the lady beetle (ladybug), the green lacewing, and the praying mantis, as well as certain flies, wasps, and beetles.

*Helpful Insects*

Fig. 14

There are also many microscopic beneficials that attack garden pests, causing disease and death. Science has begun to harness their powers, creating new, safer pesticides with no harmful residual effects. So far as it is known, these microbial insecticides are not harmful to any other life forms except the insects that they are meant to control, and unlike chemical pesticides, the insects do not develop tolerances to them. These features make them especially attractive to the home gardener since they can be used on food crops without fear, and there is no chance of accidental poisonings.

Among those being marketed today is *Bacillus thuringiensis* (BT), a disease-causing bacterium widely sold in garden centers under the trade names Dipel and Thuricide. It is an effective biological control of most caterpillars, and acts by paralyzing the intestinal tract of affected individuals. To be effective BT must be ingested in fairly large quantities and therefore is only useful against chewing insects that feed externally on plants, where it is easily applied. It is not effective against larvae of such insects as the codling moth or corn earworm, which feed within the fruit. BT must be applied frequently to remain effective.

Japanese beetles can also be controlled by a bacterium commonly known as milky spore disease *(Bacillus popilliae),* which attacks the larval stage of the beetle. But since the larvae are primarily found in lawns, the bacterium is of no use to most urban container gardeners. Better to hand-pick the one or two adults that may be found during the course of the season.

Insects are also affected by viruses but as yet these have not been able to be reproduced commercially. Viruses are extremely contagious and attack and kill their victims quickly, sometimes in a matter of hours. After death many of the affected insects split open and their bodily liquids spew out, spreading the virus further. When coming across such insects in the garden you should leave them, or you can gather a few, chop them up and place their remains in some water, which is then sprayed on your other plants.

Another way in which we can use biological control doesn't involve insects, parasites, or diseases, but rather planning. Insects usually appear about the same time each year, live a short active life, then disappear. By taking advantage of the natural insect cycles many serious pests can be outwitted. For instance, in the vicinity of New York City you can miss an infestation of Mexican bean beetles by planting your snap beans in early June. Of course, insect cycles vary throughout the country. By keeping a garden journal in which you jot down when certain insects appear and what the weather conditions are, you can learn to predict their appearance and plan accordingly.

It has also been found that healthy plants properly watered and fed, in soil that is well drained, friable, and containing a high proportion of organic matter, tend to be less susceptible to insects and disease. An imbalance of nitrogen to potash can leave plants more prone to attack, while a soil rich in compost and humus increases the micro life which in turn helps stabilize the pH factor and makes needed nutrients more readily available. Plants that are overfed are just as prone to attack as those that aren't fed enough. The secret is balance.

Two other ideas that smart gardeners take advantage of is interplanting and rotation. In the woodlands and meadows surrounding us, we find a wide variety of plants growing in the same area. This diversity is the basis for natural biological control. Some gardeners believe that by interplanting certain plants you can ward off insect attack. This idea, known as companion planting, has received much attention lately, but so far there is little scientific evidence to support these claims, although there is evidence that root exudants from marigolds and asparagus may inhibit certain nematodes. By planting a wide variety of plants you will stimulate a wide variety of insect species, including a greater variety and number of beneficials, many of whom in their adult stages are not carnivorous but live on pollen and nectar.

By grouping containers close together, you raise the humidity and create shelter for beneficials. Many of our welcomed guests are very tiny and tend to dehydrate quickly. The more hospitable your garden is for beneficial insects, the more likely they will be to lay their eggs there.

Another good practice is not planting the same varieties year after year. By changing them you may find a new variety of a favorite plant that is not as prone to attack. Plant breeders have also made advances in recent years by providing beautiful and bountiful plants that are also resistant to disease. Look for these resistant varieties when ordering new seeds and plants.

Varying the location of plants each year is called rotation, and it is a good practice to get into for several reasons. First of all, different plant species take up nutrients in different amounts. If the same marigolds are continually planted in the same place, the soil becomes depleted of the nutrients marigolds need. You are also making a permanent home for certain pests and diseases. Many insects lay their eggs near a host plant so their offspring can find it easily in the spring. If you move their favorite food, they will not find it so easily. Many soil-borne insects and certain diseases also feed only on certain plants. If the host is moved, their numbers can't build up year after year.

Good sanitation is also important. Keep the garden free of old plant debris that can act as an alternative home and breeding ground for garden pests, many of which overwinter on old plant stems and tree trunks. Dig in all old plants at the end of the season or remove them to the compost pile. Remove old mulch material, replacing it with a new, clean mulch. Keep the garden free of weeds that can act as alternate hosts. Once a week, hose your plants down with a forceful stream of water that can dislodge and discourage many garden pests from building up into large numbers. Of course a good rain storm will have the same effect, but don't be fooled by a spring or summer shower; insects are much more hardy than that.

Proper pruning techniques are also important in preventing the spread of disease. Pruning cuts should be made flush with the trunk just above a bud, leaf, or branch, leaving no stub. Prune overgrown plants to promote better air circulation and light penetration. Cut out all heavily damaged foliage, especially that already damaged by insects. Insects such as borers or leaf miners can be held in check by cutting out all infected portions of the plant. Finally, work only among plants that are dry. Most diseases are spread from plant to plant by splashing water.

# Common Plant Diseases

The largest cause of plant diseases is fungi, microscopic plants which contain no chlorophyll and therefore cannot manufacture their own food. They are responsible for such diseases as leaf spots, leaf blotches, mildews, rusts, and cankers, as well as some blights and wilts.

The main body of a fungus is composed of numerous threads (hyphae), which in mass are called mycelium. The fruiting bodies, or spores, are borne on or in specialized structures that arise from the mycelium. Some, like the common mushroom, are *saprophytes* that gain their nourishment from dead material. Others, like those responsible for disease, are parasitic. Some fungi actually live off both, which is why it is so important to clean up old plant debris.

In order for fungi to gain a foothold and flourish, weather conditions must be right. What is true of all of them is that they love moisture. Wet weather and high humidity are their invitations. As for temperature, some prefer cooler conditions while others prefer warmer ones. Another factor may be physical damage. Some fungi gain entrance through an already existing wound. This is true of many organisms that cause rot. After long periods of rainy weather, it is a good idea to dust susceptible plants with a fungicide.

Bacteria are the cause of fire blight, bacterial wilts, leaf spot, galls, scabs and some rots. These single-celled organisms enter the plant through natural opening or injuries. They are also spread by insects, wind, rain, people, and machinery. There is no cure for bacterial diseases and in most cases the entire plant must be destroyed in order to stop the spread of infection. Sometimes the infected part of the plant may be cut out and the specimen saved.

The presence of a virus most often results in some form of discoloration of foliage, which may include yellow or brown spots or streaks, ring patterns, and sometimes the complete yellowing of foliage. Leaves may exhibit dark green areas along veins (vein banding) or a loss of color (vein clearing). Flowers may exhibit color breaks or white flecks. Other symptoms may include distortion of foliage, the appearance of witch's brooms (a clump of thin, twiggy growth emerging from the trunk), fruit that is small or misshapen, or a general stunting and reduction of output.

Viruses are composed of a protein coat around a core of ribonucleic acid and can only multiply within living cells. They can change the internal structure and metabolism of other living things and these changes can be passed on genetically. Not all the results of viruses are bad, for they are responsible for many natural mutations such as dwarfing and color breaks in flowers. Sometimes the virus does very little damage and is not easily spread, as in the case of a witch's broom; at other times, however, a virus can be a highly infectious disease that causes a great deal of damage.

Viruses cannot penetrate the plant directly and can only gain entrance through a wound. Insects feeding on infected plants absorb the virus through their digestive systems and pass it into their salivary glands where it multiples. When the insect moves to an uninfected plant it carries the virus with it, spreading it as it feeds, and the insect remains a carrier for life. Viruses can also be transmitted by garden tools, or man himself as he moves from plant to plant. Plants propagated from infected material will also contain the virus.

There is no cure for virus diseases. To ensure that the infection will not spread, all affected plant material must be destroyed and a spraying program instituted to control insect carriers. Be sure to sterilize all garden tools in household bleach and to wash your hands before touching another plant. All garden debris must be cleaned up, put in bags, and immediately removed. Plants that are susceptible to the same disease should not be grown near each other, nor should they be grown on the same spot as any plant that has previously succumbed to the disease.

Recently a new organism has been found that is the true cause of more than forty diseases collectively known as yellows, which were previously attributed to viruses. Known as MLO (mycoplasma-like organism), it is transmitted by leafhoppers and little is known about it. New growth is yellow and distorted. There is no cure and affected plants must be destroyed. At the same time, a program to control leafhoppers must be instituted to stop MLO from spreading throughout the garden.

When a disease appears, it is important to act quickly; once a foothold is gained, it spreads rapidly. At the moment fungus diseases are the only diseases that are treatable with fungicides. In the case of viral, or bacterial disease, or those caused by MLO, you must discard the plant and sometimes the soil as well. Most diseases cannot attack healthy plants grown under the proper conditions and their appearance usually indicates some physiological problem. Reassess the procedures you have been following and try to make some adjustments. It would be wise in the future to choose only resistant varieties since many diseases can lie dormant in your soil for up to ten years. After treating infected plants, be sure to sterilize all garden tools in undiluted household bleach before using them on healthy ones. It is also important to wash your hands and even change your clothes before working in the garden again.

# Air Pollution

We have concentrated on problems with a biological origin. Today we must also recognize the damage to plants that can be caused by air pollution. For air pollution damage to occur a pollutant must be present in a high enough concentration for a long enough period of time. Pollution levels that affect plants are much lower than those required to produce symptoms in humans. This fact raises serious consequences that will affect the quality of life of future generations. The major pollutants often implicated are ozone, sulfur dioxide, and hydrogen fluoride.

Not all plants are susceptible to pollution damage. The sensitivity of plants varies with the species and even the culture. Individual plants are affected by age, fertility, water supply, root aeration, and exposure to light. Unlike plants affected by biological factors, plants damaged by air pollution are in general, healthy, well-fertilized, well-watered, and growing rapidly. This is due to the fact that such plants have a higher rate of transpiration and are taking in more of the pollutant. Damage becomes evident twenty-four hours after exposure. The diagnosis is based on the fact that although the damage mirrors that of insects, there is no evidence of such insects present.

Ozone damage is the most widespread and usually develops after periods of air stagnation during which accumulated automobile exhaust fumes acted upon by sunlight create significant levels of ozone in the air. Injury to foliage is seen on the upper leaf surface with little evidence on the lower surface and can take the form of either a bleached stippling effect reminiscent of spider mite damage (spinach, cucumber, zucchini, parsley, nasturtium) or a dark pigmented stippling (green beans, lima beans, white potatoes, grapes). The fact that the damage is only evident on the upper leaf surface is an indication that insects are not to blame. Severe symptoms cause the affected leaves to turn yellow and drop. Again it is the newer foliage that is affected, and damage can occur in waves throughout the season. Other insects that inflict damage that may be confused with ozone pollution may include whiteflies, lacebugs, and leafhoppers. Woody plants are in general not as susceptible.

Sulfur dioxide and hydrogen fluoride are gases which, unlike ozone, are usually emitted from a specific location such as a factory and only affect a relatively small area. The most common source of sulfur dioxide is an industrial plant or factory that burns fossil fuels, especially those with a high sulfur content. Injury appears on the plants as tan areas or spots located between the veins of leaves. The lesions go all the way through the leaf and can be seen on both upper and lower surfaces. Susceptible plants include begonias, tomatoes, apples, clover, birches, and roses. Violets and zinnias are useful indicator plants. Hydrogen fluoride originates with industries involved in the production of aluminum, ceramics, phosphate fertilizers, and steel; it causes a browning of leaf margins on sensitive plants including blueberries, cherries, corn, grapes, peaches, and tulips. Sensitive conifers develop needle tip necrosis, which in severe cases may extend to most of the affected needle. Unlike deciduous trees, the damage is irreparable. A useful indicator of the presence of hydrogen fluoride is gladiolus.

# *Diagnosing the Problem*

Even after following all the horticultural rules, you will probably still find your garden becoming someone's lunch, making it necessary to rely on some other means of control. In order to pick the proper remedy, you must first know what is wrong with your plant. Diagnosis is a process of elimination in which all factors are considered. Sometimes the diagnosis is easy and the remedy is straightforward, but in other cases the obvious cause of the symptoms may be linked to more subtle primary factors such as climate conditions or horticultural practices. Sometimes two entirely different causes produce the same symptoms. Spider mites and thrips, for instance, both have a stippling effect on foliage. Leaf spots and wilts can be caused by either bacteria or fungi. A closer examination of the foliage will provide the necessary clue.

In making a diagnosis, consider factors such as the type of plant, the time of the year, and recent climatic conditions. Some insects and diseases attack only a small number of species while others attack a wide spectrum. Caterpillars found in a mass of webs in spring are probably tent caterpillars, but in August or September probably the fall webworm. Stippled foliage in summer probably means spider mites, but twenty-four hours after a period of high temperatures and thick, still air may be air pollution.

When you do notice some damage, observe it carefully for any evidence of insects; look for the organism itself, or for any egg masses, webs, sticky secretions, or chewed leaves. Holes in leaves are usually caused by a chewing insect, but there are one or two diseases that will produce the same effect. The patterns formed by the feeding culprit are in many ways a personal signature. Tiny round perforations are most often caused by flea beetles, while skeletonized leaves or a filigree pattern may be the work of beetle larvae. Weevils cause angular openings in leaves.

If there is no evidence of insect attack, then the problem may very well be a disease caused by either a fungus, bacterium, virus, or a mycoplasma-like organism. Some diseases, such as mildew, gray molds and rusts, are easy to diagnose. Others are more difficult, since many produce similar symptoms. A leaf spot that is caused by a fungus exhibits a definite outline, which may be regular or irregular. The spot itself is usually filled with minute dark pimples. A leaf spot caused by bacteria is smooth in texture. If the leaf spot is smooth in texture but characterized by an irregular outline, then the cause is probably sunscald or windburn.

Wilts are another group of diseases that may be caused by a number of factors that range from physiological, to a fungus, bacterium, or virus.

# Using Chemical Controls

Biological control represents the promise of the future, when we can control all our insect problems without fear of poisoning or residual effects to the environment. Now that science recognizes it as a viable alternative and research is advancing, more gains will probably be made, but at the moment it would be extremely unwise to rely exclusively on this method to deal with a major insect infestation. Instead, a program that integrates biological and chemical control makes the most sense. If insecticides must be used, they should be applied only to infested plants and those likely to be seriously damaged. Excessive use doesn't control pests any better than limited applications. When choosing an insecticide, try to select one that does not affect garden beneficials or at least poses a minimal threat. Wherever possible, avoid using broad-spectrum insecticides that are meant to kill a wide assortment of insects. Choose a substance with a short-term residual effect that will control a limited number of species in order to conserve the natural balance. Gardeners are taking a new look at the older compounds, which have still proven to be effective against many garden pests. Among these are soap, rotenone, pyrethrins, nicotine, sabadilla, ryania, diatomaceous earth, dormant oils, and sulfur, all of which are definitely easier on beneficials. Some of these compounds have been used for hundreds of years with success.

One of the safest, easiest, and most inexpensive insecticides you can use is one you can make yourself, namely a dilution of soap and water. It is effective against soft-bodied insects such as aphids and mealybugs and can be made by dissolving one or two tablespoons in a gallon of water. Soaps derived from vegetable or plant material generally work better than those derived from petroleum products. Try using an old-fashioned laundry soap on a limited basis or try buying some from a health food store. Ivory soap flakes can also be tried, as can most dishwashing liquids, since they do not contain phosphates. Unfortunately, commercial soaps vary tremendously in composition and purity, and thence effectiveness. A word of caution here, though: soap should not be used on hairy plants.

Rotenone, which is also known as derris, is probably the best general-purpose, nonsynthetic garden insecticide available against chewing insects. It is a powder made from the root of a tropical plant, *Derris elliptica,* and related species, and acts as both a contact and stomach poison. It can be used as a dust or a spray and is effective against a wide range of garden pests including aphids, beetles, weevils, slugs, cabbage loopers, imported cabbage worms, fleas, thrips, and mosquitoes, but is useless against most sucking insects, such as spider mites and soil insects. Rotenone is extremely toxic to fish (it is listed as a piscicide) and is used in reservoirs to clean out unwanted species before restocking. Rotenone can be used on food crops within a few days of harvest, having a short residual effect, and although it has a longer residual action than pyrethrins, it must be applied often to remain effective.

Pyrethrins and allethrin (an insecticide chemically similar to pyrethrins), like rotenone, are derived from a plant, pyrethrum, a species of chrysanthemum, and have been used as insecticides since ancient times. Pyrethrins deliver a quick knockdown, but if the insect has not received an ample dose, it can recover; that is why this insecticide is usually combined with an activator or synergist, which makes it much more effective. Pyrethrins kill insects by contact and are mostly effective against a wide range of sucking insects such as aphids, mealybugs, leaf-hoppers, thrips, whiteflies, and others. It will not control mites or most chewing insects. It has a short residual effect, so fruits and vegetables can be eaten shortly after spraying, but it too must be applied often and like rotenone should not be used near fish ponds.

Nicotine, sold in the form of nicotine sulfate, is no longer manufactured in the United States and is difficult to obtain. Although it is organically derived, it is a deadly poison. It has a short residual effect and is much less effective when used during cool weather. Keep it away from children.

Sabadilla is an insecticidal dust that is derived from the seeds of *Schoenocaulon officinalis,* a tropical lily-like plant, and has been used since the sixteenth century. Since it is both a contact and a stomach poison it is effective against a fairly wide range of pests including aphids, armyworms, beetles, cabbage loopers, webworms, European corn borers, grasshoppers, harlequin bugs, leafhoppers and squash bugs, but it is not effective against mites. Sabadilla dust may irritate the nasal membranes if inhaled, so wear a protective mask when applying the dust. It is marked under the trade name of Red Devil Dust and is also available through the Burgess Seed Company.

Ryania is an organic insecticide derived from the roots of the tropical shrub *Ryania speciosa.* It is a contact and stomach poison that kills such pests as aphids, codling moths, corn borers, cucumber beetles, flea beetles, hornworms, leafhoppers, and the oriental fruit moth, while leaving most beneficial insects unharmed. It is usually sold as a dust under the trade name Tri-excel D.S. and is safe for mammals.

Diatomaceous earth is a nontoxic dust that consists of the silicate skeletal remains of a prehistoric class of algae that was found in both fresh and salt water. It works by puncturing the bodies of insects, causing death by dehydration, and works best on soft-bodied insects. It will also interfere with vital bodily functions if taken internally. Diatomaceous earth is the prime ingredient of an insecticide sold under the name of Perma Guard. It is best applied after a light rain, or after the plants have been sprayed with a fine mist of water. Wear a protective mask when applying the dust.

Dormant oils are derived from petroleum and act as contact poisons. Until recently their use was limited to winter use since the oils damaged plant foliage, but now, with the development of lighter products, it can also be used in summer with minimum damage. When applied in late winter or early spring, the spray is effective against the overwintering stages of such plant pests as aphids, leaf rollers, mealybugs, mites, and scale. Applying an oil spray at this time of year is the most effective way of controlling most of these pests and can actually reduce the number of pesticide applications required during the growing season and may make further spraying to control certain pests totally unnecessary. As a winter spray, it is applied heavily to dormant plants so a thick film covers every square inch of surface area. Choose a day when the temperature is expected to stay above 45°F., especially when spraying broad-leaved evergreens to prevent damage. As a summer spray, a weaker concentration is sparingly applied. The coverage should correspond to that of any other insecticide. Dormant oils are only used on woody plants and should never be applied within 30 days (before or after) of application of a sulfur product. They should also not be used in combination with or closely following an application of Orthocide garden fungicide. Do not use the oil on certain trees including Japanese maple, coco palm, and blue spruce. Oil sprays are poisonous to fish.

Elemental sulfur is a very safe fungicide; in fact, sulfur is essential to good health. It is a finely ground powder that can be used as a dust or spray and will control spider mites and many fungus diseases, especially during hot weather. It should not be used on vegetables just prior to harvest if you plan to can the produce since it can cause an off flavor or make the cans explode. Elemental sulfur should also not be applied within one month of a dormant oil, nor should it ever be used on roses or cucumbers, or any other plant that is sulfur shy.

Other safe compounds, not often thought of in the context of insect control, may be used in the garden. They are usually found in every household and include household bleach, borax, rubbing alcohol, milk, and buttermilk. Bleach is not only a wonderful sterilizing agent but it can be used to kill troublesome weeds. Spray them with bleach and kill the plants. Borax can be mixed with red pepper and sprinkled along ant trails to eliminate the pesky insects. Alcohol is effective against both scale and mealybugs. Either touch each insect with a cotton swab dipped in alcohol, or dilute 2 parts alcohol to 1 part water and spray the plants early in the morning before the sun is too strong. Alcohol can also be used as a wetting agent for powdered insecticides. Just replace one-third of the water with alcohol and the insecticide will penetrate the insects' bodies much faster. Whole milk can deactivate the mosaic virus that attacks tomatoes, eggplant, and peppers while buttermilk mixed with a little wheat flour and diluted with water can be used as a control for spider mites.

Sometimes we may find that these safer compounds cannot solve the problem we are faced with. Perhaps the garden is too small to support a steady population of beneficials or the gardener doesn't have the time to constantly respray at the necessary intervals to keep insect outbreaks under control. In these situations you may need to turn to the stronger modern insecticides. At present, nearly all garden pests can be controlled at least temporarily by various new chemical materials. Unfortunately, it is impossible to eliminate all pests by spraying, and the few that survive live to breed, passing on their resistance to the chemical. In this way, insect populations develop tolerances, making it necessary to use stronger and more frequent dosages. Every few years, new compounds must be invented to replace the old ones that are no longer effective. At the same time, scores of beneficial insects are eliminated from the environment, thus permitting problem flare-ups of insect species that had previously been held in check by biological means. In this way, the steady spiral of imbalance continues and may take years to correct even after the elimination of these chemical pesticides. Before resorting to their use, you should ask yourself seriously if they are needed and if there is no effective alternative. Have you diagnosed the cause of the problem beyond a doubt and is the pest still present in a vulnerable stage? Many insects only live for a few short weeks before disappearing. If you still feel a strong chemical compound is needed, then you must choose the best to fit your needs. Synthetic insecticides come in a wide assortment of forms, all with different advantages. There are multipurpose pesticides, broad-spectrum insecticides, those that work by making the entire plant poisonous for a certain period of time, and those with a short residual effect. Whichever you choose, be sure the pesticide is labeled for the use you put it to. Otherwise you may be creating new problems while solving old ones. You could make your fruits or vegetables unfit to eat, or, worse, you may even damage the plants you are trying to protect.

Multipurpose pesticides combine two or more compounds in one spray. This could include an insecticide combined with a miticide, and/or a fungicide, and in the case of a lawn compound, a herbicide. Multipurpose sprays are usually used for a specific plant such as a spray for roses or vegetables. The reasoning behind such sprays is that you can set up a preventive spray program before the insect arrives, or if the damage is already evident, you don't have to worry about which specific chemical is needed. One spray can save time and effort. Or can it? What you are really doing is zapping your plants with more chemical controls than are really necessary. If the only problem you are experiencing is an outbreak of spider mites or aphids, then you don't need a spray that includes a poison for chewing insects or mildew and vice versa. If in fact the plant you are trying to grow is attacked by all of these insects, then you should move it to a new location or not grow it at all. Unless you need a perfect specimen plant for exhibition, you probably do not need this type of pesticide.

A broad-spectrum insecticide usually takes care of a wide range of insects, but it doesn't include a fungicide and may in theory only include one chemical compound. In years past, insecticides were divided into contact poisons and stomach poisons to take care of sucking and chewing insects respectively. Many new modern insecticides act as both, making this distinction unimportant. Some of these new contact insecticides also have a long residual effect, making it unnecessary for the offending insect to be present when you spray. Of course their disadvantage lies in the fact that they kill more insects than may be causing the problem, and their residual life can mean they continue to kill long after the intended target has been eliminated.

A systemic is an insecticide or fungicide that is absorbed and translocated by the movement of sap, making the plant itself totally poisonous. It becomes a deadly meal to a wide variety of insects and, in some cases, to fungi that attempt to feed by sucking its sap or chewing its tissue. The effect can last for weeks, making repeated spraying or dusting unnecessary. A liquid systemic can be used as a spray or as a soil drench. A far safer method is to mix systemic granules into the soil around plant roots. This way there are no winds to blow the spray around and nothing to breathe in. There is little chance of any harm if the proper gloves are worn. Beneficial insects are not as easily affected either since there is no spray to come in contact with. The use of such compounds on the surface seems appealing, but you must remember that you are making your plants poisonous. They cannot be used on any food crops at any time. If the plant is given too large a dose, it can be severely damaged or even destroyed, or if too small a dosage is administered then the more resistant insects may survive to breed, passing on this characteristic, while beneficials feeding on the contaminated insects may in fact eventually receive a bigger dose of the poison due to a chemical buildup in their systems. They too would eventually be eliminated. Systemic dusts are also available but these are primarily used as a seed treatment to prevent damping off. Some systemic insecticides presently on the market include dimethoate (Cygon), formothion, oxydemeton methyl, di-syston (banned in some states), metasystox R, systox, and menazon.

When choosing an insecticide, the form in which it is used can be an important factor in making your decision. All pesticides come in a variety of forms, including ready-to-use aerosol sprays, dusts, and liquid concentrates. The form chosen will determine what equipment you will need. A liquid concentrate must be diluted and applied with a sprayer while a dust must be applied with a duster. When applying a spray to a glossy-leafed plant, it is also wise to mix in a tablespoon of soap to help it stick. When applying a dust it is best to do so when plants are moist from either dew, rain, or a spray from the garden hose. When the water evaporates, it will leave the pesticide tightly fastened to the leaf surface.

# Using Pesticides Safely

It must be remembered in dealing with pesticides that they are potent poisons capable of causing great harm and sometimes death. They must be handled and stored with great care. Poisoning can occur in a variety of ways including absorption through the skin (the most common cause of all pesticide poisoning), inhalation of the fumes and accidental ingestion of the material. The effects of repeated exposure can be cumulative, causing eventual poisoning. Many pesticides remain stored in the fatty tissues of our bodies as well as our livers and kidneys for years. They must be used according to the directions only and must be kept away from all children and pets. Some people are allergic to pesticides and may develop a skin rash, a burning sensation, and swelling of the lips to name a few of the symptoms reported. If any of these symptoms develop while using any pesticide, stop immediately. It may also be a good idea to consult your doctor. If at any time you suspect pesticide poisoning, call your local physician or contact your Poison Control Center (look up "Poison" in your directory or call the local health department). Have the container or label with you so the proper information can be given.

Plants also vary widely in their response to pesticides. You can reduce the chance of damage by watering them the day before you plan to treat the plant and by applying the spray early in the morning or evening when the sun is not as strong. Damage from insecticides includes burned leaf edges and tips, spotting or yellowing of leaves, and distorted growth. It is usually the new growth that is affected.

The label is the most important source of information about the product you plan to use. It should be read entirely before buying or using the contents. Pesticides are manufactured, formulated, and packaged to exacting standards and the information is all printed on the label. Be sure it hasn't been folded over and taped down so that only half of it is visible. This is a common practice especially on small bottles. The label identifies the chemical compound and the EPA registration number, categorizes the compound's toxicity, names the insects or diseases it effectively controls, states the days that must elapse before harvesting edible plants, and gives the necessary safety precautions that the applicator must follow and all directions for use.

All pesticides have been grouped under standard headings according to toxicity by the government, and this information is passed on to customers by certain code words that must appear on the label. Whenever possible, always use the safest material available. Look for the signal word "caution" on the label. Only rarely do problems arise that may require a more toxic substance bearing the word "warning." If a label calls for protective clothing beyond what is normal, or special equipment such as

## Toxicity in Pesticides

| CATEGORY OF TOXICITY | | AMOUNT NEEDED TO POISON 150-POUND PERSON | CODE WORD USED IN LABELING |
|---|---|---|---|
| I | Highly toxic | Few drops to 1 teaspoon | Danger—poison—skull and crossbones |
| II | Moderately toxic | 1 teaspoon—1 oz. | Warning |
| III | Slightly toxic | 1 oz. to 1 lb. or pt. | Caution |
| IV | Relatively non-toxic | Over 1 lb. or 1 pt. | Caution |

a respirator, don't use it. Highly toxic materials that require a *Danger—Poison* label are for the most part restricted and cannot be purchased by the home gardener.

Always keep pesticides in the original container and read the label directions carefully each and every time you use them. That includes all caution and first-aid procedures. If a damaged container is found, place it in a clearly labeled plastic or paper bag or transfer the contents to another container that has held the same compound. Never guess what the material is or the dosage required. Never handle a pesticide container for even for a second without wearing protective gloves. If the material comes in a cardboard box or paper bag, always use a sharp knife to open the container. Partially filled containers should be resealed with tape or staples to prevent spilling. Work with pesticides in a well-ventilated area and never smoke, chew gum, eat, or drink while using them. Never work with pesticides in the kitchen. Always measure amounts accurately and prepare only enough mixture for your immediate needs. To mix small amounts use the conversion tables on pages 62–63. Avoid splashing yourself, especially with concentrated material; but if you do, wash it off immediately, since the greatest amount of absorption takes place in the first few minutes. Clean up any spills right away since these can become sources of accidental poisoning of children and pets. Pesticides can be absorbed by vermiculite, cat box litter, dry dirt, or sawdust. Dispose of the absorbent material as you would an empty pesticide container. Cover any bird baths, dog dishes, or fish ponds before spraying. Choose a calm day so the wind doesn't blow the spray all over you instead of the plant. Never use a pesticide on any herbs, fruits, or vegetables unless the label says you specifically can, and be sure to check the number of days required between spraying and safely harvesting food. Always wash fruits and vegetables before eating them. Spray all foliage evenly until the liquid begins to run off the tips, and don't forget the undersides of leaves.

When you've finished spraying apply any leftover material on an alternate target. Don't throw it away or flush it down the toilet. Rinse any empty containers three times and pour the rinse water into your sprayer to be used in the garden. Take the empty container and wrap it in several layers of newspaper before placing it in the garbage. Change your clothes, including underwear, and wash them separately from the family laundry and be sure to wash your face and hands before smoking or eating. Store pesticides in a cool, dry place out of direct sunlight. If given proper storage, some pesticides may remain active for several years. However, storage conditions vary so widely that it is difficult to predict the long-term shelf life of a compound, so most manufacturers will not back their product after two years. Tightly closed lids can help extend the shelf life of most pesticides as can protection from temperature extremes. High temperature can cause many pesticides to become volatile or break down more rapidly, while liquid formulations, if allowed to freeze, may separate into their various components. Pesticides that contain low concentrations of active ingredients generally lose effectiveness faster. Some pesticides have a characteristic odor that grows stronger in the storage area. This could be an indication of a leak, spill, improperly sealed container, or a deteriorating formula. Sometimes a pesticide will give off a gas, making handling or opening the container hazardous, and sometimes the pressure can cause it to rupture or explode.

---

### *Common Pesticides and Their Estimated Shelf Life*

| | |
|---|---|
| Benomyl (Benlate) | 2 years |
| Captan | 3 years |
| Diazinon | 5–7 years |
| Di-syston | 2 years |
| Malathion | 2 years |
| Metasystox R | 2 years |

---

## *Using a Soil Drench*

A soil drench is a pesticide that is poured over the soil to knock out an insect or disease organism. Such a plant pest can cause a tremendous amount of damage before it is discovered. The first signs of any root problem can usually be seen aboveground, and are usually mistaken for a lack of water. The foliage wilts and the leaves may yellow and dry out. Watering the plant more often only contributes to the problem since constantly wet soil, especially when combined with poor drainage, often leads to root rotting. To be sure, remove the plant from its container and examine the roots. They should be healthy looking and firm—any damp or depressed patches or any discoloration is a definite indication that a fungus is present. If the roots contain large swollen areas or knots, you can be sure that the trouble is caused by nematodes (microscopic worms). Examine the soil as well for evidence of insects. Some of the pests that can cause problems include springtails, fungus gnats, and root mealybugs. If the problem is nematodes, there is little that can be done. The plant must be destroyed and the soil and possibly the container must be discarded. If the problem is a fungus or an insect, the plant can be treated. First cut away any damaged root material and dip the roots into a fungicide solution according to the directions on the label. Replant the plant in fresh soil, making sure there is ample drainage material, then water the plant thoroughly. Let the plant stand for one day, then apply a soil drench, either an insecticide or a fungicide depending on the problem.

It is important when dealing with soil drenches that you follow the directions carefully and apply only what is needed. After all, you are dealing with poisons. It is also important that the plant be watered the day before so the roots will be functioning normally and the soil will be evenly moist. Pour the drench on the soil slowly and evenly until it begins to come out the bottom, then stop and allow it to drain.

## Common Insecticides in Use Today

*Acephate.* This is sold under the trade names Orthene and PT1300 (aerosol spray) and is used to control a wide range of chewing insects as well as aphids and scale. It is primarily used on roses, carnations, and chrysanthemums, as well as trees and shrubs. It is toxic to bees, so do not spray when they are active. Do not use acephate on crabapple trees *(Malus)*.

*Carbaryl.* Sold under the trade name Sevin, carbaryl is a broad-spectrum insecticide of short persistence used against chewing insects including caterpillars, beetles, webworms, leaf miners and some soil insects. It is not effective against aphids or mites and may even increase a mite problem. Carbaryl is relatively safe for plants and people, but it may injure foliage during periods of high humidity. It should not be used on Boston ivy, virginia creeper, or cotoneaster. It is moderately toxic to fish and quite toxic to bees so try not to apply the spray when bees are active. Repeated freezing and thawing of liquid carbaryl formulations may decrease effectiveness. Wettable powders are quite stable under normal storage conditions.

*Diazinon.* This is an organophosphorus insecticide that is sold under the trade name Spectricide and is effective against sucking (but not chewing) insects including aphids, leaf miners, red spider mites, whitefly, and scale, as well as many soil insects including nematodes, root aphids, and root flies. Diazinon is also toxic to bees, so confine your spraying until after dusk. Follow the instructions strictly when treating vegetables, which cannot be harvested for two weeks following application. It should not be used on certain ferns and gardenias. Use the 4E formulation within six months of opening the container and do not store near a heat source.

*Dicofol.* This is a miticide marketed under the name Kelthane and used to control spider mites on some ornamentals, vegetables, and fruits. Since it breaks down quickly, edible plants can be harvested within seven days of spraying. It will not harm bees or beneficial insect predators if used as directed, but it is toxic to fish. Dicofol should never be used on eggplant or avocados and may also harm certain cyclamen, geraniums, lantana, kalanchoes, chrysanthemums, and nasturtiums as well as the tender new growth of other ornamentals. When in doubt spray a small portion of a plant before applying it further, and do so only in the early morning or evening to prevent sun scorch. Dicofol is not compatible with sulfur.

*Dimethoate.* This is a systemic organo-phosphorus and auticide, useful against aphids and spider mites, sold under the trade names Cygon, De-Fend, and Rebelate. It is a reasonably safe foliage spray that is also sometimes used as a soil drench, but it may be injurious to some plants, especially chrysanthemums. Vegetables shouldn't be harvested for at least one week after treatment. Liquid formulations should be stored above freezing. Dimethoate is flammable, so keep it away from heat or open flame. Its flash point range is from $163°$ to $212°F$.

*Di-syston.* A systemic insecticidal spray, di-syston is marketed under the trade names of Isotox, Science Systemic, and Bonide. It is extremely poisonous and may be restricted in some states. It is effective against a wide range of insects including aphids, whiteflies, mites, thrips, scale, leaf miners, leafhoppers, and lacebugs. Never use it on edible crops. It is extremely toxic to fish and wildlife.

*Malathion.* A broad-spectrum phosphate compound that has been in use for twenty-seven years, malathion still remains one of the safest pesticides on the market. Because it breaks down so quickly, edible plants may be sprayed a few days before harvesting. It is useful in controlling many sucking insects including scale, whitefly, mealybugs, mites, thrips, and lacebugs, and it is the most effective insecticide to use against aphids. Malathion is extremely toxic before dilution and must be handled carefully. Children should not be allowed contact with newly sprayed plants. It is also toxic to fish and bees and should not be applied when bees are active, nor should it be applied if the temperature is expected to exceed $85°$. Plants that are sensitive to malathion include many ferns, lantanas, petunias, sweet peas, violets, red carnations, crassulas, some roses, junipers, Japanese red maple, and white pine. Wettable powders are stable for at least two years. Liquid formulations should be stored above 0°. Keep away from heat.

*Methoxychlor.* This insecticide is very effective against certain chewing insects including worms, beetles, and thrips. It has a residual toxicity of one week and can be used on edible plants fairly close to harvesting. It is relatively nontoxic to bees but highly toxic to fish. Methoxychlor should not be used on chrysanthemums.

# Common Fungicides in Use Today

*Bordeaux mixture.* This is the granddaddy of fungicides. Discovered in the last century, Bordeaux mixture is a mixture of copper sulphate and lime and is the remedy for a disease that calls for a fixed copper or copper-based fungicide. Although many new compounds have been invented since World War II, this compound is not obsolete by any means. While the newer compounds tend to be more specific in their effectiveness against certain fungus diseases, Bordeaux mixture is generally useful against a wide range of diseases. It can be prepared in either a strong or weak solution depending on use. The stronger solution is used as a dormant spray on peaches to control leaf curl. It can also be used on apples and pears in the green-tip state of growth to control fire blight, while the weaker solution is usually used during the bloom period. Bordeaux mixture should never be applied to Ilex (holly), which can be injured by copper.

*Benomyl.* This is a general-purpose fungicide, sold under the trade name of Benlate, which has some systemic properties. It can be used as a bulb dip and is excellent for the control of a wide range of foliage fungus diseases including powdery mildew and rose black spot, although recently there has been an appearance by tolerant strains of botrytis, rose powdery mildew, and apple scab fungus. Benomyl can be substituted for captan and is more effective in the control of brown rot on stone fruits. It is recommended for both bloom and preharvest sprays. Benomyl is also compatible with dormant oil sprays. Dilute benomyl remains effective for only eight hours, and if you let it stand for more than twenty-four, it will actually harm the plants it is supposed to help. The wettable powder should remain stable for two years if kept dry and tightly sealed.

*Captan.* A fungicide that is sold under the name of Orthocide, captan is a very safe fungicide to handle. It is compatible with almost any insecticide except malathion and an oil spray. It can be used to control a wide range of diseases and as a seed treatment, but it will not control powdery mildew or rusts. When applied with an oil, it can cause fruit damage, and it may also cause spotting on Red Delicious apples and some sweet cherries. Use maneb instead on these fruits.

*Dinocap.* Sold under the name Karathane, Mildex, or Garden Karaspra, dinocap is an extremely efficient control of powdery mildew but little else. Surprisingly, it also seems to control mites and is sometimes recommended as such. Dinocap can be mixed with almost any other spray substance except white oil emulsion. It will damage certain varieties of chrysanthemum. Do not store liquid formulations near heat or flame.

*Ferbam.* This is sold as Fermate, Carbomate, and Karbam Black. It is a good general fungicide especially for the control of rust diseases. Ferbam may leave a black spray deposit on flowers and woodwork or other surfaces.

*Fixed copper.* This is a useful fungicide for diseases that attack tomatoes, potatoes, cabbage, and beans. Some plants have shown some sensitivity to the compound. This should never be used on Ilex (holly).

*Lesan.* Also known as dexan, lesan is used as a soil drench to prevent damping off and root rots.

*Maneb.* Sold under the trade names Manzate and Dithane M–22, maneb is a valuable general fungicide useful in the control of diseases of tomatoes, potatoes, onions, celery, cabbage, carrots, melons, squash, and cucumbers. Maneb will not control powdery mildew or rusts.

*Thiram (arasan).* This is a dithiocarbamate fungicide that controls a wide range of diseases. It is widely used as a seed treatment to protect against damping off and other root rots and will also control downy mildew, gray mold, raspberry cane spot (anthracnose), currant leaf spot, tulip fire, and rust disease. It is nontoxic, but it should be handled carefully to prevent irritation to the skin, eyes, and throat. It should not be used on fruit intended for canning or freezing since it can affect flavor unfavorably.

*Truban.* This is a compound used primarily as a treatment for stem and root rots.

*Zineb.* A compound made by combining zinc sulfate with the fungicide nabam, zineb is sold under the names Z–78 and Parzate. It is an effective control against all foliage fungus diseases including downy mildew, leaf spots, tomato and potato blight, tulip fire, and rust diseases. It is frequently a constituent of all-purpose mixtures. Zineb decomposes quickly and flammable derivatives may form upon decomposition. Keep it dry and away from heat.

# Equipment for Pesticide Application

*Hand sprayer.* Small atomizer or pump-type sprayers are good for treating a few specimens in the garden only. They usually hold no more than 1 quart of liquid spray.

*Compressed air sprayer.* These range in capacity from ½ to 5 gallons and are capable of taking care of most jobs in the garden. Pressure is built up by hand with a pumping action that has to be repeated from time to time during the course of application. They are great time savers but they cannot be used for applying dusts.

*Hose end proportioner.* This is an appliance that is attached to the end of a garden hose. In order for it to work properly, there must be sufficient water pressure coming through the hose. Hose end proportioners that spray out directly are mainly suitable for lawns, trees, and shrubs. Use the type with extension tubes and a deflector so the spray can be directed up through the foliage.

*Dusters.* These range in size and capacity from a rubber bulb or cardboard carton to motor-driven varieties. Dust guns of 1-pint to 2-quart capacity are relatively inexpensive and satisfactory for small gardens. Be sure to buy an extension tube with the duster to be able to effectively dust trees and shrubs. Remember to direct the dust toward the undersurface of leaves.

## *Beneficial Insects*

| BENEFICIAL INSECTS | CONTROLLED PESTS | COMMENTS |
|---|---|---|
| *Lady beetle, ladybug* | | |
| Adult: Shiny orange body marked with two or more black dots.<br><br>Pupae: Orange and black; can be found attached to the upper surface of a leaf.<br><br>Larvae: Black alligator-like bodies that taper at the rear. They change to blue-gray marked with orange spots, and their spines become more apparent.<br><br>Eggs: Yellow-orange and barrel shaped. They stand on end in a cluster of five to fifty. | A single larva can consume 300 to 400 aphids. Adults also feed on aphids as well as pollen and nectar. | The convergent lady beetle, although widely sold, is a bad bargain. They are migratory, flying away when released. Rely on local beetles. Do not confuse the lady beetle with its large relative the Mexican bean beetle, which is identical in shape with a tan wing cover marked with black spots. |
| *Scale-eating lady beetle* | | |
| Adult: Identical in shape to its orange cousin. Black and shiny with or without orange spots.<br><br>Pupae: The dark pupa is formed within the last larval skin, which splits down the middle to reveal it. | As with the orange lady beetle, it is the larvae that destroy the most pests. When first hatched the young larvae attack young scale crawlers. As they grow in size they attack larger prey. | Found almost exclusively on trees. They need a fairly heavy host population to support them. |

## *Beneficial Insects* (cont'd)

| BENEFICIAL INSECTS | CONTROLLED PESTS | COMMENTS |
|---|---|---|

### *Scale-eating lady beetle* (cont'd)

Larvae: They resemble the larvae of the orange beetle and are grayish in color.

Eggs: Yellow or reddish, laid singly in bark crevices or underneath the armor of a devoured scale.

### *Green lacewing*

Adult: Slender light-green body with long antennae and large delicate, gauze-like wings.

Pupae: A globular white cocoon woven from silk and found on the underside of a leaf.

Larvae: Similar in appearance to lady beetle larvae. A flat body tapered at both ends with a set of jaws that is disproportionately large for its body. It is yellowish gray marked with brown, with bristles laid out horizontally, forming stripes. These larvae like to carry trash around, which keeps them almost completely hidden.

Adults are not predaceous but feed on pollen and nectar. The larvae are known as aphid-lions, as they feed on aphids, mealybugs, mites, thrips, and certain scales and their eggs.

Available for purchase, lacewings are one of the best investments among beneficials.

## *Beneficial Insects* (cont'd)

| BENEFICIAL INSECTS | CONTROLLED PESTS | COMMENTS |
|---|---|---|
| *Praying mantis (praying mantid)* | | |
| Adult: Long and slender, measuring 4 inches long. When fully mature, they display tan wings and a green body.<br><br>Young: Except for their size and lack of wings they resemble the adult in form. When newly hatched they measure ½ inch long and are brown. They change to green as they mature.<br><br>Eggs: A large foam-like, straw-colored mass 1 inch in diameter found attached to twig stems. | They are general predators that do not distinguish between friend and foe.<br>When young, they feed on the smallest prey such as aphids. As they mature they attack larger insects including caterpillars, beetles, and flies.<br>They will also attack each other. | Their reputation as man's best friend in the garden is not entirely true since they will not reduce the population of any one insect. Instead of actively seeking out their prey they wait for their prey to come to them.<br>Egg cases may be purchased in the spring. One egg case will hold from 100 to 300 little mantids and will certainly take care of the largest roof garden. |
| *Syrhid or hover fly* | | |
| Adult: Resembles a honeybee that has been crossed with a yellow jacket. Abdomen is marked with black and yellow stripes.<br><br>Pupae: Hard and brown.<br><br>Larvae: Green, legless maggots.<br><br>Eggs: Tiny, white, and laid singly among the chosen prey. | Adult feeds on pollen and nectar. Larvae feed on aphids, mealy bugs, leafhoppers, and scales. | Adults are often seen hovering above insect-infested plants. |

## *Beneficial Insects* (cont'd)

| BENEFICIAL INSECTS | CONTROLLED PESTS | COMMENTS |
|---|---|---|
| *Gray robber fly*<br><br>Adult: Distinguished by its protruding eyes, hairy mouth and long pointed abdomen.<br><br>Larvae: Rarely seen since they live in the soil. | Adult is predaceous, attacking other winged insects including wasps, bees, dragonflies, and grasshoppers. Larvae feed on other larvae. | Makes a loud buzzing noise when flying. |
| *Tachinid fly*<br><br>Adult: Resembles the housefly, distinguished by a hairy thorax and abdomen. | Parasitic, laying its eggs internally or externally on the host (usually a caterpillar). Larvae hatch and feed internally before emerging as adults. | |
| *Wasps (various species)*<br><br>Adult: Range in size from the large paper wasp to those almost too small to see. | Various insects in all stages of development. | Vespids make up the largest group of parasitoids, laying their eggs internally or externally on a host. They emerge from the body of the host as an adult. |
| *Braconid wasp*<br><br>Adult: Unnoticeable. Larvae: Surrounded by a white cocoon resembling a grain of rice. Often seen attached to caterpillars<br><br>Eggs: unnoticeable | The larvae are parasitic, mostly feeding on caterpillars but at times on aphids, beetles, flies, mealybugs, and scales. The adult wasp eventually emerges from the cocoon. | When an infested caterpillar is spotted in the garden, do not destroy it as you would be killing the developing braconid larvae. |

## *Beneficial Insects* (cont'd)

| BENEFICIAL INSECTS | CONTROLLED PESTS | COMMENTS |
|---|---|---|
| *Trichogramma wasp*<br><br>Adult: Too small to be noticed.<br>Lays its eggs inside the eggs of its host. | Tomato hornworm, cabbage worm, cabbage looper, corn borer, corn earworm, codling moth. | The eggs of Trichogramma can be purchased commercially. |
| *Encarsia formosa*<br><br>Adult: Tiny wasp that goes unnoticed, lays its eggs in developing larvae.<br><br>Larvae: Developing larvae turn the immature form of whitefly from white to black. | Whitefly. | Primarily used for greenhouse control of whitefly. Not practical in the home garden since ideal temperature must be maintained. |
| *Soldier beetle*<br><br>Adult: Resembles the firefly in size and form. One species is yellow orange with black markings on its head and thorax and black spots on the base of each wing cover. The second species is identical in size and shape but brown in color. The larvae are predaceous. | A wide variety of insects including caterpillars, slugs, and aphids. | |
| *Assassin bug*<br><br>Adult: Small elongated head and stout beak attached to a flat sculptured body. Brown or black in color. | Feeds on the larval stage of plant-eating insects including caterpillars, aphids, and beetles. | They sometimes bite humans. |

## Where to Purchase Beneficial Insects

| COMPANY | BENEFICIALS |
|---|---|
| Better Yield Insects<br>13310 Riverside Drive East<br>Tecumseh, Ontario N8N 1B2 Canada<br>(They supply import permit and instructions) | 1, 2 |
| Bio-Control Co.<br>P.O. Box 247, 13451 Highway 174<br>Cedar Ridge, CA 95924 | 1, 2, 4, 9, 11 |
| W. Atlee Burpee Co.<br>300 Park Avenue<br>Warminster, PA 18974 | 1, 2, 9 |
| Gurney Seed & Nursery Co.<br>Gurney Building<br>Yankton, SD 57079 | 1, 2, 4, 5, 9 |
| King's Natural Pest Control<br>224 Yost Avenue<br>Spring City, PA 19475 | 1, 2, 3, 4, 5,<br>6, 9, 10, 11 |
| Lakeland Nurseries<br>340 Poplar Street<br>Hanover, PA 17331 | 1, 2 |
| Mellinger's<br>2310 W. South Range<br>North Lima, OH 44452 | 1, 2, 4, 5 |
| Natural Pest Controls<br>9397 Premier Way<br>Sacramento, CA 95826 | 1, 2, 3, 4, 5, 6<br>7, 8, 9, 10 |
| Rincon-Vitova Insectaries Inc.<br>P.O. Box 95<br>Oak View, CA 93022 | 2, 3, 4, 5, 6,<br>9, 10 |
| White Fly Control Co.<br>P.O. Box 986<br>Militas, CA 95035 | 10, 12 |

1. Chinese praying mantis
2. Convergent lady beetle
3. *Cryplolaemus* lady beetle (scale and mealybugs)
4. Green lacewings
5. Fly parasites (controls many kinds of flies)
6. Predatory mites (controls red spider mite)
7. *Aphytis melinus* (controls red scale)
8. *Metaphycus helvolus* (controls black scale)
9. *Trichogramma* wasps (controls moth and butterfly larva)
10. *Encarsia formosa* (controls whitefly)
11. Lady beetle—lacewing food
12. Safers insecticidal soap

## Plant Pests

| INSECT AND DESCRIPTION | PLANT SYMPTOMS | CONTROL |
|---|---|---|
| Aphids: Soft-bodied, pear-shaped, pink, green, or black insects; some generations have wings. | Insects cluster on succulent new shoots and buds and congregate below flowers. Flowers, shoots, and leaves are deformed, foliage curled up or cupped down, blistered, or discolored. Galls sometimes form on stems and leaves. Insects exude honeydew which covers leaves. Black sooty mold may develop on honeydew. Aphids are also vectors of many virus diseases. | Crush insects between leaves, hose off with a forceful stream of water. Spray with soap solution. Effective chemical controls include rotenone, pyrethrum, diazinon, acephate, malathion and the systemics, dimethoate, metasystox-R. Dormant oil spray will destroy overwintering eggs. |
| Woolly aphids (often confused with mealy bugs) | | Dimethoate. |
| Root aphids | Plants yellow and wilt. Growth is poor as aphids feed on roots. | Rotenone, malathion, diazinon, water in. |
| Bagworms | Difficult to detect at first. The caterpillar hides in a "bag" made of bits of leaf that hangs from the stem of infected plants. Plants are slowly defoliated. Both evergreens and deciduous trees are affected. | Hand pick and destroy bags. Sever the silken thread that attaches it to the stem to prevent girdling. Spray in June to control young worms. BT, diazinon, malathion, acephate, carbaryl. |

## *Plant Pests* (cont'd)

| INSECT AND DESCRIPTION | PLANT SYMPTOMS | CONTROL |
|---|---|---|
| Beetles and weevils: Chewing insects distinguished by the horny sheath covering their wings; only some can fly. | Chewed leaves that may be skeletonized to resemble filigree lace or leaves can have tiny round perforations or shot holes usually caused by flea beetles. Weevils produce angular openings. | Hand-pick insects. Apply a dormant oil spray. Chemical controls include rotenone, carbaryl, malathion, methoxychlor. |
| Borers: Tiny larvae of moths, beetles, sawflies or bees | Presence indicated by holes in stems or trunk sometimes including the presence of sawdust. | Stab insects with a sharp object poked into holes. Prune out infected plant parts. Spray with methoxychlor, Sevin or diazinon from mid-May to mid-June to destroy eggs. |
| Canker-worms (inch-worms): 1" long, green | Chewed leaves in spring will defoliate trees. | BT, methoxychlor, Sevin, acephate. |
| Caterpillars: The larvae of butter-flies and moths. They come in a wide variety of sizes and colors and range from smooth to hairy. | Look for chewed leaves and flowers. | Hand-pick individuals. Spray with BT, Rotenone, methoxychlor, Sevin, acephate. |

## *Plant Pests* (cont'd)

| INSECT AND DESCRIPTION | PLANT SYMPTOMS | CONTROL |
|---|---|---|
| Cutworms: 1″ soil caterpillar. | Young transplants and seedlings are cut in half just above the soil line. | Place a paper collar around seedlings when setting them out in the spring. Diazinon. |
| Flies and midges: Some are very small. Larval stage is a legless maggot. | Larvae burrow into bulbs, fruit, and roots or mine leaves. Plants wilt if roots or bulbs are affected, foliage sometimes exhibits round or conical protrusions or serpentine markings. | Remove and destroy infested fruits and bulbs. Apply diatomaceous earth, pyrethrins, diazinon. |
| Gypsy moth caterpillars: ¼″ to 2¼″ long. Tiny black larvae hatch in the spring and are spread by the wind. When mature they can be recognized by the line of blue or red spots on their backs. | Both deciduous and evergreen trees are defoliated, predisposing them to distress, other insect attack, disease and pollution damage. | They can be trapped by placing a strip of burlap around the tree, 5 feet above the ground, that is 1 foot wide and tied around the middle. The top half is then folded down to form a skirt. Pests will be trapped under the skirt during the day and easily destroyed. A second method is to place a band of heavy paper around the tree that is coated with Tanglefoot, a sticky substance. Not recommended for young or thin-barked trees. Spray infested plants during May and June with BT, acephate, carbaryl, methoxychlor. |

## *Plant Pests* (cont'd)

| INSECT AND DESCRIPTION | PLANT SYMPTOMS | CONTROL |
|---|---|---|
| Lace bugs: ⅛″ long brown or black insect with transparent lace-like wings. It should not be confused with the beneficial lacewing. | Adults and nymphs feed on lower leaf surfaces that sometimes result in a brown staining or spotting. Upper surfaces reveal a grayish stippling not unlike that resulting from spider mites. Damage is minimal. | Apply malathion in early June after all nymphs have hatched and before they become adults. Other controls include acephate and carbaryl. Dimethoate provides longer residual activity. |
| Leafhoppers: Small wedge-shaped insects that hold their wings in a roof-like position. May be brightly colored. | They suck the sap from the undersides of leaves. When disturbed the insects leap away. They are vectors of the disease called "yellows." | Diatomaceous earth, pyrethrins, rotenone, carbaryl, malathion, diazinon, methoxychlor. Systemic control includes dimethoate, Metasystox-R. |
| Leaf miners: The larval stage of some flies, moths, sawflies, and beetles. Holly leaf miner. | Serpentine marking blisters or blotches made on leaf surfaces by larvae feeding within. | Remove and destroy infested leaves. Apply dormant oils Spray with carbaryl, acephate, diazinon, or malathion during the period mid-May to mid-June when sawflies lay their eggs. Other controls include permethrin, dimethoate, Metasystox-R. |

## *Plant Pests* (cont'd)

| INSECT AND DESCRIPTION | PLANT SYMPTOMS | CONTROL |
|---|---|---|
| Leaf rollers | Leaf margins roll backward toward the midrib, creating a tunnel in which larvae feed. | Hand-pick insects. Spray with BT, carbaryl, methoxychlor, or acephate in May and June. |
| Maggots | *See* Flies and midges | |
| Mealybugs: Tiny white oval insects with a white powdery coating. Do not confuse with wooly aphids. | Soft white cottony clumps found in leaf joints and on the undersides of leaves. | They cannot survive the winter cold. Dislodge with a stream of water. Spray with soap solution. Spray with diluted alcohol (1 to 3). Other chemical controls include acephate, diazinon, carbaryl, or malathion. They are not easily controlled by systemics applied to the soil. |
| Root mealy bugs | Plants are stunted from root damage. | Malathion, diazinon, watered into soil. |
| Spider mites: Tiny sucking insects related to spiders; barely visible to the naked eyes | Leaves are stippled with white or yellowish spots on the upper surface. Small webs may be visible in leaf crotches or on the undersides of leaves. Prefer dry conditions. | Try to raise the humidity around plants and protect them from drying winds. Spray with soap solution or buttermilk. Also try rotenone and dormant oil sprays. Other chemical controls include Kelthane, malathion, Tedion, diazinon, dimethoate, and Metasystox-R. |

## *Plant Pests* (cont'd)

| INSECT AND DESCRIPTION | PLANT SYMPTOMS | CONTROL |
|---|---|---|
| Cyclamen mites | They hide in moist, dark locations on plants and are too small to be seen with the naked eye. They do not produce webs. Plants are stunted, leaves thick and deformed. Flower buds turn black. The mites thrive in moist conditions. | Where practical, immerse plant in warm (110°F) water for thirty minutes. Increase drainage and lower humidity. Chemical controls include dicofol (Kelthane) and diazinon. |
| Leaf blister mites | Reddish or yellowish pustules or galls on leaves. Do not confuse damage with rust diseases. | Spray with dormant oils or lime sulfur in early spring to catch mites as they emerge from buds. |
| Nematodes: Small microscopic wormlike insects | Plants are stunted and wilt on warm days. Growth is poor. Roots are poorly formed and are covered with lesions and/or tumor-like growths (galls). Nematodes are a major problem in the southern states where many varieties flourish. | Don't bring soil or plants into the garden from other regions that may be contaminated. Use sterile soil, practice rotation, plant resistant varieties, plant marigolds. If nematodes are suspected, seek professional help. Diagnosis cannot be made without a microscope. Chemical control of nematodes is not practical for the home gardener. If nematodes have been diagnosed, then discard the plant and soil and treat containers with Clorox. |

## *Plant Pests* (cont'd)

| INSECT AND DESCRIPTION | PLANT SYMPTOMS | CONTROL |
|---|---|---|
| Sawflies: Related to bees and wasps. Adults are usually small, yellowish, brown or black with iridescent or smoky wings. Maggots resemble caterpillars or slugs. | Depending on the space involved, damage may range from chewed leaves, to skeletonizing, leaf rolling or stem boring. | Rotenone, Methoxychlor, Sevin |
| Scale: Insects are recognized by their hard brown covering that protects them. | Hard brown spots are attached to stems and leaves. The insects secrete honeydew, which provides a medium for black sooty mold. | Dormant oils malathion, acephate, dimethoate. |
| Spittle bugs | Frothy masses that resemble slightly beaten egg whites are found at leaf axils or along stem. | Methoxychlor, malathion, dimethoate. |
| Tent caterpillars: 2" long, black with white, brown, and yellow stripes and blue spots on each side. Hairy tufts. | Nest is a webbed tent formed in tree crotches and forks. | Clean out nests with a broom and destroy. Spray infested plants with acephate, carbaryl, or methoxychlor in May. |

## *Plant Pests* (cont'd)

| INSECT AND DESCRIPTION | PLANT SYMPTOMS | CONTROL |
| --- | --- | --- |
| Thrips: Small, slender insects | They congregate in large groups on leaves and flowers, flying away when disturbed. Injured leaves are twisted and discolored and show stippled whitish streaks similar to mite damage. Flowers are streaked with brown and wither prematurely. Some thrips are vectors of spotted wilt virus. | Clean up debris at the end of the season. Diatomaceous earth, tobacco dust, nicotine. Malathion, carbaryl, acephate, diazinon, dimethoate, Metasystox-R. |
| Webworms: Hairy tufted caterpillar | Nest is similar to that of tent caterpillar, but is formed over the ends of branches. | Cut out webbed tips and destroy nest. BT, carbaryl, methoxychlor, acephate, malathion applied July and August. |
| Pine webworms | Sew the needles of evergreens together in June. | See above. Carbaryl or malathion applied in mid-June to mid-August. |
| Whitefly: Small, white, moth-like insects. Nymphs are small, flat, yellowish discs. Related to aphids, mealy bugs, scale. | Clouds of small white insects fly up from plants when disturbed. They exude honeydew, which encourages black sooty mold. | Whiteflies cannot survive cold winter temperatures. Place sticky yellow orange boards near plants to trap insects. Pyrethrum, malathion, resmethrin, diazinon, Enstar, dimethoate, Metasystox-R. |

## Plant Diseases

| DISEASE | PLANT SYMPTOMS | CONTROL |
|---|---|---|
| Anthracnose (fungus) | This disease affects leaves, fruit, twigs, or branches. Spots on leaves begin as small necrotic dots that enlarge and become black or brown, and are sometimes sunken. They are irregular in shape and several different-size spots can be present on the same leaf.<br>During wet weather the spots sometimes exude a pinkish ooze. Young leaves that are affected become distorted. Fruit that is affected may develop dark brown pock marks or sunken areas with little discoloration, as in the case of tomatoes. Affected branches are disfigured, sometimes developing sunken, dark brown lesions and cankers. | Rotate crops, grow resistant varieties.<br>Use fungicides like Bordeaux mix or lime sulfur (1 part to 9 parts water); also ziram, zineb, maneb, captan.<br>Treat seeds with a fungicide protectant.<br>The disease is most prevalent in wet weather. To avoid spreading the disease, don't work in the garden when it is wet. |
| Bacterial blight | Water-soaked spots develop on fruit, stems, and leaves. During wet weather the spots enlarge and a creamy ooze may appear. In dry weather the spots dry up. The bacteria overwinter in seed and on crop residues. | There is no cure; destroy infected plants. Don't work in the garden amid wet foliage or you will spread it. At the end of the season clean up and destroy all plant debris.<br>Do not save or use home-grown seed. |

## *Plant Diseases* (cont'd)

| DISEASE | PLANT SYMPTOMS | CONTROL |
|---|---|---|
| Bacterial soft rot | Bacterium enters through wounds inflicted mechanically or through pest damage. Small rotting spots appear on fruits and vegetables and rapidly enlarge, becoming soft and watery. Within three to five days the entire fruit becomes worthless.<br>Excessive application of nitrogen materials can cause soft growth, which is prone to attack. | Cut out infected tissue and dust wound with lime sulfur. Cut down on nitrogen fertilizers. Prune to promote air circulation. Make sure the soil is properly drained. Remove crop debris at the end of the season. |
| Bacterial wilt | Affects cucumbers, squash, melons, and carnations.<br>The leaves, runners, or the entire plant wilts and dies. To test for the disease cut a wilted stem near the crown. Touch a clean knife to the stem; if threads of white ooze stretch out between the knife and the stem, bacterial wilt is present. The disease is spread by the cucumber beetle. | Symptoms appear under hot conditions. Destroy infected plants, as there is no cure.<br>Remove infected debris. Control cucumber beetles with rotenone, Sevin or methoxychlor.<br>Do not work in the garden in wet weather and avoid splashing while watering. |
| Black rot, brown rot (fungus) | Attacks blossoms, fruit, spurs, and shoots.<br>Blossoms wilt and turn brown, persisting into summer. Small, light-colored, raised circular spots develop on fruit and eventually brown or blacken. Sometimes the fruit is destroyed in a matter of hours. In humid weather, a fuzzy, ash-gray covering develops over the spots.<br>Infected wood develops cankers that also expand. | Clean and destroy all crop residues including leaves and infected fruit. Rotate plants and treat seed with a fungicide.<br>Reduce nitrogen fertilizer, if roses are affected. Spray plants with Benomyl, captan, thiram, Bordeaux mixture, Maneb. |

## *Plant Diseases* (cont'd)

| DISEASE | PLANT SYMPTOMS | CONTROL |
|---|---|---|
| Blossom end rot (physiological) | Affects tomatoes and sometimes peppers. Tough black patches develop on the bottom (the blossom end) of the fruit, not the area that is attached to the stem. It is caused by uneven watering or a calcium deficiency. | Apply a mulch and water plants on a regular basis. Avoid excess nitrogen fertilizer. Add lime if you suspect a calcium deficiency. |
| Club root (fungus) | Growth is stunted, leaves pale, yield reduced. Plants wilt especially on hot days but usually recover at night. Rot organisms may set in. Below-ground roots become swollen and distorted, forming long, tuberous structures or a large, round gall-like mass. Spores are persistent and may remain dormant in the soil for up to ten years. | Remove and destroy infected plants and discard soil. Treat container with household bleach. Sometimes adding lime to the soil at regular intervals inhibits the disease. Call your local county agent for assistance. |
| Crown and stem rot (fungus) | Stems on crowns of affected plants turn soft and mushy. Overwatering, excessive humidity and extreme high or low temperatures cause the disease. Also see *Gray mold*. | The disease spreads rapidly. Cut out and destroy infected areas, or take cuttings from unaffected tissue. Treat the soil with lesan, terrachlor, or truban since it is a soil-borne disease. Dust wounds of cuttings with captan or Zineb. Avoid wetting foliage while watering. |

## *Plant Diseases* (cont'd)

| DISEASE | PLANT SYMPTOMS | CONTROL |
|---|---|---|
| Crown gall (bacterium) | Plants show reduced growth, yellowing of the leaves and wilting. Upon examination of the roots, swellings or tumors can be seen. | Once in the soil the pathogen can exist indefinitely. It enters through a wound made during planting, cultivating, grafting, or pruning. Practice strict hygiene and sterilize all tools frequently. Destroy infected plants and discard the soil. Sterilize containers with a bleach solution. |
| Damping off (fungus) | Seeds may rot, causing poor germination. The stem just above the soil rots, causing newly emerged seedlings to fall over and die. Roots may also rot. | Seeds should be treated with a combination of fungicides to guard against both preemergence and postemergence damping off. To prevent preemergence damping off, lesan and truban are recommended, while benomyl, terrachlor, and thiram are used for postemergence damping off. Be sure to use only sterilized pots and soil mix and do not overwater. Provide good air circulation and a temperature between 65° and 70°F. |

## *Plant Diseases* (cont'd)

| DISEASE | PLANT SYMPTOMS | CONTROL |
|---|---|---|
| Early blight (fungus) | The disease first manifests itself on lower leaves and progresses up the plant. It first appears as brown spots with inner concentric rings. The infected spots enlarge and merge, often defoliating the plant. | Buy resistant plants and use only healthy specimens. If the problem has been present previously, spray plants with Maneb or Zineb as a preventive measure. Practice rotation. |
| Fire blight (bacterium) | Attacks all ornamentals but most seriously pears and apples. The disease first appears on blossoms that blacken as if scorched and then spreads down the plant. Leaves suddenly turn brown and dry, hanging close to the stem. In the fall they fail to drop. Twigs, stems, and eventually branches are at first water soaked and ooze a creamy exudant. When cut, the tissue beneath the bark is stained red-brown. Eventually branches darken, turning either black or brown. | The disease causes much less damage to trees grown in well-drained soil that is not acidic or overfertilized. Bacteria are spread by windblown rain, insects, and pruning tools. There is no cure and most plants will have to be destroyed. Certain trees may be saved by cutting out infected portions at least 6 inches below the infection. |
| Fusarium wilt (fungus) | Leaves curl upward and there is a brown discoloration of the vascular system of the stem. Plants at first wilt only during the heat of the day, recovering at night. In the later stages the plant wilts and dies. The disease is most severe in hot, dry conditions. | Do not take cuttings. Destroy plants immediately to prevent spreading. Also discard the soil and treat containers with bleach. Grow resistant varieties in the future. It can be introduced through contaminated seed. |

## *Plant Diseases* (cont'd)

| DISEASE | PLANT SYMPTOMS | CONTROL |
|---|---|---|
| Gray mold botrytis (fungus) | Brown or black spots on leaves and stems. In humid weather a fluffy gray layer will develop over spots. The disease will attack tissue previously damaged by frost, insects, improper pruning; or it will attack the base of cuttings. It is also seen in conjunction with powdery mildew. It spreads in wet conditions and is most prevalent in cold, damp weather. | If caught early, cut out infected tissue and treat with benomyl or captan. Otherwise destroy infested plants. Try to reduce humidity. Prune to allow better air circulation. Avoid splashing and don't work in the garden when plants are wet. Clean up old plant debris. |
| Leaf spot (bacterium) | Yellowish spots with brown centers at leaf margins or wound sites. Infected tissue eventually turns brown and dry. On some plants the disease manifests itself in the form of small translucent circles that enlarge to form water-soaked spots. | Pick off infected leaves and destroy. Sterilize all pruning tools after working on each plant. Clean up all plant debris and destroy. |
| Leaf spot (fungus) | Common name applied to the appearance of spots on leaves, caused by various microbes. They may range in color from yellow to green to black. | Caused by high humidity, overwatering, low light, poor ventilation, or chilling, they are also spread by splashing water. Destroy all infected leaves and spray with a foliar fungicide such as benomyl, captan, or maneb. On roses use folpet. Prune to allow better air circulation and be sure to clean up all plant debris in the fall. |

## *Plant Diseases* (cont'd)

| DISEASE | PLANT SYMPTOMS | CONTROL |
|---|---|---|
| Downy mildew (fungus) | On the surface what is seen is a grayish patch of furry growth, but the fungus grows deeply into inner tissues causing considerable damage. The disease is much worse in moist conditions. | Avoid overhead watering, which spreads the disease. Remove infected tissue and destroy. If necessary, destroy the infected plant. Clean up leaves immediately since the disease can be transferred to the soil as they disintegrate. Spray with dinocap, Zineb, or a copper-based fungicide. Plant resistant varieties. |
| Powdery mildew (fungus) | Very little serious damage, but it does inhibit photosynthesis. A white powdery growth is prevalent on the upper leaf surfaces as well as on stems. The disease is usually worse in warm dry seasons. | Lower the humidity and provide better air circulation. Wash off affected plants to remove powdery growth. Spray with sulfur, Bordeaux mix, benomyl, dinocap, or folpet (roses). |
| Mosaic (virus) | Light green and yellow patches develop mottling leaves. In some cases they develop as streaks or stripes. Leaves may be reduced in size and distorted. Fruits may have light splotches and a warty appearance. In some cases the disease does not affect the plant very much. Spread by aphids. | Use resistant varieties. Pull and destroy affected plants. Extremely contagious; sterilize all tools, clothes. Don't touch other plants. Control aphids. |

## *Plant Diseases* (cont'd)

| DISEASE | PLANT SYMPTOMS | CONTROL |
|---|---|---|
| Ring spot (virus) | If the disease develops early in the season, plants will be stunted and resemble mosaic. Later infection results in ring spotting on leaves and fruit. The disease is spread by aphids. | There are no resistant varieties. Remove and destroy infected plants, control aphids. |
| Root rots (fungus or bacterium) | New growth is stunted and dies back. The plant wilts and at first recovers at night but finally dies. Roots may look hollow and collapsed with wet black spots, or the lesions may be drier and either black or brown. | Improve drainage and do not overwater. May also attack plants in moderately moist soil. If the roots are severely affected, take cuttings and destroy the plant. Otherwise water with lesan, truban, benomyl or terraclor. |
| Rusts (fungus) | Bright orange circular spots on leaves, sometimes with a dark spot in the center. Quince rust spots are sunken and dark green. | Condensation or moisture is needed for spore germination. Spores are spread by splashing water and enter through the lower leaf surface. Spray with Maneb or Zineb and be sure to treat the lower leaf surface. |

## *Plant Diseases* (cont'd)

| DISEASE | PLANT SYMPTOMS | CONTROL |
|---|---|---|
| Scab (bacterium or fungus) | Brown, black, or olive green spots on fruit sometimes with a suede-like texture. Spots turn corky and brown as they age. Dull green spots or blisters, or small pimply or corky spots and ring-like cracks on leaves enlarge as the disease spreads. | Clean up infected fruit and leaves and destroy. Rotate plants and check drainage for fruits and ornamentals. Spray with captan or benomyl. For potato scab check soil pH. For gladiolus scab destroy infected bulbs. Dip new bulbs in Zineb, Maneb or Ziram. |
| Smudge (fungus) | Black smudgy spots on white onions. Especially troublesome in wet weather. | Destroy infected bulbs. Dust seed and furrow with thiram or captan. Grow yellow and red varieties. Practice rotation. |
| Smut (fungus) | Attacks all members of the onion family as well as corn, carnations, and dahlias. The fungus accumulates in certain organs of the host plant, which swell and burst, emitting masses of sooty spores. This includes leaves as well as flower parts. Instead of releasing pollen and seeds, the plant releases spores. | Infected plants should be destroyed and healthy plants should be sprayed with a copper fungicide (Bordeaux mixture). Treat seeds in the future with thiram. |
| Sooty mold | Stems and leaves of plants sometimes develop a black or olive green coating as a result of attack by insects that exude honeydew. The fungus is not parasitic but does stop transpiration and photosynthesis. | Wash off affected plants with a soap and water solution. Treat plants for insect infestation. |

## *Plant Diseases* (cont'd)

| DISEASE | PLANT SYMPTOMS | CONTROL |
|---|---|---|
| Verticillium (fungus) | The fungus gains entrance through the roots. Tomato leaves develop yellow blotches and wilt during the heat of the day. A brownish discoloration of the vascular system can be seen if a cut is made longitudinally. Other plants remain vigorous when young, only developing symptoms after buds develop. Then marginal wilting of leaves occurs, followed by chlorosis. Leaves then turn brown and hang close to the stem.<br>Sometimes the disease only affects one side of the plant. | Destroy infected plants and discard or sterilize soil.<br>Treat containers with household bleach.<br>Grow resistant varieties and practice rotation. |
| Yellows (myco-plasmas) | New leaves yellow and may twist, curl, or be dwarfed in size. Lettuce balls prematurely and carrots develop a very hairy tap root.<br>The disease is spread only by leafhoppers. | There is no chemical control. Destroy affected plants.<br>Control leafhopper infestation. |

# ❧ 9 ❧
# Propagation

IF ART CAN BE DEFINED AS AN ACT of creation and self-expression and horticulture can be defined as the art of making things grow, then propagation is the soul of that art. It was not until the first seed was planted that man began to influence his environment to suit his needs, rather than being manipulated by it. Propagation is the creation of life.

Essentially all propagation can be organized into two categories: sexual and asexual. Sexual propagation involves the fertilization of an ovum by a grain of pollen and may either be the result of a cross between two plants or the product of self-fertilization. The union between male and female parts produces a seed that carries a genetic code which is similar, although not identical, to the parent or parents. The slight variation among individuals increases the specie's ability to adapt to changes in the environment. Asexual or vegetative propagation involves the removal of living tissue from the parent, which is then used to grow an entirely new plant. New plants that are vegetatively propagated are genetically identical to the parent in every way. That means that the quality of the offspring is ensured. Hybrids, which do not come true from seed or which are sterile, can be reproduced and will be identical to the parent plant. In many cases, plants that are propagated through vegetative means will also reach flowering or fruiting size faster than those propagated from seed.

The methods of vegetative propagation include division, cuttings, layering, and grafting. In all cases, successful propagation depends largely on the health of the parent plant and the care given to the offspring. Only healthy material taken from healthy stock will produce strong, vigorous plants. At the same time, a cutting or layered stem requires meticulous aftercare and close observation if it is to grow into a healthy specimen.

# Division

Division is a simple method of propagating a wide variety of plants, including fibrous-rooted perennials and shrubs that do not grow from a central crown, plants that form runners, suckers, or offsets, and bulbs. The basic procedure involves dividing the parent plant into several sections or the removal of a plantlet. Each section or plantlet is in itself complete in that it contains a main stem and a fully formed root system. There is no need to regenerate any missing parts. Division is also a very good way to renew an older plant that is no longer flowering well. Plants always put out new shoots around the perimeter of the clump, while the center grows old and woody. When you divide a plant, you remove the older growth, and you create a new central point thereby eliminating the problem. Most perennials should be divided every two to three years.

To divide a multi-stemmed, fibrous-rooted plant refer to figures 15

Fig. 15   *This overgrown perennial needs to be divided.*

*Fig. 16    To remove the plant, overturn the container and gently slide the plant out. Note that in this case the wooden container had been lined with a plastic garbage bag.*

*Fig. 17    Remove the plastic from around the root ball and cut away the matted tangle of old roots. Divide the plant in half.*

*Fig. 18  Fresh soil, with fertilizer added, has been prepared in a new container.*

*Fig. 19  The two freshly planted and mulched perennials now have plenty of growing room.*

through 19. Remove the plant from its container, loosen the roots with a hand cultivator and cut away any matted growth. Examine the stems and foliage and decide where you should divide the clump. Remember that each section must have a main stem or stems and a good piece of the root system. Cut down through the clump and the root ball with a trowel or saw, or pull the clump apart with your hands. Discard any old woody sections, leaving only young vigorous shoots. Each section should then be replanted at the same depth as the original plant. Finally, prune foliage severely to make up for the loss of roots and water the plant heavily to ensure good contact with the soil. Most plants can be divided at any time, but the best results are obtained if dividing is done when the plant is not growing too actively. A good rule is to divide spring- and summer-flowering plants in the fall, and fall-flowering plants in the spring.

A runner is a special prostrate stem that produces plantlets at its nodes or tip. It is often associated with plants, like the strawberry, that grow from a central crown. In many cases the plantlet will grow regardless of any lack of contact between the runner and the soil, but roots will not form without it. To ensure that the runner stays in contact with the soil, it may be held in place with a U-shaped wire or a stone. Once the roots have grown enough to support the new plant, it may be severed from the parent. Then lift carefully so as not to damage the young roots, taking some of the surrounding soil with it. When repotting a plant that grows from a central crown, it is important to set the plant at the proper depth or it will not survive.

Many ferns also put out runners that resemble long, green strings. They must never be allowed to dry out and turn brown while the new plant is forming. The best way to ensure that the necessary humidity is maintained is to cover the runner with clear plastic until the new plant can be severed.

A sucker is a shoot that rises from an underground stem and usually is complete with its own roots. Many garden shrubs produce suckers that can sometimes be quite a nuisance. The usual time to propagate them is in the spring or autumn. The soil is removed from around the new plant until the underground stem is located and the roots can be seen and are extensive enough to support the new plant. The underground stem may then be severed with a pair of pruning shears and the new plant lifted. Unless the plant grows from a central crown, the top growth should be pruned back to make up for the loss of small feeder roots.

Offsets or offshoots differ from suckers in that they are not formed from a horizontal, underground stem, but rather are formed at the base of a vertical stem just at or beneath the soil line. These shoots will usually produce roots where they come in contact with the soil. Before severing an offshoot from the parent, gently remove the soil from around its base to check the root system. If it is well formed sever the offset with a sharp knife and treat as you would a sucker.

Bulbs are usually propagated by division according to the kind of bulb in question. Tulips and hyacinths form bulblets at the base of the parent bulb while narcissus form offsets. These can be separated by simply breaking them off from the parent and repotting. In two or three years they will reach flowering size. Gladiolus and crocus, which are corms, can be treated in the same way.

Many bulbs can be treated to produce offspring when you want them to. To encourage tulips and narcissus they should be planted on the shallow side; hyacinths, on the other hand, may be encouraged to form bulblets by scarring the bulb in one of two ways. In August the base of the bulb may be scored deeply across its diameter to resemble the spokes of a wheel. Each cut should reach halfway through the depth of the bulb and form a V-shaped channel. Be careful not to actually cut the bulb in half or break any pieces off. The second method involves scooping out the base of the bulb and forming a conical pit, the top of which reaches halfway into the bulb. After the bulb is scarred by either method, it should be treated with a disinfectant and placed in a light, warm (68°F.), humid but airy room base up. Be sure to keep the bulb dry. After five weeks the bulblets will begin to form, and the temperature should be raised to 75°F. This can be done by placing the bulbs on top of a light fixture or on a propagating mat, if you have one. Do not place them on a radiator. By November, the entire bulb, complete with bulblets, should be planted five inches deep and protected from freezing. The following summer the bulblets can be separated from the mother plant and planted individually. In three to five years they will have reached flowering size.

Lilies can be propagated in two ways. The individual scales that make up the bulb can be separated like cloves of garlic and planted separately. In two or three years they will begin to produce flowers. Many lilies also produce bulblets along their stems as well as just at or under the soil line

*Fig. 20   Division of dahlia tuber*

and in leaf axils, while they are actively growing. When mature, these bulblets will usually fall to the ground and take root. The young plants can be transplanted and within two to three years will begin to flower. It is important when transplanting them that they be placed at the same depth they were previously. They will never survive if they are planted as deeply as a mature bulb.

Plants such as dahlias and irises that grow from tubers or rhizomes may be propagated by cutting the bulb into pieces. Each piece should include an eye or growing point from which leaves and roots will emerge. Dahlia tubers resemble long, fat, swollen fingers that radiate from a central stem and must be divided so each new piece will include a portion of that stem as well as a finger-like growth. The pieces should then be treated with an insecticide and either stored or replanted according to the individual cultural needs of the species.

# *Cuttings*

Plants possess one of the most remarkable abilities ever witnessed by science. By taking a small piece of living tissue known as a cutting, you can grow an entirely new specimen. The various types of cuttings that can be taken get their name from the plant part from which they come, and by the state of development of the tissue. For instance, a cutting taken from a branch is known as a stem or tip cutting, while a piece taken from a root or leaf is known as a root or leafbud cutting. If the stem cutting is taken in the spring when the wood is still pliable, it is known as a softwood cutting. If it is taken later in the season, it is known as a semihardwood or semiripe cutting, and if it is taken after the plant has entered its dormant period it is known as a hardwood cutting.

The key that makes taking cuttings possible can be found in plant physiology. Each plant has specialized areas that are responsible for plant growth. They are found at the tip of every stem and root and wherever a leaf or flower has been produced. It is in these areas that all cell division takes place and where it is decided whether a new leaf or flower is needed. Such growth is controlled in large part by plant hormones known as auxins or kinins which dictate the genetic code each plant possesses. The growth center at the tip of each branch, known as the terminal bud, is responsible for most plant growth. The other growth centers located further down the branch are called nodes and for the most part do no more than put out a new leaf when needed, but if the terminal bud is severed or damaged these nodes take over producing new branches. If a severed branch that contains at least two or three nodes is subjected to the proper conditions of temperature, humidity, and light, these same nodes will begin to produce roots. The process works best on young plant tissue, which is why it is easiest to root softwood cuttings. It is also true that the earlier the cutting is taken, the more time it will have to produce a strong healthy root system before winter and the greater your chances are for success.

Farmers and horticulturists have been using cuttings to increase their stock almost from the beginning, but recently with the discovery of new techniques and the invention of new products even the most difficult plants can be successfully rooted by the home gardener. Two new products that make rooting cuttings easier are synthetic rooting hormones and polyethylene plastic. Hormones are chemicals which, in extremely small concentrations, are capable of greatly affecting growth. Cuttings of many plants that root fairly well without treatment respond by producing more roots in less time. Other plants that have been difficult or impossible to root in the past can now be propagated more easily. Treated cuttings also show a better distribution of roots than untreated ones. Synthetic hormones come in a range of strengths, with the weakest being adequate for most home purposes. Some of the more difficult cuttings will require the stronger compounds. The mail order firm of Mellinger's (see page 110) offers the stronger compounds for sale. Regardless of the strength of the

*Fig. 21    This plastic Ziploc bag retains the necessary moisture for rooting cuttings.*

compound, plants are always treated in the same way. The cutting is prepared and dipped in water (very hairy or juicy cuttings need not be moistened) and then into the powder. The cutting is immediately planted, taking care not to knock the powder off the cutting in the process. The best way is to make a hole twice as large as needed in the planting medium, insert the cutting, then press the medium close around the stem.

The invention of polyethylene plastic has revolutionized propagation. Polyethylene plastic allows the passage of air while inhibiting the passage of moisture. Plants contained in polyethylene plastic receive all the air and humidity they need. After the initial watering, the rooting medium will remain moist for weeks. Polyethylene plastic has made the propagation of traditionally difficult woody plants including yew, holly, rhododendron, and azaleas a successful undertaking for even the busiest gardener.

## Preparing and Rooting Cuttings

It is best to prepare the parent plant by moving it to a shady location for one week before taking the cuttings. This gives the foliage time to acclimate to conditions that will approximate those to which the cuttings will be subject. Chosen plants must be free from any insects or diseases and should exhibit healthy compact growth. Plants that are weak and spindly, or damaged in any way, will only provide weak cuttings that will usually not take the shock of propagation or will only produce inferior plants.

Most gardeners have successfully rooted a cutting in a glass of water. If it can be done in a glass of water, why would you want to go to the trouble of rooting it in a growing medium? Very few plants will actually take root in a glass of water, and those that do produce a different kind of root, one that is brittle and prone to rot when planted in soil. They will have to produce a second set quickly if they are to survive once they have been transplanted. It may take a little practice, but the rewards associated with rooting cuttings in growing medium are far greater.

Choosing the right rooting medium can play a large part in a successful outcome. It should remain uniformly moist for long periods of time while still providing good drainage and aeration. Over the years some of the materials that have proved successful include peat and sphagnum moss, builder's sand, vermiculite, perlite, powdered Styrofoam, and gravel. Soil or compost should never be used for rooting cuttings since these harbor microorganisms including pathogens. By far the most popular mix is made up of one-half peat or sphagnum, and one-half sand or vermiculite, but what you choose will depend largely on what is available in your area and the unique conditions of your individual situation. Many gardeners prefer to mix three or more ingredients together, while others vary the proportions of the standard mix. Keep experimenting until you find the combinations that work for you. Each material has its own advantages or disadvantages. Sphagnum peat, for instance, has a slight antibiotic action that makes it almost impossible for microorganisms to exist, while its acidic nature seems to encourage the formation of roots. It will also hold moisture for long periods of time while remaining well aerated. Other kinds of horticultural peat moss possess the same qualities to a lesser degree though they all will shed water when dry. Microbes find little to survive on in sand, but sand loses moisture quickly while vermiculite doesn't. Perlite, powdered styrofoam, and gravel all remain well aerated, a quality much needed for root cuttings that rot easily such as geraniums, lantana, or fuchsia.

Any shallow garden container can be used for rooting cuttings as long as it can hold three inches of rooting medium. Flats, bulb pans, flower pots, plastic boxes, market flats or even polyethylene plastic sheets are suitable. Be sure that whatever container you choose has adequate holes for proper drainage.

If your cuttings are to survive, it is important that the tools, containers, and growing medium that you use be sterile. All tools and containers should be soaked in a 10 percent bleach solution for 20 minutes before they come into contact with the cuttings. Bags of sterilized potting materials are available at all garden centers and can be used with complete confidence as long as the bag has not been opened. If it has, then it can

*Fig. 22   Polyethelyne plastic can also make an excellent container for rooting cuttings.*

*Fig. 23   Roll up cuttings in plastic and secure with a rubber band.*

*Fig. 24   Cuttings treated in this manner can be left on a window sill to root.*

be sterilized by pouring boiling water through the mix or by placing it in a warm (180°F.) oven for 30 minutes. As an added precaution, it should be moistened with a fungicide solution before the cuttings are inserted. If any additional watering is needed while the cuttings are rooting, the water should be boiled or distilled and a fungicide added. The medium should always feel moist to the touch, with some sticking to the fingers. It should not drip when squeezed, nor should your fingers feel really wet.

The best time to take the cuttings is early in the morning, especially after a spell of wet weather when the leaves and stems will contain the most water. Use a sharp pocket knife or a pair of pruning shears that will not damage the stem. Don't worry about making a perfect cut. You will trim the cuttings later. It is best to try to keep them as short as possible since they are less apt to wilt. A cutting from any section of a branch will usually root, although tip cuttings (those that contain the terminal bud from the tip of the branch) are usually the most successful. Some shrubs, including camellia, cytisus, corylopsis, coronilla, and most narrow-leafed evergreens root better if thin side shoots are taken with a "heel." This is done by tearing the cuttings from the parent plant with a downward motion, taking a sliver of older wood along with the newer growth. Drop them immediately into a pail of cold water to increase their turgidity; you want them as plump and full of moisture as possible. Since they don't have roots, they cannot replace the moisture lost through transpiration very well.

The most common reason for failure with cuttings is that they have been allowed to dry out. Once you have finished taking all the cuttings and all your materials are assembled and prepared you can begin the final preparation of the cuttings. Begin by grouping the different kinds of cuttings together, always keeping them immersed in water. Use a clean sharp razor blade or potting knife that has been sterilized to make the final cut. Never use a scissors, which would crush the stem, inhibiting the flow of moisture and making the cutting prone to infection. When preparing softwood or semihardwood cuttings, first trim all the leaves from the lower portion, leaving two to four leaves at the top. Plants such as rhododendrons that produce large leaves should have them cut in half. The more leaf area, thet the faster rooting takes place; however, more leaves mean a faster rate of transpiration and possible wilting. Cut the stem at a 45 degree angle about one-fourth inch below a node. It has been found that cuttings root best when the stem is cut as close as possible to a growth center without damaging the internal dormant bud. A callus will then form over the wound and new roots will grow. If the cutting in question has no terminal tip, then the top of the cutting should be treated in the same manner. Cuttings that have been taken with a heel should not be trimmed but inserted in the medium as is. It is also an accepted practice when preparing semihardwood cuttings to wound the base of certain plants such as azaleas, rhododendrons, magnolias, and maples by scraping

*Fig. 25  Properly prepared tip, or stem, cuttings*

off a strip of bark to expose the green tissue just beneath for a distance of one or two inches. Leaf-bud cuttings are prepared by cutting a chosen stem into sections, each containing a leaf. Each leaf is then carefully cut out of the stem so it includes the node beneath it. They differ from leaf cuttings used to propagate certain houseplants in this respect.

As soon as they are made the cuttings should be submerged in water, which, if you wish, has been treated with a fungicide. The only exceptions to this are geraniums and plants with a milky sap; they must be allowed to dry for a period of from twelve to twenty-four hours before insertion in the medium. If the cuttings are to be kept under humid conditions, then the usual rule is to bury the bottom one-third of the stem, but if the cuttings are to be kept under normal household conditions then the bottom half should be buried. Leaf-bud cuttings are inserted so only the leaf is visible. It is best to insert all cuttings at a 45 degree angle (see Fig. 25).

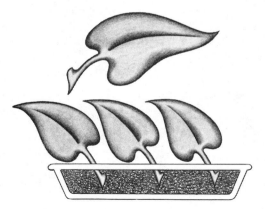

*Fig. 26   Leaf bud cuttings*

After you have finished inserting all the cuttings, gently water the containers without disturbing them. Application of a fungicide at this time is recommended. Cuttings should not be given any fertilizer while they are rooting since this tends to contribute to soft, rangy growth of both foliage and roots. Place the newly planted cuttings in a plastic bag or sweater storage box to prevent rapid loss of moisture and wilting (see Fig. 21 on page 136.).

Wilting occurs for several reasons, including lack of moisture, too little humidity, too much light or attack by stem rot. In the case of stem rot, the affected cuttings should be destroyed immediately to prevent the spread of the disease and those remaining should be treated with captan or zineb. In most other cases, the cuttings can usually be revived with a light spray of tepid water. Cuttings have a great deal of trouble absorbing the moisture they need and tend to lose moisture from their leaves faster than they can absorb it. It is important that a high humidity level be maintained throughout the rooting period. Keep the cuttings in polyethylene plastic bags or a plastic sweater box while rooting. The cuttings must be checked every day so that the proper moisture and humidity level can be adjusted. They should be moist but not soggy. If too much condensation is noted or evidence of mold is seen on the surface, the plastic covering should be removed temporarily and the air circulation increased slightly. It is best to water them from the bottom early in the morning.

Fig. 27   *This method of rooting cuttings takes advantage of the porous nature of clay pots. The small pot in the center had its drainage hole plugged and is kept filled with water. The water seeps through the clay pot into the surrounding growing medium.*

Wet foliage at night is an invitation to trouble. Never water cuttings during the heat of the day unless the water is as warm as the air. Cold water on warm foliage causes damage. Mixtures that contain a great deal of peat moss should be watered only moderately since peat absorbs a great deal of moisture. When rooting cuttings directly in the garden, plunge the containers into larger pots to help maintain a more even soil temperature and moisture level.

Cuttings need a lot of light, but they cannot handle full sun. If you do not have fluorescent lights then a sunny window or a shaded spot in the garden is best. If your apartment windows face south or if you cannot provide a shady place in the garden, you can shade the cuttings with a sheer curtain, a piece of cheesecloth, or a white plastic bag which should be removed on cloudy days.

Cuttings will root faster if the soil temperature remains 5 to 10 degrees warmer than the air. These temperatures can be maintained with a soil heating cable or mat, or by keeping a light bulb on below the container. Do not place the cuttings on a radiator, since the heat is intermittent and usually too warm for the cuttings to handle. Some plants such as delphiniums and lupines require cool (55°) temperatures if they are to be rooted successfully. If kept too warm, they will rot. You can check to see if the cuttings are rooted by giving them a gentle tug. If you feel any resistance, they have rooted. Once rooting has taken place, it is time to harden them off and transplant them into individual containers. Remove the plastic covering for two hours and gradually increase the time each day until they can remain uncovered for a full twenty-four hours. If they show any evidence of wilting, immediately spray them with tepid water and cover them with plastic again. Slowly increase the amount of light they are receiving and begin feeding them with one-quarter strength fish emulsion. When the roots are one-half to one inch long, carefully transplant them into individual containers. Do not try to remove any of the medium that sticks to their roots. Many plants will have to be transplanted to their original depth although most herbaceous perennials and annuals can be planted deeper with no ill effects. A good potting mixture for the rooted cuttings is equal parts peat moss, vermiculite, potting soil, and compost (optional). Stick with the fish emulsion at first, avoiding all mineral fertilizers. After transplanting, allow the plants to rest a week, then place them outside in a shady, sheltered spot in the garden for two hours the first day. Gradually increase their time outside each day. At the first sign of wilting bring them back inside and spray them with tepid water. Increase their exposure to direct sun in the same manner. Transfer them to their permanent locations and mulch them heavily after the first hard frost to protect them through the winter. Certain shrubs such as the flowering dogwoods, magnolias, maples, and certain viburnums root easily but do not overwinter well. These and any cuttings that were rooted late in the season should be placed in a cool spot (45°) indoors or in a cold frame and protected from freezing. Keep them on the dry side until mid-January, when they can be given more heat (50–55 °) and moisture. Most herbaceous perennials will reach blooming size in one year. Deciduous shrubs may take two to three years, while broad-leafed evergreens and conifers will become landscape plants in three to five years. Until this time, there is a greater chance of loss or damage due to climatic conditions.

Hardwood cuttings are treated differently. The finished cuttings are gathered into bundles, grouping all like kinds together. The bottom of the bundle should then be topped and leveled on a flat surface, labeled and tied together. These cuttings are then buried in a horizontal position in a moist but not wet material such as peat, sphagnum, sand, or vermiculite, and placed in a dark, cool (35–50°) place for a period of six to eight weeks. During this time, the cut ends will quickly form a thick, fleshy callus. This is the beginning of root formation and an important step in the process. The heavier the callus the better the root formation and the greater the chance of success.

After they have callused, the temperature should be maintained at a cool level, just above freezing, to keep the tops from growing. At this time the cuttings should not be subjected to drying conditions, fluctuating temperatures, or excessive moisture. Once the outside temperature has risen enough so the soil can be worked, it is time to pot up the cuttings. Unlike other cuttings, it is best to pot them directly in soil buried about two-thirds their length. At least two nodes should be underground. Once they are planted, the cuttings should be placed outside in a sheltered spot free from direct sun. The cool, early spring temperatures will prevent the leaves from growing. It is imperative that the cuttings produce roots first.

Root cuttings are taken while the parent plant is dormant. It is usually lifted in early spring or fall except in the case of the oriental poppy, which is propagated in midsummer. The pieces are then replanted with the top buried one-half to one inch below the surface of the soil, and the container is placed in a cool but frost-free location for the winter. As with any cutting, the medium must be kept moist at all times. When top growth is evident in the spring, the rooted cuttings may be moved to their permanent locations.

# *Layering*

Layering is one of the oldest methods of propagation, having been practiced by the ancient Chinese, and one of the easiest for the amateur gardener. Unlike a cutting, which is subject to wilting and damping off, a layered stem remains attached to the parent and still receives nourishment and moisture. It is a method of propagation that has been used successfully on almost every plant with an upright habit, including plants

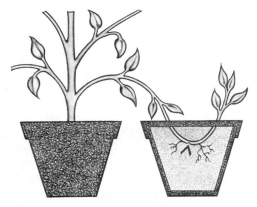

*Fig. 28   Simple layering*

that do not propagate easily by cuttings or division. Layering takes advantage of the plant's natural tendency to root when a stem comes in contact with moist soil for the necessary period of time.

There are basically four kinds of layering techniques that can be used: simple or common layering; tip layering; mound layering; and air layering. The method you choose depends largely on the plant you wish to propagate.

Simple layering can be performed on any plant with a flexible stem. First, prepare the container and soil that will be used. The container should be heavy and squat enough to act as an anchor. A good choice would be a large clay azalea pot. The medium should retain moisture and yet be well drained. A mixture of one-third peat, one-third vermiculite and one-third potting soil or compost is fine. It need not contain any fertilizer since the layered stem will receive nourishment from the parent plant.

Second, select a healthy, well-formed stem from the previous season's growth, or if the layering technique is carried out later in the growing season, a stem formed of the current season's growth. It should have the width of a lead pencil. Remove all the foliage twelve inches from the tip, exposing the stem about six inches in either direction. This is the area that will be buried. Bend the stem so it touches the soil of the prepared container and choose the node from which you want the roots to form. Then let the stem return to its natural position. With a sharp knife, notch or slit the stem in an upward direction one-third of the way through, just below the node. Take care not to make it too deep or the stem may break. The wound should be positioned on the underside of the stem when it is buried. Dampen it, apply a liberal dose of rooting hormone, then bury the stem two to three inches deep, 4 to 6 inches for rhododendrons. Secure the stem with a piece of wire, a forked stick, a large stone or a brick. It should not be allowed to work itself loose under any circumstances. Keep the layered stem well watered and in a few months it will have rooted.

Tip layering works for plants that root readily when the tip of the stem comes in contact with the soil, plants such as black raspberry, currant, and gooseberry. The foliage is removed from the top portion of the stem, rooting hormone is applied, and the tip is buried four to five inches deep. There is no need to wound the stem.

Mound layering is a good method to choose when dealing with multi-stemmed perennials and shrubs and when a lot of new plants are desired. In the case of herbaceous perennials, the parent is planted in the normal manner but set deeply in the container. The tips of all growing shoots are pinched back and the crown is buried one-half inch deep. As the shoots grow, more soil is added until the crown is buried two to three inches deep. The parent plant is left alone for eight to ten weeks (about the time it would take a cutting to root), then the plant is lifted. Carefully remove the soil with your fingers to expose each rooted stem. Sever them and pot them up individually.

When dealing with a woody shrub, the procedure is quite similar. All the branches are cut back to just above the first node on each stem. Soil is then mounded over the base of the plant until the stem stubs are buried one-half inch deep. The mound may be secured with sheet moss, plastic netting, or newspaper—anything that will hold it securely in place while allowing moisture in and the new young shoots to grow out. As they grow, more soil is added until the old stems are three to four inches deep. When they are well rooted, the new stems are uncovered, severed, and potted up.

Simple, tip, or mound layering is best carried out in early spring when growth is most rapid and the shoots are easier to bend. Some shrubs can actually be layered when they are still dormant. The rapidity with which a layered shoot roots varies with the kind of plant, age of the shoot, and conditions that prevail during the rooting period. Herbaceous plants may take a few weeks, while woody plants will generally take from one to six months. Broad-leaved evergreens such as rhododendrons may require 18 months or longer. When in doubt leave the layered stem attached to the parent plant, especially through the winter when most losses occur. Be sure to keep it moist throughout the season or the new roots may wither. The most critical time for the new plant is just after it is severed. It should be treated as you would any newly rooted cutting. Keep it moist, shaded, and feed it sparingly.

Air layering is used primarily for plants that have stems that will not bend easily, including tall rhododendrons, conifers, camellia, prunus, and liquidambars. Instead of bringing the stem to the rooting medium, the rooting medium is brought to the stem. Choose a healthy young stem the size of a lead pencil from the previous season's growth. Locate a leaf node about six inches below the tip of the stem. This is where you will layer

*Fig. 29   Air layering*

the plant. Remove all the leaves from this area so you have a piece of clear stem that measures about four to five inches long. Slit the stem below the node as previously explained or ring it. Two shallow cuts that only pierce the bark and encircle the stem are made about one inch apart. A third shallow cut is made that joins the first two together. The bark is then peeled back exposing the wood beneath. What ringing does is to allow the passage of nutrients to the upper portion of the stem while preventing their downward flow. This encourages the roots to form quickly. An added advantage is that the stem retains its strength because the woody tissue has not been cut and is less likely to break.

Once the stem has been wounded, wet it down and apply rooting powder. The area is then firmly packed with sphagnum peat moss which has been soaked and wrung out. If the stem has been slit, be sure to work some of the moss up into the wound. If you have some trouble keeping the slit open, insert a wooden match or toothpick. Splint the stem with a wooden chopstick or piece of bamboo staking; continue applying enough moss to produce a sizable bulge and secure it to the branch with some string. Wrap a strip of clear plastic around the bulging moss and secure both the top and bottom. If executed properly, no moisture should be able to escape and there should be no further need to water for several weeks. Check the moss from time to time and moisten it with a spray bottle when needed. Sphagnum peat will lighten as it dries, so use the color as an indication of the moisture level. Depending on the plant, air layering will take from one to six months. Since air-layered roots are easily damaged by frost, it is important to carry out the procedure early enough to be able to sever the stem before cold weather arrives. For this reason, it is best to do it by the end of April or early May. Once a sturdy mass of roots can be seen through the plastic, the layered stem can be severed. The string that holds the moss is removed, but the moss is left in place so as not to disturb the roots. Keep in mind that the sphagnum moss will hold moisture far longer than the surrounding soil, and it should be checked before watering. The new plant should be placed in a sheltered spot out of direct sun and protected from freezing.

# Grafting

A graft is the physical union of parts from two or more varieties to form one complete plant. Grafting is a way to propagate many species that will not come true from seed or to improve upon plants that produce lovely flowers or delicious fruit but weak roots. Sadly, this is the case with most of our fruit and nut trees as well as many of our ornamentals. It is not uncommon for gardeners to plant the seeds of such plants only to find the results disappointing. The most common form of grafting unites the root-stock of one plant (the understock) with a bud, twig, or seedling of another (the scion). Although they grow together to form one plant, the understock and scion exert little influence on each other. The foliage, fruit, and flowers of the scion retain all the characteristics of the parent plant. That is why it is possible to have one tree that produces five different kinds of apples. The same is true of the understock. If it was taken from a variety that characteristically has a vigorous root system, then it will retain this characteristic. The only instance in which one will influence the other is in the case of dwarfing. If the scion of a standard-sized apple tree is grafted onto the understock of a dwarf variety, then the finished product will be a small tree that bears the same full-sized fruit as the standard variety.

Although space permits only a brief discussion of grafting here, it is a complicated horticultural procedure that every gardener should be aware of since so many of the trees and shrubs found in gardens today are grafts. Such plants are not as hardy as nongrafted stock and may need protection in particularly bad winters. The bud union (the actual point of the graft) must never be allowed to freeze at any time. Neither should it be buried beneath the soil, or the scion will root and the benefits of the graft will be lost. Suckers or offshoots that emerge from the understock should not be allowed to develop for a similar reason. Although the flowers or fruit may be inferior, the understock is probably a vigorous grower and could eventually crowd out the scion.

# Growing Plants from Seed

For the amateur gardener, seeds are the most common means of propagating most annuals, vegetables, and certain perennials. Most local nurseries only make available a narrow range of young plants to choose from, but mail order firms with their larger lists of customers can offer much more by selling seeds as well.

All it takes to successfully master the skill of seed sowing is a little patience and attention to detail. If you have tried sowing seeds in the past without success, try again. Perhaps this discussion will help you solve your problems. The main factors that govern successful seed germination include the quality and freshness of the seed itself, planting time, a sterile growing medium, correct temperature, consistent moisture, and sufficient air.

To ensure seed of good quality and freshness, begin by selecting a few packets from a reputable store or mail order firm. Choose plants that you enjoy and that are easy to grow, such as cosmos, marigolds, zinnias, or tomatoes. If you are a novice, stay away from plants that have very fine seed or long germination periods or that require special handling.

To determine the correct planting dates for different seeds check the table of average frost dates on pages 168–169; mark the average frost date for your area on your calendar. Then sort your seeds out by the number of weeks prior to the frost-free date they may be sown. Most seeds can be started indoors six to eight weeks before they can safely be planted outside, but some such as geraniums will require ten to twelve weeks and others such as cucumbers or squash only four weeks. Some plants that prefer cool temperatures such as lettuce will tolerate some frost and can safely be set out a week or two prior to the frost-free date, but don't start any plants earlier than suggested. The most frequent mistake made by inexperienced gardeners is to start sowing seed too soon. The young plants become large and pot-bound and usually suffer from too little light. Growth is checked and any advantage of an early start is lost. Put away all those seeds that it is too early to plant and subdivide those remaining according to cultural requirements. Some will need light in order to germinate, others total darkness, and so on. Sorting them accordingly will facilitate planting and meet the individual needs of each plant.

The next step is to assemble the needed equipment and supplies including containers, plant markers, a waterproof marking pen, a sieve, a measuring cup, a bucket, scissors, sphagnum peat moss, vermiculite, a fungicide, bleach, some distilled water (optional), and Ziploc bags or sweater storage boxes.

There are many different containers designed for growing seedlings on the market today, including expandable peat pellets, compressed peat pots, and plastic containers. The peat pellet is a small disk of compressed peat usually encased in a plastic net. When water is applied, the small disk expands. The great popularity of compressed peat pellets is based on convenience, as there is no need to mix a rooting medium, and the entire pellet can be transplanted directly into the garden without disturbing the young plant. However, there are several objections to their use. First of all, they are expensive. Secondly, they take up a great deal of room and can actually limit the number of plants you can comfortably grow. Eventually all seedlings must be placed in individual pots, but some will be transplanted to the garden early, making more room on your windowsill for others. This is an important consideration when you don't have much space. The most serious objection has to do with the material itself. Peat holds moisture for a long time, and once transplanted to the garden, it holds water longer than the surrounding soil. Roots that are not contained in the peat pellet will need more water while those that remain inside may rot from overwatering. Peat moss also repels water when dry and is very difficult to rewet. My last objection concerns the netting that can obstruct root expansion into the surrounding soil. It is not uncommon to dig up spindly plants halfway through the season and find that their root systems have been constricted. If you wish to use the pellets, remove the plastic covering before planting them in the garden. Pressed peat pots have also been designed for direct transplanting to the garden, but again I have similar objections. They are expensive and they constrict the spread of roots. They do not disintegrate quickly and are often dug up in the fall completely intact. Plastic reusable containers have none of these problems. True, the initial expense may be greater, but they are reusable, and if care is used in transplanting there will be little root damage.

Satisfactory seed containers need not be limited to those specifically designed for this purpose. Cut-down milk cartons, butter or cottage cheese tubs, or Styrofoam cups can also be used. I do not recommend the use of egg cartons for starting seedlings since the cups hold too little soil. Any container you choose should be at least 3 inches deep and should hold 2½ inches of growing medium to give adequate room to the roots. I would not recommend any metal containers. For my own seedlings I use rectangular plastic containers, known as market flats, that measure 5½″ × 7½″. I can plant all the seeds of one variety in a single container, which makes keeping track of them much easier. The containers also fit nicely into Ziploc plastic bags, making daily watering and care unnecessary. Market packs are sold at many garden centers and through most mail order firms. I also save the market packs from the prestarted plants that I buy each year. It is best to keep all of your containers as uniform as possible. I find this helps when it comes to watering. Different containers of different sizes all dry out at different rates. Knowing when to water can become difficult. Be sure all containers have enough drainage holes to let excess water pass through.

All containers (except those made of peat moss), plant markers, and any equipment that may come in contact with the seeds or growing medium must be sterilized in a 10 percent bleach solution for twenty minutes and then rinsed thoroughly. This is to prevent the spread of damping off, a fungus disease that spreads rapidly and kills young seedlings in a matter of days. Pre-emergence damping off attacks and kills the sprouting seedling before it emerges from the soil while post-emergence damping off attacks the newly emerged seedling at the soil line. There is nothing quite so discouraging as damping off to gardeners who have carefully cared for their seedlings from the beginning. Sterilization is a step that should not be overlooked.

Since soil is by its very nature a wonderful medium for microorganisms, it should not be used for growing seedlings. Instead, a mixture of one-half sphagnum peat and one-half vermiculite is recommended. Moisten the growing medium before filling the containers with either distilled water, or tap water that has been boiled for five to ten minutes. The medium should feel damp enough to stick to your fingers but not really wet. Once filled, the containers should be leveled off.

Treat the seeds themselves with a fungicide (see "damping off," page 122) by placing a pinch of the powder in the seed packet and shaking. Then sprinkle the seeds on top of the growing medium. Don't worry too much about spacing. They can be thinned later with a scissors. Those that require light to germinate or those that are very fine do not need to be covered. Just press down the medium to ensure good contact. If the seeds do require a cover, a thin layer of sifted sphagnum or vermiculite can be applied. I prefer the vermiculite because the lighter color allows me to tell if the seeds have been properly covered. I just smash it up in a blender (don't worry—it's totally harmless), food processor, or by hand, using a mortar and pestle, then sprinkle it with a sieve over the seeds. After the seeds are planted, each container is labeled immediately. This is important if you don't want to find you've planted your two-foot marigolds in a hanging basket. Information noted should include the species, variety, and planting date. The average number of days to germinate is optional, but always give the seeds an extra couple of weeks beyond the average germination time before giving up on them entirely. Sometimes environmental conditions slow the process down.

The containers are then watered from the bottom by setting them in a layer pan of a diluted fungicide solution made with distilled water, until the tops are moist. They are then removed and drained.

Once watered and labeled, each container is slipped inside a plastic enclosure to maintain an even moisture level. The plastic must not touch the growing medium. Seeds that require total darkness can then be covered with several layers of newspaper or cardboard.

Improper watering is probably the biggest cause of seedling failure. Before any seed can sprout, it must absorb moisture, which softens the outer shell. The germ or kernel then swells and breaks through toward the surface. Once the seed has begun to sprout, a lack of moisture is usually fatal. Check the containers daily for dryness and don't assume the medium is wet because there is condensation on the plastic. When watering, use sterilized water only, until the first true leaves make their appearance. It is also a good idea to use water that is at room temperature to avoid hindering development. To avoid disturbing the seeds or tender seedlings, it is best to water them from the bottom or with a spray bottle. Overwatering can also prove fatal, since too much humidity encourages fungus, which appears as a fuzzy covering on the surface of the growing medium. If this growth appears, cut down on the amount of water and provide better air circulation by opening the plastic covering. You may also find it advantageous to open a window in the next room, especially on warmer days. As the seedlings grow tall enough to come in contact with the plastic covering, the covering should be removed gradually and the seedlings hardened off.

Soil temperature is also important. Satisfactory soil temperatures range from 65 to 85°F. with 70°F. being the ideal. A nighttime drop of 10° is also preferred. Generally, if you are comfortable, so are your seedlings. Some cool growing annuals, perennials, and vegetables can take even cooler conditions without any trouble as long as they receive adequate light. It is the combination of cool temperatures and lack of light that favors the spread of damping off. Most seedlings will germinate faster if provided with some bottom heat, especially if they are kept in a cool location like a windowsill, but most will do quite well without it. You can purchase one of the many soil heating cables and mats that are available at your local nursery or through a mail order house. Also invest in a good soil thermometer, since the thermostats in most heating devices are not accurate.

Germinating seedlings contain only enough stored nourishment to get them through sprouting. It is imperative that you place them where they will receive adequate light as soon as the first seedlings emerge. Unless you can provide southern exposure, I suggest that you invest in a fluorescent light fixture that will provide an ideal environment for starting seedlings. The expensive models sold through plant catalogs are not necessary. Neither is it necessary to invest in expensive "grow lights." Any inexpensive 48-inch fluorescent fixture equipped with one warm white and one cool white bulb will grow plants that are perfectly healthy.

There are many advantages to growing seedlings under fluorescents, the most obvious of which is that day after day, hour after hour your seedlings will be receiving a constant, even source of light. There are no cloudy days or short day lengths to check their progress. By investing in an inexpensive timer to complete the unit you can control the length of the growing day without the bother of turning the lights on and off. Another less obvious advantage is that fluorescents provide a constant source of heat to warm the soil and air to an optimal level. Seedlings grown under lights are not subject to the cold drafts common to windowsills or excessive heat buildup from a strong spring sun. The added warmth and constant light also discourage damping off.

When using the lights, the tops of the seedlings should be no closer than 2 inches but no further than 4 inches from a double-tubed fixture.

Fig. 30    *This plastic sweater box prevents sprouting seedlings from drying out.*

If the fixture contains four lamps, the seedlings should remain four to six inches away. The lights should remain on fourteen to sixteen hours each day. The intensity of the light falls off rapidly at the ends of the tubes. Seedlings that don't require as much light can be grouped there. Those needing more light should be rotated toward the center every few days. Seedlings that are not receiving enough light will grow long and leggy. They should be raised so they are closer to the tubes. If they are receiving too much light, their leaves will curl under or change color, turning darker or taking on a reddish tinge.

After they emerge, seedlings should be fed with fish emulsion diluted to one-quarter strength once every week. The first leaves to appear are not the true leaves but seed leaves. These will be followed by the first set of true leaves. Once these have appeared, the seedling is no longer in danger from damping-off disease and the use of sterilized water can be discontinued. The appearance of the first set of true leaves also signals that it is time to begin transplanting. This may check their progress slightly but transplanted seedlings eventually grow into more compact, bushy plants later. By the time the second set of true leaves has appeared you should have transplanted all except the smallest plants.

As with the previous containers, the individual 2½-inch and 3-inch pots should be treated in a 10 percent bleach solution and rinsed. A growing mix should be prepared that is made up of two-thirds of the seed sowing mix and one-third potting soil. If you have access to compost, the

*Fig. 31   Newly emerged seedlings ready for transplanting*

proportions can be changed to one-half seed sowing mix, one-quarter soil and one-quarter compost. To this basic mix you can add some lime, dried blood, bone meal, and greensand. Stay away from chemical fertilizers, which could be too strong for the small seedlings.

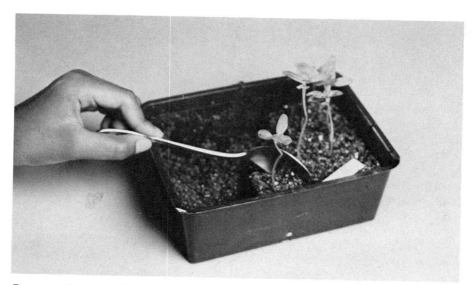

*Fig. 32   A spoon makes a good tool for pinching out seedlings.*

*Fig. 33    Newly transplanted seedlings*

Prick out the seedlings a few at a time, using a blunt instrument such as a plant label or a spoon. Gently separate the individual plants with your fingers, handling the small seedlings by their leaves only. They should be planted immediately so that their roots are not exposed for too long. Do not stuff the roots into a hole in the growing mix! Turn the pot on its side and half fill it with soil. Then lay the seedling on top and continue to fill the pot with the growing mix. Plants that grow from a central crown (that is, all the leaves emerging from a single point on the stem) must be set at the same depth they were originally. Plants that are set too deep, with their crowns below the surface, will usually rot. Plants that have an upright stem and a terminal bud can actually benefit from deeper planting. They will eventually produce roots along the buried portion of the stem. Continue to feed the young plants with one-quarter-strength fish emulsion each week. Soon it will be time to place them in the garden in a shaded location and gradually harden them off. A mist of tepid water will help them recover in the event of wilting. If there is no natural shade, you can provide some by covering the seedlings with cheesecloth. It is best to transplant the seedlings to their permanent locations when the sun is not very strong.

## Sowing Seeds in the Garden

Planting seeds directly in the garden doesn't have to be tricky. Seeds sown outdoors have the same moisture, humidity, light, and temperature requirements as those that are sown indoors. Success lies in the gardener's ability to accurately observe the events of nature and interpret them on the basis of horticultural knowledge.

By now you have a good understanding of the moisture and light requirements of sprouting seeds. It is also important to know in greater detail the subtle role soil temperature plays in chemical reactions. Water absorption and the availability of nitrogen and phosphorus all increase as the soil temperature rises. Some plants germinate, flower, and fruit long before the real heat of summer begins, while other plants don't begin their growth cycle until the warm weather makes its appearance. They have adapted themselves to very different circumstances based on temperature. Temperature in conjunction with moisture also triggers the germination of seeds.

Knowing the soil temperature can greatly reduce the guesswork involved in deciding when to plant your seeds. Seed packages tend to have vague descriptions that are of little real help. Until recently, farmers would take their cues from nature. When compared to the readings of a good soil thermometer these cues made a lot of sense. For instance, cool-weather crops such as peas or delphiniums were planted when the first buds began to open. The forsythias would not yet be in bloom but their buds would be showing color. Checked against a soil thermometer these conditions appear when the temperature is about 45°F., perfect for such plants. When the soil temperature reaches 50°F. (in New York City the first two weeks in April, for example) forsythias and some of the earliest-flowering fruit trees, such as apricots, should be in full bloom, and the red maples should be enveloped in a pink cloud. At this time, carrots, radishes, and lettuce should be planted. As spring progresses and the oak leaves grow to the size of a mouse's ear, it is time to plant most seedlings. The soil temperature should be about 60°F. and all danger of frost is past. The most tender annuals, such as tomatoes and eggplant, need a soil temperature of at least 70°F. to germinate and should not be planted outside until lilacs begin to bloom in your area.

Soil thermometers are probably sold at the nursery where you buy your supplies. They are quite simple to use; just plunge them into the soil to a depth of 2 inches. Readings should be taken around 7 A.M. and again at 2 P.M. and the readings averaged. When the proper temperature range is reached, you can plant your seeds.

Before any seeds can be sown, the soil must be prepared. Two weeks before planting, compost or peat should be added along with lime, bone meal, potash, and dried blood. If the soil is still too cold to work easily, cover it with black plastic for a week or so. Next year it can be prepared and covered in the fall to speed things up. Be sure the plastic has drainage holes so rainwater can get through. When the soil is dry enough to be worked, cultivate it deeply, breaking up any clumps and distributing the new materials. Loosen and level the surface. Water it thoroughly with a fungicide a day or two before planting. It is a good idea to treat your seeds with a seed protectant as well. The seeds may be sprinkled on top or planted in rows. If necessary, the seeds should be covered with a layer of peat or sphagnum and then gently watered in. Seeds that require total darkness to germinate can be covered with a layer of newspaper. Be sure to check under it every day when you expect the seeds to sprout. Once the seeds are covered, place a sheet of clear plastic over them to maintain an even soil temperature and conserve moisture. As with seeds planted indoors, they must be checked daily and never allowed to dry out.

## Seeds That Require Special Handling

Many seeds will germinate easily under a wide range of conditions but others, including some perennials and most trees and shrubs, will not respond to the normal germination practices employed by most amateur gardeners. These seeds must pass through a series of different conditions that help break their dormancy. Just as many seeds need exposure to light or total darkness in order to germinate, others need soaking, exposure to near freezing temperatures, or a period of after ripening before they will germinate.

One of the most common causes of seed dormancy is a hard protective seed coat that ensures the safety of its contents for long periods of time. Unfortunately what it can also do is prevent germination by not allowing the passage of air or water. This hard seed coat is meant to be worn down by the natural effects of weathering. Gardeners can mimic these effects by soaking the seeds overnight and up to twenty-four hours depending on the seed in question, or the seed can be scarified. Using a hammer, file, nutcracker or a piece of sandpaper, the shell can be nicked, cracked, or worn down. It is important when handling the seeds that you don't damage the contents. All that is needed is the slightest break on the shell to speed up germination.

For many seeds scarification of the shell is not enough to break their dormancy. They must experience a period of chilling temperatures before they will germinate. Such adaptations ensure that the new seedling will emerge at a time when weather conditions are optimal for survival. It is possible to plant such seeds directly in the garden in the fall using the techniques previously outlined, or the process can be sped up by tricking the seeds under more controlled conditions. Such treatment is called stratification and can be carried out easily by most amateur gardeners. The seeds are placed in a moist growing medium that has been treated with a fungicide. Satisfactory materials include peat moss, sphagnum, and sharp sand, or a combination of any of these. Small seeds in danger of getting lost can first be placed in cheesecloth or a paper towel that is then placed in the medium. The depth of the seeds is not important and a seed container is not needed. The seeds and the medium can be placed directly in a plastic bag or a glass jar. If a glass jar is chosen, the lid must not be screwed on too tightly. The containers are then placed at the bottom of the refrigerator, where the average temperature is 40°F. Some variation is acceptable, but try not to subject the seeds to freezing temperatures. Some plants require a period of warm temperatures followed by a period of cold temperatures. The seeds should be checked from time to time and moisture added as needed. The length of the treatment will vary from plant to plant but the usual range is from 60 to 120 days.

## Saving Seed

With the easy availability of so many varieties through nurseries and mail order catalogs, saving seed is not worth the trouble for most amateur gardeners. But there are some circumstances where it is advantageous. If you have a large garden, or grow many of the same varieties year after year, you can save the expense of purchasing the same seeds over and over again. Most seed packets contain twice the number of seeds needed for one planting. Saving seed also makes it possible to grow unusual or older varieties that are not always offered for sale. It also makes the propagation of wild plants possible without disturbing them in their natural surroundings.

Not all seed can be saved. Many of the varieties grown today are hybrids and do not come true from seed. These hybrids result from crossbreeding several closely related species and varieties, and usually result in improved flowers, or yields, and better disease resistance. That is not to say that nonhybrids, or open-pollinated varieties as they are called, are not worthwhile plants. Many are just as beautiful and free from disease. Because they are not easily reproduced hybrids are also more expensive. Seed saved from open-pollinated varieties will be true to the parent plant.

If you wish to save seed from a favorite flower or vegetable, allow only your best plants to set seed. Choose plants that exhibit the best characteristics of the variety that you would like to see in next year's garden. If you are interested in an earlier vegetable crop, save the seed of the earliest fruiting plants. If you are interested in larger flowers or a plant that is a prolific bloomer, save the seed from plants that exhibit these characteristics. The chosen plants must be protected from chance pollination by other varieties growing in the area. Cover the flowers with tissue or paper bags from the moment they begin to open until they fade. Pollination should take place by hand, using a soft brush to spread the pollen from the stamens to the pistil. Allow the seed to completely mature on the plant. The flower heads should turn brown and brittle, and fruit should be allowed to overripen on the vine before being gathered. Once the seed is completely mature, it can be stored in plastic bags. Choose a day with low humidity to do so and the seed will remain fresh much longer. They should be stored in a cool (50°F.), dark location until they are needed.

Be sure to keep accurate notes on your crosses for future reference and enjoyment. By looking back you can judge your success. Important information to jot down includes the general health of the parent, any susceptibility to disease or insects, and the general growth pattern and yield.

Each year before purchasing any new seeds the viability of those that you have saved should be checked. Count out a few seeds of each variety (I find units of 10 the easiest) and place them between moist paper towels. Then wrap the towels in plastic. Subject the seeds to the necessary conditions needed for germination for the correct period of time, then count the number that have sprouted. If the total is less than 70 percent the seed is not fresh and the subsequent seedlings will probably be weak and spindly. Some seeds remain viable for a long period of time but most will last about two years. Plants whose seed remains viable for only one year include delphinium, gerbera, regal lily, flax, thalictium, and viola.

Over the last few years a grass-roots movement of seed collectors has begun to spring up all across the country. Horticulturists, farmers, and amateur gardeners have all banded together to form seed exchanges for the purpose of locating, preserving, and distributing seeds of heirloom varieties and unusual plants. If you care to get further acquainted with the seed exchanges contact the following organizations:

The Seed Saver's Exchange
Rural Route 2
Princeton, MO 64673

Wanigan Associates
262 Salem Street
Lynnfield, MA 01940

Ray K. Walker
N.A.F.E.X.
Box 711
St. Louis, MO 63188

## *Division*

The following perennials can be increased by division:

| | |
|---|---|
| Aquilegia | Lilium |
| Aster | Monarda |
| Astilbe[1] | Myosotis[1] |
| Campanula | Oenothera |
| Chrysanthemum[1] | Oriental poppy |
| Coreopsis | Phlox (tall herbaceous) |
| Delphinium[1,3] | Phlox (alpine) |
| Digitalis | Physostegia |
| Helenium | Rudbeckia |
| Hemerocallis | Veronica |
| Hypericum[3] | Viola |
| Iris | |

The following trees and shrubs can be increased by division:

| | |
|---|---|
| Ailanthus[2] | Kerria |
| Amelanchier[3] | Pernettya |
| Berberis[2,3] | Philadelphus[3] |
| Buxus | Rose[4] |
| Juniperus[3] | Spireas |

[1]Divide in spring.
[2]Divide by removing suckers.
[3]Some species only.
[4]Divide clumps or suckers.

## Softwood Cuttings

The following annuals and perennials can be propagated from softwood cuttings:

| | | |
|---|---|---|
| Aster | Delphinium[2] | Myosotis[3] |
| Begonia[1] | Dianthus | Nepeta |
| Campanula | Dicentra[3] | Pelargonium[7] |
| Chrysanthemum[2, 3] | Fuchsia[4] | Petunia[3] |
| Coleus | Gaillardia[5] | Phlox (tall herbaceous) |
| Dahlia (annual)[2] | Iberis[6] | Verbena[2] |
| | Lantana[1] | |

[1]Cuttings rot easily.
[2]Keep cuttings at 55°F.
[3]Take in early spring.
[4]Difficult to root.
[5]Take in late summer.
[6]Take right after flowering.
[7]Allow cuttings to callus.

The following trees and shrubs are propagated by softwood cuttings:

| | | |
|---|---|---|
| Acer spp. | Flowering dogwood | Magnolia |
| Azalea[1] | Golden rain tree | Privet |
| Berberis | Ilex (Japanese) | Pyracantha |
| Corylopsis[3] | Lonicera | Rose[2] |
| Cotoneaster | Parthenocissus | Spirea |
| Deutzia | (Boston ivy) | Weigelia |
| Forsythia | Philadelphus | Viburnum |
| Camellia[3] | | |

[1]Take in June.
[2]Take after the first bloom.
[3]Take with a heel.

## *Semihardwood Cuttings*

The following shrubs may be propagated from semihardwood cuttings:

| | | |
|---|---|---|
| Arborvitae[1] | Hedera | Parthenocissus |
| Azalea | Hypericum | (Virginia creeper) |
| Buxus | Ilex (English) | Rhododendron |
| Cotoneaster | Juniperus[1] | Rose |
| Deutzia | Kerria | Spirea |
| Euonymous (evergreen) | Kolkwitzia | Taxus[1] |
| | Pachysandra | Weigela |

[1]Take with a heel.

## *Hardwood Cuttings*

The following plants can be propagated from hardwood cuttings:

| | |
|---|---|
| Buxus | Privet |
| Deutzia | Rose |
| Forsythia | Syringa |
| Ilex (Japanese) | Viburnum |
| Philadelphus | Weigelia |

## *Root Cuttings*

The following plants can be propagated from root cuttings:

| | | |
|---|---|---|
| Anchusas | Dicentra | Poppy (Oriental) |
| Apple | Gaillardia | Romneya |
| Aster | Golden rain tree | Rose (some) |
| Blackberry | Gypsophila | Sea kale |
| Bouvardia | Horseradish | Trumpet creeper |
| Cherry | Oenothera | Verbascum |
| Daphne | Phlox (tall herbaceous) | Viola |

## Leafbud Cuttings

The following plants may be propagated by leafbud cuttings:

Azalea
Ilex (Japanese)
Rhododendron

## Layering

Trees and shrubs to propagate by layering:

| | | |
|---|---|---|
| Berberis | Fig | Loganberry |
| Blackberry | Heather | Lonicera[1] |
| Buxus | Jasmine | Magnolia |
| Clematis[1] | Kerria | Rhododendron |
| Cotoneaster | Laburnum | Syringa |

[1]Layer wood that is 18 months old.

## Cuttings

| TYPE OF CUTTING AND DEFINITION | WHEN TO TAKE | LENGTH OF CUTTING (IN INCHES) | HOW TO MAKE THE CUT | HOW LONG TO ROOT | COMMENTS |
|---|---|---|---|---|---|
| *Softwood (slips, greenwood)* | | | | | |
| Taken from vigorous, actively growing plants whose foliage has begun to darken. The stem must be flexible but mature enough to break. If when bent it becomes crushed, it is too immature. If it does not break, it is too old. Not suitable for conifers | May-June Cuttings of early-flowering plants are taken after flowering. Those that flower later are taken before flowering. Cuttings of annuals and perennials are also taken in the fall for indoor color. | Rock garden plants—2 Annuals and perennials —3–4 Geraniums —4 Shrubs—6 | Cuttings must contain at least 2 nodes. The cut is made at a 45° angle ¼ inch below the bottom node. If the cutting does not include the terminal tip then the top cut should be made ¼ inch above the uppermost node. | Annuals and perennials 10 days to 2 weeks. Shrubs 6–10 weeks. | Easy to propagate. The earlier propagation takes place, the better chance for success. Protect newly rooted shrub cuttings from freezing but keep cool (40° –45°) until mid-January, then raise temp. to 50°–55°. Many shrubs root easily but are destroyed by severe conditions. |

| | Description | Season | Preparation | | Time to root | Notes |
|---|---|---|---|---|---|---|
| *Pips* | A special type of softwood cutting used to propagate members of the dianthus family. | May-June | Instead of cutting the stem the tip of a young shoot is held between thumb and forefinger and pulled out. No other preparation is necessary. | | 10 days to 2 weeks | Easy to propagate. |
| *Semihardwood (halfripe)* | Taken from wood that has finished growing but has not yet fully matured. Useful for the propagation of conifers. | July-September | See softwood. Cutting will require a slight heel. | See softwood | Some 5–25 weeks | Difficult to propagate. Conifers will not form roots unless a cool temperature of 50°–55°F. can be maintained throughout the entire rooting period. Even then many will not form roots until spring. Spraying the cuttings daily with tepid |

## Cuttings (cont'd)

| TYPE OF CUTTING AND DEFINITION | WHEN TO TAKE | LENGTH OF CUTTING (IN INCHES) | HOW TO MAKE THE CUT | HOW LONG TO ROOT | COMMENTS |
|---|---|---|---|---|---|
| | | | | | water will help maintain moisture. Protect newly rooted plants from freezing. |
| *Hardwood*<br>Taken from mature wood in a dormant state. | November–March. Can be taken any time up to 10 weeks prior to the average frost-free date. | 6–12 inches and the thickness of a pencil | Cuttings must contain at least 3–4 nodes but the inclusion of the terminal bud is not important. The base cut is made ¼ inch below the bottom node. Top cut is made at least 1 inch above the top node to allow for some dieback. | 15–36 weeks | Moderately hard to propagate. Plants that are easily damaged by frost should have cuttings taken before the temperature drops considerably. A success rate of 80 percent is considered excellent. |

| | | | | |
|---|---|---|---|---|
| *Root* | Used to propagate plants with fleshy roots | Early spring or fall while the plant is dormant. Oriental poppies are propagated in mid-summer. | 2–3 inches long and pencil thick. Cuttings should contain at least 1 node, bud or sprout and may also contain some feeder roots. | Traditionally the top cut is made at an angle and the bottom cut is made straight across to distinguish top from bottom. | Easy to propagate. Replant the pieces ½ to 1 inch below the surface. Keep from freezing. Cuttings taken from grafted stock will produce plants from the understock only. |
| *Leafbud* | Used to propagate many plants that produce leaves along a stem. | Early summer. | Each leaf is carefully cut out of the stem so the node is included. | See softwood. | Easy to propagate. Treat as you would a softwood cutting. |

## *Average Frost Dates for Major American Cities*

These dates constitute an average only and should not be considered safe planting dates for tender plants.

| CITY | LAST FROST (SPRING) | FIRST FROST (AUTUMN) |
|---|---|---|
| Alabama: Birmingham | Apr. 1 | Nov. 7 |
| Alaska: Anchorage | May 15 | Aug. 15 |
| Arizona: Phoenix | Mar. 1 | Dec. 1 |
| Arkansas: Little Rock | Apr. 7 | Nov. 1 |
| California: Los Angeles* | Feb. 1 | Jan. 1 |
| Colorado: Denver | May 15 | Oct. 1 |
| Connecticut: Hartford | May 1 | Oct. 15 |
| D.C.: Washington | Apr. 15 | Nov. 1 |
| Florida: Jacksonville | Mar. 1 | Dec. 1 |
| Miami* | Feb. 1 | Jan. 1 |
| Georgia: Atlanta | Apr. 7 | Nov. 15 |
| Illinois: Chicago | May 1 | Oct. 15 |
| Indiana: Indianapolis | Apr. 15 | Oct. 10 |
| Iowa: Des Moines | May 3 | Oct. 7 |
| Kansas: Wichita | Apr. 15 | Oct. 7 |
| Kentucky: Louisville | Apr. 15 | Oct. 21 |
| Louisiana: New Orleans | Feb. 7 | Dec. 7 |
| Massachusetts: Boston | Apr. 21 | Oct. 15 |
| Michigan: Detroit | May 1 | Oct. 15 |
| Minnesota: Minneapolis | May 10 | Oct. 1 |
| Mississippi: Jackson | Mar. 20 | Nov. 15 |
| Missouri: Kansas City | May 21 | Oct. 7 |
| St. Louis | Apr. 15 | Oct. 7 |
| Nebraska: Omaha | May 1 | Oct. 7 |
| Nevada: Las Vegas | Apr. 1 | Nov. 1 |

## Average Frost Dates for Major American Cities (cont'd)

| CITY | LAST FROST (SPRING) | FIRST FROST (AUTUMN) |
|---|---|---|
| New Mexico: Albuquerque | May 1 | Oct. 1 |
| New York: Buffalo | May 1 | Nov. 1 |
| New York | Apr. 15 | Nov. 1 |
| North Carolina: Charlotte | Apr. 7 | Nov. 21 |
| South Carolina: Columbia | Mar. 21 | Nov. 15 |
| Ohio: Cleveland | May 1 | Nov. 1 |
| Cincinnati | Apr. 21 | Oct. 15 |
| Columbus | May 1 | Oct. 15 |
| Oklahoma: Oklahoma City | Apr. 7 | Nov. 1 |
| Oregon: Portland | May 1 | Nov. 1 |
| Pennsylvania: Philadelphia | Apr. 21 | Nov. 7 |
| Pittsburgh | May 1 | Oct. 15 |
| Rhode Island: Providence | May 1 | Nov. 1 |
| Tennessee: Memphis | Mar 25 | Nov. 5 |
| Texas: Dallas | Mar. 20 | Nov. 10 |
| Houston | Feb. 20 | Dec. 1 |
| Utah: Salt Lake City | May 1 | Oct. 1 |
| Virginia: Norfolk | Apr. 1 | Nov. 25 |
| Richmond | Apr. 15 | Nov. 1 |
| Washington: Seattle | Apr. 1 | Nov. 1 |
| Wisconsin: Milwaukee | May 1 | Oct. 15 |
| Canada: Montreal | May 15 | Oct. 1 |
| Toronto | May 5 | Oct. 7 |

*Indicates cities where freezing temperatures occur rarely.

## Seed Germination Requirements

### Plants Requiring a Soil Temperature of 45–55°F.

| | | |
|---|---|---|
| Cabbage | Leek | Pea |
| Carrot | Lettuce | Radish |
| Chicory | Lupine | Scallion |
| Delphinium | Mustard | Spinach |
| Endive | Onion | Sweet pea |
| Kale | Pansy | Swiss chard |
| Kohlrabi | Parsley | |
| Larkspur | Parsnip | |

### Plants Requiring a Soil Temperature of 60–65°F.

| | | |
|---|---|---|
| Achillea | Gazania | Penstemon |
| Ageratum | Hesperis | Phlox |
| Alyssum | Hollyhock (p.)[2] | Platycodon |
| Aster | Lantana | Veronica |
| Cyclamen[1] | Lunaria | |
| Dictamnus | Matricaria | |

[1]Soak seeds for 24 hours.
[2]p—perennial; a—annual

### Plants Requiring a Soil Temperature of 65–70°F.

| | | |
|---|---|---|
| Artichoke | Dianthus (p.)[3] | Potato |
| Asparagus | Dimorphotheca | Primula |
| Bean | Dill | Pyrethrum |
| Calendula | Dusty miller | Rudbeckia |
| Campanula | Globe amaranth | Sage |
| Candytuft | Gypsophila | Scabiosa |
| Carnation[1] | Hollyhock (a.) | Snapdragon |
| Celery | Linum | Sunflower |
| Centaurea[2] | Lobelia | Sweet William |
| Columbine | Morning glory[4] | Turnip |
| Coreopsis | Nasturtium | Zinnia |
| Cosmos | Petunia | |
| Cucumber | Physalis | |
| Dahlia | Poppy | |

[1]Freeze seed for 5 days.
[2]Prechill seed for 5 days at 40°F.
[3]Freeze seed for 14 days.
[4]Soak seed for 8 hours.

## *Seed Germination Requirements* (cont'd)

### Plants Requiring a Soil Temperature of 70°F. or More

| | | |
|---|---|---|
| Amaranthus | Four o'clock | Oenthera |
| Armeria[1] | Foxglove | Ornamental pepper |
| Balsam | Gaillardia | Passiflora |
| Basil | Geranium | Pepper |
| Begonia | Gypsophila | Portulaca |
| Browallia | Helichrysum | Salvia |
| Celosia | Hibiscus[4] | Saponaria |
| Cerastium | Impatiens | Squash |
| Cleome[2] | Kochia | Statice |
| Coleus | Marigold | Tomato |
| Eggplant | Melon | Venidium |
| Euphorbia[3] | Mesembryanthemum | Verbena |
| Flowering Kale | Mimosa | |

[1]Soak seed overnight.
[2]Prechill at 40° for 5 days.
[3]Poisonous.
[4]Soak seed for 24 hours.

### Plants That Require a Soil Temperature of 75°F.

| | |
|---|---|
| Gloxinia | Strawberry |
| Gourd | Thunbergia |
| Nicotiana | Tritoma |

### Plants That Require Light to Germinate

| | |
|---|---|
| Trailing arbutus | Lobelia |
| Alpine strawberry | Matricaria |
| Begonia | Mesembryanthemum |
| Bellis | Monkey flower |
| Browallia | Nicotiana |
| Clarkia | Petunia |
| Coleus | Pine |
| Draba azoides | Primula |
| Fir | Salvia |
| Gentiana | Spruce |
| Grass | Stock |
| Impatiens | Sultana |
| Jacobinia | |

## Plants That Need Total Darkness to Germinate

Calendula
Centaurea
Cyclamen
Dimorphotheca
Gazania
Larkspur
Myosotis
Nasturtium
Globe amaranth

Nemesia
Pansy
Penstemon
Salpiglossis
Schizanthus
Sweet pea
Verbena
Viola

## Plants with a Double Dormancy

The following plants must be subjected to warm stratification, then cold stratification. Store from 34–40°F. during the cold period, at room temperature during warm period.

| SCIENTIFIC NAME | COMMON NAME | WARM TEMP. | PERIOD | COLD TEMP. | PERIOD |
|---|---|---|---|---|---|
| Cotoneaster | Cotoneaster spp. | 58–77 | 90–120 | 35–41 | 90–120 |
| Crataegus (some) | Hawthorn | 77 | 120 | 41 | 180 |
| Halesia | Silverbell | 68 | 30–90 | 41 | 60–90 |
| Lindera benzoin | Spice bush | 77 | 15–30 | 34–41 | 90–120 |
| Taxus | Yew spp. | 68 | 90 | 41 | 120 |
| Viburnum opulus | European cranberry | 68–86 | 60–90 | 41 | 30–60 |
| Viburnum trilobum | American cranberry | 68–86 | 90–150 | 41 | 60 |

## Woody Plants That Need a Cold Period

The following plants should be subject to a period of cool (41–45°F.) temperatures.

| SCIENTIFIC NAME | COMMON NAME | APPROX. LENGTH OF TREATMENT IN DAYS |
|---|---|---|
| Abies spp. | Fir | 60–90 |
| Acer palmatum | Red Japanese maple | 100–120 |
| Amelanchier spp. | Shadbush or juneberry | 90–180 |
| Berberis spp. | Barberry | 15–40 |
| Celastrus spp. | Bittersweet | 90 |
| Chionanthus virginicus | Fringe tree | 90–120 |
| Cornus florida | Flowering dogwood | 100–130 |
| Cornus kousa | Kousa dogwood | 120 |
| Diospyros virginiana | Persimmon | 60–90 |
| Elaeagnus angustifolia | Russian olive | 90 |
| Fagus spp. | Beech | 90 |
| Fraxinus spp. | Ash | 30–90 |
| Juniperus spp. | Juniper | 90–120 |
| Ligustrum spp. | Privet | 60–90 |
| Lonicera spp. | Honeysuckle | 30–60 |
| Magnolia spp. | Magnolia | 120–180 |
| Malus spp. | Apple | 30–90 |
| Picea glauca | White spruce | 60–90 |
| Picea pungens | Blue spruce | 30–90 |
| Pinus spp. | Pine | 30–90 |
| Prunus spp. | Apricot, cherry | 60–120 |
| | Peach, plum | 120 or more |
| Rosa spp. & hybrids | Rose | 60–120 |
| Sorbus spp. | Mountain ash | 90 |
| Vitex agnus-castus | Chaste tree | |

# PART TWO

# The Plants

# ❧ 10 ❧

# Trees and Shrubs

THE ROLE OF TREES AND SHRUBS in the garden is an important one. They add stability and a sense of permanence. They are the backbone, the support on which the garden design is built. Trees and shrubs add volume, vertical dimension, and year-long interest. They can be used to create privacy, hide an unattractive area, and direct traffic. Thorny bushes placed on a roof's edge will do more to keep small children away than any fence.

Trees and shrubs come in a wide array of sizes and shapes, colors, and textures, making it possible to find one to suit every situation. The most important things to remember when choosing a tree or shrub are the eventual height and spread of a particular plant and its basic shape. The illustration (Fig. 34) on page 178 should help. It is best to choose dwarf varieties and slow growers. Two shrubs may both reach an eventual height of ten feet but one may take twice as long to get there. Many trees and shrubs will eventually grow too tall for container culture, but those that grow slowly will be enjoyed for many more years. There is nothing worse than trying to force a tree with the potential of reaching sixty feet to maintain a height of six feet, or a tall spreading shrub into a long, narrow area. Not only is it a tremendous amount of work, but the results are always less than pleasing. While we are on the subject, be sure to keep in mind the maximum height a tree can attain if you have a covered terrace; you'd be surprised at how quickly a badly chosen tree will reach it. Another point to remember is that an immature sapling rarely looks like the mature tree seen in pictures. Often they are rather spindly and bare with few branches. They look more like fence posts than trees. Since

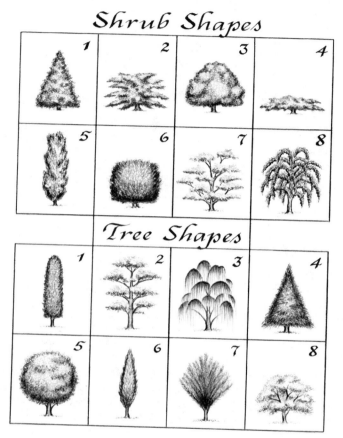

Fig. 34   Different shrub and tree shapes

SHRUB SHAPES

1. Pyramidal        5. Columnar
2. Low branching    6. Compact
3. Roundheaded      7. Open
4. Prostrate        8. Weeping

TREE SHAPES

1. Columnar                5. Globe
2. Openheaded irregular    6. Fastigate
3. Weeping                 7. Vase
4. Broad cone              8. Horizontal
                              spread

the immature form is the most important to a container gardener, never order a tree from a catalog unless you are sure of what it looks like. When purchasing a tree or shrub at a garden center, try to imagine it in relation to the other plants you already have and not just as an individual. Once you get it home, it just might not look right.

The type of root system is another important factor when choosing a tree or shrub. Those that develop long tap roots do not make good container subjects. A better choice is a plant with a shallow fibrous root system that could develop normally. If you wish to grow a plant with a long tap root, then prune the root back. This will encourage it to form laterals and develop a root pattern that more closely resembles a fibrous system.

When considering a tree or shrub for your terrace, examine its interest in all seasons. Trees and shrubs are on display in the garden twelve months a year, unlike other plants. In spring and summer many add beautiful flowers to the garden, but their bloom period is usually short. Their foliage on the other hand is on display throughout the growing season. When considering the foliage, think of color. There are many shades of green, some light, some dark, some tinged or marked with hues of another color. Many trees and shrubs are noted for their autumn displays, while some have interesting bark or persistent berries that add winter interest.

Trees and shrubs can also be divided into background plants and specimens. Background plants perform a special function by acting as a backdrop for more flamboyant individuals. Even so, this does not mean they do not have their own moments of glory. An azalea makes a bright splash for a few weeks but then settles down to a more subdued existence for the rest of the year. A tree or shrub singled out as a specimen draws attention to itself. Specimens should be placed where they will stand out and where their special qualities are seen at their best advantage. Although you may wish to include several specimens in your garden, limit your choices to one or two. If you choose too many, their special qualities will be lost.

When dealing with trees and shrubs texture becomes important. Texture is produced by leaf size and pattern. Small leaves regularly spaced produce a neat, fine texture, while larger leaves with a serrated edge are said to produce a coarse texture. Coarse-textured plants do not lend themselves to clipping or shearing, since the leaves are cut in half and the plant tends to look butchered. Large-leaved plants also tend to look even larger when confined in a small area, an important consideration for a small terrace. As a general rule, place fine-textured plants in front of coarse-textured ones for a better feeling of balance.

As with other plants, different trees and shrubs have different cultural requirements including light, moisture, soil preference, and cold hardiness. It is important to choose a tree or shrub that will do well in your area. All plants have minimum and maximum temperature tolerances. When planted in containers, this range of tolerance becomes even narrower. To determine if a tree or shrub will survive in your area, use the hardiness zone map illustrated in Fig. 35 on page 180. This map illustrates the various climatic zones found throughout the country. Plants will survive in some zones and not in others. To be safe, choose plants that are hardy one zone further north from your area. Many plants also require a period of cold temperatures (below 45°F.) in order to break dormancy

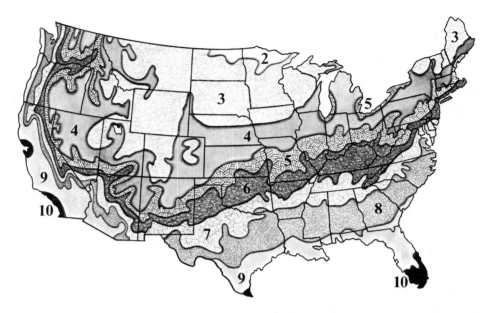

*Fig. 35 Hardiness zone map. Compiled by The Arnold Arboretum, Harvard University, May 1, 1967.*

of flower and fruit properly. At the other end of the spectrum, plants have a maximum high temperature they can handle without being placed under too much stress. A prolonged period of high temperatures will weaken the plant. When choosing shrubs, keep in mind that sites facing west that are very hot are considered to have full sun exposure. At the same time, plants that prefer full sun in New England may need partial shade in Virginia.

Trees and shrubs may be purchased from a local garden center or through a mail order firm. Both have their advantages and disadvantages. By purchasing your plant at a garden center you can see the actual plant you are getting. You can also purchase plants that are older, a bit larger in size, and usually grown locally, but the cost will be higher and the choice of varieties not as great. Large mail order firms on the other hand generally carry a wider selection with many unusual plants that cannot be offered by a smaller nursery. The specimens are usually younger and smaller for purposes of shipping, and your purchase is sight unseen. I have found through all my years of dealing with mail order companies that the quality of the plants is very high, often better than what I can purchase at the local garden center. Of course, because of their size, these plants will take longer to become full-sized specimens. For this reason I suggest you purchase one or two good-sized plants from a local nursery and fill in with younger plants purchased through mail order.

It may not always be easy to find a specific plant you are looking for no matter how wide the selection offered. For this reason the Brooklyn Botanic Garden publishes a booklet called *The Nursery Source Guide* each year that lists 1,200 trees and shrubs and a list of both wholesale and retail companies where they may be purchased.

Trees and shrubs are sold in three forms: bare root, balled and burlapped, and container grown. Plants that are sold bare root are dormant; all soil has been washed from their roots, which are then cut back. Most trees and shrubs sold through mail order are shipped this way to prevent the spread of disease and to keep down shipping costs. They are usually available early in the spring or in the fall while the ground is still workable. It is best to purchase them in the spring for container culture since some winter damage is inevitable. If the damage to the roots is extensive, the tree may never develop into a strong specimen. Spring planting should take place as soon as the ground is workable to give the plant a chance to make as much root growth as possible before green growth begins. Plants that are sold through garden centers are usually balled and burlapped (B&B). These are field grown, then dug up with a good amount of the surrounding soil. Plants that are handled in this way have a generous supply of healthy roots (though some severing of small feeder roots is inevitable) and a high success rate. Container-grown plants have spent their entire life in a container. Plants handled in this way are used to confined quarters and will have no trouble adapting. The soil the plants are grown in is probably a mix not too dissimilar to what they will be subjected to in your garden. There is little need to worry about the quality of the soil surrounding the roots.

When selecting a plant at a garden center, look for one of average size whose top growth and root development are in balance. Do not pick the smallest or the largest of a group. The smallest may have a weak root system or may have been damaged when younger. The largest probably had a considerable number of roots severed. Be sure to measure your elevation before making a final selection. Remember that plants are flexible and can be bent, and that the diagonal measurement of an elevation will be longer than its height. Plants that are extremely large can be raised to the roof with a block and tackle, but this will considerably increase the expense of the plant.

Select a tree that is at least three years old. By that time it will exhibit more of its mature structure. A one-year-old sapling, known as a whip, is usually nothing more than a single, straight trunk. It will take a great deal of care and pruning to produce a good specimen. Shrubs are most commonly sold in one- and five-gallon-sized containers. A smaller plant in a one-gallon container will be considerably less expensive. You can save quite a bit by choosing the smaller plant. In a year or two it will have grown considerably and in the meantime you can fill in with flowering annuals.

When choosing a tree or shrub never fail to examine the roots. The

*Fig. 36  Special arrangements are often required to hoist large specimens to rooftop gardens.*

quality and importance of the roots cannot be overestimated, for defects can result in poor growth that no amount of care can overcome. A container-grown or balled-and-burlapped plant should have a well-developed root ball. A well-formed root system will be symmetrical, with several main roots that radiate out and down for support. The root ball itself should hold together and maintain its shape when unwrapped or removed from the container. Don't choose a balled-and-burlapped plant with a broken or cracked root ball or a plant in a container that is split, smashed, or rusted. These conditions could indicate the roots were damaged in transit. Also bypass any plant whose roots are noticeably bent or circle the container or trunk. Such roots will eventually strangle the tree or shrub as it grows. To check for kinked or circling roots stick your finger down into the top two or three inches of soil near the trunk. A container-grown plant with masses of roots on the surface is seriously bound and will need considerable pruning to straighten out. An oversized plant in a small container should also be avoided.

After checking the roots visually, lift the plant by the trunk; if the plant moves up before the soil does the roots are probably not well developed and it should be avoided. The trunk itself should be straight and slightly tapered. If the tree is staked, untie it. A tree should be able to stand alone without staking. If it bends, it has a weak trunk. Choose a different one.

The branches should be evenly spaced, indicating that the plant was grown under ideal conditions and has a well-formed root system. New shoots should be present all over. Half the leaf area should be along the lower two-thirds of the tree, but often this is not the case since growers regularly prune away growth from the bottom half. If the tree is in leaf, the foliage should be green with no evidence of yellowing or scorching. There should be little needle drop off evergreens when shaken. Do not choose a plant that shows evidence of being recently cut back hard. This may indicate that the plant has outgrown its container or has recently been infected with some disease.

It is also possible to find a seedling tree on a trip to the country, but this is not recommended. Often these plants have a difficult time adapting to new surroundings, and it is quite likely that along with the tree you will be introducing a host of new bugs and diseases. Seedlings of questionable parentage will also grow so quickly that within a few years they will be too large for container culture. Still, if you really fall in love with one, get permission from the owner before moving it and never, never take one off public land. Choose a small specimen, since these are most likely to be more adaptable.

The most immediate concern when handling a new plant is to get it in the ground as soon as possible. Although most plants other than bare-root stock can be planted at any time during the growing season, the best time is when root growth is greatest in the spring and fall. In most areas April to May and September to October are the best months, in warmer regions February to March, and October to November are good. The roots of most trees and shrubs will continue to grow at temperatures as low as 40°F., much lower than the temperature needed for top growth. At this time all the plant's energies will be diverted to the roots instead of into leaf production, and the plant will be established that much sooner. In colder areas, spring is best since there will be little winter damage to contend with (see the spring and fall planting guide below). If you must plant in the fall, be sure to watch the plant closely, give it plenty of water, and mulch it well.

---

## Spring and Fall Planting Guide

---

North of zone 7 plant the following in spring only:

> Cornus florida (flowering dogwood)
> Crataegus (hawthorn)
> Koelreuteria paniculata (golden rain tree)
> Prunus (cherry, peach, plum, and other stone fruits)

Plant the following in late summer or early fall:

> Berberis thunbergii (Japanese barberry)
> Cotoneaster spp.
> Ilex crenata (Japanese holly)
> Ilex opaca (American holly)
> Pinus mugo (dwarf mugho pine)
> Pinus thunbergiana (Japanese black pine)
> Rhododendron spp.

---

Once you get your plant home, keep it cool and moist in a shaded location. Try not to pick it up by the trunk, since this will damage small feeder roots; always support it from the bottom. Plant it as soon as possible. If you cannot and the plant is in a metal container, do not have the can cut at the nursery. Instead slip the plant out of the container as you would for any house plant. Bare-root stock should be planted within two days of receiving. If this is not possible, place it in a carton that has been lined with a plastic garbage bag and cover it with moist peat moss. Some growers like to place bare-root plants in a pail of water for a few hours before planting, but under no circumstances should your plant be left in the pail for more than eight hours.

When choosing a container for your tree or shrub be sure it is large enough to accommodate your plant for several years. The larger container will not only make annual transplanting unnecessary but will help protect the roots at this critical time. If the plant seems small in proportion, underplant it with annuals and group it with other containers.

Prepare enough soil mix to accommodate the plant and place two inches of drainage material in the bottom of the container. Planting the tree or shrub at the proper depth is important. Be particularly mindful of the graft or bud union. It must be at least one inch above the level of the soil.

It will be easy to spot by the bulge or kink at the base of the trunk. You will be able to tell where the tree or shrub emerged originally from the soil line by the color of the bark: The woody material that was submerged will be darker in color. It is important to plant the tree or shrub at the same depth as it was previously. Raising or lowering the plant may result in root or stem rot and insect damage.

When removing a tree or shrub from a container do not break the root ball trying to get it out. This could permanently damage the plant. Instead, run a knife around the sides to loosen it, then gently tap the bottom of the container with a hammer. It should then slip out easily. If it does not, cut away the container, do not pull on the plant.

When planting balled-and-burlapped stock, set the plant, burlap and all, in the container. Position the plant so it faces the direction you wish, then unwrap the burlap. Gently rock the plant to one side, exposing the bottom of the root ball, and cut away as much of the burlap as you can. Repeat the process until most of the material is removed. Although plain burlap will rot away in time, synthetic materials or burlap that has been treated with preservatives will not. If left in place, it will hamper root development.

Once the plant is in place, loosen the roots and spread them out. Pull away all circled or matted roots with a hand cultivator, and prune any injured or diseased ones. Begin to work in soil around the loosened roots and continue until the root ball is half buried. Water the soil to remove any air pockets, then continue to fill the container. Water again when fully planted.

To compensate for the loss of roots, trim the foliage. You can reduce the leaf area by thinning out individual branches instead of topping the tree; this will result in a better specimen. Bare-root trees will need more extensive pruning but some may already have been removed at the nursery prior to the sale. If so, little extra pruning will be needed.

Avoid chemical fertilizers at planting time and for a month or two afterward. Bone meal, dried manure, and greensand can be incorporated into the planting mix. Wait until further growth begins before adding anything else. If a stake is necessary, place it on the side of the prevailing winds or use two stakes. Tie the plant loosely to the stake. A certain amount of give is necessary for the proper development of the roots and trunk. A staked tree will be weaker than one that is unstaked. Wrap the trunk of a young tree with a commercial tree wrap to discourage insects and protect it from sunscald. Your newly planted tree or shrub should quickly adapt to its new surroundings.

Be sure to water your new plant faithfully. Remember that transplanting is a bit of a shock to begin with. Lack of water will only compound the problem. Signs that the plant is suffering from a lack of water include wilting, a change in leaf color (shiny to dull or dark green to gray green), and premature leaf fall.

Trees and shrubs do not need heavy concentrations of fertilizer. Low formulas such as 1–1–1 or 1–2–2 are adequate. Applications of nitrogen will make trees and shrubs grow rapidly but will also make them outgrow their containers and their surroundings. This does not mean that you should not fertilize your trees and shrubs—because of constant watering, nutrients are leached out quickly—but a light application in the spring and another in the summer should be enough. Beyond that, let your plants tell you when they need to be fed. As long as the leaf color remains good and they grow reasonably well, no further feeding is necessary. If leaf color is pale, apply more. If growth is excessive, apply less or none until next year. Since nitrogen promotes leaf growth, use it in moderation on any shrub that must be pruned regularly, like a hedge. As with other plants, high-nitrogen formulas are used in spring when plants are making rapid green growth and high phosphorus formulas are used during flower bud formation. Never feed woody plants with a high-nitrogen formula after midsummer. It promotes late green growth that is easily damaged in winter.

Plants grown in containers are much more susceptible to frost damage than plants grown in the ground. Although plant foliage can take very low temperatures before any damage will occur, most plant roots can be damaged by prolonged temperatures below 0°F. Roots located near exposed sides of containers suffer more damage than those near the trunk. One solution is to line containers with blocks of styrofoam. The blocks can be made to fit round containers by scoring one side at one-inch intervals and bending the blocks. Grouping containers together also affords greater protection. Gardeners who live in really cold areas should choose plants that can withstand the cold such as the dwarf Amur maple or the paper birch. Other plants that make good choices for cold localities include most pines, junipers, and spruces. Other precautions that can be taken include mulching, thorough watering during thaws, treating plants with an antidesiccant, constructing windbreaks, and wrapping trees.

Wind is the chief menace in winter. It can break brittle branches and dry out plants. A windbreak of burlap strung between stakes will break the force of a cold wind. Wrapping trees with burlap and layers of straw can also mean the difference between survival and certain death for some. Desiccation or the drying out of foliage is a form of winter injury most commonly associated with broad-leaved evergreens, but it has also been found to occur on occasion to narrow-leaved evergreens and even deciduous plants. On sunny days, even though the air temperature may be low, the temperature of plant leaves is high, causing transpiration to take place. The moisture lost through the leaves and stems cannot be replaced because the soil is frozen. As a result, leaves turn brown and curl. (It is normal for rhododendron leaves to curl but the edges should not be brown.) The problem can be prevented by shading certain plants and applying an antidesiccant when the air temperature is well above 40° F.

Snow for the most part is a gardener's best friend in winter. It acts as an insulating cover, protecting roots, though it can be a problem for evergreens. The weight of heavy snow on branches can damage or break them. It should be removed from evergreens.

Eventually, all plants grown in containers will become root-bound. When that happens you can either transplant them to a larger container or prune the roots. Root pruning accomplishes two things: new root growth is encouraged and the plants are kept dwarfed. Root pruning can be accomplished in one of two ways. If the plant is not too large it can be slipped out of its container and the outermost roots can be removed and replaced with fresh soil. For larger specimens, root pruning must take place from above. Dig down into the container with a sharp trowel and remove sections of the roots, replacing them with fresh soil mix. Be sure to dig deep and remove a few good-sized portions from several different areas around the plant. Repeat the process every two or three years for deciduous trees and every three or four years for evergreens. At the same time remember to prune the top back to keep it in balance.

Pruning is by far the most confusing gardening procedure for new gardeners. Once you understand the basic principles it will become easier. All plants have their own individual characteristics that set them apart from all others just like individual human beings. The natural characteristics of different kinds of trees and shrubs should be taken into account when pruning. The aim of the procedure is to promote good form and overall plant health. A good branching structure must be encouraged while top growth is kept in balance with the roots. At the same time all dead, diseased, or weak growth is being eliminated. When a portion of green growth is removed, the moisture and nutrients that would have gone into its maintenance are redistributed to the rest of the plant. At the same time, because the leaf area is diminished, transpiration and the manufacturing of sugars is reduced. The result is a healthier but smaller plant.

The time to prune different plants depends on when they flower and fruit. The timing of reproduction has been adapted to give the offspring every advantage of survival. Spring-flowering plants have the advantage of reproducing early, ensuring the establishment of the seedlings by the end of the growing season. Many flower and fruit on wood that was produced the year before. Early pruning would result in a loss of flowers or fruit. Summer- and fall-flowering plants reproduce on wood that is produced the same year, while some plants flower and fruit on wood that is at least two years old.

The pruning of plants that flower on wood that was produced the previous season is best carried out right after the blooms fade. The flowers can then be enjoyed while there is still enough time for the plant to produce enough new wood to ensure flowering the following year. Plants that flower on wood produced in the same year are best pruned before

*Fig. 37   How to shape a shrub by thinning*

buds break in early spring. Plants that bloom on wood that is at least two years old can be lightly pruned in early spring without seriously affecting flowering and fruiting, but heavy pruning will result in the subsequent loss of flowers in seasons to come. If you are unsure of exactly when the plant blooms, you can always wait until after the plant flowers to carry out the bulk of the pruning. The drawbacks to this method are twofold. A late-flowering plant will spend an entire season putting energy into the production of wood that is undesirable while winter damage will necessitate repruning in the spring. This will make more work for you at a time when you can least afford it.

The most pleasing style of pruning for most trees and shrubs follows the natural branching habit of the plant. Unless your objective is to produce a formal hedge the best results are obtained by thinning, which results in a healthier plant of greater size even though the overall leaf area is reduced. The effect is one of a more open, less formal appearance and less work for you. Thinning is carried out by removing whole branches back to their place of origin. In the case of a plant that produces long canes that originate from the ground, the branches are removed at the soil line. Overly long branches are cut back to one-quarter inch above an outside-facing bud. Buds always face in the direction they will grow, and the bud located just below a cut will usually take over and become the new terminal shoot. The cut itself should be planted toward the direction you wish the new bud to grow. This will result in better healing and a neater appearance. Be sure to make all pruning cuts close to the trunk, leaving no stub (see Fig. 38). However, it is important not to cut into the trunk itself. Using clean, sharp tools is important. Large branches will require three cuts to remove them. The first is a shallow cut made on the underside of the branch several inches above where you wish it removed. Its purpose is to prevent the bark from tearing when you remove the bulk of the branch. The second cut is made clear through the branch several inches above the first. The third cut removes the remaining stub.

The first step when pruning a tree or shrub is the removal of all dead and diseased wood. The next step is to remove all material that grows back toward the center of the plant. Such wood will eventually weaken

*Fig. 38    How to prune a young tree*

the plant by inhibiting the flow of air and light. Such plants are more prone to disease and will drop their lower leaves. The next step is to remove any branches that are growing toward each other as well as any weak or spindly growth. Small limbs, water sprouts, or suckers should be cut off close to the trunk to prevent new shoots from sprouting. The idea here is to build a strong framework to support any subsequent growth. The last step is to prune for a pleasing form. Prune back any overly long branches or those that seem out of balance with the rest of the plant.

Not all branches will need pruning; it is possible and more advantageous to redirect the stem or branch by mechanical means. If a young branch emerges from a crotch that is too narrow, it can be trained to grow at a wider angle by the insertion of a spreader. A spreader is a piece of wood that is wedged between the branch and the trunk until it forces the branch into a better position. It is left in place for a year and then is removed. Branches can also be tied with a cord and redirected. After a year or so they will have assumed the new shape and the cord can be removed.

Recent studies have shown that sealing large wounds with black tree paint does little to prevent disease and may in fact hamper the healing process. It will, however, improve the appearance. If you wish to use it, apply only a thin coat to darken the wound.

Proper pruning can keep old shrubs that produce long canes from the ground young, vigorous, and within bounds for years. Every year the three-year-old canes should be pruned out at the soil line, leaving only the youngest and most vigorous canes. The approach can be modified over a five-year period for slower-growing plants. By removing the oldest canes, larger, healthier flowers are produced.

"Heading back" is a method of pruning used to create a formal hedge or when a bushier compact appearance is desired. Pinching is a form of heading back. By removing the terminal bud you force dormant buds to be activated all the way down the branch. In some cases, when the growth of a tree has been too rapid, resulting in a sparse appearance, heading back can be advantageous, but it will usually result in an unnatural growth pattern and disfigurement. To head back a tree or shrub just cut off all green growth beyond the desired perimeter of the plant.

The proper tools are important to any job and pruning is no exception. Every gardener should have a good pair of sharp pruning shears for pruning small twigs and branches up to ½ inch in diameter. Get a good one—inexpensive models will only have to be replaced quickly. For branches that measure over ½ inch to 1½ inches in diameter, lopping shears will be necessary. These long-handled cutters are also good for getting at hard-to-reach places. A pruning saw is necessary for large limbs that cannot be cut with lopping shears. It is designed to cut greenwood on the pull stroke. Do not use a regular carpenter's saw! The teeth are wrong and they cannot cut cleanly. Hedge shears are a must for anyone with a formal hedge or practicing the art of topiary. They have long scissor-like blades and make fast work of a hedgerow.

Any tool, no matter how well made, will not perform well without the proper care. Plant juices and dirt will eventually gum up the blade and a less than clean cut will allow entrance of disease organisms and inhibit healing. So clean your blades after each use and sharpen them yearly. Proper oiling is also essential and will help prevent rusting.

# Creative Pruning

At the beginning of the seventeenth century, when the wealthy could afford to employ an army of gardeners, the formal garden came into being. Pruning was raised from mere utilitarian purposes to an art form. Hedgerows and topiary dotted the garden while fruit trees were espaliered along walls. Today these gardening practices have been rediscovered and modified to fit our modern lifestyles. The well-ordered geometric shapes of such formal techniques blend well with the straight architectural lines inherent in a roof or terrace garden. Hedges give privacy and direct traffic, while espaliering makes it possible to grow trees where there is little shade. Plants trained in these ways do require a great deal of maintenance but this shouldn't be too burdensome in a small garden with few plants.

The formal hedge is by far the most familiar of these techniques and

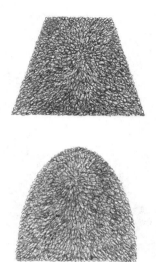

*Fig. 39    How to shape a hedge*

has never truly gone out of fashion. It makes a wonderful backdrop for other more flamboyant plants, or it can itself become the focal point, depending on the type of plant chosen. Lots of different shrubs can be used. Your choice will largely depend on the desired effect and the amount of pruning you are willing to do. For a formal garden, small-leaved plants such as privet, boxwood, and rosemary are chosen because they look good when sheared. Larger-leaved plants tend to look butchered. Save them for more informal effects where clipping isn't required. Instead, cut back individual branches with pruning shears to avoid cutting their leaves in half.

The proper spacing of individual plants will vary from species to species. Close spacing may result in a thicker hedge sooner, but as the plants mature they will crowd each other out. If plants are spaced too far apart, the desired effect may never be achieved. Hedges should be shaped like a wedge with a narrow top and a wider bottom. More often than not they are shaped improperly, resulting in bare patches. All plants will drop any leaves that are not receiving enough light. By shaping a hedge wider at the bottom, the lower foliage will remain full.

Allow a newly planted hedgerow to develop naturally the first year. It will need its foliage to produce enough food to develop a strong root system. A light pruning to make up for the loss of roots at planting time is all that is needed. Bare-root stock should be pruned back halfway. The second year, trim it back once or twice to encourage thicker growth and to begin forming its basic shape. The third year regular shearing can begin. Once the desired height has been reached, each time you clip leave ¼ inch of new growth. This will help avoid the development of clusters of cut

*Fig. 40 Well-designed topiary*

branches and bare patches. The hedge will also have a covering of young, healthy foliage for the best appearance. In time, when the hedge has grown too large, you can prune it back severely and begin again. To rejuvenate a neglected or bare hedge cut it back to a height of a few inches and new growth will emerge.

Topiary is a form of pruning that results in a piece of living sculpture. One or more plants are shaped into an ornamental form that is often geometric in nature. But topiary need not be limited to this aspect. In England, where gardening is a national passion, hedgerows have been turned into battleships, while in Disneyland, topiary figures have taken on the shape of cartoon characters. Animals are also a favorite subject, but you need not stop there. I would love to see a sculptor use topiary to create a modern work of art.

Before training begins, have a design in mind. Choose a plant that lends itself to the desired shape and takes well to pruning. Boxwood is a good choice for formal designs but rosemary would make an interesting teddy bear. In developing forms such as animals, the pruning is done freeform. You make a cut here and there until the desired shape is created. In many cases a wire form can be purchased or made to help with the process. It is placed over a young plant, which then grows up around it. Foliage that grows out of the frame is clipped. A simple geometric design can be achieved with the use of cord. The cord is strung between stakes to achieve the desired form; as the plant grows beyond the cord, it is clipped.

Topiary requires a great deal of patience and is therefore not for every-

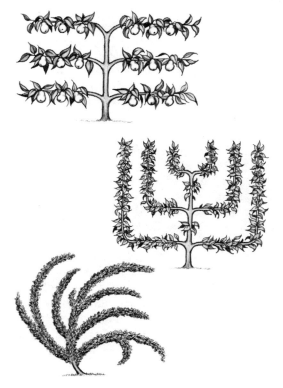

*Fig. 41    Examples of espalier*

one. It can take years before the final effect is achieved. If you don't want to wait that long, pretrained plants can be purchased at some garden centers.

The word espalier is derived from a Latin word meaning broad or flat piece. Trees or shrubs are shaped to grow in a narrow vertical plane with their branches trained into intricate patterns. This process makes it possible to grow normally large plants on the smallest balcony. A mature tree will grow in a space 18 inches wide by 4 to 6 feet long. Almost any tree or shrub can be handled in this manner as long as it has flexible branches. A favorite subject is the fruit tree, which, because each branch receives full sun, produces an abundance of fruit, outstripping the production of trees allowed to grow normally. Other popular espalier subjects include flowering cherries, flowering dogwoods, flowering quince, ornamental crabapple, hawthorn, rhododendron, forsythia, American holly, cotoneaster, euonymus, pyracantha, yew, and viburnum.

Espaliers are quite ornamental with their intricate patterns and changing seasonal interest. In spring and summer the lovely light-green foliage and masses of flowers highlight the garden, while in the fall, fruit, berries, or brilliantly colored leaves become the focal point. In winter, while evergreens still put on a display, the intricate design of deciduous shrubs can be appreciated.

You should remember that it takes time to fill out the desired form. A good-sized espalier can take up to eight years to fill out the basic form. Start by selecting a plant with the right cultural requirements for the chosen site. Keep in mind that walls absorb heat, and choose your plants accordingly. In a warm, sunny, sheltered position, you might even experiment with a plant that normally would not survive the winter in your area. Plants that require full sun may be perfect for a western exposure, while areas that are very hot, with temperatures that range in the high 90s, often may require an eastern exposure for fruit trees. Try not to place thorny plants next to a walkway. Also keep in mind that eastern and northern exposures will provide the least protection from desiccation in winter.

Have a definite design in mind before you begin—and stick to it. When laying out the necessary supports, measure them accurately; the finished design will depend on it. Traditionally, the most common designs have been symmetrical and geometric, although whole words have been spelled out. Today a more modern informal approach has developed that achieves a graceful balance with asymmetrical designs that rely on sweeps and curves.

Almost any woody plant can be trained to grow into any design as long as you start early enough. A one-year-old whip is better than an older plant that has already begun to form branches. If you are planning to espalier a shrub, choose one with a strong central stem. Begin by running the supports on which the plant will be trained. Proper support is vital. On masonry, drill holes and cement in rustproof hooks, or run wire supports. Wire makes a more permanent support than wood. Be sure to measure accurately, keeping your final design in mind and remembering the height of the container. For most trees the height of the first support wire should be eighteen inches above the soil line; for shrubs it is usually placed much closer.

Plant the tree or shrub in the container, the cut of the main stem just below the first wire. Allow only three new shoots to grow. Train two horizontally and allow the third to grow vertically as an extension of the main trunk. When this central stem reaches the second wire, pinch out the growing tip and repeat the process until the basic frame of the design is filled. Any stem that must be bent to conform to the design should have this done early in the season when the new growth is pliable. Once the basic design is completed, keep all new growth severely restricted. Pinch out the tips of the selected branches when they reach their desired length. Throughout the growing season, pinch out any new growth that doesn't conform to the design. If the espaliered plant is a fruit tree, let the side branches that develop off the main laterals reach twelve inches before cutting them back to form two-inch fruiting spurs. These should each have a few leaves. Leave the short fruiting spurs unless they become too crowded. If you are not sure which are the fruiting spurs, wait until the plant flowers. Heavy yearly pruning is best done in the spring or, in the case of spring-blooming plants, just after flowering.

# The Care of Evergreens

Evergreens play an important role in the garden in all seasons. Their foliage provides a contrast of color and texture to brighter flowering plants in spring and summer, while in the fall their dark green hue sets off the brilliant autumn shades of deciduous shrubs. In the winter we most appreciate evergreens when their bright berries, interesting cones, and foliage add color to a dreary time of year.

Evergreens can be broken down into two main groups; conifers and the broad-leaved evergreens. Conifers for the most part produce long narrow leaves that resemble needles. Their seeds are produced in cones that when mature break open to distribute the seeds. Arborvitae, cedar, cypress, fir, hemlock, juniper, pine, sequoia, spruce, and yew are all conifers. Broad-leaved evergreens include andromeda, aucuba, azalea, barberry, boxwood, cotoneaster, camellia, gardenia, holly, kalmia, magnolia and privet (south of Washington, D.C.), and rhododendron. They produce leaves that more closely resemble those of deciduous shrubs in appearance. The broad-leaved evergreens include some of the most beloved plants grown in American gardens today.

Although these plants are evergreen, their leaves are not everlasting and some annual shedding is normal. However, because the leaves persist for several years dirt and pollutants that clog the pores can be a problem as it interferes with their normal function. It is important that the foliage, including the undersides of the leaves, is washed down regularly. Most pollution damage occurs under dry conditions, so it is important that evergreens receive adequate moisture. For the harshest conditions, pines make the best choice since they will sustain the least amount of damage.

Most evergreens prefer a soil that ranges from near neutral to very acid. This is especially true of such broad-leaved evergreens as the rhododendrons and azaleas, which prefer a pH of 4.5 to 5.5. They prefer a rich soil loaded with peat and leaf mold. The amount of light they require will vary from species to species.

For the most part, conifers need little pruning, but when it is necessary caution must be exercised. Improper pruning can result in disfigurement. Studying the general growth pattern of a particular plant will give you a clue as to how it should be treated. Conifers fall into two categories: those with branches that radiate from the trunk in whorls and those that grow branches in a random pattern. Whorl types include pine, spruce, and fir, while those with a random branching habit include arborvitae, hemlock, juniper, cedar, taxus, yew, and cypress. Those that grow in whorls are incapable of regenerating from older wood and should not be cut back beyond the point where green growth begins. (An exception may be certain pines.) Instead you must cut back only to an inside bud or lateral. Narrow-leaved evergreens also do not take shearing well. Once the plant has reached the size you want, the terminal tips can be pinched out in early spring to control growth. To make pines more compact or to control their size one-half of each candle (the new terminal growth at the end of each branch from which new needles will emerge) can be removed. Sometimes secondary leaders will develop and should be removed immediately. Do not pinch back the top of the tree unless you wish to limit the tree's height, or unless the growth of the leader is so vigorous that the whorls are spaced far apart causing a leggy appearance. Then trim it back to half its original size. This and all other pruning can only be carried out during the spring. Do not attempt it too early before growth is well underway nor after the new growth has begun to harden in midsummer. Conifers cannot form a new terminal bud from hardened wood.

Conifers with an irregular branching habit are easier to prune and take shearing well. Cuts can easily be hidden and mistakes will eventually be remedied. Prune as you would any deciduous shrub. The best time to prune any conifer is in the evening after a thorough watering. This way you will avoid a condition known as needle burn, which occurs when a dry conifer is pruned.

Both types of conifers, those that grow in a regular whorl pattern and those of irregular habit, can be trained to form a new central leader if the old one is damaged. Early in the spring, before the foliage has begun to harden, bend one of the uppermost laterals into a vertical position and splint it securely with a bamboo stake. The stake must be long enough to extend down along the main trunk and gain support. Keep the splint in place for a period of one year.

The sale of live Christmas trees has become quite popular in the last few years as the price of cut trees has risen. Such trees are almost always fast-growing forest stock that is not really suited to container culture. It is better to bypass such specimens. If you still wish to have a live tree or if you can find a dwarf variety that will not outgrow its surroundings then by all means purchase the plant. It may be possible to buy topsoil at a garden center even in winter, but if not, and you know you intend to buy a live tree, then purchase the container and soil in the fall. Keep all materials in a frost-free place and plant the tree immediately. Live trees should not remain indoors for long. Three or four days or at most a week is all they can handle. Place the tree in a cool spot away from any source of heat and water it well. Use only the smallest Christmas-tree lights sparingly so as not to dry out the tree. Remember many of the roots have been severed and the plant may not be able to replace all the moisture that

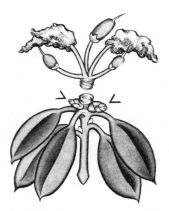

*Fig. 42   When pruning rhododendrons, you must take care not to damage the buds.*

has been lost through transpiration. Avoid the use of canned snow or preparations to prevent needle drop since they will hamper the proper functioning of the leaves. Once the tree is placed outside, mulch it heavily, apply an antidesiccant and water well.

Broad-leaved evergreens comprise one of our most favorite plant groups, with lovely foliage, beautiful flowers, and interesting berries. Most prefer cultural conditions that duplicate their natural forest habitat including partial or light shade, shelter from strong, drying winds (though they can take more than you might think), and a rich acidic soil loaded with humus. Many have shallow, fibrous root systems that take well to container culture, but they resent drying out. These plants are fairly heavy feeders and should be given regular applications of fertilizer from mid-May to mid-August.

Among the most popular of the broad-leaved evergreens are the rhododendrons and their subgroup the azaleas. The distinguishing difference between these two groups is where their buds are formed. Rhododendrons only produce their buds at the branch tips behind the flowers and just in front of the leaf rosette. If these buds are removed or damaged, no new growth or flowers will be produced. Azaleas, on the other hand, produce dormant buds under the bark all along the length of the branches. This fact becomes important where pruning is concerned. Spent rhododendron blooms are best removed by hand, snapping them off carefully once they have browned. Azaleas can be cut back at any point and in fact heading back these plants is recommended, for it will encourage strong compact growth and larger blooms.

The ilexes or hollies are best known to us at Christmas, when their decorative foliage and berries decorate our homes. Many hollies are best left for cultivation in southern areas, but there are some that will be quite at home in northern locations. It is important to know that some species produce their berries on old wood. If they are pruned too heavily during the holidays, you will remove many of the flower buds and subsequent berries for the following season. Hollies that produce on old wood include *Ilex latifolia* (luster-leaf holly), *I. aquifolium* (English holly), and *I. cornuta* (Chinese holly). Hollies that produce flowers and berries on new wood include *I. opaca* (American holly), *I. vomitoria* (yaupon holly), *I. chinensis,* and *I. pedunculosa. I. crenata* (Japanese holly) and *I. glabra* (inkberry) should be pruned in the spring before new growth begins. Both produce inconspicuous black fruits. In order to guarantee the formation of the berries, both a male and female plant should be purchased.

The blossoms and fruit of pyracantha (firethorn) are produced on short spurlike branches from two-year-old wood. Heavy pruning one year will reduce the berry crop next year. Instead, prune by pinching out the growing tips regularly to produce compact shrubs. Pyracantha is a good subject for a formal hedge topiary or espalier. Severe pruning will, however, reduce berry production. For confined areas, choose dwarf varieties that will not need extensive cutting to keep them in line.

*Kalmia latifolia* (mountain laurel), *Pieris japonica,* and *P. floribunda* are all evergreen shrubs that produce their flowers on old wood and should be pruned after flowering.

# Roses

Roses are by far the most popular flowering shrub of all time, and why not, with their beautiful form, wide color range, and unforgettable fragrance. All roses are classified into three main groups: the wild species, old garden roses, and the modern roses. The first two groups are rarely for sale and are characterized by a short flowering season. Modern roses generally either flower continually or flower once in the spring and again in the fall. The main classifications of modern roses include hybrid teas, floribundas, grandifloras, patio roses, miniatures, and climbers.

Hybrid teas were derived from a cross between the less hardy tea roses and the hybrid perpetuals. These are by far the most popular of all the roses and are characterized by large well-formed symmetrical flowers, and long, pointed buds that are born singly on strong stems suitable for cutting. The plants grow from 2½ to 5 feet tall and produce blooms all season.

Floribundas are derived from a cross between the polyanthas and the hybrid teas. Like the polyanthas, the flowers are borne in clusters and are produced in waves throughout the season; the individual flowers measure 2 to 3 inches across, and may be either single or double. The plants themselves are smaller than hybrid teas, measuring eighteen to forty-two inches in height.

Grandifloras are a relatively new class of rose with the flower form and size of the hybrid tea, and the free flowering habit of the floribundas. They produce an abundance of flowers all season on long stems suitable for cutting. Flowers may be produced singly or in clusters, and plants are usually larger than the hybrid teas.

Patio roses are a relatively new development and are most promising for container culture. Large flowers are born on moderate sized plants. They are smaller than hybrid teas but larger than the miniatures and well suited to container culture.

Miniatures have been increasing in popularity recently, and with good reason. Small flowers that measure less than one inch across are produced on tiny demure plants, many less than twelve inches high. Miniatures are often more hardy than standard roses, surviving where the larger plants would not. There are upright varieties, cascading varieties (perfect for hanging baskets), and climbers. Don't be misled by these climbers; some can reach twelve feet in height.

Climbers are divided into ramblers and large flowering climbers. They should not be confused with climbing hybrid teas, floribundas, and grandifloras, all of which are classified under those headings. Climbing roses will need some support. Since they do not have tendrils you will have to tie the canes to the support. Basically there are two kinds of climbers, pillar roses and fan-shaped climbers. Pillar roses include climbing hybrid teas, floribundas, and grandifloras and should be trained to grow vertically. These will bear flowers along the entire length of the canes. Fan-shaped roses include the large flowering climbers and ramblers. Ramblers are characterized by thick clusters of small flowers that appear only in June. As a general rule they are susceptible to mildew. Large flowering climbers generally bloom repeatedly throughout the season on old wood. If you have had trouble wintering over climbing hybrid teas, you might try a large flowering climber, since they tend to be hardier. These roses need to be trained to arch with the growing tips pointed down in order to flower well. As long as the canes are held in a vertical position, they will continue to grow and produce their flowers only at the tops of the canes.

Tree roses are really grafted plants. A bush is grafted onto a long understock, which acts as a sturdy stem. Tree roses come in several sizes, a standard tree rose stands 30 to 36 inches high while patio tree roses measure 18 to 24 inches, miniatures stand only 10 to 15 inches high.

The American Rose Society publishes a booklet called the "Handbook for Selecting Roses" that lists all the roses in commercial cultivation and rates them. It is published each year to help gardeners choose among the different cultivars. Container gardeners in northern areas should stick to the smaller types such as the hybrid teas, floribundas, patio roses, and miniatures since these are easier to winter over.

Roses can be purchased in containers or bare root, from either garden centers or mail order companies. Mail order firms that specialize in roses are considered the best buy, offering the choicest stock and widest selection. Some roses are offered for sale in a cardboard container that is said to be biodegradable. You are supposed to plant the rose, container and all. I have found these to be unsatisfactory since they do not decompose fast enough. Instead, remove the cardboard container and plant the rose as you would any other container-grown stock.

Roses need a rich soil mix with lots of organic matter. A good formula is made up of ¼ topsoil, ¼ vermiculite, ¼ peat, and ¼ compost, leafmold, or well-rotted manure. The depth at which the plant is set depends on the climate in your area. In most localities where the temperature drops to 0°F. or lower for a prolonged period, set the plant so the bud union is an inch or two below the level of the soil. In warmer areas, set it at ground level. Most growers cut back the plants to the correct height before shipping and so no further pruning will be necessary. If your plant has not been pruned, cut it back to ten to twelve inches above the bud union.

Feed rose plants with a balanced 5–10–5 formula or a prepared rose food at least three times a year, once in the spring as growth begins, after the first flush of blooms in June, and again about two months before the first frost. Do not use a fertilizer high in nitrogen or you will get too much green growth and few flowers. Along with a rich soil mix, roses need at least six hours of direct sun a day and plenty of moisture. The soil should never be allowed to dry out. Watch miniatures in hanging baskets closely. At the beginning of each season remove the top two or three inches of soil and replace with a fresh mix. If the plant is root bound, trim some of the roots.

It is often difficult to ensure the survival of container-grown roses through the winter in northern areas. The container size can make a difference. Standard roses should be planted in an 18-inch container. Miniatures in smaller pots should be buried to the rim in larger ones. Placing all the containers together against an inside wall and mulching them heavily with marsh hay will help. Pack the canes with hay and cover with plastic netting. Roses are so inexpensive that they can be treated like annuals and planted in a 12-inch container, so even if they will not survive in your area there is no reason not to grow them.

Roses perform best with a regular program of pruning. Most modern roses are best cut back at the end of the dormant season just before buds swell. The best time is when the forsythia is in bloom. The job should certainly be completed before the new leaves emerge, or the canes will bleed. Old-fashioned roses, those that bloom on old wood, or those that only bloom once in the spring, should not be cut back until after they flower. If you aren't sure what type of rose you have, then wait until the first flush of blooms. Begin by removing all dead and diseased wood and any weak growth thinner than a pencil. Since the best blooms are produced on young canes, all those older than three years should be removed.

The color of the canes darkens as they age, so it will not be difficult to spot the ones to be removed. The three-year-old will be dark brown or black while two-year-old canes will be green-brown in color. After removing the old canes choose three or four strong canes and eliminate all the rest. More vigorous plants can be left with six. Cut these back according to type. Floribundas should be pruned back to three quarters their original size while other roses should be pruned back by two thirds. When shortening the remaining canes, don't cut back to the oldest wood since this can cause dieback. Most climbers and old garden roses bloom on old wood. The long vertical canes are produced the first year while short flower-bearing laterals are produced the second. Prune out the oldest of the long canes, leaving three to five of the strongest. If the rose is a pillar type, pinch out the growing tip when it reaches the desired height. Fan-shaped roses should not have their canes shortened. Instead, arch the canes to discourage further vertical growth. On all climbers, cut back the side laterals that bloomed previously to two or three buds. Tree roses should be pruned to keep their crowns symmetrical. Remove all dead and diseased wood as well as any weak or twiggy growth. Cut back all canes to an outside facing bud.

## Fruit Trees

Just because you garden in containers doesn't mean you cannot enjoy the pleasure of fruit trees. I have had an apricot tree for three years now that gives me tons of fruit each summer. What makes this possible is the new genetic dwarfs that have been developed in the last few years. Don't let the small size of these trees fool you; they produce full-sized fruit that is every bit as good as the larger trees.

Standard fruit trees can reach 25 to 35 feet when mature while semi-dwarfs range from 12 to 18 feet. Grafted dwarfs will usually reach about 10 to 12 feet but will still eventually outgrow their containers. Genetic dwarfs, on the other hand, will usually top out at 6 or 7 feet, a perfect size for containers. Almost every kind of fruit tree is now available as a genetic dwarf.

One of the most important things to know when choosing a fruit tree is if the tree is self-fruitful. A tree that is not will need a second tree of a compatible variety to set fruit. If you only have room for one tree, or if you wish to raise several kinds of fruit trees, this is an important consideration. Most of the genetic dwarfs are self-fruitful, and most will also bear fruit within a year or two of planting.

Some garden centers have begun to carry these genetic dwarfs but the widest selection will come from mail order companies. Be sure when ordering that the tree you choose is suitable for your area. Generally apple trees are the hardiest and can handle temperatures down to −20°F., followed by pears, European plums, sour cherries, sweet cherries, and Japanese plums. Peaches and apricots are the least hardy, handling a minimum temperature of about −10° F. Choose a tree that is at least three years old, unless you wish to train it as an espalier. Most will have developed a strong framework of branches with most of the early (and most important!) pruning having been completed by the grower. Mail order trees will be shipped bare root with their roots wrapped in moist sphagnum. As with other trees, the best time to plant is in the spring or fall.

Fruit trees need a minimum of five hours of direct sun each day. A half whiskey barrel is the right size container. If you choose a grafted dwarf, be sure to plant the tree with bud union above the soil level.

Fruit trees are pruned according to the type of fruit produced. Cherries, European plums, and quinces need little pruning as long as bad crotches do not develop. Remove all dead and diseased wood as well as any crossed branches. Apples, figs, pears, and citrus trees are pruned to form a central leader, while apricots, peaches, nectarines, and Japanese plums are pruned in the open center or vase shape. Trees that are trained to form a central leader have a main trunk that runs the full length of the tree and is surrounded by four or five main branches. Open-centered trees have the leader removed while a basic framework of three or four scaffold branches radiate from the trunk. This basic framework allows more light and air to penetrate, increasing fruit production.

If you have not purchased a three-year-old tree, you will have to do the early pruning yourself. If the tree is to be trained to have a central leader, cut back the trunk of a one-year-old whip by one third the first year. A two-year-old sapling will have developed side branches. Choose four strong laterals that are spaced six to eight inches apart that radiate evenly around the central leader. They should form an angle of 35° to 60° with the trunk. If the angle is too narrow, a length of wood can be wedged between the chosen branch and the trunk to increase the angle further. Remove all other lateral branches. Cut back the central leader to a point 12 inches above the highest lateral and cut back the laterals to 10 inches. The following year select two or three side branches that have formed along the main laterals and remove all the others. In subsequent years as the tree matures, allow new branches to develop at 6-inch intervals along the limbs and prune as you would any other tree.

If the tree is to be trained to have an open center, prune back the trunk of a one-year-old whip to 2 feet after planting. Nick the bark below the uppermost bud. This will help prevent it from taking over and becoming the new leader. The bud will still develop, but because nutrients were diverted it will be weak and can be removed the following year. Next year choose three or four strong branches to train as the main laterals and

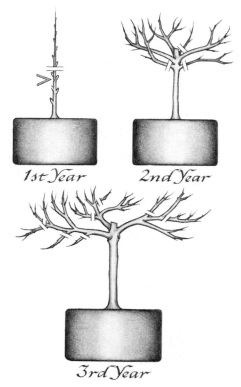

1st Year     2nd Year

3rd Year

*Fig. 43    Training a young fruit tree*

remove all the others. As with central-leader pruning they should radiate evenly around the trunk, joining it at a 45° to 60° angle. Unlike central-leader pruning they may be closer together. At the beginning of the third year, choose one or two side branches that develop from the chosen laterals and remove all others. Do not remove twiggy growth. In succeeding years prune as you would any other tree in early spring before the buds break and allow side branches to develop every five or six inches along the limbs. Apricots are the exception, and will need at least one third of their new wood removed each year.

When your fruit trees reach three years of age they can be allowed to bear fruit. They must, however, not be allowed to produce so much one year that they cannot produce the next. To ensure against this, the fruit must be thinned. Nature is somewhat helpful by having the trees drop many of their immature fruits in June. This, however, is never enough and the trees must be thinned in early July. (Cherries are the only exception.) Thin apricots until 2 to 3 inches remain between fruits. Plums need 3 to 4 inches, nectarines 4 to 5 inches. Peaches need 5 to 6 inches, while apples and pears require 8 inches between developing fruits.

# *The Berry Fruits*

There is nothing like fresh berries to grace a table in summer, and there is no reason why they can't be on yours. Berries are no more difficult to grow than fruit trees, but there are certain cultural practices that will ensure satisfactory results.

## Strawberries

The strawberry is the only garden fruit that is in fact a herbaceous perennial. Not only can it be grown in containers, but it makes a good subject for a hanging basket. There are three types of strawberries in general cultivation today. These include the June-bearing and everbearing hybrids and the alpine strawberry *(Fragaria vesca)*. The alpine strawberry is a species that produces small, pointed fruits with a distinctive flavor. The plants are propagated each year from seed or purchased at garden centers since they produce no runners. The hybrids, which are more widely grown in this country, produce the large, red fruit we are all so familiar with. The June-bearing varieties are the most flavorful, producing larger, juicier berries than the everbearing varieties. Everbearing strawberries can produce berries throughout the season but it is best if they are only allowed to produce two crops, one in the spring and another in the fall. Continual production, especially in hot weather, will exhaust the plant and give you smaller, inferior fruit.

When purchasing plants, select healthy plants from a reputable source and be sure the variety you select will do well in your area. Day length, temperature, and soil type and culture can change the flavor of the berries. Strawberries are heavy feeders and prefer a soil rich in organic material. The addition of compost or leafmold and a dressing of 5–10–5 fertilizer is desirable. When planting, be sure to set the crowns at the same level they were previously. Setting the plants too high or low can result in death. Soon after the appearance of the first berries, most hybrid varieties will begin to produce runners. Allow only enough to take root to give you a fresh supply of plants for next year without crowding. Pinching out all unnecessary runners will also divert the plant's energies into further fruit production. Strawberries should be mulched in winter to prevent the crowns from freezing, which would result in the loss of the plants.

## Blueberries

Blueberries are beautiful, compact shrubs that make wonderful container subjects. In late spring or early summer they are covered with attractive, white, bell-like flowers that attract bees. Blueberries must be cross-pollinated to set fruit, so it is essential that you have at least two plants of different varieties. They prefer an acid soil with a pH of 4.5 to 5.5 and will take less sun than other fruits but not total shade. It is also important that some canes be thinned to the ground to guarantee larger berries. Blueberries tend to overproduce.

## Blackberries

Blackberries make a wonderful addition to the garden since they are so difficult to come by in the stores. They will need lots of sun and some support for the long prickly canes. They produce berries once on year-old wood and will not bear again. Each year after harvesting the berries choose four or five new canes and eliminate the rest. Allow these to reach 36 inches in height then pinch out the tips to encourage the formation of laterals. In early spring while the plants are dormant, cut these back to 18 inches to encourage better fruit production.

## Raspberries

Raspberries do not ship well and consequently are very expensive when purchased at the supermarket. This doesn't mean, though, that they are difficult to raise. A good choice for container culture and limited space are the everbearing varieties that produce two crops, one in the spring and another in the fall, on the same cane. Single crop raspberries should be treated like blackberries: The canes that have borne fruit should be pruned to the ground after bearing, though the everbearing kind need special handling. Contrary to what you might think, the first crop of berries is produced in the fall while the second crop is produced in the spring on the same cane. Therefore, those canes that bear in the spring should be cut down to the soil line after harvesting. The new canes that have formed will begin to produce a crop in September, after which they should be cut back to 5 feet. Be sure to provide raspberries with proper support.

## Grapes

Grapes are a wonderful addition to any garden, but require a certain amount of annual pruning to keep them producing well. Young plants should be set in fairly large containers. When planting set them deep, the deeper the better. You can bury them all the way to their tops if you wish, just allowing the buds to show. Give them plenty of water, sun, and the proper support. Grapes can be trained in any one of three ways. The method you choose will depend largely on the type of grape you plan to grow. Most European grapes are spur-pruned, while most American grapes as well as *Vitus vinifera* (Thompson seedless) are long-cane pruned. It is also possible to modify both of these basic methods to arbor training.

The first season after planting, allow the plants to develop normally and

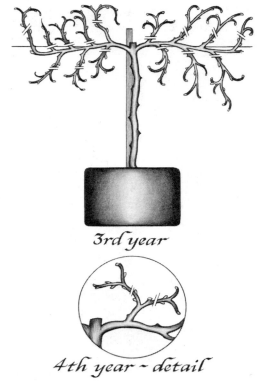

3rd year

4th year ~ detail

*Fig. 44  Grape: spur pruning, third and fourth year*

do not prune. The following spring, choose the strongest cane and cut off all the rest. Prune back the chosen cane to three buds. Let these three buds develop until the canes reach about 12 inches in length, then select one and cut off the rest. From this point on, train the plants according to the type of pruning called for.

Spur pruning calls for a main trunk and two laterals to form a capital T. A wire is stretched 30 inches above the soil line. Train the plant as just described, allowing the selected cane to reach a foot above the wire then cut it back so it is even with the support. Allow two buds at the top to develop, training each to run along the wire to form a T. These are the two main support branches. The following spring while the plant is still dormant, cut back to one bud the laterals that have formed along the two main branches. The third year after planting, the laterals that have formed along the two main branches are thinned to stand 6 to 10 inches apart. Cut back all the selected laterals to two buds to form the spurs. The two canes that develop from each spur will begin to bear fruit. The following spring and every year thereafter while the plant is dormant, the canes that have developed the previous season from the spur are cut back in the following manner: The cane nearest the main trunk is cut back to two buds while the furthest is removed completely. The two new buds will develop and bear fruit.

When long-cane pruning is employed, two wires are stretched above the soil level at 18-inch intervals. As with spur pruning, the selected cane is allowed to develop until it reaches above the top wire, then it is cut back. The cut should be made right through a bud. Remove all side shoots that develop below the first wire but allow the upper half to develop normally. The following season select four side shoots to train along the wires and cut these back to two bud spurs. Eliminate all the others. These two buds will develop into side shoots. At the beginning of the third season, while the plant is still dormant, cut back the lower of the canes to a two-bud spur and the upper to a ten-bud fruiting cane. Train the fruiting canes along the wires. The following season and every year thereafter, cut off the old fruiting cane and cut back the two canes that have developed from last year's two-bud spur into a new two-bud spur and ten-bud fruiting cane.

To train a grape vine to grow up an arbor or wall, do not pinch out the

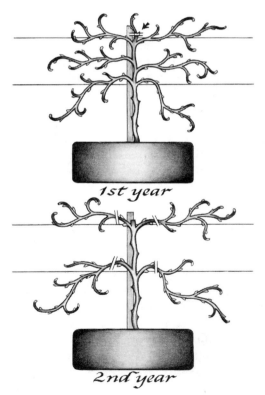

*Fig. 45    Grape: Long-cane pruning, first and second year*

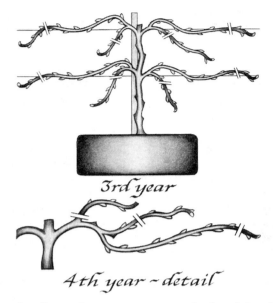

*3rd year*

*4th year ~ detail*

Fig. 46    Grape: Long-cane pruning, third and fourth year

main trunk. Let it develop and instead pinch out the side branches. The following year cut back the trunk to wood that is at least the thickness of a pencil. Allow the vine to continue to grow and develop side shoots. At the beginning of the third season, thin out all side shoots to 12 inches apart and cut them back to 6 inches in length. The following year train as you would for either spur- or long-cane pruning.

The following list describes a wide variety of trees and shrubs that may be used for container gardening. This is by no means complete, but it affords the gardener a representative list of possible choices for container gardening.

# Recommended Trees

*Acer* (maple). The best varieties for container gardening would be the amur maple and the Japanese maple. These trees grow well year round in city conditions and provide exceptional beauty in leaf and bark. The leaf can range in color from white to yellow and various shades of green, changing in the fall to brilliant shades of red and maroon. They grow in a variety of sizes, from quite large to dwarf.

*Cercis canadensis* (eastern redbud). A hardy, beautiful tree that grows well in poor conditions, this tree is attractive year round. The tree flowers earlier than most trees (early spring) and in the winter the reddish brown bark shows off the interesting structure of the branches.

*Chamaecyparis obtusa* (false cypress). This large tree is a good subject for bonsai. It provides an interesting and lovely branch appearance as the branches grow horizontally, and can also grow in a "weeping" form as the ends of the branches droop downward.

*Chionanthus virginicus* (fringe tree). Grows in a short, bushy manner and produces lovely white, aromatic flowers that bloom in late spring and last into early summer. Interesting in more than one season, the female tree will bear clusters of dark blue berries that will last into the winter.

*Cornus* (dogwood). A lovely flowering variety of trees, the dogwood produces not only beautiful varieties of flowers but glossy red berries and an interesting bark. Many varieties of dogwood are winter hardy, they attract birds, and the configuration of the branches makes the trees, even after they have shed their leaves, attractive in the winter months. Suitable varieties are the Japanese and the flowering dogwoods.

*Cotinus Coggygria* (smoke tree). This is a good subject for bonsai and is very durable even when subjected to the harsh conditions of poor soil and drying winds. The flowers produced by this tree provide a smoky, soft appearance throughout the summer.

*Crataegus Lavallei* (hawthorn). Produces an abundance of flowers and grows well in the harsh conditions of a city. Shiny green leaves in the summer turn bronze and red in the fall, producing many months of bright color. The best variety for city conditions is the English hawthorn. Some groups will not produce many fruits but will produce large quantities of flowers that range from deep scarlet to rosy reds. The tree will develop a full and well-rounded appearance when it matures.

*Fagus* (European beech). The beech not only produces nuts that attract birds, it has an unusual bark that can be the most attractive feature in a garden. The bark is smooth and gray with wrinkles on some parts of it. The tree is a good bonsai subject and grows well in small spaces. The branches droop down to produce a dramatic "weeping" effect.

*Ginkgo* (maidenhair). A slow grower that can be pruned to remain small and will grow well in city conditions. The ginkgo when young is sparse in appearance but with age will become dense and full with a conical shape. The tree is easily sheared to fit any space, tolerates pollution, and is pest free.

*Ilex* (holly). These species range from very large to dwarf varieties. This tree will tolerate pollution conditions and will grow well in partial shade or full sun. The tree produces waxy green leaves and clusters of red berries that last well into the winter and attract birds. The tree can be sheared and designed into its space.

*Koelreuteria paniculata* (golden rain tree). A large tree that produces great amounts of yellow flowers and fruits that will attract birds, this very hardy tree tolerates harsh city conditions of drying winds, full sun, and pollution. In the spring the leaves develop quickly, and the flowers begin to bloom in early summer, producing fruits that will remain on the tree into late fall.

*Laurus nobilis* (sweet bay, laurel bay). This is a compact tree that will not withstand freezing temperatures, but can be brought in in the winter. It can be pruned to remain small and is very tolerant of harsh city conditions. It can be sheared or works well as a wall tree. Its small berries and aromatic leaves attract plenty of birds.

*Malus* (crabapple). This species is one of the most common of flowering trees because of its adaptation to harsh city conditions. The edible fruits it produces attract birds. It can be pruned to maintain a manageable size and is largely pest free. Crabapples produce brilliant flowers.

*Juniper.* These trees are hardy and can be used to screen most terraces and roof gardens. Size varies from low, sprawling growth to tall, conical trees. The foliage ranges from bright green to dark bluish-gray, and the small juniper berries will attract birds.

*Pine.* This is a very large group of hardy plants that are often used as bonsai subjects due to their interesting form. Some varieties are quite suitable to tolerate city conditions. The single-leaf piñon pine is especially suited to container growing and will produce edible pine nuts.

*Prunus.* This is a very large genus of stone-fruit bearing trees that includes almonds, cherries, apricots, peaches, and plums. The varieties produce masses of lovely flowers and abundant edible fruits. These trees have dark, attractive bark that emphasizes the beauty of the design of their branches. They are hardy and will withstand winter conditions.

*Thuja occidentalis* (white cedar). The branches of this tree sweep dramatically upward and produce a foliage that ranges from dark green to yellow-green. They range in height from fairly short and hedgelike to quite tall for use as a screen. They can be sheared and designed for their particular space.

*These bright yellow flowers draw attention to the splendid view.*
Designed by Halstead Welles.   Project designer: Bill Hutchinson.   Photo: Ruth Russell.

*The organization of this garden reflects the simple architectural lines of the building.*
*Designed by Robert A. M. Stern.    Photo: Robert Ermerins.*

*This colorful little terrace garden is perched high above street level.*
Designed by Halstead Welles.    Photo: Stanley Schnier.


*An inviting corner with a dramatic city view.*
Designed by Mason-Nielsen, Inc.    Photo: Signe Nielsen.

*This young Atlas cedar adds sculptural interest to a terrace garden.*

*Designed by Robert Ermerins.    Photo: Signe Nielsen.*

*This modern urban garden has a rustic woodland feeling.*
*Designed by Halstead Welles.   Photo: Stanley Schnier.*

*The thoughtful placement of plants, rocks, and water in this small Japanese garden produces a feeling of tranquility.*

*Designed by Hal Inoue.   Photo: Toshiro Kan.*

*This refreshing water garden is most appropriate for warmer urban climates.*
Courtesy of William Tricker, Inc.    Photo: Erwin Zimmer.

# *Shrubs*

*Aucuba japonica* (Japanese aucuba). This is a popular shrub for container growing. This very hardy broad-leafed evergreen is tolerant of heavy shade, drought conditions, and almost any soil. The Japanese aucuba can be dwarfed by careful pruning of its roots and shoots. Varieties are available in many foliage colors, variegations, and shapes. Male and female plants are necessary to set fruit and red berries appear in fall and winter. Care should be taken to protect this shrub from the hot sun.

*Berberis thunbergii* (Japanese barberry). This is a deciduous shrub that is extremely easy to grow. Its lovely shearable foliage and impenetrable thorns make it a most popular hedge and barrier plant. This shrub does not seem to mind pollution and grows easily in a container in any soil, with full sun or partial shade. Foliage is colored in reds, yellows, and variegated leaf design, but those varieties with colored leaves generally retain their color only if kept in full sun. Dense foliage and thorny stems make it a good choice for a barrier or border shrub that is relatively pest-free and bears winter fruit. Of moderate growth rate, this barberry will grow 3 to 6 feet high.

*Cotoneaster divaricata* (spreading cotoneaster). This is an outstanding shrub known for the beauty of its summer and fall foliage, fruit, and lovely shape. Grown as a border or informal hedge, the shrub produces rose-colored flowers in May and bright to dark red berries appear profusely from September through November. A deciduous shrub whose foliage is a dark, glossy green in the summer, the foliage turns to dazzling bright yellow and red combinations that are long-lasting since this shrub defoliates very late in the season. This cotoneaster should be planted in well-drained, moist, and fertile soil. It is also fairly wind-tolerant and will do well in full sun or light shade. Though this shrub will need repotting often, it is trouble free and hardy.

*Cotoneaster horizontalis* (rockspray cotoneaster). This will add an unusual texture to the garden because of the layered form of growth and semi-evergreen appearance of its branches. It is a good choice for ground cover since it grows 2 to 3 feet high and will spread out. The foliage is deciduous in northern climates with blue-green leaves that have a finely textured appearance in the spring and summer and in the fall will turn orange to red before dropping. Abundant pink flowers bloom in May and early June and red berries appear in August and last through November. Like the spreading cotoneaster, this shrub is very hardy and pest-free, tolerant to wind, full sun or light shade.

*Eleagnus pungens* (silverberry). This is a broad-leafed evergreen that produces small but wildly fragrant flowers in October. The tough olive-colored leaves, the thorny branches, and edible red fruit in the spring make this an exceptional shrub. These plants are wonderfully hardy and adaptable, and do well in city conditions. They tolerate full sun, poor soil, and excessive wind. Since the plant will sprawl if not pruned, it should be sheared to maintain the shape and density of its foliage.

*Euonymus fortunei* (wintercreeper). This is a broad-leafed evergreen whose season is fall when the bush produces exotic pink, red, or more rarely white fruits among brilliant red autumn leaves. The shorter dwarf varieties are very good for container growing. In the spring the bush has moderately attractive leaves and later produces tiny white flowers. This is not a dense, bushy plant, but the fall show of color makes it worthwhile. All euonymus are easy to care for and grow. They require no special soil and do well in full sun or light shade. They seldom require pruning. Another euonymus to consider is the *Euonymus japonica,* which is small and grows to an eight-foot spread. This shrub is very hardy and requires little maintenance, which makes it a good selection for particularly rough conditions. Though it tends to be susceptible to pests, if it has good air circulation and is well-drained, it will do very well.

*Ilex cornuta* (Chinese holly). This is another broad-leafed evergreen. Though some species can grow quite tall, there are many species of this holly that are smaller, denser variety. The large leaves of this shrub are tough, and a dark, shiny green in all seasons. This holly can be dwarfed and does not need a female and male plant to bear its abundant red berries. Dwarf varieties grow very slowly but are dense and easy to care for. Like the *Ilex cornuta,* the *Ilex crenata* (Japanese holly) will transplant easily into moist, well-drained soil that is slightly acid. They both do well in sun and shade and will tolerate pollution well. The foliage of the Japanese holly is smaller and more delicate in appearance than the Chinese holly, but it too has the dense, lustrous dark green leaves. Like the Chinese holly, it too responds well to shearing and will maintain a neat, rounded shape when pruned. The Japanese holly produces smaller berries that are black and unobtrusive. Both do well in sun and will tolerate pollution well.

*Juniper.* This is a conifer that remains a very common choice of shrub in a garden. Junipers come in a confusing variety of forms and sizes adding to the versatility of this shrub. Juniper varieties are extremely adaptable and very easy to care for and maintain. They do, however, tend to be susceptible to pests, root rot, and water molds if not properly cared for, so it is necessary to be careful about drainage in containers. The fine texture of the evergreen makes it very attractive to gardeners in northern climates because of their winter color. They respond well to shearing and when located in a sunny spot they will keep a good color and shape. The juniper prefers a sandy soil, bright sun, and good drainage.

*Kerria japonica* (Japanese kerria). This is a deciduous shrub that is noted for its bright yellow flowers in the spring, and stems that remain bright green throughout the winter. It is a tough shrub, easy to care for, that has a tendency to look gangly if it is planted alone—it should be planted in masses or groups. The shrub should be potted in average soil and set in the shade because its flowers will fade in full sun. Find a protected location for it in the winter and provide it with good drainage to avoid winter damage. It will grow three to six feet high and spread six to nine feet. This shrub does well in pollution and drought conditions, making it very suitable to city life.

*Ligustrum* (privet). This shrub comes in varieties that are semi-evergreen and deciduous. Privets in the northern climates are deciduous while some in the southern climates are evergreen. This shrub grows very fast, is pest-free, adaptable, and easy to grow. Privet is used most often for hedges and informal borders. It becomes fuller and bushier when sheared. All privets transplant easily bare-root, and do well in any soil except a wet one. Most privets produce white, very fragrant blooms in the spring. They do well in full sun to partial shade, and pollution and drought do not harm them. This plant can get quite large but many dwarf varieties are available.

*Lonicera tatarica* (Tartarian honeysuckle). This is a deciduous shrub whose main attraction is the fragrant flowers produced in spring in the widest array of colors of any honeysuckle (whites, pinks, and reds). Then altering its appearance again, in early summer masses of showy, bright red berries appear. This honeysuckle must be pruned because it has a tendency to spread. The plant responds well to shearing and can be shaped into a full, dense bush with bluish-green leaves of a medium texture. This shrub is not an especially attractive plant in the winter, but a very easy one to transplant and it adapts well to many soils. It is a very hardy city dweller and does not seem to mind pollution. Pruning should be done just after blooming. Honeysuckle, as it gets older, will get gangly but can be revitalized by cutting it to the ground.

*Malus Sargentii* (Sargent's crabapple). This is a crabapple that is small enough to be a shrub rather than a tree, a hardy deciduous plant that does well in city conditions and drought situations. It is easy to grow and is a superb choice in any garden, with a definite horizontal growth pattern that will spread to twice its height. It will do well in a variety of soils and prefers full sun and average moisture. The foliage is dense and dark green, and it produces a profusion of white, fragrant flowers in spring that transform into branches ladened with red, tiny apples in fall and early winter, attracting birds. Unlike most crabapple trees, this variety is extremely resistant to diseases. This tree can be dwarfed from eighteen inches to twenty-four inches and will spread two to three feet wide. It is not necessary to prune often but if done, do it after flowering, before next year's buds set.

*Picea glauca "Conica"* (dwarf Alberta spruce). This is an extremely slow-growing conifer (about one to two inches a year). Its very interesting shape (full at the bottom and narrow to a point at the top) make it a good selection for variety in a garden. The attractive, finely textured, light green needles enhance its beauty year-round. This spruce has a vulnerability to red spider mite but a drenching with a strong jet of water will help control this problem. The plant performs well when placed in sandy soil with good drainage and set in full sun or light shade. Care should be taken to place this shrub out of hot, windy locations since it is not very tolerant of heat. It does well, though, in cold, damp, winter conditions.

*Pinus mugo* (dwarf mugho pine). This is a conifer that grows from two to four feet high and should be pruned yearly to keep it small. When young, this plant is quite small but can become a monster. The mugho pine should be potted in moist, deep loam and set in full sun or partial shade. The mugho pine is very good for masses of low-lying ground cover with its soft, green cushion of needles that produce spikey "candles" of new growth, and looks good year-round.

*Pittosporum Tobira* (Tobira; Japanese pittosporum). This is a broad-leafed evergreen whose foliage is dark green and leathery in appearance. The spring flowers in creamy yellow, with a scent like orange blossoms, are lovely against the clean, rounded leaves. The density of this plant makes it suitable for screens or borders. As a dwarf, this shrub does very well in containers and is fairly drought resistant but will appreciate an annual fertilizer and adequate watering. Full sun or partial shade is best, but the pittosporum will tolerate dense shade as well.

*Potentilla fruticosa* (bush cinquefoil). This is a deciduous shrub that has many advantages either as a border, facing plant, or just for massing. It produces flowers for a very long time (early summer until frost) and in masses. The one-inch blooms will range in color depending on the cultivar (white, yellow, orange, and red) and set against the finely textured, bright green leaves, this plant has a neat, rounded, and rather dainty appearance. Though the shrub will flower most profusely in full sun, it will tolerate partial shade very well. It is an easy plant to grow and care for and is relatively pest-free. Pot in any soil, from wet to dry. This shrub is very hardy and will do well in extreme cold or drought.

*Prunus tomentosa* (Nanking cherry; Manchu cherry). This is a very good-looking deciduous shrub. The branches point upward as the plant spreads out to almost twice its height. It is a good shrub for shearing and is easy to control. It has a lovely dark, reddish-brown bark, that when defoliated in the winter, is a real attraction. The best aspect of its appearance is in early spring when the shrub becomes massed with pink buds that open to white fragrant flowers. The fruit is abundant and delicious.

*Pyracantha coccinea* (scarlet firethorn). This is a broad-leafed evergreen that is semi-deciduous in the north, a spectacular shrub whose appearance changes as the seasons come and go. Dazzling white flowers against the evergreen foliage bloom in the spring and change in the fall and winter to masses of red and orange fruit. This shrub comes in many dwarf varieties and can grow upright, or layered and close to the ground. It produces some nasty thorns, too, that make it an excellent border or hedge, though somewhat difficult to prune. The pyracantha grows easily and fast. It should be set in full sun and well-drained soil, and once it is established, it should not be moved.

*Rhododendron.* This is an incredibly complicated genus containing over nine hundred species of which there are thousands of varieties. They are an extremely popular shrub because of their large and lovely foliage and dazzling array of flowers. Most rhododendrons are evergreen, though some are deciduous and many are available as dwarfs. Rhododendrons are not a difficult plant to care for and grow; actually, when conditions are right they are easy, carefree, and long-living plants. The soil must have good drainage but hold moisture well, and should also be acidic. Filtered shade in a protected location is best, since the heat of the sun in summer and the winds of winter can damage the shrub. Rhododendrons will not tolerate drought and should be watered regularly but never allowed to get soggy. Rhododendrons are prized for their appearance, which is large and rounded. They hold their shape well and seldom need pruning. Many of these shrubs produce abundant clusters of huge, bright-colored flowers. Proper care and a good selection will provide a lovely garden addition.

*Rosa* (Rose). Like the rhododendron, this genus numbers its species in the thousands. The rose bush is a much-loved and very common selection for a garden. The choice of which type to plant will come from such considerations as color, shape, size, and amount of care. The rose species are mostly deciduous, though there are some evergreen varieties. The shrub can range in size from climbing and viny, free-spreading, to tiny dwarfs. Generally the rose is pest-free, very easy to prune, and requires little special attention. They do well in city conditions and because of the beauty of the fragrant flowers, the rose is an enchantment in the garden.

*Spirea.* This is a very common and much loved shrub. Though most grow quite large and spreading, there are many dwarf varieties that are compact and neat in appearance. Like the honeysuckle, the spirea is not a particularly pretty shrub when not in season. The full, dense, finely textured foliage with its colorful clusters of bright-colored flowers in the spring and summer give way to an uninspiring look in the winter. It is a deciduous shrub that defoliates without changing color in the autumn. The spirea is easily transplanted, and with little care will grow rapidly. It is not particular about its soil or the amount of sun it gets.

*Taxus* (yew). This shrub is a conifer very suited to landscaping: It accepts pruning well and can be easily shaped to fit its location. The yew can get quite large, so it is necessary to find one of the dwarf varieties that will fit into the space provided for it. Yew is an elegant-looking evergreen, with branches of bright green needles that remain lovely year-round. If good drainage is provided, the yew will be an easy plant to care for. While pest-free and amenable to sun or shade, it will not tolerate heavy, wet soils and it should be protected from hot, drying winds. In extremely hot conditions, the shrub should be misted or hosed frequently. The tiny red berries are poisonous.

*Thuja occidentalis* (American arborvitae). This is a conifer that can actually grow to sixty feet tall. There are varieties though that are dwarfs and come in sizes of bushy ground cover to twenty feet high. Most varieties will turn a yellow-brown in cold weather, though there are varieties that retain a good color all winter long. The dark green, finely textured branches make it a very attractive shrub year round. The plant is fairly easy to care for, though the branches and foliage can be damaged by winter winds, snow and ice. This conifer will do well in places with high moisture and soil that is alkaline.

*Viburnum.* A diverse genus that contains a wide variety of shrubs for the garden, many species produce large and beautiful flowers and fruit; some are evergreen while some are deciduous. Viburnum are generally trouble-free plants and are very adaptable. They should be set in moist, slightly acid soil with good drainage. The foliage is moderately attractive, with some varieties changing color in fall. Many will produce a multitude of fruits that remain on the bush into winter.

## Recommended Plants for Different Regional Areas

### Southeastern States

| | |
|---|---|
| *Araucaria heterophylla | Norfolk Island pine |
| Acer palmatum | Japanese maple |
| Aucuba japonica | Japanese aucuba |
| Azalea | Evergreen azalea |
| *Bauhinia | Orchid tree |
| *Bougainvillea | |
| Buxus sempervirens | Common boxwood |
| Calycanthus floridus | Carolina allspice |
| Camellia japonica | Camellia, common |
| Chamaecyparis | False cypress |
| *Citrus | Orange, lemon, lime, etc. |
| Cotoneaster | Cotoneaster |
| Euonymus japonica | Evergreen euonymus |
| Gardenia jasminoides | Gardenia |
| *Hibiscus rosasinensis | Chinese hibiscus |
| Juniperus | Juniper |
| Lagerstroemia indica | Crape myrtle |
| *Laurus nobilis | Sweet bay |
| Ligustrum | Privet |
| Malus | Crabapple |
| *Nerium oleander | Oleander (poisonous) |
| Pittosporum | Pittosporum |
| Punica granatum | Pomegranate |

*Florida only

### Southwestern States

Many of these plants have been chosen for their beauty and adaptability to container culture and not their drought tolerance.

| | |
|---|---|
| Acer palmatum | Japanese maple |
| Arbutus unedo | Strawberry tree |
| Chamaecyparis spp. | False cypress |
| Cistus | Rock rose |
| Cotoneaster | Cotoneaster |
| Elaeagnus pungens | Silverberry |
| Halesia carolinia | Snowdrop tree |
| Ilex | Holly |
| Juniperus | Juniper |
| Lagerstroemia indica | Crape myrtle |
| Malus floribunda | Japanese flowering crabapple |

## Southwestern (cont'd)

| | |
|---|---|
| Nerium oleander | Oleander (poisonous) |
| Osmanthus fragrans | Sweet olive |
| Pinus | Pine |
| Pittosporum tobira | Japanese pittosporum |
| Prunus | Flowering cherry |
| Punica granatum | Pomegranate |
| Pyracantha | Pyracantha |
| Sophoria japonica | Japanese pagoda tree |
| Ziziphus jujuba | Chinese jujube |

## Southern California

| | |
|---|---|
| Aucuba japonica | Aucuba |
| Bauhinia | Orchid tree |
| Berberis Darwinii | Darwin barberry |
| Caesalpinia Gilliesii | |
| Camellia japonica | Camellia |
| Ceanothus spp. | Wild lilac (California lilacs) |
| Choisya ternata | Mexican orange |
| Cistus | Rock rose |
| Cotoneaster | Cotoneaster |
| Elaeagnus pungens | Silverberry |
| Eriobotrya japonica | Loquat |
| Ilex | Holly |
| Juniperus | Juniper |
| Laurus nobilis | Sweet bay |
| Leptospermum scoparium | New Zealand tea tree |
| Ligustrum | Privet |
| Myrtus communis | Myrtle |
| Nerium oleander | Oleander (poisonous) |
| Osmanthus fragrans | Sweet olive |
| Pittosporum | Pittosporum |
| Prunus ilicifolia | Hollyleaf cherry |
| Punica granatum | Pomegranate |
| Pyracantha coccinea | Scarlet firethorn |
| Raphiolepsis indica | India hawthorn |

## Pacific Northwest

| | |
|---|---|
| Arbutus menziesii | Madrone |
| Arbutus unedo | Strawberry tree |
| Berberis | Barberry |
| Calluna vulgaris | Scotch heather |

## Pacific Northwest (cont'd)

| | |
|---|---|
| Cytisus | Broom |
| Erica | Heath |
| Euonymus | Euonymus |
| Hamamelis mollis | Chinese witch hazel |
| Ilex | Holly |
| Juniperus | Juniper |
| Kalmia latifolia | Mountain laurel |
| Ligustrum | Privet |
| Magnolia | Magnolia |
| Mahonia Aquifolium | Oregon grape |
| Malus | Crabapple |
| Photinia × fraseri | |
| Pieris japonica | |
| Prunus | Flowering cherry |
| Pyracantha coccinea | Scarlet firethorn |
| Rhododendron | Rhododendron, azalea |
| Ribes sanguineum | Red flowering currant |
| Rosa | Rose |
| Styrax japonicus | Japanese snowbell |

## Rocky Mountain Region

| | |
|---|---|
| Caragana arborescens | Siberian pea shrub |
| Chamaecyparis | False cypress |
| Cornus alba | Tartarian dogwood |
| Elaeagnus angustifolia | Russian olive |
| Euonymus alatus | Winged euonymus |
| Forsythia ovata | |
| Ilex glabra | Inkberry |
| Juniperus horizontalis | |
| Juniperus scopulorum | Rocky Mountain juniper |
| Lonicera tatarica | Tartarian honeysuckle |
| Malus | Crabapple |
| Myrica pensylvanica | Northern bayberry |
| Pinus mugo | Mugho pine |
| Potentilla fruticosa | Bush cinquefoil |
| Prunus tomentosa | Nanking cherry |
| Rhododendron canadense | |
| Rhododendron nudiflorum | |
| Ribes aureum | Golden currant |
| Ribes cereum | Wax currant |
| Rosa rugosa | |
| Viburnum trilobum | American cranberry bush |
| Thuja occidentalis | American arborvitae |

# ❧ 11 ❧

# Perennials

PERENNIALS ARE PLANTS THAT LIVE and flower over several years. Trees, shrubs, and many bulbous plants are in fact perennials. All such plants are divided into two categories according to stem type. Those with woody stems that persist above ground throughout the year are *ligneous* perennials. They survive because their stems and trunks are extremely resistant to winter conditions. *Herbaceous* perennials have soft, fleshy stems and survive cold weather by dying down to the ground in late fall. Beneath the ground their roots are alive and dormant, waiting the return of kinder growing conditions. With the onset of spring, the roots awaken and send up new shoots.

Of course the reason that perennials are a favorite among gardeners lies in their varied and brilliant flowers. Unlike annuals, perennials usually bloom for only a short time. The constant changing images add freshness and help forecast the changing of the seasons. The perennial garden is always changing. In April, the pink clusters of *Bergenia cordifolia* rise above the leaves to be followed by *Viola odorata.* In summer the cheerful face of the painted daisy is followed by the vivid blooms of *Hemerocallis.* Asters and chrysanthemums end the season in a burst of fall color.

The majority of perennials bloom for only two to four weeks so it is important to keep in mind their various bloom periods to ensure a colorful array all season. Despite catalog claims, there are no perennials that will bloom continuously all season, although there are a few that will bloom in waves throughout the summer, especially if the foliage is cut back after the initial bloom period. For most of the active life of a perennial, its leaves will be its most visible feature.

*Fig. 47 A hybrid day lily*

Perennials can be started from seed or bought as young plants from a nursery. If you decide to start some plants from seed, consult the chapter on propagation. When purchasing plants, select those that are bushy and compact, with healthy green foliage. It's best if the plants are not in bloom. Ask your nurseryman when they receive fresh stock and purchase the plants on that day. This will not only ensure your obtaining plants in the best condition, but will also allow you the widest selection.

Perennials that are hard to find can be ordered through catalogs. They are shipped in one of two ways: (1) dormant bare-root stock (no top growth) with the roots enclosed in damp sphagnum moss and plastic; (2) potted, with some top growth visible. Companies usually ship orders timed to arrive during the best possible time for establishing the plants.

Because perennials are well adapted to the changing seasons, most require minimal care. The vast majority are tolerant of a wide range of conditions including poor soil, though a little attention to soil quality will practically guarantee success in growing these plants. For one thing, good soil will greatly increase the height and flower production of the plant. But more important, most perennials will stay in the same container for three years or more before being lifted and divided. The recommended soil mix outlined in Chapter 4 will get your plants off to a good start. Plenty of peat, manure, or compost should be included. Most perennials like a neutral or slightly acid soil, though some prefer a soil that is alkaline. After selecting the plants for your garden, prepare the soil to meet their needs. A little effort early on will avoid the disappointing experience of undernourished, unhealthy plants.

Since most perennials can be planted in either the spring or the fall, it's best to plant according to the bloom period of the plant. Spring-flowering plants should be planted in the fall, and fall-flowering plants in the spring. The containers ought to be large enough to provide plenty of room for the mature plant's root system. Plants with long tap roots will need deep containers.

If the plant is already actively growing, plant it on a cloudy day or in the evening. Dormant plants that come from mail order firms arrive looking pretty lifeless and must be treated with care. If you can't plant them immediately, store them in a cool, dark place and keep them moist. To plant, partially fill the container with soil. Set the plant on top and gently spread out the roots. Continue to fill the container with soil until the crown is set at the depth it was previously. Placing the crown too shallow or too deep can result in the death of certain species. Once planted, give them a thorough soaking, but do not add any chemical fertilizers. This will give the plant a chance to replace some of the feeder roots that were lost in the transplanting process. Instead, feed the plant two weeks later with a solution of fish emulsion. Avoid any chemical fertilizers until the plant is well established. In general, perennials should be fed once in early spring just as the green shoots appear, and again in midsummer. A generous handful of bone meal and some cow manure should be worked into the soil. If your plants begin to look pale or off-color, or if their growth seems slow, give them a boost with a solution of fish emulsion. Do not feed them late in the season with nitrogen fertilizers since this will only retard their preparation for winter and may result in severe frost damage.

Since perennials survive to return each spring, some amount of attention must be paid to their winter care. After the first killing frost, the dead foliage should be cut back. A handful of bone meal can be worked into the soil to nourish the roots in winter. Then a winter mulch should be applied to protect the plants from changes in temperature. It is not the freezing of the soil that is injurious but repeated freezing and thawing. This can result in the forced raising of the roots known as *heaving.* For those plants that are particularly tender, an inverted flower pot placed over the plant will afford greater protection. This is also a good technique for protecting already emerged plants from a threatened late spring frost. In early spring, wait for the emergence of new green shoots before removing the mulch. Begin first by removing it from the earliest flowering plants. Those that are particularly tender should not have the mulch removed until all danger of frost is past.

Once perennials become well established they will grow larger and larger and most will need to be divided every three years to remain healthy and bloom well. Perennials grow in an outward direction from the center of the crown. In small containers plants will quickly become root-bound and produce few blooms or none at all. In larger containers, while new foliage is produced around the perimeter, the older foliage in the center dies and turns brown and few flowers appear. Division can correct or prevent these conditions. For more information about division consult the chapter on propagation.

The following plants have been chosen for their dependability, beauty, availability, and adaptability to container culture in a roof or terrace situation. They are by no means the only plants that will grow in a container, but they make a good starting point.

*Achillea* (fern-leaf yarrow). This plant is long-lived and requires little care. It bears flat-topped umbels of tiny flowers, usually in shades of yellow but there are also rose and white species. Various species range in height from one and a half to four feet. It is best to consider the shorter varieties for container culture. One of the most popular varieties is *A. filipendulina* (Coronation Gold), which stands two and one-half to three feet high. Another especially nice variety, *A. millefolium* (Fire King), blooms white and changes to a deep rosy red. It stands one and one-half feet tall with foliage that is more finely textured than most yarrows. *Achillea* can be planted in either spring or fall in soil that is well drained and not too rich. Yarrows do well in full sun or partial shade and will tolerate drought. The flowers appear in late June to mid-July but the bloom period can be prolonged if the spent flowers are removed judiciously. The foliage is gray-green in color and presents a nice contrast to other plants.

*Agapanthus* (African lily). This plant is not hardy, but is worth raising for its large exotic flowers. It grows well in a large pot and starting in July, the white or blue blossoms last up to sixty days. It needs plenty of water and should be fed bi-weekly with a nitrogen fertilizer to ensure yearly blooms. Bring it inside before a hard frost and divide the old plants in the spring.

*Alchemilla* (lady's mantle). This is a hardy member of the rose family. Grayish-green leaves surround a yellow or chartreuse flower, creating an incredibly soft and delicate appearance. The plant, which grows eighteen inches high, is long-lived and has a reputation for being invasive when planted in the open but is more easily controlled when planted in containers. Pick off faded flowers to prevent unwanted volunteers from springing up all over the garden. *Alchemilla* can be easily started from seed or purchased as young plants. They require average soil, good drainage, plenty of moisture, and a shady location.

*Aquilegia* (columbine). A member of the buttercup family that sports curious but exquisite long, spurred flowers, these plants are found growing wild in high mountains of much of the world. The flowers are not their only attraction. They also possess lovely airy-looking foliage that resembles the maidenhair fern. The flowers appear in May and June in a variety of colors including purple, blue, pink, yellow, red, white, and many bicolors. The plants stand eighteen to thirty-six inches high with most hybrids remaining under thirty inches. As you may have already guessed, this plant prefers moist, shady situations, but I have found that it will do quite well in full sun provided it is grouped with other plants and given plenty of water and a rich humus soil. Drainage is most important with this plant; it will not survive without it. Picking spent blooms will prolong the bloom period. They are sometimes bothered by leaf miners but this is easily controlled by picking off affected leaves.

*Armeria maritima.* This is also called sea pink or sea thrift and is a member of the leadwort family. This hardy evergreen is the answer to a lazy gardener's dream. It forms small grass-like mounds and bears demure, pink, cushion-like flowers on six- to twelve-inch stems in May and June. This plant does best when it is totally neglected. It thrives in poor soil provided it is well drained. Do not feed or mulch, and do not water too often. It may be purchased at garden centers or started easily from seeds provided they are soaked for several hours before planting.

*Artemisia schmidtiana.* This plant is also called silver mound or wormwood and is grown for its very fine silver-green foliage. About the only way to describe it is to compare it to a puffy cloud or silver cotton candy. It also is quite pleasing to another sense not often thought of when discussing plants, the sense of touch. This plant is one of the softest things you have ever felt. The only thing softer perhaps is baby's hair. This is a spreader, wider than it is tall. It stands about twelve inches high and eighteen inches across. It prefers poor, sandy soils that are not overly rich in organic material. It tolerates heat and dryness well and prefers full sun.

*Aster.* This relative of the daisy produces lovely bright flowers in many shades of blue, white, pink, purple, and red. The flowers appear in August and continue until frost and may be either single or double. Ranging in height from nine inches to three feet, they are easily started from seed, though the germination rate may be rather low. They are not necessarily long-lived and can often be treated as annuals. Give them full sun or partial shade and plenty of water. Do not feed them too often as this can result in lush foliage at the expense of flowers. Pinch out the growing tip to produce more compact plants.

*Bergenia.* This plant is native to Siberia and Mongolia, which makes it extremely hardy and easy to care for. It is excellent when used as a ground cover and in borders, growing well in a variety of soils and conditions. The plant has broad, flat, thick leaves that project out from the base. Pink or white flowers appear in April and May in spike-like clusters above the leaves. It spreads slowly and if not fed too generously will not need division for years. In hotter areas it is best given a shady location; be careful not to overwater.

*Brunnera.* Also called Siberian bugloss, this plant produces sprays of tiny sky-blue flowers that resemble myosotis in April and May. The twelve-to-fifteen-inch leaves are covered with large, heart-shaped leaves that reach six to eight inches in length by July. The plant is quite easy to care for and will adapt to either full sun or shade. It needs regular feeding and ample water and rarely needs division.

*Campanula carpatica.* This is also called the Carpathian bellflower, and produces bell-shaped blooms at the top of the medium green foliage. Blue, purple, and white flowers grow throughout the summer. Soil must be well drained and of normal fertility. Water often, but feed infrequently. Division is usually necessary in the third or fourth year. It's best to start campanula from nursery plants since seeds are seldom true to type. Another species, *C. persicifolia,* is known as the peach leaf bellflower because the foliage resembles peach tree leaves. They grow a bit taller (up to two feet) and need a well-drained soil. Campanula should be protected during the winter.

*Chrysanthemums.* These plants come in over a hundred and fifty different varieties of hybrids providing an amazing array of spectacular colors and shapes. They are difficult to raise because they bloom so late in the season. There are basically two kinds—the hardy bedding mums found growing in gardens, and the larger flowering hybrids that are grown under glass for the florist trade. Chrysanthemums come in every color of the spectrum but blue and can measure from one to four inches across for bedding mums, with the hothouse varieties measuring six inches or more. They come in a variety of forms including globes, buttons, bursting stars, or soft daisies. Take care in selecting varieties where winters come early, since many varieties bloom late. If you live in a short-season area, choose only the earliest blooming varieties. Chrysanthemums require average soil with a neutral pH, plenty of moisture, and full sun. Mums must be divided every other year in the spring to promote better blooms. A few that are especially vigorous growers will need it annually. Be careful of crowding the plants. They need at least a twelve-inch container each. Pinch back young shoots to promote bushier growth. To promote larger blooms, disbud, leaving only one per stem. For show quality flowers, do not pinch back the stem. Instead allow only one stem and one flower bud to develop. Besides division, mums can be propagated from cuttings or raised from seed.

*Chrysanthemum coccineum* (painted daisy, pyrethrum). This is a relative of the more familiar hybrids but has been known to horticulturists for generations for it is the source of the insecticide pyrethrin. It produces lovely white, pink, or red daisy-like flowers in June and early July. Give them full sun or light shade, good soil, and adequate moisture. They are heavy feeders and need to be fertilized often. Like annuals, painted daisies will flower again if the spent blooms are removed before forming seeds.

*Chrysanthemum parthenium* (feverfew). This plant produces small, white, daisy-like blooms with yellow centers. There are also double forms that are quite popular. They are prolific, bursting into bloom in July and August. Pinch back the new shoots to produce bushy plants and help prevent sprawling. They sometimes become so top-heavy that the branches fall over, leaving an open center. This can be prevented by tying and staking the plant. Feverfew likes full sun and almost any soil as long as it is well-drained. Plants grown from seed will flower the same year. They can also be propagated easily from cuttings and of course from division. Like all chrysanthemums they make excellent cut flowers.

*Chrysanthemum maximum* (shasta daisy). This plant is a familiar sight in flower shops in the spring, with its white petals and yellow centers. There are both single and double varieties that produce flowers measuring two to three inches across and grow on strong stems well-suited for cutting. The blooms are produced over a long period (from June to October) and often last long enough to be showy all season. Give these plants full sun or partial shade, a rich, moist, well-drained soil and plenty of fertilizer. Remove spent blooms to keep the plants blooming well and to keep unwanted seedlings from popping up.

*Coreopsis lanceolata.* This plant produces a bright, golden daisy with a serrated edge and is extremely easy to raise. The plant produces blooms in waves from June through September and grows in compact clumps that need division every three years. Easily started from seed indoors five or six weeks before the last frost, or outdoors in early spring or up to two months before the first frost, it is very hardy.

*Coreopsis verticillata* (threadleaf coreopsis). This has very dense, fern-like foliage covered with little golden, star-shaped flowers in summer. Cut it back after its initial bloom period to encourage further flowering. This plant is very easy to start and hardy even in dry soils. It thrives especially well in full sun. Its bushy dark green foliage gives an exceptional appearance. *C. verticillata* spreads slowly and will not need division often.

*Dianthus plumarius* (Scotch pink). This plant offers a neat and compact look. The flowers can be rose, pink, red, or white and bloom through May and June. The grass-like leaves are produced in a low and bushy mound six to eight inches high, and the flowers extend above the plant to a height of twelve inches. Well-drained, alkaline soil will produce sturdy, long-lived plants. Pinch out flowers toward the end of blossoming to prevent reseeding and to promote a longer bloom period. Division is the best way to increase Scotch pinks and should be done in early spring. Otherwise, divide every third or fourth year to prevent overcrowding.

*Dianthus deltoides* (maiden pink). Like the Scotch pink, this plant is easy to raise and produces great amounts of flowers in June. The foliage continues growth into winter.

*Dicentra eximia.* This is popularly known as fringed bleeding heart because of its delicate fringed flowers. This plant will bloom continuously for most of the summer. Flowers are usually pink but there is a white variety that is more satisfactory since the pink variety eventually fades to an ugly brown. The plant does well in partial shade and a rich, moist soil high in organic matter. Regular feedings will keep it at its best. Plants should be purchased in the spring. *D. eximia* rarely needs dividing.

*Dicentra spectabilis* (bleeding heart). This is a much prettier plant than *D. eximia* and has the same cultural requirements. It is taller, reaching a height of twenty-four inches, and blooms in May and June. It has a tendency to die down and go completely dormant in hotter areas.

*Dictamnus.* This is a large, unusual perennial also known as the gas plant. It gets its common name from the fact that a lit match held below a blossom will, with a soft pop, ignite the tiny amount of gas the flower produces without injuring the plant at all. The plant itself is large (three feet) and bushy, and produces spikes of white, pink, or purplish flowers in May and June. The plant is long-lived and has a wonderful lemony fragrance. Dictamnus is easy to care for, preferring full sun or light shade and a rich, well-drained soil. The plant resents disturbances of any kind and rarely needs dividing. It is best to purchase nursery-grown plants, since seedlings take up to four years to reach flowering size.

*Geranium sanguineum* (bloodred geranium). This is a true geranium and should not be confused with the tender perennial pelargonium, which is often called geranium. The blooms are purplish-pink, white, or red. They have five petals that rise on stems about eight inches above the foliage and bloom from May through August. The leaves turn bright red in the fall, giving the plant its common name. It thrives in full sun or partial shade, and under moist conditions tends to spread. Division is necessary every three or four years and is usually carried out in the spring. Plants may also be propagated by cuttings or by sowing the seed about five weeks prior to the last frost.

*Hemerocallis* (daylily). This is very easy to care for, long-lived and produces striking, large star-shaped flowers in an array of colors that range from yellow, orange, gold, maroon, pink, wine, and near black. The common name is derived from the fact that each bloom only lasts for one day, but this is no problem since a new one opens as another fades. Individual flowers will appear continuously for three to four weeks. It is possible to have blooms all season if several plants are grown with different bloom periods. Early-flowering plants bear flowers in May and June, followed by midseason and late-blooming varieties, which begin to flower in July and August, into September. They range in height from twenty inches (including flowers) to thirty-six inches. The taller plants present no problems in wind since the stems are flexible and bend easily. The foliage is grass-like and forms dense mounds twelve to eighteen inches high. Set the crowns at the soil line in full sun or partial shade. Propagation is by division.

*Hosta* (plantain lily or ribbon plant). The foliage of this plant is its biggest feature, although it does bear spikes of white, purple, or blue flowers. The foliage forms a rosette with the variations between species being so great it is possible to build an entire garden around them without being redundant. The color can range from an almost-blue to a varigated light green. Shape and texture is just as varied as their colors. Most species bloom in July, with some flowering late in October. Since full sun burns the leaves, partial to full shade is best. It thrives in a broad range of soils but does best in one that is well drained and rich in organic matter. Since it takes three years for seedlings to develop, you should purchase nursery-grown plants. It can also be propagated by division, but the crowns are difficult to separate.

*Phlox.* This plant produces boldly colored flowers that are so profuse it creates masses of color in the garden. The most common species is the garden phlox or *P. paniculata.* I find it totally unsuitable for urban container culture, but it has a couple of close relations that should not be overlooked. *P. subulata,* also known as moss pink, is very different in appearance. It forms dense mats that in April are covered with brightly colored flowers in shades of lavender, pink, white, and red. Give it full sun and a light, fast-draining soil. *P. divartica* is another species suitable for container culture. It grows in an upright manner, reaching a height of fifteen inches, and is covered with blooms in April making it a good companion for early spring bulbs. It prefers partial shade. Both species can be purchased in the fall for planting.

*Physostegia* (false dragonhead). This is a native of North America. It and its hybrids make a lovely addition to the flower border, blooming from July into October. The flowers resemble those of foxgloves and are borne in spikes on tall stems that measure from eighteen inches to three and one-half feet. The blooms are colored either pink or white and look best in groups. Give them a sunny location and divide every other year in the spring.

*Platycodon* (balloon flower). This produces lovely pink, blue, or white flowers in July and August, and sometimes into September. Before they open, they resemble little globes, hence their common name. They are best purchased as nursery-grown plants, since seedlings take three years to reach blooming size. They are easy plants to grow, preferring full sun or partial shade and average soil that barely covers the crown. They can be propagated by division, but resent disturbance of any kind. Fortunately this is rarely necessary. Platycodon will tolerate hot, dry locations and will reach a height of between two and three feet.

*Santolina.* This is a very agreeable, small, shrub-like plant that has wonderfully aromatic foliage. Very easy to grow, santolina blooms in June and July. It has small, delicate yellow flowers and gray foliage. This plant is not winter hardy and should be kept indoors in a sunny window as a houseplant. Plant in normal, well-drained soil and water regularly, since it likes plenty of direct sun.

*Sedum.* These plants prefer hot, dry, desert-like conditions. The species are quite varied and interesting to look at: Some are rather low and creeping, never reaching more than two or three inches in height, while others measure eighteen inches or more. Of particular merit is *S. spectabile,* which bears flat-topped umbels of pink, red, or white that change to rust as they mature. Other sedums bear blooms in shades of yellow, red, pink, or rust: some also have mahogany or bronze-toned foliage. An outstanding group of plants, these are easily propagated by division and are perfect for urban container culture.

*Stokesia.* This is also called Stokes aster and is a sturdy perennial that is easily grown and cared for. The flowers resemble cornflowers or asters and are blue, white, and purple. They bloom from July to August on long stems above large clumps of leaves. The plant is easy to start from divisions. The plant will not tolerate wet soil in winter—otherwise it is long-lived. Stokesia should be divided about every four years to prevent crowding.

*Veronica.* The common name is speedwell. This is a member of the snapdragon family and produces lovely small flower spikes in June and

July. The blooms are usually in shades of blue, but there are also pink, white, and purple varieties. It is a neat-looking plant that is not at all invasive and does not need dividing very often. To start, plant seeds or nursery divisions in the spring. Use average well-drained soil and plenty of sun. It enjoys being left on the dry side, and if you remove spent flowers, it will bloom again.

*Viola cornuta.* This plant is better known as the tufted pansy and is probably the easiest and most prolific bloomer of all the violas. It resembles the better-known annual species and has the same cultural requirements. Give it a shady location and moist, rich soil. A close relation to the tufted pansy is *V. odorata,* or sweet violet. It flowers in early spring and again in the fall, producing lovely blue, sweetly scented blooms. It too needs the same conditions.

## *Perennial Plant and Seed Distributors*

Bluestone Perennials
7211 Middle Ridge Road
Madison, OH 44057

Busse Gardens
635 East 7th Street
Route 2, Box 13
Cokato, MN 55321

Caroll Gardens
P.O. Box 310
444 East Main Street
Westminster, MD 21157

Garden Place
6780 Heisley Road
Mentor, OH 44060

Holbrook Farm & Nursery
Route 2, Box 223 B
Fletcher, NC 28732

Lamb Nurseries
E 101 Sharp Avenue
Spokane, WA 99202

Wayside Gardens
Hodges, SC 29695

White Flower Farm
Litchfield, CT 06759

# ✺12✺
# Flowering
# Bulbs

BULBS ARE EXTREMELY POPULAR because they yield so much in return for so little. These small storehouses of energy provide more brilliant color and spectacular form than any other group of plants. They are the first to arrive in the spring and continue to enrich the garden with their beauty throughout the growing season. Botanically, bulbs are subterranean buds consisting of layers of fleshy rudimentary leaves, called scales, attached to abbreviated stems. Depending on their shape and some slight botanical differences, they are classified as bulbs, corms, rhizomes, or tubers. Regardless of what they are called, their function is the same—to store food and moisture for use during periods of adverse conditions.

All bulbs, regardless of shape or classification, have common characteristics and life cycles that set them apart from other plants. They exist in nature in parts of the world associated with hot blistering summers and extremely harsh winters. The best conditions for their growth really only exist for a few short weeks, when temperatures are more moderate and rains provide ample moisture. Under these conditions they grow rapidly, flower quickly, and then begin to prepare for their long rest. What makes these plants even more remarkable is the fact that while the plant is growing and flowering above ground this year, next year's plant is already forming deep within the recesses of the bulb, complete with flowers and leaves. This special adaptation means the plant can flower almost immediately, taking full advantage of the best growing conditions.

As the seasons change and the sources of moisture begin to disappear,

*Fig. 48    Tall bearded iris*

their leaves shrivel and they die back. Below ground their roots continue to make some growth and store more moisture and nutrients until they too are halted by harsh climate conditions. Well-protected in its subterranean home, the bulb lies dormant. It contains enough food and moisture to sustain the miniature plant within until the following season.

## Bulb Care and Culture

When ordering, always purchase good sized bulbs from a reputable mail order house or your local nursery. Your plants can never be any better than the stock you begin with, and on a roof or terrace where they are subject to closer scrutiny, their quality becomes even more apparent. Early ordering will assure you of the freshest stock and the widest selection. Begin planning your spring garden in July and order your bulbs in August. The same principle holds true for your summer garden as well.

Most bulbs should be planted immediately upon arrival. If this is not possible, open the bags for ventilation and place the bulbs in a cool, dry place. The planting period for bulbs depends largely on their flowering season. Spring flowering bulbs are usually planted between September 1 and December 15, but the sooner the better, since they will begin to make root growth right away and will continue to do so until the ground freezes hard. Narcissus bulbs should be planted by the end of October. Summer-flowering bulbs are usually planted in April or May, with gladiolus planted at intervals through June. June-blooming lilies should be planted in the fall, while later-blooming varieties are planted in the spring. Autumn-flowering crocus and colchicums should be planted in early August to give them time to make some growth.

It is important to plant the bulbs at the proper depth. If a bulb is supposed to be planted six inches deep, then the top or neck of the bulb should be six inches below the surface of the soil. Bulbs that can withstand freezing winter conditions usually do so because they are protected by several inches of soil. This fact must be remembered at all times when planting bulbs in containers. If a bulb is supposed to be planted six inches deep and the bulb itself measures two inches long then the bulb should preferably be placed at least eight inches, but never closer than six inches from an exposed side of a container. The depth of the soil beneath the bulb is also important and must include some space for root growth without frost damage. The above-mentioned bulb would then need ten

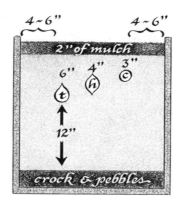

Fig. 49   Planting depths for large and small containers
   T—tulips        H—hyacinth        C—crocus

to twelve inches of soil beneath its base. As you can see, to enjoy certain plants you may need some very large containers. You could also try lining slightly smaller containers with one-inch-thick styrofoam blocks for insulation. This could reduce the necessary size of the container considerably. Other methods that could be used for planting bulbs are modified versions of methods used to force bulbs for winter bloom. What is usually suggested is to plant the bulbs in containers so their necks are just at the soil line, then either store them in a cool frost-free place such as a cold frame or bury them in a trench so the bulbs set at the proper depth. In this way the containers need not be nearly so large, and some may be brought inside to add some color to an otherwise drab time of year.

An inexpensive cold frame can easily be built and placed along an inside wall so it can receive some heat from the building. Be sure, though, to place it on a deck of some kind and pack it with straw or leaves. Styrofoam blocks or styrofoam packing pieces can be added for extra insulation. The styrofoam blocks can be purchased at lumber yards and do-it-yourself home centers. The cold frame should be deep enough to hold all your containers and several inches of straw, leaves, or styrofoam that has been placed on top of the containers. The cold frame should also be equipped with an inexpensive, solar-operated device to open the top of the cold frame when the temperature reaches 70° F. inside. They are available through many mail order catalogues.

Another method that could be used involves building a chicken wire or wide screen pen on a raised platform. On the floor of the pen, place a generous amount of straw, pine boughs, leaves, fiberglass insulation, or packing material to a depth of at least six inches, then place your planted containers on this material. Leave at least six inches or more of space between the containers and the chicken wire. Group plants by period of bloom, with the earlier placed in front. The rims of all the containers should be at approximately the same level, which means shorter containers must be raised. Pack the space around and between the pots with more straw, styrofoam, or other material, and then cover the tops of the containers. Secure the material down with an old sheet or other porous substance that allows moisture in and then wait until spring. Begin checking the containers in March for signs of growth. Remove only those with green tips showing and secure the rest.

Still another very simple method can be used if only a handful of bulbs is involved. Just place them in the crisper of your refrigerator for eight to ten weeks and then plant them with their necks at the soil line, and water. They will begin flowering in a few short weeks.

Bulbs grown in smaller containers can be moved around easily and can even be brought inside to brighten up a room. Containers that are meant to be brought in early should be clearly marked with the planting date so the necessary eight- to ten-week cold period is given to ensure flowering. The disadvantage to shallow planting and small containers is that the bulbs should really be discarded after one season. They usually will not flower again or will have such inferior blooms as not to make the effort worthwhile.

When planting the bulbs themselves, place all the ones of a particular kind at a uniform depth so they will flower at the same time. Give each a half twist to ensure good contact with the soil: Air pockets left at the base may allow rotting or delay root growth and flowering. When planting spring bulbs in large containers that will receive no additional winter protection or when planting more than one kind of bulb in a container, it is best to mark the planting areas with stakes. This way there is little chance of planting them too close to the edge of the container or of planting shallower bulbs on top of deeper planted ones. Once planted, water them well. After the first hard frost, lay down a winter mulch to protect the bulbs from heaving. They should need no other additional winter care except an occasional watering. Let me stress at this time that the biggest reason for failure with spring bulbs is not improper planting, but lack of water. Even when dormant, some moisture is needed. Water them thoroughly once a month and check down below the top few inches to be sure there is moisture below. It is not uncommon for the top two inches to be quite moist, freeze solid, and yet the soil around the bulbs be bone dry.

Most bulbs will do quite well in almost any soil as long as it is well-drained. They cannot survive wet, soggy conditions for any length of time. Bulbs also seem to do best when fed with a slow-acting organic fertilizer. The soil beneath the bulb should be enriched at planting time with bone meal, compost or peat, and potash. Summer-flowering bulbs planted in the spring can also be given a feeding with a complete fertilizer such as a 5–10–10 formula. Such formulations are found in fertilizers meant for use on root crops such as potatoes. Well-rotted manure should never be allowed in contact with any bulb at any time since it promotes rotting. It can, however, be worked into the soil four inches below the bulb, where it is most beneficial. Once top growth becomes evident, all bulbs benefit from a feeding of 5–10–10 fertilizer. Plants that bloom briefly but whose foliage remains green should be fed with a 10–10–10 or similarly balanced formula once the flowers fade. A few weeks before the foliage begins to yellow, all bulbs should be given a generous dressing of phosphorus and potash to promote good root growth. Avoid nitrogen fertilizers that encourage green growth and allow all foliage to fade naturally.

While actively growing, all bulbs need adequate moisture. Check the soil several inches beneath the surface for signs of dryness and be sure to water deeply. To encourage summer-flowering bulbs to prepare for dormancy, gradually begin to withhold water in September. By the end of the month, they should be receiving no water at all except in times of drought. Once the foliage has yellowed or has been blackened by frost, the bulbs may be lifted. Shake off any excess soil and allow the bulbs to dry in the shade for several hours, then place them on screens in a cool, dark, dry location for two to three weeks before placing them in paper (never plastic) bags or containers, and covering them with dry sand or peat moss. As an added precaution, they should be dusted with a fungicide to prevent rotting during storage. Shallow-rooted spring bulbs such as crocuses and hyacinths should also be lifted in June to prevent damage from cultivation. They may be stored for a few months and then replanted in October.

Not everyone may wish to save bulbs from year to year. Instead, they may wish to purchase new stock annually. There is a lot to be said in defense of this practice, especially when space is at a premium. The plants can be cut down and discarded right after blooming, making more space for annuals and eliminating the need to look at faded foliage. Often there is no room to store the bulbs properly under conditions that will ensure good results the following year. I have also found that very often blooms produced in subsequent years are just not as spectacular. So if you really don't feel like saving your bulbs, discard them with no second thoughts.

Most bulbs are relatively free from pests and diseases. Spring-flowering bulbs are sometimes attacked by the narcissus bulb fly. There is no treatment other than destroying the infected bulbs. By far the biggest problem associated with bulbs is rot. This occurs when they are planted in containers with poor drainage or if they are not stored properly. If a disease should appear among a planting, lift all the infected specimens and discard. Do not compost. Disinfect those that remain and move them to a new container. Avoid planting any bulbs or root crops in the old containers for several years.

## Crocus

A crocus in bloom is probably greeted with more joy than any other flower. It is the first real sign that the end of a long, dreary winter is near. The large Dutch hybrids make a spectacular display in shades of pure yellow, white, deep purple, and lavender and brighten up the entire garden. But these are not the only plants in this genus to be admired, nor is spring the only season in which to enjoy them. There are at least two dozen species that await discovery by the unknowing gardener: Many begin to bloom several weeks ahead of the large Dutch hybrids and are known collectively as the snow crocus. It is not uncommon to find them blooming by mid-February as far north as New York City. What these little plants lack in size they usually make up for in profusion, with each plant producing several little cup-like flowers. The color range is similar to that of the hybrids and includes many bicolors not found among the larger blooms.

If you enjoy crocus in the spring, you can also do so in the fall. Among the autumn-flowering species is *C. sativus,* which is an important cash crop in many parts of southern Europe and the Near East. It is grown for its bright red stigma that is the source of saffron. Autumn-flowering crocuses resemble the spring flowering species, but there is one important difference. Instead of producing foliage in the fall, they wait and do so in the spring. They are often confused with colchicums, which bloom at the same time.

Crocuses lend themselves easily to pot culture. Plant them in masses, burying the corms three inches deep and one inch apart. They should be placed no closer than four inches from the side of a container. The spring-flowering species and hybrids may be planted from mid-September to December, while the autumn flowering kinds should be planted in August through mid-September. They prefer full sun but will tolerate partial shade.

# *Narcissus*

The name narcissus is derived from the Greek word *Narke,* which means stupor, or *Narkae,* to be stupefied, as some species have narcotic properties. The Greeks were so intrigued by the beauty of these flowers and at the same time their deadly properties that they gave them an important place in Greek mythology. The nymph Echo fell madly in love with a beautiful but self-centered youth by the name of Narcissus, but when her love went unreturned she slowly pined away until nothing but her voice remained. Nemesis, the goddess of retribution and vengeance, knowing how vain Narcissus was, offered him a long and happy life if he never looked upon his own reflection. One spring while drinking from a pool he gazed at his own image and fell madly in love. He could not bear to leave the pool and finally died there. From that spot sprang a beautiful yellow flower with narcotic properties to remind all those of the hidden flaw of vanity.

The terms narcissus, daffodil, and jonquil are often misused when describing these flowers. Narcissus is the botanical name that is used to describe the entire genus, which includes the yellow trumpet species commonly known as daffodils. Jonquil is the name of a specific yellow species and its hybrids, which are marked by a sweet scent, slender round flower stalks, and rush-like leaves. Today there are over ten thousand registered narcissus hybrids, although only five hundred are in commercial production. Horticulturists have invented eleven different classifications to describe the color, shape, and proportion of the flower. All but a few are hardy, tolerant, and adaptable plants that will grow almost anywhere except in deep shade or under soggy conditions. Those that are descendants of *N. Tazetta* include the paper whites so popular for forcing, and are hardy in warmer (zone 8, see page 180) parts of the country. Descendants of *N. Bulbocodium, N. cyclamineus,* and *N. juncifolius* are hardy only to zone 6.

With proper planning, narcissus can begin to bloom in your garden in late February and continue to bloom through May. Among the many hybrids available are miniatures that range in height from three inches to ten or twelve inches. The flowers themselves vary tremendously in form and include large trumpets, small trumpets, double flowering varieties and those with lovely frilled centers that don't resemble trumpets at all.

Narcissus bulbs should be planted by the end of October or as soon as the bulbs are received. The earlier the better, since they really need the time to make strong root growth. Early planting will also ensure early blooms. Plant the bulbs six to seven inches deep and three inches apart. Miniatures should be planted four to five inches deep and two inches apart. Deep planting encourages strong flowering and discourages the formation of offsets, making transplanting necessary less often. When transplanting is needed, it is best done before mid-July. Narcissus begin growing roots early and are easily damaged if moved too late. The larger hybrids are heavy feeders and prefer a soil rich in organic material and bone meal. The miniatures do not like fertilizers, so use them sparingly. Narcissus will do well in full sun or light shade.

# Hyacinth

The hyacinth (*Hyacinthus*) takes its name from Hyakinthos, who according to Greek mythology was accidentally killed by Apollo. Where his blood touched the soil, flowers sprang up that possessed a sweet scent that was almost overpowering.

Hyacinths are closely related to both scilla and muscari. The many splendid varieties available today were derived by the Dutch from a single cultivar, *H. orientalis.* Hyacinths lend themselves to both formal and informal displays and exhibit a color range from yellow to deep violet. They are classified according to the size of the bulb with the largest bulbs (seven to seven and a half inches) producing the largest, fullest flower stems. These are known as exhibition hyacinths and make wonderful subjects for forcing. Unfortunately, their heavy flower heads become a liability in the garden where the stems are often broken by the wind. The best hyacinths for garden use are the bedding-sized hyacinths, which are a little smaller and a little less expensive. When ordering, be sure that the bulb measures at least six inches in size or the blooms will be disappointing.

The large Dutch hyacinths are not the only species worth growing. There are several smaller species that are quite charming when planted in clumps. Look for them in specialty catalogs if you'd like something a little different.

Hyacinths prefer a light sandy soil and a sunny position. Best results are obtained when the bulbs are planted in late October. Hyacinths are deep rooting plants and need twelve inches of soil beneath their bulbs. They are also heavy feeders, so work in a generous amount of bone meal and potash. For bedding hyacinths, the neck of the bulb should be six inches below the surface and the bulbs should be placed five inches apart. Exhibition hyacinths will need six inches between them. Plant the smaller species of hyacinths two to three inches deep. Where winters are severe, slightly deeper planting is recommended. In some areas the bulbs may have to be buried fully six inches deep and under these conditions, they will also benefit from a winter mulch. Exhibition hyacinths may be brought inside when their foliage is four to five inches high and the flower buds show some color. Keep the plants in a cool room until their buds open. They may then be placed in a warmer location, but it has been found that the cooler the room, the longer the flowers last.

## *Tulip*

The tulip is the most popular of all garden bulbs, offering the widest choice of color, form, and bloom period. Many mimic other flowers or birds, with ruffled or fringed petals, while others appear to be hand-painted. Tulips bloom from mid-April through the end of May and like other garden bulbs, require little effort. They were first discovered by Europeans over four hundred years ago when the ambassador of Emperor Frederick I went to Turkey around 1554 and reported seeing them between Adrianople and Constantinople. The Turks referred to the flower as *tul-ban* or *tulipans,* which means turban.

The first bulbs were introduced to Europe by this diplomatic mission, and over the years the horticulturists of the Haarlem area in Holland nurtured them into a meager living. In 1634 the tulip craze hit Holland and speculation rose to such fantastic heights that a handful of bulbs were traded for fields of crops, wine, and money. In Haarlem an entire house was purchased for the ridiculous price of one tulip bulb. Things had gotten so out of hand by 1637, that the Dutch government had to intervene and make all transactions illegal. Since that time, breeders have developed over three thousand cultivars and today about eight hundred are still in commercial production. These are classified into twenty-three groups arranged in four divisions. Classification of the first three divisions is by period of bloom, while the fourth is made up of species tulips and botanicals.

The first division is made up of those that flower in mid-April. These

*Fig. 50    Tulips are always a cheerful addition to your spring garden.*

include the single early and double early tulips, and the Duc Van Thol tulips that are not generally available to the public. These early-flowering varieties are generally shorter than the later blooming kinds and exhibit a round form.

The second division is made up of the mid-season hybrids that flower in early May. These consist of three groups—the Mendels and the Triumphs and the Darwin hybrids. The Triumphs bloom a few days after the Mendels on strong stems. They are large-cupped, weather resistant, and vigorous growers, and are a good choice for locations that require sturdy plants. The earliest of the group are the Darwin hybrids, which should not be confused with the later flowering Darwins. These have the largest flowers and the most brilliant colors, mostly noted for their shades of red. They are the result of a cross between the Darwins and a species tulip, *T. Fosterana,* and bloom just after the Triumphs.

The late-flowering division makes up the largest group of tulips and their hybrids. They are the tallest and by far the ones that most often come to mind when one thinks of tulips. They have the most beautiful and varied flower heads, straight perfect stems, and the widest color selection. Included in this group are the Darwins, the lily-flowered tulips, cottage tulips, the Rembrandt tulips, the parrots, and the double late or peony-flowered tulips.

The lily-flowered tulips were created a century ago by crossing the Darwins with another species tulip, *T. retrofexia.* They are recognized by their long, narrow flowers with long pointed petals that gracefully curve outward to form a chalice. They are one of the earliest flowering of the late division, blooming just after the Triumphs.

The Darwins are the tallest, most stately of the tulips, with classic egg-shaped flower heads. They are sturdy and wind resistant, and encompass the largest color variations. Some varieties have fringed petals. Darwins have been used extensively in breeding and are the basis of many other hybrids including the Mendels, Triumphs, Rembrandts, and Darwin hybrids.

The cottage tulips are similar to the Darwins in appearance but exhibit slightly rounder flower heads on shorter stems. There is also more variation in form from one variety to the next. Cottage tulips perform well in hot weather and are recommended for southern gardens.

The breeder tulips are derivations of the Darwin group and were thought by Dutch growers to be the most likely to "break" and produce striped or streaked flowers. They are mainly kept for breeding purposes and are not generally available.

Tulips that have already "broken" are classified as either Bizarre, bybloemen, or Rembrandts. Each tulip is one of a kind, individually streaked as if painted by hand. The Rembrandts are broken Darwins. The Bizarre and bybloemen tulips are broken breeder and cottage tulips. Only the Rembrandts are generally available with the others used for breeding purposes. Broken tulips look best when planted in small groups of no more than six.

The heavily ruffled petals of the parrot tulip are often streaked with a contrasting color. So exotic-looking they often resemble tropical birds, they have been known since the seventeenth century, but until recently their stems have been too weak to support the large blooms. To ensure satisfaction, purchase only high-quality bulbs from reputable sources. Space parrot tulips at least eight inches apart.

The double late or peony tulips are a little shorter than the other late-flowering tulips. They have beautiful fluted petals in single shades and bicolors.

The remaining division consists of the botanicals or species tulips. The three most important groups are the Kaufmanniana or water lily tulips; the Fosterana tulips, which include the famous Emperor hybrids; and the Greigii tulips with their brilliant flowers and mottled foliage. The Kaufmanniana or water lily tulips are the first to bloom, sometimes in late March. They have large cone-shaped flowers with petals that curve gracefully back to form stars. They are quite short, growing from only four to nine inches high, and are extremely sturdy. *T. Fosterana* and its hybrids are the next to bloom in early April, about the same time as daffodils and hyacinths. Included in this group are the ever-popular Emperor tulips. They are best planted in clumps so their brilliant color can be appreciated. For their small size they have extremely large flowers.

The Greigii tulips can easily be distinguished from all other tulips by their beautifully marked foliage and bright flower heads. Long after the flowers fade, the foliage can be appreciated.

Although tulips can be planted any time in the fall until mid-December, best results are obtained when the bulbs are planted in October. Location can make a difference in the quality and time of bloom. Most tulips will tolerate partial shade, and the late-flowering varieties will bloom even longer if given such a location. If early-flowering varieties are given a sunny, sheltered spot, they will bloom earlier. Botanicals and species tulips require full sun. Tulips should be planted six inches deep except for the botanicals, which should be planted four inches deep. Fosteriana tulips, including the Emperors, should be set five inches deep.

Tulips, like other bulbs, are basically pest and disease free. An occasional aphid may be spotted on late-flowering varieties but by and large the biggest pest associated with them is the narcissus bulb fly. If an infestation occurs, lift and discard all infected bulbs. Dip the remaining ones in an insecticide and store until planting time. If the blooms develop blisters and brown, water-soaked spots, or the leaves develop greenish spots that gradually increase in size, your plants may be suffering from fire blight. Discard all infected plants immediately. Treat all nonaffected plants with a fungicide. If your plants just refuse to bloom, they may be underfed or they may just be spent. Tulips tend to run out faster than many other bulbs. Dig up and discard.

# *Iris*

According to Greek mythology, Iris was the goddess of the rainbow, and as such offers a perfect name for these plants. Four or five large, delicately ruffled, paper-thin blooms appear on each stem, towering above neat, swordlike foliage. Each flower is made up of three petals (the standard), which often stand erect and are held above the sepals (the falls). Not only are these flowers beautiful, they thrive on neglect, and with the many different species available, you can enjoy their blooms from March through July. Each species falls under one of five main groups: bearded, bulbous, beardless, crested, or cushion (Regelia).

The bearded irises are the most important group and the ones most often brought to mind when the name is mentioned. They all exhibit beards on their falls. The most important species and hybrids are the dwarf bearded, intermediate bearded, and tall bearded, or German, iris. The dwarf bearded irises are the first to flower, beginning in April and continuing into early May. They range in height from three to twelve inches, with most varieties measuring under ten inches. The intermediates are the next to bloom, in mid- to late-May, and range in height from fifteen to twenty-eight inches. They are mostly crosses between the dwarf and tall varieties. The tall bearded, or German, irises are the next to flower in late May, continuing into June. They range in height from twenty-eight inches to four feet and are not the best suited to windy situations. Bearded irises have the largest color range of all the species. The only color of the spectrum that is not represented is green.

Bulbous irises are natives of southern Europe, Africa, and Asia Minor, and are true bulbs. The earliest to flower is *I. danfordiae* in March just after the crocus, with yellow blooms that measure three to four inches across, borne on four- to six-inch stems. They are followed by *I. reticulata,* a species of similar size and height bearing blooms in shades of blue. Both species are easily forced for a winter display in your living room. The Dutch irises are the next to bloom in June, after the tall bearded varieties fade. They can easily be confused with *I. reticulata* because of their shape and color range but these plants stand sixteen inches high with slightly larger blooms. Their color range includes white, yellow, bronze, violet, and blue. The Spanish iris flowers just after the Dutch iris in June, and closely resembles the bearded species in form. They come in shades of blue, yellow, white, and are heavily veined. The English iris is the last of the bulbous iris to flower, beginning at the end of June and continuing into July. These range in color from pale lilac through purple and white. Their sepals are marked with yellow, and the flower is heavily flecked with a deeper purple. Their form closely resembles that of the Dutch iris.

Beardless irises are a large group of plants that flower after the bearded species. They are also rhizomatous but that is where the resemblance ends. Beardless irises are moisture-loving plants that prefer an acid soil. They are found growing in and around ponds and streams throughout the world. If you wish to know more about these plants, please turn to the chapter on bog and water gardens. The species in this group include *I. kaempferi* (the Japanese iris), *I. sibirica* (the siberian iris), spuria iris, the Louisiana hybrids, and the Pacific Coast hybrids.

The crested irises are a small group of plants that resemble Japanese irises in appearance but which are more closely related to the bearded iris. They are distinguished by the small linear crest at the base of each sepal. The plants are generally small, growing under one foot, and are quite beautiful and easy to grow. Crested irises bloom in April and May, preferring cooler conditions, lots of humus, and damp porous soil. They are best given afternoon shade to protect them from the summer heat. Treat as you would bearded iris.

The cushion or Regelia irises consist of only two species native to Turkestan. They are hardy plants that bloom in May and prefer a sunny, sheltered spot and a calcareous soil. Treat as you would bearded iris.

## Culture of Rhizomatous Iris

Rhizomatous irises prefer a sunny location but will tolerate light shade in hot climates and locations especially during the afternoon. They prefer a porous, fast-draining soil that is neutral or slightly alkaline. They are not heavy feeders and a heavy application of a high nitrogen fertilizer will only encourage green growth at the expense of flowers. In mid-March give the clumps a light dressing of a mixture made up of one part bone meal to one part lime.

The rhizomes are best planted from about July 1 to September 15, giving them plenty of time to make solid root growth before the cold weather commences. It is possible to plant them later, but the results will not be as good. They can also be planted in the spring, but will not flower the first year. The most common reason for a lack of flowers is deep planting. The tops of the rhizomes should be just at the soil level or slightly deeper if the soil is very light. Irises grow in an outward direction, so place the rhizomes at least six inches apart and be sure that the growing tips are not facing each other and have plenty of head room. When they do need dividing it is best done just after flowering. Avoid excess water in winter and summer but give ample moisture during the growing season. Pick faded flowers daily and cut the stems back after the bloom season ends.

Irises have very few natural pests or diseases, but one to watch for is the iris borer, which feeds on rhizomes. To prevent an infestation, clean up all debris and old foliage. Treat plants with Sevin or Diazinon before the blooming season. Rhizome rot is more a cultural problem than a disease. It occurs when plants experience too much water, too much heat, and bad air circulation. Cut out affected parts and discard. Coat the remaining rhizomes with a sulfur fungicide, and replant in less crowded containers in a cooler location.

## Culture of Bulbous Iris

All bulbous iris species should be planted four inches deep and three inches apart in a sunny location. The early flowering *I. reticulata* and related species should be planted in September, while the later-flowering species should be planted in October. Treat as you would any other bulbous plant. The Dutch and Spanish species should be lifted and reset annually, while the English species may be left undisturbed for two to three years or until they become overcrowded.

# *Tuberous Begonias*

Tuberous begonias are the crowning glory of any shady summer garden, whether they are planted in beds or hanging baskets. The spectacular blooms that can measure four inches across come in every shade and hue except violet, blue, and green, including many bicolors. The flower form can take the shape of camellias, carnations, and even roses. Once they begin to flower, they will continue to do so right up until the first frost.

Unlike most other garden plants, begonias actually produce separate male and female flowers on the same plant. It is the male flowers that are spectacular. The female flowers are usually removed unless crossbreeding is desired. This is not a common practice, since raising begonias from seed is extremely difficult, although not impossible for the home gardener.

Tuberous begonias flower best in light or partial shade. An eastern exposure is best, especially if there is some kind of overhang above the plants to cut off direct sun in the middle of the day. They will also do quite well in a northern exposure provided they are planted in a more open environment unobstructed by other foliage. If the shade is too dense, they will produce few blooms.

Begonias are heavy feeders and require a rich humus soil that is kept evenly moist but not soggy. A good soil mix for these plants is made up of two thirds of the general mix discussed in Chapter 4, and one-third peat or compost. To this add a generous portion of bone meal and well-rotted cow manure. It is better to err on the side of too much organic material than not enough. Many horticulturists recommend planting them in 100 percent organic matter.

Begonias will usually begin flowering in July if the tubers are planted out after all danger of frost is past. It is possible to have blooms in June if the tubers are started indoors six to eight weeks earlier. This can be done by placing the tubers in shallow containers filled with moist peat and vermiculite, hollow side up. The tops of the tubers should be level with the soil line or just barely covered and kept evenly moist. Place the containers in bright but not direct sunlight and keep them at 65–75° F. After roots have formed and the plants have produced two leaves, they may be potted up individually or planted out in the garden.

Set them out about the same time as you would tomatoes. The tubers should be placed not closer than two inches from the sides of the container. If you plan to pot them up individually, you will need at least a

6-inch container for each tuber. It is wise to remember that begonia blooms always face the same direction as the tips of the leaves, so position them accordingly for the best viewing.

Begonias should not be fed until they have produced at least two leaves. They have enough stored energy to sustain them until this stage of development. They should then be fed with a high phosphorus formula every two to three weeks. You can always tell when a begonia needs fertilizer. The leaves will turn light green and cup upward. A healthy plant has dark green leaves that curl downward.

In hot weather begonias will need to be watered every day. In humid areas it is best not to wet the foliage. Water the plants early enough to ensure that they are dry by nightfall. In drier climates wetting down the foliage increases humidity and is advantageous.

If you wish to save the tubers for next year, you will have to encourage the plants to go dormant in the fall. Begin to withhold water gradually. When the leaves yellow and the stems separate from the tuber, it is time to lift them for storage. Brush off the soil and cure them in the sun for a few days until they are hard and dry. Remove any portion of the old stem that may be attached, for very often it can cause the tubers to rot. Store them in a cool dry place until next year.

# *Dahlia*

Dahlias are practically unbeatable for show-stopping summer color from July until frost. Unlike most other bulbous plants they flower almost continuously with proper care. Today's hybrids are also relatively easy to grow, with strong stems that will hold the blooms erect even when cut, no matter how large. They will tolerate almost any soil as long as it is fairly neutral, and they are not bothered too much by insects except for an occasional aphid or spider mite. Diseases include verticillium wilt, leaf spot, and some viruses.

Dahlias cross-pollinate readily, making hybridization easy. As a result, flower forms are quite varied and are now classified under ten divisions. Of these, the most important are the formal decorative, informal decorative, cactus, semi-cactus, and pompons. Formal decorative blooms are fully double with broad, neatly spaced petals or rays. They can measure from four to twelve inches across or more. Informal decorative flowers have irregular rays and are somewhat shaggy in appearance. They have the same size range as the formal decoratives. Cactus-flowered dahlias have narrow rays that curl under, giving them the appearance of quills, while the semi-cactus form indicates a flower with petals that curl back for only half of its distance. Pompons are smaller, measuring under two inches in diameter with small, evenly spaced, tubular petals. The flower has a tight, roundish form that resembles a little ball. Other categories include the anemone-flowered collarette, singles, ball type, and a miscellaneous category that includes everything else.

Dahlias come in an extensive range of colors and bicolors. Only true blue is not represented. Heights can range from ten inches to four or five feet for a full-sized variety.

Dahlias prefer full sun and cool temperatures. In hot, dry situations some shade, especially in the afternoon, is helpful but six to seven hours of direct exposure is mandatory. The taller kinds will need staking and a spot sheltered from the wind. Give them plenty of water since they are somewhat thirsty plants, and be sure when watering that you moisten the soil down deep. They don't mind a little dryness but once a plant wilts it is difficult to bring it back into growth and flowering. At the same time good drainage is most important—they don't like their roots to remain wet.

Dwarf bedding dahlias can be started early from seed indoors and will produce blooming-sized plants as quickly as any of those grown from a tuber. However, plants grown from seed will show some variation from plant to plant within the same variety.

Dahlias grown from tubers are best planted out about the same time as tomatoes. For large plants you'll need at least a sixteen-inch container. Place an inch of drainage material in the bottom and cover with five inches of soil that has been enriched with lots of organic matter such as compost and well-rotted manure. Avoid poultry manure (super manure) since it may produce rangy growth. Also work in about a cup of bone meal and a generous portion of potash. Cover this with four inches of plain soil and place the tuber on top. The eye or bud should be positioned in the center. Drive in a stake about two inches from the bud and cover with another three inches of soil. Water well. Dahlias prepared and planted in this way should need no additional feeding for the rest of the season. Overfeeding will only result in rangy growth at the expense of flowers. Apply a mulch at the end of June to help keep the soil cool and moist. Dahlias put out lots of shallow feeder roots that are easily injured by cultivation.

Allow only one main stem to develop from each tuber. When the plant forms three sets of leaves, pinch out the center to promote bushy growth. When buds form, pinch out all but one on each stem. This will conserve the plant's energy and will promote a longer flowering season as well as larger blooms. Small bedding dahlias will not need disbudding. As each flower fades cut back the entire stalk one joint above the main stem and new flower producing laterals will develop.

At the end of the season the tubers may be lifted and stored for the winter. They are quite brittle and easily broken, so handle them carefully. Some horticulturists prefer dividing them at this time when the tuber is easy to cut and the buds are relatively recognizable. Others prefer to do so two to four weeks prior to planting in the spring and run less risk of the tubers shriveling in storage. If you wait until the eyes sprout, you can see them quite easily. It is important that the tubers be divided every year if the flowering quality is to remain high.

# *Gladiolus*

Gladioli are among the easiest and showiest garden flowers to grow. Even a novice can have blooms that rival the local florist's. Glads also have other attributes worth mentioning. They take up very little space, making them a perfect choice for containers while adding a much needed vertical dimension to the garden. They also come in one of the widest color ranges available for a single cultivar, and with continuous planting will bloom in your garden from June until frost.

Although most catalogs will list hybrids under four basic categories, including large-flowering hybrids, butterfly glads, miniature glads, and baby glads, the terms *large* and *miniature* refer to the flower size only. Most gladioli will grow four feet tall. There is such wide variation in color and form within these categories that most gladiolus societies do not recognize this system of classification. Instead they list cultivars by the size of the bloom only. Sizes 400 and 500 indicate that the individual florets measure at least four and a half inches across. Such blooms, of course, are borne on the largest plants. Size 300 indicates medium-sized florets that measure three and a half to four and a half inches across while small-flowered cultivars produce blooms that measure two and a half to three and a half inches. Such plants have been categorized as size 200. Size 100 indicates a miniature with blooms that measure less than two and a half inches across. These size listings are often found in catalogs in parentheses next to a description of the plant.

The large-flowering hybrids range in height from four to six feet. The largest are generally self-colored although there are quite a few that exhibit contrasting flecks or blotches at the throat. Such large specimens can be subject to a great deal of damage from winds and storms and as a result breeders have developed newer, shorter hybrids that make much better subjects for container gardening. These shorter varieties are generally heavily ruffled with multicolored florets that can exhibit three colors or more. They also tend to bloom a little sooner after planting.

Butterfly gladioli are usually a little smaller than the large-flowering hybrids and exhibit hooded florets that measure three to four inches across. They get their name from the fact that they are extremely colorful and unusually marked. They usually bloom a little earlier than the larger hybrids.

Miniature glads generally grow to a height of twenty-four to thirty inches and bear florets that measure two and a half inches across. These smaller glads make excellent cut flowers and are well suited to arrangements.

Baby glads prefer cool, humid coastal areas, making them a wonderful subject for the mild winter areas of the south and northwest. North of Washington, D.C., they are usually grown under glass. They flower early, in May and June, and sport lovely two-and-a-half- to three-inch florets that are arranged loosely along the spike. They come in an assortment of pink, red, rose, and white, many with diamond-shaped blotches on their lower petals. The plants only reach a height of fifteen inches, making them the daintiest of the glads commercially available.

For top quality blooms select high-crowned corms that measure one and a half inches in diameter. The time of planting will vary depending on the local climatic conditions. In parts of southern California for instance, gladioli can be planted at any time. In hotter areas the corms should be planted between November and February to avoid the heat of summer. In the midwest and northeast, gladioli are planted from May to June, while in the humid northwest, April to June are the months to do so. To keep a succession of blooms coming until frost, continue to plant the corms at five-week intervals. There are some new hybrids that can actually begin to flower six weeks after planting, but most will take about two and a half months if top-sized bulbs are used. The smaller the corm, the longer it takes.

Gladioli are heavy feeders and do best if given a rich soil and a sunny position. However, in hotter areas later-planted specimens may prefer a little light shade. Use a container at least fourteen inches deep and add plenty of organic matter, bone meal, and a complete 5–10–10 fertilizer down in the root zone. If you decide to add any animal manures, keep it well away from the corms.

The proper planting depth is approximately four times the thickness of the corm. This can vary slightly depending on the lightness of the soil. In good soils, place large corms about five inches deep and six inches apart. If the soil is very light, a depth of six inches is preferred, while in heavy soils four inches is adequate. Medium-sized corms should be placed three to four inches deep, while small corms and cormels should be planted just two to two and a half inches deep. Insert a stake at the time of planting so there is no chance of injuring the corm later. Side-dress the plants every three or four weeks with a high phosphorus fertilizer and water liberally during dry spells.

Gladioli are relatively disease-free but are occasionally attacked by thrips, aphids, and caterpillars. If you wish to save the corm until next year, be sure to cut down the flower stalk (not the foliage) after flowering as this could be a source of infection. Dust the bulbs with malathion before storage. The corms may be gathered and braided like onions, then hung for the winter.

# *Lilium*

Lilies make wonderful container plants and lovely cut flowers. They come in a wide variety of forms and colors, and since they originate in fairly extreme climatic areas, they are quite hardy and will stand up to most U.S. weather conditions. In the past fifty years lily hybridization has come into its own, producing healthier, hardier plants than were known previously; these new hybrids have a wider range of blooming periods, making it possible to have some lilies always in bloom from June to October.

Sorting out all the different hybrid groups and subgroups can be a bit confusing but there really are only a few main groups of any real importance.

The Asiatic hybrids are generally the earliest to flower, starting in June and continuing until the middle of July. They stand between two and five feet in height and bear lovely flowers that measure four to six inches across. Included in this group are the mid-century hybrids, which are descendants of the tiger lilies, the fiesta hybrids, and the harlequin hybrids. Named varieties include Enchantment, Harmony, and Citronella. They are strong-growing, very hardy, tolerant of most soils, and prefer full sun. The color range includes yellow, orange, red, pink, white, and lavender.

The Martagon hybrids are descendants of *L. Martagon* (Turk's cap lily), and have lovely pendant flowers that measure three to four inches across on three to six foot stems. The paisley strain is a subgroup. The Martagon hybrids prefer light shade and flower in June. The color range is the same as that of the Asiatics with the addition of mahogany.

The candidum hybrids sport four- to five-inch flowers that are borne on three- or four-foot stems and also flower in late spring to early summer.

The American hybrids include the subgroup Bellingham hybrids as well as the San Gabriel strains. They stand four to six feet tall and bear four- to six-inch flowers. These are the result of crosses of species native to the west coast and flower in midseason—late June to July.

The Aurelian hybrids are quite popular and are offered for sale almost everywhere. Flowers in this group may be trumpet-shaped, bowl-shaped, pendant, or sunburst-shaped. Many are marked by a light color on the outside. They stand from three to six feet in height and flower in late July and August. Included in this group are the Olympic hybrids. Popular varieties include Pink Perfection and Black Dragon.

The longiflorum hybrids represent the Easter lilies, which normally flower in midsummer but are forced into bloom for Easter. As a group they are quite tender and must be grown under glass except in warmer climates.

The Oriental hybrids are late-season plants, flowering in August. Included in this group are the imperial strains and the gold band hybrids. Plants stand two to eight feet tall, thus many are too tall for rooftop culture. They are tolerant of heat and cold, many preferring partial shade. They are also quite disease resistant.

Other species often grown include *L. auratum* (yellow-banded lily), *L. candidum* (white madonna lily), *L. regale* (regal lily), *L. speciosum* (a large white fragrant lily), and *L. Martagon* (Turk's cap lily).

A lily strain usually refers to plants that are grown from seed, and there may be slight variations in color from plant to plant. A named variety is usually a vegetatively produced clone and all plants will be identical.

All lilies are either stem rooted or basal rooted. What this means is that they either produce roots along the stem above the bulb or they produce them from the basal plate below the bulb. It is very important to know what kind of lily you are dealing with since its culture is dependent on it (see Classification chart on page 263).

Stem-rooted lilies are planted six to nine inches deep, depending on the variety grown. They are then covered with a rich potting mix made up of one quarter topsoil, one half compost and peat, and one quarter vermiculite. A generous amount of bone meal and a complete 5–10–10 fertilizer should be worked in. Adding manure is controversial. Some growers use it, while others don't. If you use it, never put it in direct contact with the bulb.

Basal-rooted plants are set with their tops two to three inches deep in a fourteen-inch container that has been filled with the same rich mixture. Most lilies do prefer a soil that is slightly acid with a pH of 5.5 to 6.5, although *L. candidum* and *L. Martagon* will tolerate some lime. They all respond well to a monthly side-dressing while actively growing.

Most lilies prefer full sun, although there are a few that will tolerate light shade. In hot locations a little afternoon shade will be appreciated by all. They all prefer cooler conditions for their roots and will benefit from a year-round mulching program. The basal-rooted kinds can even be overplanted with shallow-rooted annuals.

Unlike other bulbs, lilies never go completely dormant and have no protective outer layer. They must be handled carefully and not remain unplanted for long. That is why it is important to purchase American-grown bulbs and plant them as soon as they are received. If the bulbs appear dried out when they arrive, place them in moist sand or peat until the scales become plump again. If the bulbs arrive too late, cover them in the same way until they can be planted.

Lilies need a constant supply of moisture both winter and summer. It is best to lift and transplant them just after they flower so they have plenty of time to make good root growth before the cold weather slows their progress.

Lilies are relatively insect- and disease-free but they will occasionally be bothered by aphids or thrips. Diseases include botrytis, mosaic, or fusarium wilt. Do not use malathion on lilies since it can mark the flowers. To protect the bulbs when they are lifted, dust them with malathion powder.

# Miscellaneous Bulbs

*Agapanthus* (African lily). These tender plants are at their best when grouped in containers. Depending on the species, large umbels of blue or white flowers are produced over a sixty-day period on one and one-half- to three-foot stalks. They make wonderful cut flowers since they last for quite a while. The strap-like foliage is quite handsome, making this plant an attractive garden addition in all seasons. Give it plenty of water and a sunny position. They resent frequent division or transplanting, preferring to remain restricted. Just place the pots in an out-of-the-way, frost-free place for the winter.

*Allium giganteum.* Large umbels of purple, star-like flowers form perfect spheres atop five-foot stems. In July this plant is not to be missed, especially when planted in groups. Give it a sunny location and well-drained soil. Hardy zones 6 to 10.

*Allium Moly* (luteum). Many bright yellow flowers, borne in clusters on stems one to one and one-half feet high, bloom in May and June. This plant is best set in groups in a sunny location. In some very cold areas they may not be permanent. Hardy zones 4 to 10.

*Anemone blanda* (Grecian windflower). This is a hardy plant that produces two-inch daisy-like flowers that bloom in early spring. They look wonderful when teamed up with daffodils forming a 5-inch-tall mat. They come in shades of blue, pink, and white, with some bicolors, and look best planted in clumps. Bury the tubers three inches deep and two inches apart in a partially shaded location.

*Brodiaea.* Native to the western United States, Brodiaea blooms in spring or early summer depending on the species. It produces round clusters of one-half- to one and one-half-inch flowers on stems that grow from twelve to thirty-six inches high. The color range is mostly blue, but some species are yellow or red. Brodiaea produces grass-like foliage and prefers a gritty, well-drained soil. It does not do well if given too much water. In zones 5 and 6, it will require some winter protection in the form of a mulch, while north of zone 5 it is not hardy.

*Caladium.* This tender plant produces large tropical-looking, arrow-shaped leaves that are edged and mottled with white, pink, or red markings. They make a colorful display in fairly heavy shade but require four full months of growing time if you wish to save the bulbs. Treat them as you would tuberous begonias. They may be started indoors for an earlier display.

*Camassia.* This bulb produces two and one-half- to three-foot flower stalks that are covered in blue star-like blooms reminiscent of hyacinths. They thrive under ordinary conditions in full sun but will also do well in partial shade. They prefer moist conditions and bloom in May and June.

*Canna.* With its broad, tropical-looking leaves, this handsome plant adds a touch of the exotic to the summer garden. Its form resembles that of the banana plant, with foliage that can range in color from light green to bronze. It grows quickly and, depending on the species, can range in height from eighteen inches to six feet. It is topped by a flower spike that bears several blossoms measuring four to five inches across. They come in shades of red, white, yellow, coral, and pink and can be blotched with a contrasting hue. It prefers full sun and a rich soil.

*Chionodoxa.* This plant, also called glory-of-the-snow, produces small white, blue, or pink star-like flowers on five- to seven-inch stems. They bloom in March and April about the same time as crocus. Give them a sunny or partially shaded location.

*Eranthis hyemalis.* This is also known as winter aconite and produces fragrant yellow buttercup-like flowers sometimes ahead of crocus. It prefers a moist location in partial shade or full sun. Soak the tubers for twenty-four hours before planting in the fall.

*Fritillaria imperialis.* This plant, also known as the crown imperial, has stately drooping flowers which are borne on two and one-half- to four-foot stems. The flowers, in shades of yellow, orange, or red, are topped with a tuft of green foliage like a cap. The stem is covered with broad, lily-like foliage. *F. imperialis* makes a fine specimen plant but its musky fragrance may be objectionable. It needs full sun, good soil, and should be protected from strong winds. Hardy in zones 5 to 8.

*Fritillaria Meleagris* (the checkered lily). This plant has bell-shaped, pendant blooms that resemble tulips. It takes its name from the curious white-and-burgundy checkered pattern of the petals. *F. Meleagris* blooms in early April on one-foot stems. Other similar species such as *F. lanceolata, F. pudica,* and *F. recurva* are native to the American northwest and do not perform well outside that area. The checkered lily requires a dry location and is hardy in zones 3 to 8.

*Galanthus.* This plant is also known as snowdrops and consists of small white drooping flowers that bloom in early spring with the hybrid crocus. They come in both single and double varieties, blooming on six- to nine-inch stems. They require little attention and do well in sun or partial shade. Plant them thickly in clumps for the best effect. Hardy in zones 3 to 9.

*Galtonia.* Also known as summer hyacinth, this is a tender plant that produces strap-like leaves that measure two to three feet long. Greenish-white, bell-shaped flowers that measure one to one and one-half inches across are loosely placed along a two- to four-foot stout flower spike. For the best effect, plant in groups in the spring after danger of frost is past.

*Gloriosa Rothschildiana.* This is better known by its common name, gloriosa lily. If you have ever seen its flowers, you know you will never forget them. The lovely lily-like blooms are heavily reflexed and measure four inches across. The waxy petals are red, banded with yellow. They make wonderful cut flowers and will last for several days. The plant is a climber and supports itself by tendrils that are produced from the ends of its leaves. Plant the rhizomes horizontally four inches deep in a sunny location, or one that receives partial shade. It is hardy in zones 8 to 10. In all other zones, store the tubers over winter.

*Ixia.* Also known as the African cornflower, this plant is somewhat reminiscent of the gladiolus in form. The eighteen- to twenty-inch stem is topped with flowers in May or June. They can range in color from cream, yellow, and orange to red or pink, all with darker contrasting centers. The flowers open flat on sunny days and will last up to two weeks after being cut. The foliage is grassy with a sword-like appearance. Ixias are tender and will not withstand freezing temperatures. Plant them in clumps one inch deep.

*Leucojum* (snowflake). This plant grows to a height of twelve inches and produces small white bells that look like lily of the valley. There is an early and a late variety. The early variety blooms in late March and early April. The late variety blooms in late April into early May. They prefer full sun or light shade. The flowers become larger if bulbs are left undisturbed. Hardy in zones 4 to 8.

*Muscari.* This plant, also called grape hyacinth, blooms as the crocus fades. Small spikes of blue or white bells stand six to twelve inches tall. They are particularly effective when planted in thick groups with yellow daffodils.

*Scilla hispanica* (wood hyacinth). Formally called *S. campanulata,* this plant blooms at tulip time. Pink, white, or blue bells are held loosely on fifteen- to twenty-inch stems. The foliage is grassy and strap-like. Plant in full sun or partial shade in soil high in humus. This species needs plenty of moisture when actively growing but once established lasts forever. Hardy in zones 4 to 10.

*Scilla sibirica* (Siberian squill). This plant is very hardy with pretty blue bells, not unlike *S. hispanica.* Its bloom period is between the crocus and narcissus, and the flowers are borne on six-inch stems. Plant the bulbs in groups of a dozen or more to form colorful clumps. Culture is the same as *S. hispanica.* Hardy in zones 1 to 8.

*Tigridia* (Mexican shell flower). This plant is a striking garden addition. The five- to six-inch flowers are triangle-shaped, made up of three large outer segments and three smaller inner ones. Colors range from white, yellow, and orange, to pink or red. All have heavily spotted centers. Each bloom is borne individually on a two-foot stem and only lasts for one day but others follow quickly. The plants have a fairly long bloom period from July into August. For best results, plant in clumps of ten or more where they will receive afternoon shade. *Tigridia* is not hardy north of zone 7.

*Zantedeschia.* This plant is more widely known as the calla lily, and is a remarkably beautiful plant with a romantic quality. The small nondescript flowers are borne on a spadix that is cloaked in a heavy white bract that measures eight inches long. The blooms are borne on three-foot stalks that rise from the base of the plant. The large, tropical-looking, arrow-shaped leaves form a clump two to four feet tall. They make wonderful container plants and can handle a great deal of shade although they do prefer some sun in the morning. There is also a miniature white variety as well as a yellow and pink. Both the white and the yellow stand eighteen inches tall and sport six-inch blooms, while the pink variety has four-inch blooms. Both the yellow and pink callas have white spotted foliage that some gardeners may find objectionable. Set the rhizomes four to six inches deep for full-sized plants and two inches deep for the miniatures. Zantedeschia cannot withstand freezing temperature.

## Planting Bulbs in Containers

| PLANT | DEPTH BELOW SURFACE | HEIGHT OF BULB | DEPTH BELOW BULB | DISTANCE FROM SIDE OF CONTAINER | TOTAL DEPTH OF CONTAINER NEEDED |
|---|---|---|---|---|---|
| Tulip | 6" | 2" | 12" | 8–10" | 20" |
| Hyacinth | 4–6" | 2–2½" | 12–14" | 6–8" | 18–23" |
| Crocus | 3" | 1" | 6" | 4–6" | 10" |
| Narcissus | 5–6" | 3" | 14" | 9" | 22–24" |
| Min. narcissus | 4" | 2" | 10" | 6–8" | 16" |
| Dutch iris | 3" | 1½" | 8" | 5–6" | 13–14" |

## Tulips

| DIVISION | GROUP | HEIGHT IN INCHES | DESCRIPTION | COLORS |
|---|---|---|---|---|
| *Early* (mid-April) | Duc Van Thol | 6 | Used for breeding, and not generally available | |
| | Single early | 10–14 | Single-cupped. Flowers just after Dutch crocus | Red, orange, yellow, pink, white, bicolor |
| | Double early | 10–14 | Double flowered, graceful, ruffled petals, some fringed | Red, orange, yellow, pink, white, bicolor, flecked, feathered, edged |
| *Mid* (early May) | Mendel | 16–20 | Single cupped, self-colored, or edged in a deeper hue. Valuable for forcing | Apricot, white, rose red, crimson, pink, yellow, orange, and bicolors |
| | Triumph | 16–20 | Single-cupped, strong-stemmed, weather resistant, vigorous in habit, flowers right after Mendels | Wider range self-colored, bicolors, edged, flushed, striped, margined broken, two tone |

## *Tulips* (cont'd)

| DIVISION | GROUP | HEIGHT IN INCHES | DESCRIPTION | COLORS |
|---|---|---|---|---|
| | Darwin hybrid | 22–28 | Earliest to flower in this division. Has the largest flowers of any tulip. Brilliantly colored but not as formal as the Darwins | Mostly red, some varieties are bicolors. |
| *Late* (mid-May) | Cottage | 20–32 | Slender buds with long pointed or rounded petals, square or rounded base. More variation between different varieties than any other group, recommended for southern states | Red, yellow, white, lilac, purple, pink, orange, flecked, edged, feathered. |
| | Lily-flowered | 20–24 | Long, pointed flower petals curve outward | Reds, bright pinks, yellows, rust, lilac, violet, white, edged, bicolors |

## *Tulips* (cont'd)

| DIVISION | GROUP | HEIGHT IN INCHES | DESCRIPTION | COLORS |
|---|---|---|---|---|
| | Darwin | 26–32 | One of the oldest strains and the largest group of cultivars. Pointed or rounded petals with a rectangular base includes fringed varieties, sturdy, wind and rain resistant. | Red, yellow, white, pink, orange, black, purple, lilac, edged, striped, feathered, bicolors |
| | Breeder | 24–36 | Large, long oval flower heads, not generally available | Purple, gold, bronze, orange, yellow, soft copper, and combination of rich tints, bicolors with yellow base |
| | Rembrandt | 20–24 | Broken Darwins with large single squarish cups that look best planted in small groups | Striped and streaked |

## *Tulips* (cont'd)

| DIVISION | GROUP | HEIGHT IN INCHES | DESCRIPTION | COLORS |
|---|---|---|---|---|
| | Bizarre | 20–24 | Single cupped, broken breeder or cottage tulips. Not generally available. | Yellow with brown and purple markings |
| | Bybloemens | 24–36 | Single cupped, broken breeder or cottage tulips. Not generally available. | White background with rose, purple or lilac markings |
| *Late* | Parrot | 20–26 | Ruffled petals that resemble birds. In recent years varieties with strong stems have been introduced. Plant 8 inches apart. | Fields of white, yellow, pink, purple, red, marked with contrasting colors including green, black, also tricolors, especially yellow, red, green |
| | Peony | 20–24 | Large double flowers, with ruffled and fluted petals | Red, violet, yellow, white, bicolors including green, also edged, feathered |

## *Tulips* (cont'd)

| DIVISION | GROUP | HEIGHT IN INCHES | DESCRIPTION | COLORS |
|---|---|---|---|---|
| *Botanicals* (flowering period varies) | *T. batalinii* | 4–6 | Creeping ribbonlike leaves, single flowers. | Yellow |
| | *T. biflora* | 6 | Bouquet tulips, 3 to 8 blooms per stem, petals delicately pointed | Pointed greenish petals, gray-purple outside, yellow base |
| | *T. Celsiana* | 12 | Known as lady, peppermint stick, or candlestick tulip. Blooms late April. | Pointed petals, white outside flamed or striped in crimson, blue base |
| | *T. Eichleri* | 12–20 | Flowers with the early daffodils in April. Long flower heads with pointed petals and a fluted edge. | Scarlet with black center surrounded by yellow band, scarlet and white stripes. |
| | *T. Fosterana* | 12–18 | Rectangular blooms with pointed petals includes the Emperor tulips; flowers late March or early April, as hyacinths, narcissus, and muscari. | Red, yellow, orange, white, striped, bicolors. |

## *Tulips* (cont'd)

| DIVISION | GROUP | HEIGHT IN INCHES | DESCRIPTION | COLORS |
|---|---|---|---|---|
| | T. Greigii | 5–16 | Brilliant colored flowers with a pyramid shape and pointed petals, species marked by mottled foliage. Blooms in April, later than other botanicals. | Red, yellow, white edged, striped, two-tone. |
| | T. Kaufman-niana | 4–9 | Large cone-shaped flowers curling gracefully back to form stars; first tulips to bloom, March–April. | Bicolor, tricolors, shades of yellow, red, white, bronze, orange, outside petal usually striped in contrasting color, sometimes with yellow base. |
| | T. Hageri | 5 | April-May, 2 to 3 flowers per stem. | Copper-red. |
| | T. linifolia | 6 | Blooms in April | Scarlet, black center |

## *Tulips* (cont'd)

| DIVISION | GROUP | HEIGHT IN INCHES | DESCRIPTION | COLORS |
|---|---|---|---|---|
| | T. *marjolettii* | | Difficult to obtain. Available from P. de Jaeger & Sons. | |
| | T. *praestans* | 12 | Late April, 3 to 4 blooms per stem. | Red |
| | T. *tarda* (T. dasys- temon) | 3 | April, up to 4 star-like flowers per stem | White, green, yellow |
| | T. *turkes- tanica* | 6–8 | Bouquet, flowers in March– April, 5 to 8 flowers per stem | Gray-green outside, shading to yellow at base |
| | T. *tuber- geniana* | 18 | Bunch tulip, 3 to 5 blooms per stem. Difficult to obtain. | Scarlet flowers, yellow base |

## *Bloom Periods for Lily Hybrids*

| JUNE | JULY | AUGUST |
|---|---|---|
| Asiatic | Harlequin | Potomac |
| Mid-Century | Fiesta | Imperial |
| Del Norte | Bellingham | Olympic |
| Candidum | Aurelian | Gold band |
| Martagon | Longiflorum | |

## *Lily Rooting Classifications*

**STEM-ROOTED LILIES**

Asiatic trumpet hybrids
Chinese trumpet hybrids
Gold band hybrids
Hansen hybrids
Henry hybrids
Japanese hybrids
Longiflorum hybrids
Martagon hybrids
Royal hybrids
L. speciosum
Tiger lilies
Yellow Martagon

**BASAL-ROOTED LILIES**

L. candidum
L. caucasian
L. martagon
Nankeen lily
Scarlet lily

[BLOOM PERIOD TABLES *follow*]

## Bloom Periods of Recommended Bulbs

| PLANT | FEBRUARY | MARCH | APRIL | MAY | JUNE | JULY | AUGUST | SEPTEMBER | OCTOBER | NOVEMBER |
|---|---|---|---|---|---|---|---|---|---|---|
| Agapanthus | | | | | | ——— | ——— | | | |
| Allium | | | | | ——— | ——— | ——— | | | |
|   *A. giganteum* | | | | | — | | | | | |
|   *A. Moly* | | | | — | | | | | | |
| Anemone blanda | | ——— | | | | | | | | |
| Begonia, tuberous | | | | | ——— | ——— | ——— | ——— | ——— | |
| Brodiaea | | | | | — | | | | | |
| Caladium | | | | | ——— | ——— | ——— | ——— | | |
| Camassia | | | | — | | | | | | |
| Canna | | | | | | ——— | ——— | ——— | | |
| Chionodoxa | | — | | | | | | | | |
| Crocus | ——— | ——— | | | | | | | | |
|   Dutch Hybrids | | ——— | | | | | | | | |
|   *C. biflorus* | — | | | | | | | | | |
|   *C. imperati* | — | | | | | | | | | |
|   *C. kolschyanus* | | | | | | | | | ——— | |
|   *C. medius* | | | | | | | | | | ——— |
|   *C. sativa* | | | | | | | | | ——— | |
|   *C. Sieberi* | ——— | ——— | | | | | | | | |
|   *C. speciosus* | | | | | | | | | ——— | |
| Dahlia | | | | | | ——— | ——— | ——— | ——— | |
| Eranthis | | ——— | | | | | | | | |
| Fritillaria | | | ——— | ——— | | | | | | |
|   *F. imperialis* | | | | — | | | | | | |
|   *F. Meleagris* | | | — | | | | | | | |
| Galanthus | | — | | | | | | | | |
| Galtonia | | | | | | | ——— | ——— | | |
| Gladiolus | | | | | | ——— | ——— | ——— | ——— | |
| *Gloriosa Rothschildiana* | | | | | ——— | ——— | | | | |
| Hyacinth | | | — | | | | | | | |
| Iris | | | ——— | ——— | ——— | ——— | | | | |
|   Dwarf bearded | | | ——— | | | | | | | |
|   Intermediate bearded | | | ——— | ——— | | | | | | |
|   Tall bearded | | | | ——— | | | | | | |
|   *I. reticulata* | ——— | ——— | | | | | | | | |
|   Dutch iris | | | | — | | | | | | |
|   English iris | | | | | | — | | | | |
|   Spanish iris | | | | | — | | | | | |

## Bloom Periods of Recommended Bulbs

| | FEBRUARY | MARCH | APRIL | MAY | JUNE | JULY | AUGUST | SEPTEMBER | OCTOBER | NOVEMBER |
|---|---|---|---|---|---|---|---|---|---|---|
| Ixia | | | | | | | | | | |
| Leucojum | | — | | | | | | | | |
| Lilium | | | | | | | | | | |
|   Asiatic hybrids | | | | | — | | | | | |
|   Mid-century hybrids | | | | | — | | | | | |
|   Harlequin hybrids | | | | | — | | | | | |
|   Fiesta hybrids | | | | | — | | | | | |
|   Martagon hybrids | | | | | — | | | | | |
|   Candidum hybrids | | | | | —— | | | | | |
|   American hybrids | | | | | | — | | | | |
|   Bellingham hybrids | | | | | —— | | | | | |
|   Aurelian hybrids | | | | | | — | | | | |
|   Olympic hybrids | | | | | | — | | | | |
|   Oriental hybrids | | | | | | —— | | | | |
|   *L. auratum* | | | | | | | — | | | |
|   *L. candidum* | | | | | | | | | | |
|   *L. regale* | | | | | | | | | | |
|   *L. speciousum* | | | | | | | | — | | |
|   *L. martagon* | | | | | | | | | | |
| Muscari | | | — | | | | | | | |
| Narcissus | | | — | | | | | | | |
| Miniature daffodils | | | — | | | | | | | |
| Trumpet daffodils | | | — | | | | | | | |
| Small-cupped narcissus | | | — | | | | | | | |
| Scilla | | | —— | | | | | | | |
|   *S. hispanica* | | | | — | | | | | | |
|   *S. sibirica* | | — | | — | | | | | | |
| Tigridia | | | | | | —— | | | | |
| Tulipa | | | —— | | | | | | | |
|   Early hybrids | | | — | | | | | | | |
|   Midseason | | | — | | | | | | | |
|   Late | | | | — | | | | | | |
|   *T. Kaufmanniana* | | — | | | | | | | | |
|   *T. Fosterana* | | | — | | | | | | | |
|   *T. Turkestanica* | | | —— | | | | | | | |
|   *T. Tarda* | | | —— | | | | | | | |
|   *T. greigii* | | — | | | | | | | | |
|   *T. praestans* | | | — | | | | | | | |
| Zantedeschia | | | | —— | | | | | | |

# ❧ 13 ❧
# Annuals
# and Biennials

What do you call a plant that blooms profusely in a wide range of striking colors, shapes, and forms, and is easy to grow, requiring only minimal care? In addition to all of these qualities, a plant that is inexpensive and well-suited to container culture? There is only one kind of plant that embodies all of these qualities and that is an annual.

Annuals are plants that complete their life cycle in one season, from the sowing of the seed to their eventual death. Because they are so short-lived, they grow quickly and bloom brilliantly in an effort to perpetuate their kind. If the flowers are cut before the seeds form, the plants will bloom again and again. As a group, annuals have the largest blooms and offer the widest range of flower shape and color. They range in height from just three or four inches to more than five feet. They may be prostrate, trailing, or climbing, and there are those that are grown for their beautiful and colorful foliage. There are annuals to grow in full sun and there are those that lend their beauty in bright shady situations. They are such a versatile group of plants that you can certainly find one to put in any corner under any growing conditions.

Traditionally, annuals have been used as "aesthetic fillers" among more permanent plants and shrubs, especially those that have not reached their mature size. Unlike perennials, most annuals bloom continuously, adding much-needed color throughout the season, and because they are temporary and grow quickly, they are capable of changing the nature and flavor of a garden each year. These same qualities also make them an ideal choice for the renter who doesn't want to spend too much on a roof or terrace garden.

Annuals are classified by degrees of hardiness. A hardy annual is a plant that can tolerate some freezing, while half-hardy annuals need some warmth to get a good start but will tolerate cool conditions thereafter. They may be sown indoors in the early spring and transplanted to the garden after danger of frost is past. Once these plants are established, they are quite hardy. A tender annual is easily injured by frost and their progress is slowed considerably by cold weather. They should not be planted in the garden until conditions are warm and settled.

Most annuals prefer well-drained, average garden soil. A monthly application of a high phosphorus fertilizer formula will help replenish the energy that goes into producing each new batch of flowers. They have small root systems that make them good container subjects and can be planted a little closer together than is usually recommended. I find spacing them a distance equal to half their mature height quite adequate. What most do require is a container that holds at least eight inches of soil. The larger kinds, of course, will require larger containers.

Annuals may be grown from seed or they may be purchased at garden centers at planting time. When buying plants look for husky, properly labeled plants that are not yet in bloom. Avoid plants that are spindly, wilting, or exhibit yellowing leaves. Such plants are probably pot-bound or neglected and will never make good sturdy plants. Be sure to look for signs of insects or any evidence of disease—there is no sense in introducing these elements into your garden.

*Fig. 51  The pansy*

*Fig. 52    Annuals provide color in a shady garden.*

As the plants develop they should be pinched back to promote bushier growth and increase the number of flowers. Some plants, if not pruned in this way, will only produce one stem. The best time to do this is when the plants are from two to four inches tall. Spent blooms should also be removed immediately. Called *dead heading,* this careful pruning keeps the plant flowering profusely by preventing the formation of seeds. Because time is always running out for annuals, they will quickly produce more blooms. Some plants such as China asters will also benefit from *disbudding.* The idea here is to remove all the lateral flower buds along a stem, leaving only one remaining at the tip. The plant will then put all its energies into producing one large, spectacular flower per stem, instead of a lot of little ones. Disbudding is a technique used by many horticulturists when entering their plants in competition.

# Biennials

Biennials are plants that have a two-year life cycle. The seeds of such plants are usually sown from June onward for blooms the following season. Because the plants spend their first year storing energy, the quantity of blooms they produce is far greater than even that of annuals.

The term *biennial* is not used too strictly. Some short-lived perennials as well as certain hardy annuals are given biennial treatment. This is especially true in the milder parts of the country where seeds can be planted in the fall for blooms the following spring. Treated in this manner, most hardy annuals will grow into much larger plants.

As with annuals, biennials are divided into hardy and half-hardy plants. Hardy biennials such as foxgloves, hollyhocks, and sweet Williams can survive northern winter conditions with a minimum of protection, while half-hardy biennials such as the English daisy will not survive in northern areas. Such plants may live through a mild winter as far north as zone 7 if given adequate protection, but this cannot be guaranteed.

The biggest drawback to biennials is the garden space they take up the first year when they aren't flowering. This is a major concern for roof and terrace gardeners where space is at a premium. It may be preferable to purchase prestarted plants that are already a year old and ready to flower.

## *Recommended Plants*

Here is a list of annuals and biennials well-suited to urban container gardening. They have been chosen for their beauty, diversity of form, and ease of culture. Whether you use them in containers, hanging baskets, or window boxes, you'll discover that they are a delight to experiment with. This list is, however, limited and by no means the only plants you may choose.

*Ageratum* (half-hardy annual). This is also called floss flower, and has a misty blue or pink cluster of fuzzy blossoms. The plants grow in compact mounds and need lots of sun—at least five hours of morning sun or exposure to strong midday light. They like rich soil and benefit from additional applications of a high phosphorus fertilizer. Pinch out the growing tips when they are two inches tall to promote bushy growth and remove faded blooms to encourage further flower production. Ageratums develop slowly and should be started indoors in early spring and set out in the garden after all danger of frost is past.

*Antirrhinum* (snapdragon). This is a tender perennial treated as a half-hardy annual and comes in a wide assortment of bright colors. The lovely flower spikes are wonderful for cutting. They are classified according to height under three categories: small (6–9 inches), intermediate (18–24 inches), and large (up to 3–4 feet). The large ones are prone to wind damage and are not particularly good subjects for urban roof gardens, but the shorter varieties are marvelous. A single plant may produce as many as seven or eight spikes during the course of a season, especially when cut frequently for bouquets. They do best in full sun but will tolerate some shade. Sow seeds indoors six to ten weeks before the last frost. In the south, the seeds can be sown in the fall for blooms the following spring.

*Begonia, fibrous rooted* (tender perennial treated as a tender annual). This plant is a native of Brazil, usually growing six to nine inches tall with clusters of delicate pink, white, or red flowers and waxy green or bronze leaves. Widely grown as house plants, they are ideal for most roof gardens. They brighten up a shady corner and will even flower in full sun as long as the temperature doesn't exceed 90°F. I find the bronze-leaved types are better for full sun. Begonias prefer a rich, moist soil and require some skill in growing from seed. It is best to purchase prestarted plants at garden centers.

*Browallia* (tender perennial treated as half-hardy annual). This plant grows well in sun or partial shade and is a wonderful subject for hanging baskets. A profusion of star-shaped blue or white flowers begins to cover the plant twelve weeks after the seeds are planted. If faded blooms are religiously removed, the plant will continue to flower freely.

*Callistephus* (half-hardy annual). Also called China aster, this plant blooms in a wide variety of forms and colors. The blossoms can be shaped like chrysanthemums, daisies, or pompons and the color range encompasses everything but orange. They vary in height from eight inches to three feet. The early varieties begin blooming in midsummer, followed by the midseason and late varieties. They have a short bloom season, so plant all three kinds for a succession of bloom. Unlike other annuals, they tend to stop blooming when cut. China asters need a sunny or lightly shaded location and a rich well-drained soil. Because they are shallow rooted, they benefit greatly from a one-inch mulch.

*Campanula medium* (half-hardy biennial). Known as Canterbury bells, this plant has delicate, bell-shaped pink, blue, or white flowers, two inches across. The plant reaches a height of two and one-half feet and needs a sunny location. Although they are easy to grow from seed, it is best to buy prestarted plants if you live in the northern parts of the country. It will survive in mild winters as far north as zone 7 with adequate protection but have often failed to survive in zones 3 to 5. In milder areas they will flower the same season if given a long enough growing period. *Campanula* needs six months to grow from seed to flowers.

*Capsicum* (tender perennial grown as a half-hardy annual). Also known as ornamental pepper, this plant is grown for its colorful fruit that is borne on top of the foliage in clusters. The fruits are at first green then change to yellow and red, and have the added advantage of being edible and quite hot! The plants themselves range in height from six to twelve inches and prefer a sunny location.

*Centaurea cineraria* (hardy annual). This plant is also known as dusty miller, and is prized for its fern-like, silver gray leaves that add contrast to any summer garden. It is quite easy to grow, preferring a sunny location but will do quite well in partial shade. It needs a well-drained soil and will tolerate dry conditions. *C. cineraria* is quite hardy and can be sown outdoors in early spring as soon as the last frost passes. Southern gardeners can treat it as a biennial, planting it in August for plants the following spring.

*Cleome* (half-hardy annual). Also known as the spider flower, this is an excellent terrace plant that grows to the height of three to four feet with lovely pink or white flower clusters that can measure eight inches across and have a lovely pungent fragrance. Each individual flower is characterized by long stamens that give the plant its common name. Cleomes remain in bloom from June until frost and will tolerate dry conditions.

*Coleus* (tender perennial treated as a half-hardy annual). This is the dearest friend of the shade gardener who wants to add a bit of color. Its colorful leaves are produced in multicolored shades that include yellow, white, pink, red, green, and brown. No two are ever quite the same. They can easily be grown from seed or they can be purchased at garden centers. Pinch out the growing tips to promote bushier growth. Coleus ranges in height from eight inches to two feet. It will also do well in a sunny location provided it is given ample water and the temperature stays below 90°F.

*Cosmos bipinnatus* (half-hardy annual). This is a native of Mexico that bears lovely daisy-like flowers in shades of white, pink, and deep rose measuring three or four inches across. The plants reach three to four feet in height and need staking, but this presents little problem since the stalks are not easily broken in the wind. The foliage itself is finely cut and fern-like. They need full sun but will tolerate dry conditions.

*Cosmos sulphureus* (half-hardy annual). A close relation of *C. bipinnatus*, *C. sulphureus* has lovely golden-yellow, orange, and red flowers on two-foot plants. These plants look best when several are planted close together.

*Dianthus* (hardy annual). Annual carnations, Chinese, and Indian pinks are all members of the genus *Dianthus*. The flowers are quite fragrant with a wonderful spicy clove scent. They range in height from six inches to eighteen inches and come in shades of white, pink, and red. The annual carnation is best purchased as a prestarted plant since they take five months to come into flower. *Dianthus* prefers a neutral or alkaline soil and a sunny location.

*Dianthus barbatus* (hardy biennial). Also called sweet William, this is a favorite showy garden flower that blooms profusely in May and June. It can range in height from six inches to two feet. Sow seeds in June for blooms the following season or buy prestarted plants. It often reseeds itself.

*Digitalis* (hardy biennial, annual). Known as foxglove, this is a graceful vertical that grows three to six feet tall and bears delicate white, cream, rose, yellow, lavender, and red flowers. The shorter varieties will be suitable for container culture if properly staked to prevent breakage. This plant is not a good choice for windy situations. Recently, plant breeders have developed an annual strain named Foxy that will flower five months from seed. If they are sown in January, you will have blooms by June. Foxgloves are among the few plants that flower well in shady situations.

*Fuchsia* (tender perennial treated as a tender annual or biennial). This is grown for its beautiful pendulous flowers that resemble earrings. They range in color from white, pink, and purple with many bicolors. Tolerant of partial shade and easily grown in hanging baskets, these plants will appreciate a less windy corner of your garden.

*Gazania* (half-hardy perennial treated as a half-hardy annual in northern areas). This is an ideal plant for hot, dry city summers when temperatures soar in the 80s and 90s. The daisy-like blossoms—which can be up to four inches across—come in a variety of colors, that range from yellow through bronze and pink. Many display a dark zone around a yellow center which is itself ringed by a band of yet another color. Others have a truly spectacular contrasting colored stripe that runs down the center of each daisy-like petal. Gazanias need plenty of sun and thrive best in a sandy soil. Since their blossoms close at night or on cloudy days, they cannot be cut for bouquets.

*Impatiens* (half-hardy annual). Also known as Patient Lucy, this is a delightfully bright and cheerful addition to the shady or partially shady garden. Lovely one- to two-inch blooms cover mound-like, neat-looking plants all summer long. The plant is of a spreading habit, only growing six to fifteen inches tall and ten to twenty-four inches across. They are ideal subjects for hanging baskets as well as containers and window boxes. The flowers are in shades of pink, red, white, and orange with many bicolors. The plants may be started from seed or may be purchased as prestarts at garden centers. They do well in a rich, light soil that is kept evenly moist.

*Ipomoea* (half-hardy annual). This morning glory is a lovely vining plant that will rapidly cover a wall or climb a trellis. It is so named for its white, purple, pink, or blue trumpet flowers that can measure up to six inches across, and that open at dawn and fade by midmorning. They will last a little longer if they are not located in direct sun. Morning glories can grow up to ten feet in two months' time, making them a good choice to cover an unsightly structure or view. Give them direct sun for at least half the day and a light soil that is not too fertile or moist.

*Kochia* (half-hardy annual). This plant has been given the common name of burning bush because in the fall its leaves turn bright red. It is grown for its foliage only and will form a mound two to three feet tall, making it an excellent temporary hedge or background plant. They thrive in hot conditions, prefer plenty of sun, and will tolerate windy locations well. This plant is a real performer in the heat; while other plants stop growing, this one takes off. *Kochia* can become a nuisance because it easily reproduces itself.

*Lantana* (tender perennial grown as a half-hardy annual). This is a lovely plant for southern gardens. In northern regions plants may be treated as annuals and if given plenty of sun, wintered over as a house plant. The dwarf trailing varieties make wonderful displays in hanging baskets. The globular clusters of tiny flowers come in shades of pink, orange, yellow, white, and bicolored. Give this plant a rich soil that is allowed to dry out between watering. The plant is difficult to grow from seed.

*Lobelia* (half-hardy annual). This is a wonderful compact little plant that is covered in a cloud of dark blue or pink flowers. It's a wonderful subject for hanging baskets as well as containers and makes a fine backdrop for other plants. It should be started from seed six to eight weeks before the frost for earlier blooms, or they may be purchased as prestarts. This plant is at its best in partial shade although it will tolerate full sun if the temperature does not get too hot.

*Lobularia* (perennial but treated as a hardy annual). This is also called sweet alyssum or sweet Alison and is one of the most popular flowering annuals. Its dainty clusters of white, clear pink, and deep lavender flowers give off a pleasant, honey-like fragrance. Most varieties grow to be only three or four inches tall, but some hybrids may reach ten inches. They are easy to transplant, prosper in almost any soil, and happiest in full sun. Although in hot situations it will tolerate partial shade, *Lobularia* is at its best during the cool days of spring and will usually stop flowering in the heat of summer. Cut back the foliage and blooms will appear again in the fall.

*Lunaria* (hardy biennial). This plant is grown chiefly for its round, paper-thin, translucent seed pods that are used in dried flower arrangements, but the plant also has lovely purple flowers that adorn it in May and June. It reaches a height of two and one-half feet and does best in partial shade. It has a penchant for reseeding itself easily in the garden. Plant seeds in June for blooms the following year.

*Myosotis* (half-hardy perennial). The forget-me-not is a lovely blue springtime flower for shade and partial shade. The plants reach a height of nine to twelve inches and do well in almost any soil. There are also pink and white cultivars. Myosotis has similar cultural requirements to the pansy. The seeds are planted in late summer for blooms the following spring. It is not reliably hardy north of zone 7 and needs the protection of a cold frame. Forget-me-nots reseed themselves easily.

*Nicotiana* (tender perennial treated as a half-hardy annual). Flowering tobacco is a pleasant plant, neat in habit, and bearing lovely star-shaped blossoms that are held above the foliage and produce a heavy fragrance especially noticeable in the evening. The flowers range in color from white, red, pink, and chartreuse. The plants reach twelve inches to two and one-half feet in height in partial sun or shady situations including northern exposures.

*Oenothera* (hardy biennial). This is also known as sundrops or evening primrose and is mostly noted for its sweetly scented cupped flowers. The flowers open in the evening, perfuming the air and remaining open through the following day. The plants grow to be twelve to eighteen inches tall and are offered in shades of white and yellow. It does well in full sun or partial shade.

*Pelargonium* (tender perennial treated as a half-hardy annual). This is the proper name for the geranium. These plants will grow almost anywhere under a wide range of conditions, including full sun and partial shade, and since they tolerate dryness well, they are good subjects for containers. There are many kinds available for the home gardener, including the upright zonal geranium, the trailing ivy-leaf geranium, which is a good subject for hanging baskets, and the scented geraniums, which are discussed in the chapter on herbs. Martha Washington geraniums do not make good summer garden subjects since they need a temperature below 60°F. to bud, but may make good subjects for a winter garden in milder areas. Geraniums are found in shades of white, pink, and red, with many bicolors. A new yellow variety has been bred that should be available in a few years. Although they can grow to a height of six feet in zones 9 and 10, in most gardens geraniums will grow about one to two feet. They can be raised from seed if started early enough (they need five months from seed to flower), but most gardeners prefer to buy prestarted plants.

*Petunia* (tender perennial treated as a half-hardy annual). This is a classic summer flower that is indispensable in the garden. Its wide trumpet-shaped blooms come in a variety of colors including white, red, blue, violet, pink, yellow, and bicolored. It may be single, double, fringed, or ruffled. The eighteen-inch plants are broken down into two main categories: grandifloras and multifloras. Grandifloras have blooms that can measure from three to five inches across, while multifloras are smaller (two to three inches) but produce many more blooms. Petunias are equally at home in containers and hanging baskets, and are some of the most prolific of garden plants if the faded blooms are continuously removed. They need at least half a day of direct sun, good soil, and adequate moisture to do well. Be sure to pinch out the plants to promote bushy growth and prune back the stems to prevent legginess, otherwise they thrive on neglect.

*Phlox Drummondii* (hardy annual). Also called annual phlox, this is a lovely floriferous plant that grows six to eighteen inches high, and is completely covered in blue, pink, red, yellow, white, or bicolored flowers from July on. It is a good plant to use in hot locations in full sun or partial shade. It prefers a good, rich soil with adequate moisture. Annual phlox makes a good subject for a hanging basket and has a nice fragrance. To promote continuous flowering, cut back to the ground after the first bloom.

*Salvia splendens* (tender perennial grown as a half-hardy annual). Scarlet sage is noted for its red tubular flowers that are borne along a spike. The plants range in height from six inches to two and one-half feet and are also available in shades of white, pink, and purple. Give it good soil, full sun for half a day, and let the soil dry out a little between waterings.

*Tagetes* (half-hardy annual). This is better known as marigold and brings a note of cheeriness to every garden. Its bright flowers produced in shades of yellow, orange, mahogany, and brown are a delight to behold and even more of a delight to the novice gardener, for *Tagetes* is also one of the easiest garden flowers to grow. They are usually divided into three main categories. The Africans are taller generally, growing from eighteen to thirty-six inches, while the French are shorter, from six inches to eighteen inches. African-French hybrids usually range from twelve to eighteen inches. These categories have nothing really to do with origin, since they are all originally from Mexico. There are many cultivars of *Tagetes* to choose from and many different forms they can take. The taller ones are also quite wind resistant. One more important asset worth mentioning: It repels nematodes. All of this and easy to grow, too!

*Venidium* (half-hardy annual). Also called monarch-of-the-veld, this is a bright daisy-like flower, usually with a darker zone around the center. The flowers are usually a bright yellow-orange, but sometimes white, cream, or lemon yellow are available. Since the blossoms close at night and on cloudy days, the spectacular blooms cannot be enjoyed in bouquets. It thrives in hot, dry, sunny situations.

*Verbena* (tender perennial grown as a half-hardy annual). This produces flat clusters of blossoms that measure up to two to three inches across in shades of white, red, blue, pink, and purple. Often the colored flowers will have contrasting white centers. The plants themselves are usually of a low spreading habit, making them ideal for hanging baskets although there are erect forms. Sow the seeds indoors about three months before the last frost is due and move outdoors when the temperature remains above 50°F. Give them a sunny location and pinch out the growing tips to promote bushy growth.

*Viola tricolor* (half-hardy biennial). Also known as the pansy, this is one of the best loved of all garden flowers. The blooms are made up of five petals in shades of cream, yellow, orange, red, mahogany, blue, or lavender usually marked with one or two contrasting colors. The plants themselves grow six to eight inches tall and are best planted in full sun unless the temperature exceeds 90°F., in which case give them partial shade. They also require rich, moist soil. In southern areas violas can be planted in the fall and will flower in the spring. In the north, they can be sown twelve weeks before the last frost and will produce flowers by late spring. If it is not possible to give the seedlings full sun all day, it is best to purchase prestarts.

*Zinnia* (half-hardy annual). This is last, but certainly not least, of the annuals listed here. Another native of Mexico, zinnias are one of the most common annuals found in gardens because they are easy to grow and produce abundant, stunning flowers in a wide variety of colors, some marked with stripes or multicolored. The plants range in height from six inches to three feet. The tallest are not recommended for roof or terrace culture. Zinnias need full sun and grow best when the weather turns really hot. They flower best in average soil, producing too much foliage if overfertilized.

## Bloom Periods
## of Recommended Annuals and Biennials

| NAME | APRIL | MAY | JUNE | JULY | AUGUST | SEPTEMBER | OCTOBER |
|---|---|---|---|---|---|---|---|
| Ageratum | | | | ——— | ——— | — | |
| Antirrhinum | | | ——— | ——— | ——— | — | |
| Begonia | ——— | ——— | ——— | ——— | ——— | ——— | — |
| Browallia | | | ——— | ——— | — | | |
| Callistephus | | | | | | ——— | — |
| Campanula | | | ——— | ——— | — | | |
| Capsicum | | | | ——— | ——— | ——— | — |
| Centaurea | ——— | ——— | ——— | ——— | ——— | ——— | — |
| Cleome | | | ——— | ——— | ——— | — | |
| Coleus | ——— | ——— | ——— | ——— | ——— | ——— | — |
| Cosmos | | —Short varieties—tall varieties—— | | | | | |
| Dianthus (annual) | ——— | —depends on variety—— | | | | | |
| Dianthus (biennial) | | ——— | — | | | | |
| Digitalis | | | ——— | ——— | — | | |
| Fuchsia | | | ——— | ——— | ——— | ——— | — |
| Gazania | | | | ——— | — | | |
| Impatiens | | | ——— | ——— | ——— | ——— | — |
| Ipomoea | | | ——— | ——— | ——— | ——— | — |
| Kochia | ——— | ——— | ——— | ——— | ——— | ——— | — |
| Lantana | | | ——— | ——— | ——— | ——— | — |
| Lobelia | | | ——— | ——— | ——— | ——— | — |
| Lobularia | ——— | — | | | | ——— | — |
| Lunaria | | —flowers— | | | —— | seed pods—— | — |
| Myosotis | ——— | — | | | | | |
| Nicotiana | | | ——— | ——— | ——— | — | |
| Oenothera | | | ——— | ——— | ——— | ——— | — |
| Pelargonium | | —from starts——from seed—— | | | | | |
| Petunia | | | ——— | ——— | ——— | ——— | — |
| Phlox | | | | ——— | ——— | ——— | — |
| Salvia | | | | ——— | ——— | ——— | — |
| Tagetes | | | ——— | ——— | ——— | ——— | — |
| Venidium | | | | | ——— | ——— | — |
| Verbena | | | ——— | ——— | ——— | ——— | — |
| Viola | ——— | ——— | — | | | | |
| Zinnia | | | | ——— | ——— | ——— | — |

Please note: The dates given have been generalized and may include the bloom periods of closely related species. For more exact bloom periods check the seed packet or ask your nurseryman. Shorter varieties will generally bloom first.

# ⁓ 14 ⁓
# Vegetables

FOR MANY PEOPLE, vegetable gardens are as much a memory of childhood as flower gardens. Who doesn't remember the tomato patch that was planted on Memorial Day and produced juicy ripe Big Boys for tomato sandwiches in August? Or neat rows of peas with pod clusters hanging in front of blooming marigolds and nasturtiums? Studies predict that more than 50 percent of all households will have food gardens by the late 1980s. The reason lies not only in rising food prices, but perhaps in a basic need. Since the beginning of time, man gathered nuts and seeds and cultivated them as a way of surviving. The reward of harvesting an abundant vegetable crop makes gardening a fulfilling activity—particularly in crowded, technocratic cities. Perhaps this is why so many people find gardening therapeutic, if not necessary.

Another consideration for growing vegetables in your roof garden concerns design. Vegetables are a distinctly different-looking plant group. Though their flowers and foliages may not be breathtaking, their hanging pods, gourds, and fruits can look quite exotic, especially when mixed with a variety of annuals, perennials, and colorful shrubs. Nothing makes a more lovely border than a row of bright green leaf lettuce. A trellis of pole beans, peas, or cucumbers will give your garden a sense of vertical design, peppers look terrific when surrounded by marigolds. Careful selection and placement of containers can give your garden a unique appearance that visitors will always admire.

Probably the biggest reason people choose not to raise vegetables cen-

Fig. 53    *This pepper plant thrives in a roof garden.*

ters on the extra care they need. But it must be pointed out that *all* plants require a a little daily attention if they are to grow especially well, and the care vegetables need is really no different from flowering plants. Weeding, checking regularly for insects, careful watering, and fertilizing are the main jobs in growing healthy vegetables, and these chores can be taken care of a few minutes each day while simply relaxing in your garden.

The hardest work comes at the beginning of the year when preparing containers and selecting the plants. It is especially important to consider how much soil each plant requires, since crowding will always produce poor crops. Depending on the variety and species, plants will usually require about one and a half gallons of soil to grow in. Some varieties of tomatoes need as much as four gallons per plant, while several Tiny Sweet carrots can be planted in a one-gallon container and spaced only one and one-half to two inches apart.

If you do not buy your potting soil, but take it from a lot, carefully consider the surrounding environment. Vegetables grown in New York City lots have been found to contain concentrations of lead and cadmium *five times* the average amount. Reserve soil from empty lots for flowers and use specially prepared soil for vegetables. Also, be careful to check the pH balance of the soil, because most vegetables (particularly beets and spinach) have a very narrow range of tolerance. The best pH for vegetables is a range between 6.0 and 6.8.

Another condition necessary for vegetables is plenty of sun, at least four to eight hours a day. Flowering plants use the energy from sunlight for drawing nutrients from the soil in order to produce bursting blossoms; vegetables convert this energy into peppers, ears of corn, pumpkins, and turnips. Inadequate sunlight will result in fruitless crops—no matter how diligently watered, fertilized, and weeded. When you plan the arrangement of your garden, consider what areas get the most amount of light. Also, be careful about planting tall plants (such as pole beans, corn, or large varieties of tomatoes) in locations that will shade other plants. Usually, taller plants should be located on the north side of the garden. Trellises ought to be placed in areas that provide shade for patio chairs, not other plants.

In some cases, too much sun can be a problem, but this is easy to remedy. During especially hot periods of weather you may shade tender plants with a sheet of burlap, a deck umbrella, or similar device. Most vegetables grown for their greens, such as leaf lettuce, Swiss chard, mustard and collard greens, need only about four hours of sunlight and should be shaded during hot weather. Root crops such as turnips, carrots, and radishes will also tolerate less than full sunlight.

Most vegetables are well suited for container gardening. Half barrels, tubs, plastic-lined bushel baskets, and buckets are ideal for large plants or a combination of smaller ones. Since the size of the average household has decreased over the last two decades, a demand for smaller-sized vegetables has created new mini-varieties. These midget vegetables are excellent for container cultures, and they mature quickly, producing tender fruits. Mini-varieties of cabbage, carrot, cucumber, eggplant, peas, squash, and tomato grow easily in hanging baskets. The biggest consideration when choosing containers is that the plants have enough soil. Generally, a four-gallon container will grow any plant that is discussed in this chapter. If you aren't sure whether a container is large enough for a particular plant, it is better to have too much soil than not enough. Make sure that the containers have adequate drainage.

When planning your garden, think about which vegetables look attractive as well as how many harvests your growing season will allow and how large a crop you want to produce. Efficient use of space and crop selection are two of the most basic principles in farming, and they deserve careful consideration. April radishes can be replaced by snap beans and tomatoes; early lettuce might be replaced with carrots. In a large container, rows of lettuce, peas, and radishes can be planted between squash since they will be harvested before the squash plants can cause crowding. It takes a bit of calculation to plan a garden that will constantly produce fruits—just as it takes careful planning to have a garden that is in constant bloom. But a skillful vegetable gardener will have crops to harvest from late spring through early winter. Since cities are usually warmer than the surrounding areas—and since buildings tend to retain heat—growing seasons can last almost nine months. Kale, carrots, beets, and turnips can be planted as late as August for fall and early winter crops. Snap beans, broccoli, cabbage, Chinese cabbage, lettuce, mustard, spinach, and peas can be planted in very early spring and harvested throughout the summer. Second and even third plantings are possible in most areas of the country. Keep in mind the hardiness of fall crops as well as the average date of the first killing frost, and use a mulch to protect late fall crops.

Something that is more difficult to determine is how many plants will feed a person, and some trial and error is the only way to be sure. This depends on how much sun the plants get, how diligently you care for them, the quality of the seeds or seedlings, and the quality of the soil. This is a very general list of how many plants should be grown to feed one person:

| | |
|---|---|
| Broccoli | 5 |
| Brussels sprouts | 5 |
| Cabbages | 5–10 |
| Cucumbers | 3–5 foot row |
| Eggplants | 3–5 |
| Peas | 10 foot row |
| Peppers | 4–5 |
| Pole beans | 2 |
| Tomatoes | 3–5 plants |

Of course, the number of plants you decide on should correspond to individual taste—if you only like an occasional tomato, you'll want only a couple plants; if you have a fondness for pickles, you'll want several cucumber vines.

Many vegetables can be started indoors as early as February or March. Leeks, broccoli, brussels sprouts, and cabbage are good candidates. Peas, spinach, scallions, and radishes can be started indoors or out as soon as the soil is easily worked. Transplanting the young seedlings is much the same as transplanting annuals and perennials. Treat the plants tenderly in July and August, transplanting on a damp, drizzly or cloudy day. It's also possible to transplant seedlings in the evening. Some wilting after transplanting is normal, and it is wise to use a pine bark mulch all through the summer to help the soil retain its moisture. The newly transplanted seedlings should be introduced gradually to full sun.

Cool-weather plants can be difficult to replant in the middle of summer, but there are a few tricks to ensure second and third crops. Lettuce seeds can be chilled in the refrigerator for five or six days and then planted indoors to break dormancy. Keep pots in an east window where they will get only the morning sun until sprouts begin to form. Don't cover the seeds, since light helps them germinate.

Cold and rainy weather will sometimes affect the pollination of plants, which means smaller fruit yields. Particularly with tomatoes, poor weather conditions may cause flowers to fall off. There are some good commercial setting hormones available to help "fasten" the flowers. These hormones can be sprayed on the plants when flowers first bloom. If the plants drop many blossoms, they are probably getting too much water or not enough light.

Once you have the plants established out in the garden, you will need to feed them regularly. A once-a-week feeding will not only produce stronger, better-looking plants, but it will help each plant bear its maximum amount of fruit. A water soluble 5–10–10 fertilizer can be used for most plants, while some varieties such as leafy greens require a higher nitrogen solution. It's also important not to overfeed plants, since tomatoes, eggplants, and peppers will produce too much foliage and not enough fruit.

Vegetables require large amounts of fertilizer when they come to fruition, so it is a good idea to top-dress the soil about once a month. This is done simply by adding solid fertilizer to the top layer of soil—near, but not touching the roots—and then mixing it in with the soil. The color of the stems and foliage will quickly tell you if you are over- or underfeeding your plants. For more information on this subject, see Chapter 5.

Next to the thrill of spotting the first immature bean pods, peppers, tomatoes, and lettuce heads, the real satisfaction of vegetable gardening lies in picking ripe fruit that can be washed and served on the dinner table, all in a matter of a few minutes. There is no real secret to harvesting plants other than the sharp eye and sensitive touch that is used for picking fruit at the vegetable stand. Color, firmness, and size are usually the best indicators of ripeness. A few other hints are included in this section on plants.

# The Nightshade Family: Tomatoes, Peppers, Eggplants

The nightshade family is a group of warm-season plants native to America and first cultivated by Mexican Indians long before the Spanish conquest. The family includes such diverse species as potatoes, tobacco, belladonnas, and petunias, and requires plenty of sun and hot weather. Scientifically known as *Solanaceae,* many of these plants grew originally in tropical areas of the Americas.

Tomatoes, peppers, and eggplants make up one of the most popular home gardening trios. Though at first it may seem odd to link them together, all three require similar growing conditions. And as you watch them grow, you will see they all bring fruit from similar blossoms, and take a long period of time—at least two and one-half months—to produce ripe fruit.

# Tomato

There are about as many different varieties of tomatoes as there are tastes. Since tomatoes need plenty of soil, the smaller hybrids are best for container cultures. Not only do they require less space, but they mature more quickly, bearing ripe fruit in about fifty-five days. Basket King was specially developed to grow in hanging baskets, and they produce bushy, sturdy plants that cascade over the sides of the containers. They produce dozens of cherry tomatoes in eight or nine weeks. Pixie and Small Fry are also cherry hybrids that grow to a height of fourteen to eighteen inches. Full-sized tomatoes are produced on larger plants that are categorized as either being *determinate* or *indeterminate.* Varieties that are determinate stop growing when they reach a certain height, usually three to four feet. Indeterminate varieties never stop growing and can reach heights of six feet or more. Determinate types are usually early producers while indeterminate types are usually late fruiters. For container culture, choose only determinate types. The space requirements of indeterminate varieties are too great for container culture.

Tomatoes will continually bear fruit once they reach maturity; they are among the most abundant producers for the amount of space they assume. As soon as the first blossoms appear they should be mulched and top-dressed. The more light they get, the better they will grow, but make sure they are placed in an area that gets at least six to eight hours of full sun a day. Cool and rainy weather will cause the plants to grow sluggishly, so make sure tomatoes are among the last plants you put in your garden. If your growing season is short, make sure you choose early varieties. In some southern areas, midsummer temperatures will be too hot, so you should plant early enough to harvest before the dog days of summer.

When transplanting tomato seedlings, pinch off the lowest leaves and set the root clumps deep into the soil. The pinched-off leaves will come back as roots, helping to establish the plants. Generally, tomatoes like plenty of moisture as long as they are not standing in puddles. As the seedlings develop, watch for suckers, which branch out from the axils of the main stems. These should be pinched off since they "suck" energy from the plant, limiting fruit production.

Most tomato problems are the result of improper watering. Blossom end rot on fruit occurs during drought and shows up after periods of vigorous growth. The first sign is that the blossom-end of the fruit turns black and becomes sunken. Add a little lime to the soil and make sure the plants get plenty of moisture. Cracking of fruit may occur during warm rainy periods, especially if the plants have been dry. It is caused simply by the fruit expanding too quickly. Sunscald will occur if the plants are overpruned. It shows up as bleached areas on the fruit.

None of these problems make the fruit unfit to eat, but they do detract from the physical appearance of the tomatoes. More serious problems are diseases like verticillium or fusarium wilt, which are not treatable. Insects such as hornworms, cutworms, aphids, and whiteflies can also be controlled with sprays or dusts. One thing to remember is that many pests that attack tomato plants will live from year to year in the soil; that's why most tomato growers will never plant crops in the same area two years in a row.

Tomatoes are best when they are vine ripened, picked a day or two before they turn deep red. Be careful not to let them become overripe. Fruit that falls off the plant before it is ready can be set in a window in order to ripen. If you go on vacation while your plants are producing fruit, make sure a friend or neighbor will check on them from time to time. The fruit that ripens while they tend your garden always makes a delicious payment.

# Eggplant

An easier plant to grow than the tomato, eggplant is an unusual vegetable that can be baked, fried, and served with cheeses or as an ingredient in main dishes such as mousaka. The large fruit matures in about one hundred twenty days from seed and should be harvested as soon as the skin looks glossy and slick. Be careful to pick the fruit before the skin loses its gloss, since overripening causes the fruit to become bitter.

Eggplant can be planted indoors in March or April, and set outside when temperatures remain above 55°F. If you don't want to start them from seed, buy six-week-old plants. Allow about two gallons of soil per plant, and set them in the warmest part of the garden. Eggplants send out deep root systems and require lots of feeding. Good varieties for container cultures include Black Beauty and Morden Midget. One plant will bear about eight fruits.

# Pepper

There are more than fifteen different varieties of peppers, ranging from popular Sweet Bells to hot jalapeños and little Cherry Sweets, which are ideal for drying or pickling. Both hot and sweet varieties are easy to grow in containers.

Peppers are a little fidgety about weather conditions and grow best when temperatures are between 70° and 75°F. The biggest problem with temperatures above or below this range is blossom drop, which means the pepper flowers fall off the plant without becoming fertilized. Night temperatures below 60°F. and day temperatures above 90°F. almost always cause blossom drop, so pay attention to forecasts and bring plants in during these weather conditions.

Peppers are a very slow-growing plant. Seeds should be sown in early February. They can be started in two-inch containers, but will require two gallons of soil when they mature. Like tomatoes, they need to be staked in windy environments.

Most of the common market varieties like the Canapé or Lady Bell mature to a deep red (though they are usually solid green at the market). This longer ripening makes the fruit sweeter, not hotter. The hot varieties like Portugal or Hungarian Wax mature more quickly and are especially ornamental in a garden.

## Legumes (Peas and Beans)

The vegetable group *legumes* gets its name from its clusters of fruit that gather in pods. Snap beans, lima beans, pole beans, and peas fall into this category. Many members of this group develop nodules along their roots that house nitrogen-fixing bacteria, increasing soil fertility. Because of this, nitrogen fertilizers are rarely needed. Legumes also make a good choice to follow other vegetables such as lettuce or broccoli that deplete the nitrogen present in the soil. Peas make a good early-season choice to be followed by tomatoes, which are notoriously heavy feeders. The nitrogen-fixing ability of these plants can be increased with inoculates that are sold at most garden centers. Be sure to choose the right inoculate for the specific plant you are growing. Once harvesting is complete, the roots should be left in the soil so the full benefits may be derived.

### Peas

Pea plants range in height from fifteen inches for bush varieties, to well over three feet for pole varieties. The plants are somewhat bushy with lots of foliage, and the pods hang vertically in rows of vine-like stems. Peas generally come in early varieties (which mature in about seventy days), or sweet varieties. The sweet varieties with edible pods—such as snow peas or sugar snaps—can be harvested as soon as the bulge of the developing peas can be seen through the pod. If the pods are allowed to ripen fully, the peas can be shelled like regular peas for the incredibly sweet fruit inside. Thus edible pod peas have the longest harvest and are in fact the best choice for limited space.

Peas should be planted outdoors as soon as the soil can be worked. In New York City, St. Patrick's Day is an excellent time to sow your seeds. Snap peas generally prefer warmer growing conditions and will not produce a crop as early as other garden peas. Once harvested they can be followed by fall vegetables. Allow about one quart of soil for the small varieties, and about a half gallon of soil for the larger vine types. (A six-inch-deep container is ideal for a single plant.) The sweetest varieties of peas sprout from wrinkled seeds, but the most frost resistant plants are grown from smooth seeds. Since peas are a cool weather crop, climates with short springs and hot summers are not good for peas and may result in crop failure. If you have a window box or a fairly large container, you can plant a row of peas. The taller varieties will climb on a small trellis.

Pick regular peas in the morning when the pods are a bright green and well filled and place them in the refrigerator to keep them sweet. If the pods turn yellow, the peas will contain large amounts of starch.

## Beans

Beans need to be planted after all danger of frost is past. Most beans, especially wax and green beans, will tolerate even poor growing conditions and yield a good crop, making them very suitable for container culture. Bush beans can be harvested fifty to sixty days after planting, and will continue to produce for ten to twenty days. The first planting of either prestarted seedlings or seeds should be made about the second week in May and followed at two-week intervals with further plantings until early July. This will keep you in fresh beans all summer. Pole beans will need to grow on a trellis or fence and are the most abundant producers of the legume family. They will not need to be replanted to keep the harvest going and will need about two gallons of soil per plant. Lima beans enjoy warm temperatures and come in both bush and pole varieties. Give them plenty of room since they resent crowding and will not produce well under such conditions.

Feed young plants with a 5–10–10 formula, but do not overfeed since this tends to produce lots of foliage but reduces yield. Pole beans, which bear all season, will need a richer soil and supplemental feedings from time to time.

## *Vegetable Greens*

Vegetable greens like lettuce, Swiss chard, spinach, and kale are easy to grow and take up less space than most other vegetables. They are also abundant producers, which is a prime consideration for container gardens. Most varieties of greens raised in your home garden will be far superior to those available in markets, since many types of lettuce and other greens simply do not ship well.

Greens are generally cool weather crops, which means they should be planted about the same time as peas in both spring and fall. If you have a shady area of the garden, some will do well in summer. Because these plants have shallow root systems, they can be placed fairly close together and have minimum soil requirements. Most will need plenty of nitrogen, as well as large amounts of water. One of the nicest qualities about greens is their appearance—their foliage is decorative.

# Lettuce

There are four different types of lettuce: head, loosehead, leaf, and romaine. Most head varieties—such as iceberg or great lakes—are tough and especially crisp, which make them popular market varieties because they withstand shipping. Loosehead and leaf varieties are more popular for home gardens because of their better flavor. Some of the best varieties for container cultures include Tom Thumb (which produces tennis-ball-sized heads and is served whole as an individual salad), Red Salad Bowl and Black Seeded Simpson (these are leaf varieties, which not only make appetizing salads but attractive garden borders), buttercrunch and Bibb (which form delicate, leafy rose-shaped heads).

Seeds can be sown indoors in March or they can be planted outdoors about two weeks before the last frost. A flat of soil is ideal for starting seedlings, which can be transplanted into soil rich in humus when they are two or three inches tall. Since the root system of lettuce is so shallow, it's a good idea to side dress plants with fertilizer occasionally. The leaves of loose head and leaf varieties can be picked as soon as they are big enough to be used in a salad. If you snap off a few outside leaves as needed, the plants last longer and harvesting will be prolonged. This means you can have a good deal of lettuce from just a few plants. If you use individual pots for plants, make sure they are between six and eight inches deep. Moisture is the most important requirement for all greens, so water often. You can easily tell when plants need water because their leaves will begin to droop.

You can buy prestarted lettuce from a garden center, which will save time and produce an earlier crop. Once your spring crop has been harvested, pull up the old plants and use the containers to plant beans. A second crop of lettuce can be sown in late July or early August. Lettuce that is allowed to grow past its prime will taste bitter and become dull-looking, and when broken oozes a milk-like sap. The plants will eventually elongate and form tiny clusters of flowers.

# Mustard Greens and Swiss Chard

These two greens are essential to the art of salad making, as well as for garnishes and additions on sandwiches. Both have beautiful foliage.

Though mustard is usually thought of as a boiled green, the young raw leaves make a tasty complement to lettuce. The plants will grow in partial shade and are tolerant of some frost, which means they can be grown in the winter in mild parts of the country. Mustard tastes best during the period when plants are growing rapidly, about thirty to thirty-five days old.

Swiss chard is one green that thrives on summer heat. A type of bulbless beet, chard is an excellent substitute for spinach during hot months.

The leaves can be steamed and served as a hot vegetable or cold in salads. If the leaves are harvested above the stems, chard will produce greens throughout the summer. The whole plant can be harvested, with the stems cooked like asparagus. Chard needs plenty of water, and will survive in both full and partial sun.

## Spinach, Collards, Kale, Beet and Turnip Greens

All these types of greens can be served raw in salads, but are more commonly boiled or steamed and served with cheeses or a touch of vinegar. They can also be used in casseroles. All but turnips are cool weather crops and should be planted successively during the months from March through early May. They can be replanted for fall crops late in July.

Good spinach varieties for containers are America and Melody hybrid. The outer leaves can be harvested about forty days after planting, and each plant needs only a six-inch-deep container. Spinach requires the same care as most head lettuce varieties.

Collards taste like a mild cabbage and are grown all over the south. But it is interesting to know that collards prefer cooler climates; in fact they taste better after a touch of frost. Leaves should be harvested while tender. Collards grow from a single strong stem with bunches of leaves spreading out from the center.

Kale is a cool weather plant and can usually be grown throughout the winter. Pick the leaves after a couple of hard frosts in the fall, and harvest until first snow. The leaves will be especially sweet and tender. Many kale plants will survive outdoors through the very cold months and produce new leaves the following spring.

Turnip and beet greens are much like spinach. Check seed catalogs for varieties that produce especially nice greens.

## *The Cucurbit Family*

The cucurbit family includes squash, melon, and cucumber. They produce some of the oddest shaped fruit, as well as some of the largest and most ornamental. Most plants in the cucurbit family grow as vines, though there are some varieties such as zucchini that are bush-like. Since these plants produce such large pieces of fruit, they take the longest to mature and need long, hot growing seasons. They also tend to take up larger amounts of space, so you'll want to select plants wisely.

Generally, cucurbits are finicky about soil content, and need a pH of 6 or higher. They like applications of organic matter including manure and compost, and a black plastic mulch will generally help them to stay warm during cool stretches of weather, as well as keep the soil moist.

Seeds should be planted indoors about four weeks before the last frost. Seeds won't germinate if temperatures during the day are below 70°F., so put the pots in a warm room of your house. Three or four seeds can be planted per pot. After the young sprouts appear, grow them under lights or move them to a window that gets full sun. Once the plants reach their mature size, they will produce an abundance of male and female flowers. The female flowers have small ovaries at their base that are shaped like miniature fruits. Since fruit is only produced from the female blossoms, try to choose hybrids that produce large amounts of female flowers. (Naturally, cucurbits produce flowers in a ratio of 20 males to 1 female!)

Cucumber beetles, aphids, squash bugs, and squash vine borers are the most common insects that attack cucurbits. These pests can be controlled with insecticides, but since cucurbits require crosspollination for proper fruit set, sprays should not be used when bees are at work. Another essential because of the crosspollination requirement: Plant at least two plants of each variety of cucumber, muskmelon, summer squash, or whatever other cucurbits you choose.

# Cucumber

Most cucumbers mature sixty to seventy days after they are planted. Most hybrids and all standard varieties produce both male and female flowers, which means crosspollination will occur fairly easily. Some of the all-female plants that produce very heavy yields will need to be planted with a pollinator (male and female producing plants), so make sure you check your seed catalog or garden center before planting. The all-female hybrids require extra attention because they produce so much fruit. Cucumbers are 90 percent water, so they need large amounts of moisture in order to develop properly. Vine types are easily trained on a trellis or fence. They stay healthier this way because they get better air circulation, and they are less prone to disease. If you plan to trellis the plants, prune the first lateral shoots that appear at the leaf axils. This will encourage vegetative growth, which is necessary to shade the fruit from too much sun. Plants that don't develop enough vegetation are subject to bleaching, which causes the fruit to be bitter.

A one half whiskey barrel or ten-gallon container will support two large cucumber vines. A five-gallon container will be large enough for up to two bush varieties. Be careful to keep ripening fruit up off the ground (otherwise it will rot), and pick cucumbers before they become soft. Harvesting fruit that is barely ripe will keep the vines producing for several weeks.

There are some good varieties for containers that grow as bushes rather than vines. Spacemaster is excellent as a hanging plant and will produce high yields. Its trails hang down about a foot or two out of the pot. Bush Champion is also very good for growing in a container.

# Squash

Zucchini, Acorn, Butternut, and Golden Nugget are all varieties of summer and winter squash. Summer squashes are eaten before they are fully mature. Winter squashes are left on the vine to develop a hard rind, allowing them to be stored. Burpee has developed three types of squash that are excellent for container gardens. One is Butterbush, a butternut type summer squash that can be planted in a half whiskey barrel, producing four to five fruits per plant. Each fruit serves two people, and can be stored for winter meals. For trellising, Burpee's Butterboy hybrid is a smaller vining squash that produces lots of large-sized fruit. These plants are heavy feeders but will bear all season long. Richgreen hybrid zucchini is an excellent summer squash that needs a deep container but will produce extraordinary amounts of fruit throughout the summer. Golden Nugget and Gold Rush are also good varieties of zucchini for roof and terrace gardens.

Winter squashes such as Acorn or Table Queen should be carefully stored in a dry, warm area. Be careful not to bruise the skins since this will cause the fruit to rot. Check the fruit every week and throw out or use any that have begun to decay. Once the rinds have fully toughened, squash can be stored in a cool, dry area for several weeks.

# Melons

Watermelons and muskmelons—which include different varieties of cantaloupes—need several weeks of warm weather in order to develop sugars in their fruit. Melons raised in cool, rainy climates simply will not taste very good. There are a few early, short-seasoned melons that can be grown well in the north—honey dew and Persian are the best choices. For other areas of the country, container gardeners do best sticking to small melon varieties such as Sugar Bush watermelons, which produce two to four oval melons weighing about eight pounds each and can be grown in a whiskey barrel.

Plant seeds indoors several weeks before the last frost, and when you set them out in the garden use a plastic mulch to keep the soil warm and moist. Melons are ripe when they detach from the vine easily. Vines can be trained on a trellis if the fruits are carefully supported so that they won't fall off the vine. A mesh bag (such as ones that onions come in at the store) can be tied around the fruit onto the trellis. Trellised fruit avoids bottom rot.

One drawback to growing melons is their susceptibility to virus diseases, which can be severe in the north. If a plant is attacked by a virus, the crop will be ruined. Unfortunately, there is no treatment to help melon plants fight these diseases, and affected plants must be destroyed to prevent the spread of the disease.

# *Asparagus and Rhubarb*

These two plants are perennials and can be harvested year after year once they are established. Asparagus is an old vegetable that has been grown in the United States for more than three hundred years. Its chief drawback for roof and terrace gardens is the space it needs—asparagus plants grow feathery stalks up to five feet long. This can make it a striking addition to a medium-sized or larger garden.

Requiring two years to become established, most asparagus can be planted from a root crown. Use a large container, at least twenty-four inches deep, since this is a deep-rooted plant. Fill the container with about nine inches of soil, laying the crown on top with the buds pointing up. Most asparagus will do well in a soil rich in humus, with a pH between 6.0 and 6.8. Cover the crown with soil—a layer one to two inches thick is good—and then once the plant grows to be about a foot tall, add layers of additional soil. By midsummer the soil line should be about two inches below the rim of the container.

Asparagus can be harvested *after* the second year of growth and will produce crops for up to fifteen years. This makes it a plant well worth the initial trouble. Give asparagus periodic treatments with a 10–10–10 fertilizer (at least two treatments a year if the soil is not particularly rich). When you begin cutting asparagus spears, be careful to limit it to a three-to-four-week period during the first year of harvesting, and don't remove more than a quarter of the emerging spears. After that, spears can be harvested freely, but don't remove more than half the spears in any given year. Spears emerge in the middle of June and should be cut about an inch beneath the soil's surface. Don't let the spears develop leaves or they will be too tough to eat—harvest as soon as the spears form little buds.

Rhubarb thrives best in cooler climates and takes up as much space as you allow. Raised for its stalks, rhubarb is a favorite in pies and preserves. The leaves of rhubarb are poisonous and must never be eaten.

MacDonald, Ruby, and Valentine are the most popular varieties and are easily accommodated in a half whiskey barrel. Rhubarb is the heaviest feeder in the garden and also likes large amounts of water, but the plant will grow for five to ten years producing nice crops before it needs to be divided. Use a soil rich in organic matter and about a half pound of 5–10–5 fertilizer worked into the upper layers of soil. Remove seed stalks as soon as they form, or the plant will not produce good leaf stalks for harvesting. The plant can be harvested after its second year of growth by pulling or twisting stalks near the base. Don't pull more than two thirds of the plant's stalks at any given time. Remove the leaves and wash the stalks well before cooking.

# *Edible Roots*

Onions, shallots, radishes, and carrots are all hardy root crops that can be raised in containers. Most of these plants are easy to care for, can be planted in the spring, and left in the garden until late fall. One of the best ways to raise a variety of roots in a container garden is to use a large wooden box with a mixture of plants.

Onions grow best in cool climates with plenty of water, though they do need a spell of hot, dry weather in order to ripen. Seeds may be started indoors during January, moved to the garden in late March, where they will bulb during the long daylight hours of June and July. When leaves begin to weaken and fall over, its a sign that onions are ready to harvest. Onions can be stored easily if they are allowed to stand a week in the shade after harvesting. This allows the bulbs to dry thoroughly, preventing rotting.

Shallots are a member of the onion family and especially good for growing in pots. One bulb can be planted in a six-inch pot, making a decorative plant. They need full sun and a sweet soil with humus or peat. A single bulb will produce eight to fifteen bulbs for harvest.

Radishes are probably the fastest vegetable crop and can be planted outdoors as soon as the soil thaws. They will mature in just twenty to forty days and can be stored in your refrigerator for up to one month after harvesting. Since they take up little space and time, they can be planted two or three times in a season.

A window box is an excellent container for radishes, allowing you to plant two or three varieties with different maturing times. Plant seeds one inch apart in a rich, well-aerated soil, about a half inch below the surface layer. When the second set of leaves appears, mulch the plants to keep them cool and moist. This helps them grow quickly, which is the secret to producing good tasting and finely textured crops. If foliage looks yellow, feed with a nitrogen fertilizer. Radishes do not thrive in hot weather, so in climates with warm summers they should be grown in the spring or early fall. Good varieties for eight-inch pots include Cherry Belle, Scarlet Globe, White Icicle, and Champion.

Beets and carrots are fun vegetables to grow, especially for households with children. Both produce attractive foliage, and with beets the greens can be boiled or steamed, and eaten the same way as spinach. Both vegetables need a soil low in acid and should be planted in containers that are 14 inches deep. If the soil is too acidic, add lime (a good pH for both is 6.5). Mix a solid fertilizer into the top four inches of soil before planting, and space the seeds about sixteen inches apart. Beet seeds need to be placed about one inch below the surface; carrots about a half inch. Since it takes both plants a while to germinate, beets and carrots are often planted with radishes. The radishes won't crowd either plant since they're harvested so quickly.

Carrots do not like long periods of cool weather, especially when the plants are very young. Extended periods of temperatures below 50°F. will cause them to produce seed stalks, resulting in bitter tasting crops. If temperatures remain cool for longer than a week, they will need to be brought indoors until the days warm up.

Beets can be harvested as soon as the roots are large enough to eat. If the beet greens have matured enough to pick, the roots are also ready. Carrots can be harvested the same way, or when they are smaller, "finger-sized." A good way to judge the root size is by the size of the plant's foliage—when the plants look fairly mature, the roots are too. Varieties of carrots include Nantes, Superstar, Short n' Sweet, and Cored Chantenay; beets suited for home gardens are Early Wonder and Detroit Dark Red.

# How to Calculate the Last Safe Planting Date

Because space is so limited when gardening in containers, you have to make it count. One way of course is succession planting. In order to achieve the end result you have to know how to calculate planting your seeds or starts so as not to get caught by a frost before you have had a chance to enjoy the fruits of your labor. First add together the number of days a seed takes to germinate with its number of days to maturity. If a seed takes seven days to germinate and sixty-five days to mature, we get a total of seventy-two days. The maturity date of some plants, though, are only given from the time of transplanting. For these add another twenty-one days to the figure. Our seventy-two days now becomes ninety-three days. If the plant in question is frost tender, then we add another fourteen days onto this figure, which then becomes 107 days. Our seeds must be planted 107 days before the average first frost date in order to ensure that we will receive a crop. If the average first frost was November 15, then our seeds would have to be planted by July 1st.

## Succession Planting Schedule

| PLANT | MARCH | APRIL | MAY | JUNE | JULY | AUGUST | SEPTEMBER | OCTOBER | NOVEMBER |
|---|---|---|---|---|---|---|---|---|---|
| Bean, bush | | | —— | —— | | | | | |
| Bean, pole | | | —— | —— | —— | —— | | | |
| Bean, lima | | | —— | —— | —— | —— | | | |
| Bean, fava | —— | —— | —— | —— | —— | | | | |
| Cabbage | —— | —— | —— | —— | | —— | —— | —— | |
| Chinese cabbage | —— | —— | —— | —— | | —— | —— | —— | |
| Carrots | | —— | —— | —— | | —— | —— | —— | —— |
| Collards | —— | —— | —— | —— | | —— | —— | —— | —— |
| Cucumber | | | —— | —— | —— | —— | | | |
| Eggplant | | | —— | —— | —— | —— | | | |
| Endive | —— | —— | —— | —— | | —— | —— | —— | |
| Kale | —— | —— | —— | —— | | —— | —— | —— | —— |
| Leek | —— | —— | —— | —— | —— | —— | —— | —— | —— |
| Lettuce | —— | —— | —— | —— | | —— | —— | —— | |
| Muskmelon | | | —— | —— | —— | —— | | | |
| Mustard | —— | —— | —— | —— | | —— | —— | | |
| Onion | —— | —— | —— | —— | —— | | | | |
| Peas | —— | —— | —— | | | | | | |
| Pepper | | | —— | —— | —— | —— | —— | | |
| Radish | —— | —— | —— | | | —— | —— | | |
| Shallot | —— | —— | —— | —— | —— | —— | —— | —— | —— |
| Spinach | —— | —— | —— | | | | —— | —— | |
| Squash, summer | | | —— | —— | —— | —— | —— | | |
| Squash, winter | | | —— | —— | —— | —— | —— | | |
| Swiss chard | | —— | —— | —— | —— | —— | —— | | |
| Tomato | | | —— | —— | —— | —— | —— | | |
| Turnip | | | | —— | —— | —— | —— | —— | —— |
| Watermelon | | | —— | —— | —— | —— | | | |

## Approximate Planting Dates of Vegetables

Plant out 2 to 4 weeks before the last frost:

| | | |
|---|---|---|
| Cabbage | Kale | Peas |
| Carrot | Leek | Radish |
| Chinese cabbage | Lettuce | Spinach |
| Collard | Mustard | |
| Endive | Onion | |

Plant out after the frost-free date:

| | |
|---|---|
| Beans | Pepper |
| Cucumber | Squash |
| Eggplant | Tomato |
| Muskmelon | Watermelon |
| New Zealand spinach | |

Plant out mid-July and continue up until 8 weeks before the first freeze:

| | |
|---|---|
| Cabbage | Leek |
| Carrot | Lettuce |
| Chinese cabbage | Mustard |
| Collard | Radish |
| Endive | Turnip |
| Kale | |

## Minimum Container Size and Plant Spacing

| PLANT | SPACING BETWEEN PLANTS (IN INCHES) | MINIMUM DEPTH OF CONTAINER (IN INCHES) | VOLUME OF SOIL PER PLANT (IN GALLONS) | NUMBER OF PLANTS PER CONTAINER |
|---|---|---|---|---|
| Bean, bush | 6 | 12 | 1 | 18 per ½ whiskey barrel |
| Bean, pole | 4–6 | 12 | 1–2 | 12 per ½ whiskey barrel |
| Cabbage (miniature) | 12–15 | 8 | 1–2 | 1 per 8″ pot |
| Cabbage (full size) | 18 | 12 | 3 | 1 per 12″ pot |
| Canteloupe (bush) | 24 | 12 | 5 | 1 to 2 per ½ whiskey barrel |
| Carrot (short varieties) | 2–3 | 10–12 | ¼ | 25 thinned to 16 per 12″ pot |
| Chinese cabbage (bok choi) | 6–8 | 8 | ½–¾ | 1 per 8″ pot |
| Collard | 12–14 | 6–8 | ½ | 1 per 8″ pot |
| Cucumber (bush) | 6–8 | 12 | 3 | 3 per half whiskey barrel |
| Eggplant | 18 | 12 | 3 | 1 per 12″ pot |
| Endive | 8 | 6 | ½ | 1 per 8″ pot |
| Kale | 12 | 12 | 3 | 1 per 12″ pot |
| Leek | 6 | 12 | ¼ | 4 per 12″ container |
| Lettuce (small) | 4 | 6 | ¼ | 4 per 12″ pot |
| Lettuce, leaf (full size) | 6 | 6 | ¼–½ | 1 per 8″ pot |
| Mustard green | 4 | 6 | ¼ | 2 per 8″ pot |

| | | | | |
|---|---|---|---|---|
| Onion | 1–4 | 8 | ¼ | 80 thinned to 16 per 12-inch pot |
| Peas | 2–4 | 8 | ½–1 | 10 per 12" pot |
| Pepper (small) | 6–8 | 8 | ½ | 1 per 8" pot |
| pepper (full size) | 18 | 12 | 3 | 1 per 12" pot |
| radish | 2–3 | 6 | ⅛ | 12 per 8" pot |
| Shallot | 4 | 8 | ½ | 9 thinned to 4 per 12" pot |
| Spinach | 3–6 | 8 | ¼ | 4 per 12" pot |
| Swiss chard | 4–6 | 6 | 1 | 1–2 per ½ whiskey |
| Squash (bush) | 24 | 12 | 5 | 1 per 8" pot |
| Tomato, (small) | 12–18 | 8–10 | 1–2 | 1 per 12" pot |
| Tomato, (full size) | 18–24 | 12–14 | 3–5 | 1 per ½ whiskey barrel |
| Turnip (root) | 4 | 8 | 1 | 3 per 12" pot |
| Turnip (greens) | 4 | 6 | ¼ | 2 per 8" pot |
| Watermelon (bush) | 24 | 12 | 5 | 1–2 per ½ whiskey barrel |

# ❧ 15 ❧

# Herbs

LESS THAN ONE HUNDRED YEARS AGO, many of the herbs and spices that we now take for granted were considered rare and exotic. Today, herbs still constitute one of the most valuable plant groups.

The word *herb* is derived from the Latin *herba.* Its true definition describes any plant with a nonwoody stem, but when talking about herbs one generally is referring to any plant whose parts or whole is used for flavoring, medicine, fragrance, dyes, or cosmetics. Thus a spice is in fact an herb, yet not all herbs are spices. Spices, unlike herbs, are tropical plants. This in itself though is not the only distinction. When one refers to herbs one is generally referring to the entire plant, which may be used either dry or fresh. When one speaks of a spice, one is referring to only the dried, useful portion of the plant. These distinctions in definition arose during the Middle Ages, when spices had to be dried in order to be transported thousands of miles by ship, caravan, and horseback to Europe.

Traditionally herbs were placed in a separate garden, but today they have found their way into larger landscapes. Many herbs are quite beautiful and right at home in the flower border. Purple leaf basil, tricolor sage, pineapple mint, and English lavender are herbs with exceptionally attractive foliage and flowers. Rosemary and oregano, which are woody-stemmed herbs, can be trained as bonsai or formal standards, or pruned to form low-growing hedges. Low-growing herbs such as thyme, germander, chives, and parsley make wonderful borders for other flowering

Fig. 54    A collection of herbs grown in baskets

plants, and chamomile can be planted as a fragrant carpet beneath trees. For terrace gardens, pots and hanging baskets are excellent for growing herbs. Herbs planted in the open spread quickly and can soon take over a garden, but if they are kept in containers the confinement problem is solved.

Herbs are categorized as perennials and annuals. The tender perennials rosemary, bay, lemon verbena, tarragon, and some of the thymes will need to be brought indoors if they are to survive the winter. Sage, lavender, chives, and mint are hardy and can be left in the garden year-round. Like flowering perennials the hardy herbs do best when mulched in winter and will need to be divided every two to four years.

Annual herbs include anise, the basils, borage, chamomile, chervil, coriander, dill, fennel, marjoram, parsley, and summer savory. They are quick growing and often dried, but their strongest flavors come out when they are picked fresh and used in salads, stews, and main dishes. Annuals, as well as many perennial herbs, can be propagated from cuttings, but are most often started from seed. They are usually sown indoors several weeks before the first frost or planted outside as soon as the ground is workable. The annual herbs generally need two weeks to germinate, the perennials three to four weeks. Generally one or two plants will provide enough foliage for plenty of seasoning.

With few exceptions, most herbs prefer hot, dry conditions, and plenty of sunshine. At least five or six hours of direct sunshine is best. Herbs with long tap roots such as anise, borage, and caraway need to be planted in large containers since they resent any kind of disturbance. Plant three or four seeds together and thin out the sprouts. Be careful not to disturb their roots if you have to transplant them.

One of the most basic considerations for herbs is their need for a well-draining soil. In fact, various thymes, marjorams, and savories can be grown in rock gardens and practically neglected, producing crops for twenty years. However, a well-enriched garden soil will result in more flavorful plants with a longer life expectancy.

Since they don't require frequent feedings, you'll want to be careful about planting them with heavy feeders. Too much fertilizer results in herbs rich in foliage but poor in oils, and as you will see, oils give herbs their fragrance and flavor. The oils in some herbs also repel bugs, which is why they've been used to keep vegetables disease-free and to keep mosquitoes and gnats away from patios. Most herbs should be fed with a 5–10–5 fertilizer once in the spring and once in the summer.

Some herbs will attract aphids or spider mites, and these should be washed off with a hose. Do not use insecticide sprays or dusts on herbs, and do not combine them in containers with plants that are sprayed. Since herbs are raised for use in cooking, it makes sense to keep the leaves free of insect poisons (which are hard to wash off and may find their way onto the dinner table). The best way to control insects is to keep them off nearby plants.

Most herbs can be harvested from the moment seedlings are ready to be thinned. Leaves and stems can be snapped almost continuously as long as you are careful about how much you take from each plant. In fact, as you harvest leaves from new plants, you are actually creating bushier plants. There are even some herbs that should only be harvested when the leaves are young, because the older leaves become too tough to eat. These include sorrel, borage, burnet, and nasturtium. But the majority of herbs are best picked just as their flowers are about to open, when the oils are most heavily concentrated. This ensures that the leaves will be their most aromatic—and aroma might be the single largest contributor to taste.

Always harvest herbs in the morning, just after the dew has dried but before the hot sun begins to dry the plant's oils. You will want to gently wash the leaves and set them to dry on a paper towel. Herbs with grassy foliage, such as dill, should be cut just above the ground in order to preserve the plant's appearance and growth habits. Leaves that are to be used fresh in various dishes can be added directly after picking. Generally, when substituting fresh herbs for dried ones, use two or three times the called for amount: one tablespoon fresh for every half tablespoon dried.

Make sure you keep herbs separate from each other when you pick them and prepare them for storage. Once they have been washed, tie them in bunches and hang them upside down in a breezy hallway or in a kitchen doorway. Make sure they are out of direct sunlight. Herbs usually dry in about two weeks, when they will feel crisp and crumble easily. To test for dryness, place a few leaves in an airtight glass container and let sit for a couple days. If they become moldy or if condensation forms in the glass, the leaves need to be dried longer. Seedheads from dill, celery, caraway, and poppy should also be hung upside down, but with a paper bag tied around the buds to catch the falling seeds. All dried herbs should be stored in airtight glass containers in a cool, dark place. Don't hang a spice rack conveniently above the stove, since heat dries out the oils, causing them to lose their flavor more quickly. Store leaves whole, and crush them just before using in food. If you have a large freezer, herbs such as basil, burnet, fennel, tarragon, chives, dill, and parsley can be placed in plastic bags and frozen fresh. This is a good way to have fresh herbs for use in winter months. When using, do not defrost the leaves, but take them from the freezer and put them in stews, soups, or sauces. (They should not be used as garnishes.) With chives, basil, and fennel, parboil for several seconds before freezing. (This prevents them from getting slimy.)

Another good way to store fresh herbs—and a method for restoring taste to dried herbs—is to pack them in vinegar or oil. Stored for about six weeks and then removed, the herbs give a rich flavor to the vinegar or oil, and can be used separately in many recipes.

There are many uses for herbs outside the kitchen, and after a season or two of experimenting with various plants, the especially ambitious gardener may want to raise plants for home dyes, medicines, perfumes, and incense.

## *Herbs for Dyes*

Natural dyes are generally more subtle and softer than synthetic types, and the colors produced from a single plant can vary greatly from one batch to the next. Most dyes are made from boiling various plants to get a strongly colored liquid. Flowers are the most common plant part used to make dyes, but leaves, stems, and roots can be used to produce a wide variety of colors. Sometimes different parts from the same plant will produce different colors. For instance, barberry stems and roots will make a yellow dye, while the leaves will make a black dye. Colors also depend on the mordant that is used to set the dye in the fabric. Common mordants are alum, acetic acid, ammonia, and potassium dichromate. Depending on the mordant used, colors will turn out completely different. Coreopsis yields a lovely yellow dye when used with alum, but turns brick red when combined with potassium dichromate. Soil conditions, amount of moisture, and light, as well as season, are other factors that determine colors. All this makes dyeing a tricky and complex science.

# Herbs for Medicines

In matters of health, the doctor's office and hospital lab are much more precise and informed about treating various illnesses than almost all home remedies. Nonetheless, the earliest medicines were made from herbs, and many modern medicines still find their origins in plants. For example, the most common medicine to every household is probably aspirin, which can be made from willow bark. Of course, laboratory-manufactured medicines are much stronger and scientifically produced, but there are many herbs that—like foods such as fruit or cereals—can be used naturally and effectively to relieve indigestion, constipation, burns, or diarrhea.

A doctor who is oriented to prescribing natural medicines before chemical ones is a good person to ask about which herbs and plants can be safely ingested and for what ailments. He will tell you that aloe vera is one of the best treatments for burns, which is why this plant is found so frequently in a kitchen window. He will also say that peppermint can be chewed to relieve indigestion, and that garlic juice is a good antiseptic. But make sure you thoroughly investigate which plants to take and how to ingest them, as well as what quantities are safe before making brews or chewing leaves.

# Which Herbs to Grow

The following list includes the most common and useful herbs that are suitable for a container garden, as well as a note about their use in the kitchen.

*Anise.* A deep rooted herb, anise is grown primarily for its seeds, though its leaves are often used in salads. Characterized by its licorice flavor, the seeds give flavor to cookies, cakes, and the Italian favorite, anisette toast. It is an annual that grows eighteen to twenty-four inches tall and produces clusters of yellow flowers that are often dried and used for decorations. Anise seed should be started early indoors since the herb needs a long growing season to produce the prized seeds. It needs full sun and a rich, well-drained soil. It resents transplanting once it is established, so be sure to place it in a large enough container from the beginning.

*Basil.* This is among the oldest herbs, and at one time was considered rare and expensive in most of Europe. There are many kinds of basil that are worth growing and some offer new taste treats worth exploring. Among the many types of basil is sweet basil, the most well-known, as well as bush basil, baby basil, lemon basil, and lettuce leaf basil. All are well suited to container culture. Basil produces especially fragrant leaves that can be used in tomato dishes, with fish and eggs, and in salads. It grows best in full sun or partial shade and a rich but unfertilized soil. It should be pinched back to make a fuller plant. In Italy, this pretty herb is cut into small bouquets, placed in bud vases, and set on the table during meals.

*Bay (Laurus nobilis).* This herb is best started from a nursery plant and placed in bright light with moderate shade during hot weather. Bay is an evergreen shrub that with proper care and good conditions will grow into a medium-sized tree. The soil should be well-drained and the plant should dry out between waterings. Bay is a versatile herb and should be used sparingly in dishes with meat, vegetables, stock, stews. The leaves are quite fragrant and unattractive to insects. The stiff, bright green foliage makes this an especially attractive plant. Bay is quite tender and should be brought inside for the winter. This is a plus since the plant makes an attractive houseplant.

*Bergamot (bee balm).* This plant is a perennial whose leaves have a fragrant lemony flavor used in tea, fruit punch, and fruit soups. Nursery plants are best to use since seedlings can take a long time to start. Bergamot does well in full sun and humus-rich soil that is kept moist. The large, bright red flowers it produces are very aromatic. In the first year, cut the flower heads back before they bloom to strengthen the plant. Prune the plant to the ground in the fall. Bergamot will get quite large—growing to three feet tall.

*Burnet (salad burnet).* This plant has a lingering cucumber-like flavor. It doesn't dry well but will remain green on the plant all winter and can be picked at any time. Burnet is a perennial with round, serrated leaves that grow close to the ground. It is best to pick the center leaves, since the older ones tend to be bitter and tough. Burnet produces unusual and lovely rose-colored flowers that bloom on stems above the foliage. The plant will grow to two feet but cutting back flower stems will make this a good possibility for use as a low border. Burnet is easily grown in full sun and well-drained soil. It will start fast and well from seed.

*Chamomile.* This plant not only will produce a great cup of tea, but the flowers of this evergreen perennial make a lovely border and good ground cover. Chamomile produces masses of small daisy-like flowers. When dried, the petals are removed and the prized center of the flower is used for medicinal and culinary purposes as well as in hair rinse, sachets, and so on. Chamomile can be started from seed or nursery plants. They should be set in full sun or bright shade, in moist soil that has good drainage. The bright flowers will attract bees, and repel unwanted insects. When the plant starts to spread, cut it back to keep its delicate, viny foliage lush and full.

*Catnip.* Though very appealing to cats, catnip should be protected from them until the plant is well established. This perennial produces green leaves and white to lavender flower spikes that bloom in midsummer. The plant will grow about eighteen inches tall in containers and should be cut back each year to keep it from getting too rangy. Not for cats only, the sweet, minty catnip leaves can be used in tea and as a seasoning in salads and various dishes. Catnip will do well in full sun or partial shade. The soil should be kept evenly moist. This plant makes a lovely houseplant and can be started from seed, cuttings, or by division.

*Chervil.* This plant resembles parsley in appearance, though it is more delicate and ferny. Like parsley, the foliage is used for seasoning as well as garnish. The finely textured green leaves, which produce clusters of small white flowers in the summer, will turn to pink in the fall. The sweet-smelling plant will self-seed if it is allowed to flower. Chervil should be placed in bright shade and moist, fairly rich soil.

*Chives.* This plant will form a nice border with its thin grass-like leaves that grow up to ten inches tall. Unlike with other herbs, do not snip the growing tips; instead cut the mild onion-flavored leaves close to the ground several times during the season to keep the plant from getting tough. Leaves will be more tender after each cutting. Take care when cutting, though, not to cut one plant too often because like all plants, they rely on their leaves to manufacture food. Start chives from seed or purchase young nursery-grown plants. Set them in full sun or partial shade in a fairly moist, light soil.

*Dill.* This herb produces both seeds and leaves for seasoning and pickling many foods. This familiar annual with its light, feathery green foliage grows easily in full sun and well-drained soil. Dill self-seeds and doesn't transplant well. It forms umbels of tiny yellowish flowers on stems above the plant. Very ferny in appearance, dill grows to eighteen inches in containers.

*Egyptian onion.* The most striking feature about this plant is that it develops bulbs at the top of its shoots instead of below ground. The weight of the developing bulb eventually causes the stalk to fall over, bringing the new bulb in contact with the soil where it takes root. Visually it is quite interesting and grows to about three feet. The Egyptian onion can be used in the same way as any regular onion and its foliage can be substituted for chives. Like many other herbs, the Egyptian onion prefers a rich, well-draining soil, and as with most bulbs, the use of manure should be avoided. Give it plenty of sun, but allow the soil to dry out between waterings. The young bulbs appear in July.

*Garlic.* A familiar herb, garlic closely resembles the onion. It produces long slender shoots and a flower stalk that is topped with a white or lavender cluster of blooms. You can use the tender young shoots to season food, but it is the bulb that is the most valued part of the plant. Individual cloves should be planted in March to be ready for harvest in July and August. Garlic bulbs bought in a grocery store are not suitable for planting, since they have dried out too much. Instead, purchase cloves at nursery centers or through mail order firms. The plant needs full sun and rich soil with good drainage. Propagate by dividing the cloves. Before use in cooking, be sure to sun-dry the cloves until they are white.

*Lavender.* An old perennial favorite, lavender has a woody stem that produces fragrant blooms of lavender and deep purple that repel insects and attract bees. The foliage can be bright green to gray-green. The bitter, pungent leaves can be used in salads, but the more common use for lavender is in scented sachets or perfumes. Lavender grows one and one-half to four feet high and its color adds a soft beauty to the herb garden. The plant requires full sun and very fast-draining soil. It is best to purchase young plants since germination from seed may be sporadic. English lavender is the most popular species.

*Marjoram.* An annual that grows to two feet high, marjoram is a very pungent herb used in many dishes as well as in tea. The small oval leaves are a light green with gray on the underside and covered with a fine hair. Marjoram produces small, tight clusters of flowers that range in color from white to lilac. The plant needs full sun and a somewhat akaline soil. Propagate by seed or cuttings.

*Mints.* These are perennials and grow abundantly in rich, well-drained soil and partial shade. Mint has a tendency to spread, so it should be planted in containers to control the roots. Flowering stalks should be cut before they go to seed. Propagate by stem cutting or division. The most common mints are peppermint and spearmint, but there are other mints worth growing, like the curly-leafed varieties and the apple, orange, and pineapple mints. These are just as refreshing in flavor and lovely in appearance. Pineapple mint, with its varigated foliage, is a wonderful addition to the flower border. The leaves, fresh or candied, can be used as garnishes as well as crushed just before using in many dishes and beverages.

*Nasturtium.* This is a cheerful addition to an herb garden, producing flowers in shades of cream, yellow, orange, and red. The climbing varieties are charming subjects for hanging baskets. All parts of the plant, including the flowers, seeds, and leaves, are used in cooking and have a wonderful peppery taste. The flowers are quite good in salads and the pods, picked just after the flowers drop, can be pickled and substituted for capers. Nasturtiums grow very easily in full sun and well-drained soil. The soil should be of average fertility because if it is too rich you will get plenty of the round, olive colored leaves and few flowers.

*Oregano.* This is a perennial that is related to sweet marjoram. It has a similar but stronger flavor and can be used fresh or dried. Oregano is shrub-like and can reach a height of two and one half feet, making it a good subject for a low hedge. A pretty plant, it produces tiny, pinkish white blooms. The fragrant leaves are used primarily for cooking, though they are also used for dyeing. It needs a fast draining soil and full sun. Propagation is by seed, cuttings, or division. The plants should be replaced when the stems become woody.

*Parsley.* Although a biennial, parsley is usually treated as an annual. All parts of the plant are high in vitamin A and quite nutritious. There is hardly a culinary dish that it cannot be used in. It is flavorful, but it is also useful in blending the flavors of other herbs and aids digestion and in dyeing. Give this plant a rich soil and full sun. Propagation is by seed sown in early spring. The curly-leaf varieties are the most popular and grow about one foot in height. It makes a lovely dark green border around taller plants.

*Rosemary.* This is another very commonly grown herb. It is an evergreen and can winter over in the gardens in milder areas of the country, where it has been known to reach a height of six feet. In northern areas it will have to be brought inside or treated as an annual. Under these conditions, it rarely exceeds two feet. Rosemary can be used as a hedge or border and also makes a good subject for bonsai. Leaves are needle-like and green or gray-green. Blooms appear in clusters and are lavender or blue. It is a fragrant plant and should be used sparingly in cooking. Rosemary also has medicinal uses since it aids digestion and stimulates the appetite. Give it a sunny location and well-drained soil. It is best to purchase nursery-grown plants, since it is difficult to start from seed.

*Sage.* Perhaps the best known of the American seasonings, sage is used for meats like pork, sausages, duck, and goose. Though sage will grow to two feet, there is also a dwarf variety of this hardy perennial. The foliage is gray-green with spikes that carry violet-blue flowers projecting above the leaves. Sage will do well in full sun and average to poor soil that is well-drained and somewhat dry. Easy to grow, sage can be propagated by seed or stem cuttings. There are many varieties of sage and beyond its use in cooking, it can also be used in teas and for dyeing. The full, bushy appearance of the plant makes it a good candidate for use as a hedge or low border. Tricolor sage makes a wonderful addition to the flower border.

*Savory.* There are two kinds of savory: summer savory and winter savory. Summer savory is an annual, while winter savory is a perennial. Summer savory is larger and has a finer flavor. The winter variety can stand temperatures down to 10°F. Both plants produce small, narrow leaves that grow thickly along the stem and small pinkish white flowers. Give them full sun and well-draining soil. Summer savory prefers a richer soil mix than the winter kind, which prefers drier conditions. Propagate summer savory by seed or cuttings and winter savory by division.

*Scented geraniums.* These are some of the most fragrant plants to include in the herb garden. Various species grow from two to four feet tall and produce a range of scents that include rose, nutmeg, ginger, lime, lemon, peppermint, apple, apricot, and strawberry. Geranium leaves are used in teas, compotes, pound cake, jellies, and even as floaters in finger bowls. The fragrance of the plants' scent is given off in hot sun or by touching the leaves. There are many variations in the appearance of the geranium, from feathery, fern-like foliage to rounded leaves in many shades of green. The plant produces small colorful flowers in light and dark rose. The scented geraniums should be given full sun and potted in fertilized, well-drained soil that stays somewhat dry. Pinching back the foliage will keep the plants bushy and full. Propagate by root or stem cuttings.

*Tarragon.* This is an herb that must be used fresh since it loses most of its flavor in drying. It is possible to preserve some in vinegar for winter use. It is a perennial that grows by producing rhizomes and does not come true from seeds. The slender dark green leaves grow along the stem, and the plant produces greenish blooms. Tarragon should be planted in full sun or partial shade and in well-drained soil. To propagage, divide or use root cuttings.

*Thyme.* This herb comes in so many varieties and flavors that it could make a garden by itself. All thymes have woody stems. Some varieties are bushy, like common thyme with its tiny oval leaves or lemon thyme with its strongly scented leaves. Other thymes, like the creeping varieties and wild thyme, are more delicate and finely textured in appearance. All thymes require full sun and light, well-drained soil. Clip back stems to keep the plants from becoming woody. All varieties are fragrant and will produce flowers in abundance. Thyme is used in many dishes for its gently pungent flavor, in tea, and in sachets. It is a perennial that can be propagated by division, stem, or root cuttings. Thyme has a lovely appearance and makes a very nice houseplant in winter.

# ❧ 16 ❧
# Houseplants in Your Garden

YOUR FAITHFUL HOUSE GREENERY will reward you all winter long for a vacation in the garden during the summer months. Just as people feel the need to get out of the city when spring is fully in bloom, houseplants also begin to stir and awaken from drowsy winter survival. Leaves that have become sparse and small will increase in size and number when they are moved outdoors for just a few months. But there's a wonderful tradeoff coming as you clear plants from windowsills, tables, and hangers; you will have plenty of space and light all summer long. Are you going to miss these old friends who sat out the winter so patiently with you? No—because their place is easily filled with freshly cut bouquets of annuals and perennials straight from your garden. And outside on your terrace, your garden benefits from the addition of several mature and colorful plants.

A few weeks before moving them into the garden, check your plants and repot any that need it. Remember that once outdoors, many will grow quickly so be sure to choose containers that are at least one to two inches bigger than their present containers. All this renewed growth will also mean greater use of the nutrients present in the soil. Be sure to add some bone meal and cow manure. If you have any compost, add that too and your plants will really benefit from it.

As you begin to bring plants outside, be sure to watch for weather reports. Mid-May still brings an occasional drop in temperatures that can damage tender houseplants. If the temperature threatens to fall to 45°F.

Fig. 55   These houseplants add texture and interest to an outdoor garden.

or below, bring your houseplants back inside. Cactus can remain outdoors. Another thing to consider is the change of climate from indoors to
your terrace. Even the hardiest of plants will be damaged by hours of
direct sunlight and high winds if it is accustomed to a calm window with
a southern exposure. It's a good idea to bring plants out slowly—that is,
let them adapt to their new conditions step by step. Begin by setting them
out in a shady corner for a few hours the first day and gradually increase
the length of time. If they show any signs of distress, bring them back
inside immediately. After a week or so, they should be able to remain out
overnight. Then slowly move them to locations where they will receive
more light. Many plants will actually benefit from a location in full sun
if introduced to it gradually. You should be able to see the difference in
a plant very quickly. The leaves will grow greener and more numerous
and the stems will become stronger. Some plants, of course, may not
respond well at all. If it cannot adjust and the move seems to be damaging
the plant, take it back inside. If you aren't sure whether a plant is respond-
ing, give it time. You have at least four months of good weather ahead.
     The biggest danger in moving plants outdoors is burning them. Even
shade may not be enough to protect houseplants from hot, dry conditions.
Be extra cautious with variegated varieties like spider plants and devil's
ivy; remember that deep shade outdoors may be much brighter than the

dark corner they are used to on top of the bureau. Plants that are actively growing in a location that receives more sun or bright light than they are used to will require more water. Also remember that even though these plants continue to grow all year, their growth rate still varies with the seasons. In spring and summer, as the days lengthen, they grow more quickly than in the fall or winter. This also explains the need to water frequently during periods of active growth. If you find yourself watering your houseplants every day and they still seem to wilt often, they may need to be transplanted to larger containers. Small plants should be grouped together and buried to their rims in larger pots.

Many plants, such as begonias and African violets, are found in nature in shady areas while others, such as certain philodendrons, prefer full sun. When placing these plants outside, it is important to keep this fact in mind. It is also important to feed them more frequently than you may be used to. Begin withholding fertilizer in midsummer as you would with other perennials in the garden to help prepare the plants for their move back indoors in the fall.

When it is time to move plants indoors at the end of summer or in early autumn, remember to use the same hardening-off procedure. Move the plants back to the shady corner for a few weeks and then into the house. Not only will your plants be stronger and larger, but many that you never thought could flower will burst into bloom.

Many plants that are sold for enjoyment indoors can also increase the design possibilities of your garden in summer. Most of these plants are appreciated for some special characteristic of color or plant form, and these same qualities can help create an intriguing garden. It need not be expensive to use these plants either. Some are available at local dime stores and make a suitable alternative for annuals. When placed outdoors, they grow quickly from pint-sized plants into luxurious specimens. These plants can go a long way toward solving certain design problems. Whether your aim is to create a tropical retreat or just fill a densely shaded corner where little else will grow, houseplants offer a terrific choice.

The following is a list of some of the most common and adaptable houseplants to consider for your garden.

*Aglaonema modestum* (Chinese evergreen). This plant displays lovely, long, pointed leaves that are often marked yellow, light green, or silver. Planted in groups in densely shaded areas, it makes a striking display. As a matter of fact, this plant is noted for its shade tolerance.

*Anthurium.* This plant produces large leaves that resemble those of caladium, but that is where the resemblance ends. Anthurium leaves are thicker, dark green, and up to two feet long. The leaf veins are colored ivory and are quite prominent. Keep it moist and give it a location in bright shade.

*Asparagus Sprengeri.* A common sight in many homes, this is a beautiful plant that is easy to care for. When placed outdoors and given enough light, the feathery foliage is enhanced by the production of small white flowers that are followed by the appearance of green berries. In the autumn, these berries turn bright red and persist for a month or more. Give it a location in full sun or partial to light shade. Allow the plant to dry out inbetween waterings. Asparagus can withstand drought for short periods of time.

*Begonias.* These plants come in a variety of shapes, sizes, and colors. Aside from varieties with interesting leaves, many are flowering and can provide an extra bright spot in a garden. Hanging pots in partial sunlight are the most favorable conditions for these waxy plants. Since they do especially well in moist conditions, keep them well watered and out of a drying wind. Repot begonias annually in the spring and propagate by division.

*Cacti.* Used so often as a traditional houseplant, few people realize how well cacti thrive in a garden. They are a hardy family and can remain outdoors usually into late October. Desert varieties are most common, but there are a few forest varieties such as the famous Christmas cactus. These forest types are more tender and need the protection of moderate shade and moist soil conditions. Desert cacti are easier to find, cheaper to buy, and like direct sunlight. They aren't bothered by wind or dry soil conditions. If you have several small cacti, you can make a dish garden with four or five plants arranged in a shallow clay or plastic container and potted in loose soil for good drainage. Water regularly, especially in late spring and summer, when cacti most actively grow. Occasional feeding with a diluted fertilizer low in nitrogen will promote the best growth. Cacti usually flower after three years.

*Chlorophytum comosum* (spider plant). This is also called the airplane plant because of the little plantlets sent out from the mother plant. This is a very attractive plant with thin, grassy green and white foliage that grows quickly and is easy to care for. When it becomes root-bound, it sends out long shoots with little plantlets. It likes to be watered regularly through the summer and occasionally misted. Give it a shady location and watch it carefully since the foliage is burned easily.

*Cissus rhombifolia* (grape ivy). This is a member of the grape family. However, it does resemble ivy and is an inexpensive and common houseplant that is easy to set in a garden. It can be placed in pots or hanging baskets and makes a wonderful ground cover beneath taller plants. For rapid, leafy growth, water frequently from spring through summer in a normal soil mixture with a neutral pH. This plant is ideal for terraces because it tolerates dry or moist, hot or cool conditions. Give it a position in sun or shade.

*Crassula argentea* (jade plant). This is a succulent and, like cacti, should be placed in well-draining soil and watered regularly. This plant has the appearance of a small Oriental tree with its thick, olive-colored leaves. It thrives in sun or bright light. This is not a particularly fussy plant, and repotting is seldom necessary. A mature jade plant that has been outdoors through the summer will often produce tiny pinkish white flowers in the fall. Containers should be shallow rather than deep.

*Dieffenbachia.* Also known by the common name of dumb cane, this makes a wonderful addition for a tropical effect. The large variegated leaves are produced along a central cane or stem. It will reach a height of five feet eventually but will not grow quite that large in a summer. Give it a lightly shaded location, but avoid it altogether if there are small children around since it is poisonous.

*Fittonia.* A low-growing creeper, fittonia makes a wonderful ground-cover for a shaded location. The textured oval leaves are about one inch long and are heavily veined in pink or white. Direct sun must be avoided with this plant and adequate moisture must be given.

*Gynura* (purple passion vine). This is a wonderful trailer to hang in a garden. It is a tough, fast-growing plant with thick, velvet-like leaves that are scalloped and covered with shiny purple hairs. It has no special needs and keeps its bright purple color if set in direct morning sun. Placed in an average soil, it can be pinched back to promote leaf production. Water regularly and keep the soil moist to touch.

*Hedera helix* (common ivy). This is a hardy houseplant and a natural choice for the garden. A climbing plant, it grows rapidly and is an excellent choice for hanging baskets, window boxes, and as a ground cover. It is practically self-sufficient, requiring average moisture and only occasional feedings. Give this plant bright light and indirect sun.

*Maranta.* This plant and its close relatives include such indoor favorites as the prayer plant, the herringbone plant, and the zebra plant. They are mostly low growing, rarely exceeding eight inches in height, and all bear strikingly beautiful foliage. The leaves are usually oval and marked with contrasting blotches and/or veins in shades of brown, black, green, white, and pink. Some species have the curious habit of folding up at night. Give them a shaded location and keep them constantly moist.

*Peperomia.* Like coleus, this is very common, inexpensive, and easy to grow. It is a hardy but slow-growing plant. The foliage is amazingly varied, growing upright or long and trailing; compact or bushy. A long-lived plant, peperomia often looks nice in hanging baskets, or as a compact border around taller-growing plants. Peperomia comes in three different varieties: those with thick, waxy leaves; those with deeply ridged and dark leaves; and those with flat, smooth leaves. Color varies from solid dark green to variegated green with white or yellow streaks. They should be potted in a peat-based compost with some sand or perlite mixed in to ensure proper drainage. Avoid placing them in direct sun, and if the area they inhabit becomes especially dry or hot, mist occasionally.

*Philodendron.* A plant that is easy to grow, it can be used to fill any garden corner. Philodendrons fall into two categories: vining or climbing, and self-heading or nonclimbing. Both types are suitable for the garden. The *P. scandens,* or sweetheart, is the most popular vining plant. Its heart-shaped leaves grow in rosette fashion on tall stems from a central point. They should be staked and well-supported (though they will withstand neglect and poor conditions). Self-heading philodendrons grow much larger than their vining cousins. *P. selloums* are popular, dark green self-headers that come in a variety of shapes. It is commonly used as a decoration in commercial spaces. In the garden, philodendrons should be kept out of direct sun and placed behind shorter plants or in shady corners where growing conditions are difficult. They like a regular misting when weather gets dry. Pot in a rich soil that is slightly acidic. Philodendrons should be fed every two or three months to promote healthy leaf growth.

*Pilea.* A genus of widely grown houseplants, *Pilea* includes such favorites as the aluminum plant, the friendship plant, the moon valley plant, and many others. As a group they are low growing, generally remaining less than eight inches tall. The leaves are best described as a pointed oval and are heavily textured and usually variegated. Some species are green marked with white, while others are mahogany-brown and silver. It makes a wonderful low-growing border or ground cover for a shady location. Water liberally but allow the soil to dry out slightly between waterings.

*Plectranthus* (Swedish ivy). This is actually a member of the mint family, and is one of the most popular hanging plants. The lovely, thick, bright green leaves grow quickly and fill out a basket in a matter of months. Avoid direct sun but place the plant in a bright spot. Swedish ivies like regular, loosely potted soil. Pinch out the growing tips to keep it bushy.

*Saintpaulia.* Also known as the African violet, this makes a wonderful addition to the shade garden. The small flowers are produced in a variety of colors that include pink, blue, purple, and white. The petals may be single, double, or frilled. What the individual flowers lack in size is made up in profusion. The plants are usually covered in flowers for much of the year. The attractiveness of this plant does not stop with its flowers. The foliage is also handsome and in some cases variegated. Give these plants a lightly shaded location and keep them moist but wait for the surface soil to dry slightly before rewatering. Feed them once a month to keep the flowers coming.

*Sansevieria.* This is available in more than twenty-five different varieties. Inexpensive, popular, and practically indestructible, they like full sunlight and hot, windy conditions. The most common species (S. *trifasciata*) has tall, sword-like leaves with dark bands running cross-wise up each leaf. Allow the soil to dry between waterings. Pot in clay and fertilize occasionally. To propagate, divide rhizomes of mature plants or take leaf cuttings and plant in new pots.

*Saxifraga.* This is better known as the strawberry begonia, and produces roundish leaves from a central crown. The leaves are usually heavily veined with white and sometimes variegated with pink and white markings. The plant gets its name from the fact that it reproduces by producing plantlets at the end of long runners. Saxifraga would make a good subject for a ground cover under taller-growing plants. Give it a shady but bright spot in the garden and adequate moisture. Allow the surface of the soil to dry out between waterings.

*Schefflera.* This is a plant that becomes quite large as it matures. Its foliage is not only very attractive but unusual for a garden. Leaves grow out of stalks that project from stems of the plant. They spread into sections of four or five leaflets at the end of each stalk, giving an umbrella effect. Mature plants grow to six feet in height. They like plenty of water in spring and summer will thrive in full sun or partial shade.

*Scindapsus.* More commonly known as pothos or devil's ivy, this plant is another pseudo ivy. A good climber, it is well-suited to the outdoors in summer and spring, since it thrives in warm, humid conditions. Too much direct sun can scorch the leaves, so a semi-shaded location is best. Allow the soil to dry between waterings. The devil's ivy will be variegated with green, yellow, and white-streaked leaves.

*Senecio mikanioides* (wax ivy or German ivy). This plant closely resembles the true common ivies. Its foliage is shiny with bright streaks of white and yellow running through them. Though the shape and color is much like the true ivy, the leaves of the wax ivy are thicker and tend to be more pointed on the edges. Wax ivy is unique when set outdoors; it suddenly produces sprays of yellow flowers that cascade down the stems of the plant. Less affected by warm and dry conditions than common ivies, they should be potted in normal soil and watered regularly. Repot every two years in the spring and propagate by stem cuttings.

*Streptocarpus* (Cape primrose). This is another popular gift and holiday plant. When conditions are right, the plant blooms from May to October. The lovely flowers are trumpet-shaped and come in many colors including salmon, pink, lavender, orange, red, white, and many bicolors. Some of the blooms have ruffled petals. *Streptocarpus* should be placed in a shallow container so that the long leaves can extend over the soil and not dry out. The plant does not tolerate drafts and should be placed in a bright spot, but out of direct sunlight. Water liberally, but let the soil dry before watering again. Mist occasionally and feed lightly at each watering. *Streptocarpus* is not particularly tolerant of extreme heat or cold, and should not be placed out of doors until temperatures are fairly moderate. Propagate by seeds sown in the spring, by division, or leaf cutting. Remove faded blooms to encourage budding.

*Tradescantia albi flora* and *Zebrina pendula.* These plants are creepers that are popularly known as wandering Jew. Usually displayed in hanging baskets or window boxes, these plants grow easily and quickly. Foliage develops in variegated shades of green, white, or white with silver stripes. The underside of the leaves are deep purple, which makes them especially interesting to hang. Bright light will intensify colors of the *Zebrina*. The plant should be potted in normal soil and watered liberally spring through autumn. Occasional misting is very good during especially hot, dry weather. Propagate easily by stem cuttings taken in spring, summer, or fall.

# PART THREE

# Special Gardens

# ❧ 17 ❧

# A Shady Wild Flower Garden

WITH PROPER PLANNING A WILD FLOWER GARDEN can be quite successful. It requires none of the fertilizers and expensive pesticides of common domestic gardening and little in the way of cultivation short of providing the proper raw materials. Once established, it will renew itself year after year with little help or prodding from you. Trilliums, lady slippers, star violets, and wild columbime are only a few of the plants that may be grown. What one must have in order to deal with them successfully is some understanding of their environmental needs. Each forest is the result of an interaction of a multitude of factors, and each species has adapted itself to a particular set of circumstances that must be duplicated faithfully. The most important factors that govern the well-being of these plants are the same as those that govern any domestic plant: light, temperature, moisture, and humidity. Other factors include a fast-draining, acidic soil containing large amounts of organic material, and a protected location free from strong winds and the harsh effects of the seasons. Most of these conditions can be provided by the experienced gardener.

## Light and Temperature

In the early spring, before the trees leaf out, woodland plants receive the full force of the sun. Many species take this opportunity and flower at this

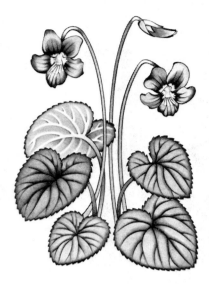

*Fig. 56   Wild violets*

time. As the season progresses and the temperature climbs, the trees leaf out, protecting the wild flowers from the heat of summer and locking in moisture. The forest floor remains damp and cool, rarely rising above 80°F. Plants that once stood in full sun may now be in dense shade.

Many urban high-rise buildings have small covered terraces that help to create this seasonal light change. During the winter months, the sun is much lower in the sky and can penetrate the terrace directly. As the year progresses and the angle of the sun changes, the terrace will be shaded for a longer period of time. You can also alter the amount of sun that you receive by planting the perimeter with deciduous trees, shrubs, and vines, as well as hanging baskets of annuals. Such plants will also break the force of the wind and help protect the wild flowers in winter. More shade will also mean better moisture retention and cooler temperatures. On a sunny rooftop it is possible to provide needed shade by constructing an inexpensive lathe house and treating it in the same manner.

## Moisture and Humidity

Woodland wild flowers are moisture lovers. They will not tolerate dry conditions even for a short time without suffering severe damage. They may need water every day, and in extremely hot weather, twice a day. All this watering can turn an otherwise relaxing experience into a bothersome chore; to make it easier, use large containers or group medium-sized ones closer together. Be sure to provide shade and some protection from drying winds. A misting in the afternoon using lukewarm water is also helpful.

If this is your first attempt at gardening with wild flowers, then I suggest that you begin small, choosing only those wildlings that tolerate dry conditions. As you succeed with these, you can add a wider selection. Of course few people will follow this advice, since the very plants that attracted them in the first place, such as the lady slipper orchids, are moisture lovers.

## *The Soil*

Woodland wild flowers are very specific in their soil requirements. They will tolerate only a narrow range of conditions. To fully understand the requirements, it is best that we understand the nature of the soil. Woodland soil is formed in natural geological layers that form a pattern that can easily be seen and identified. Each layer has a different color, texture, and chemical reaction that can be measured. This basic soil pattern holds true everywhere although wide variations including soil pH, mineral content, and depth of the different layers can be found from spot to spot, even in a small area. That is why it is possible to find species needing quite different requirements growing quite close together.

If we were to dig down into the soil and uncover and study the various soil layers, the first one we would notice is made up of a layer of debris that blankets the forest floor. Every square inch is covered in fallen leaves, twigs, and other litter discarded by all living things in the forest. It forms a natural mulch several inches thick, which protects plants by insulating them from extremes in temperature and locks in precious moisture. What grows in any given area is largely dependent on what makes up this layer of ground litter. As this organic matter breaks down, it becomes part of the forest soil. Nutrients once contained in the organic matter are released. These nutrients impart a chemical reaction to the soil. Ground litter made up primarily of pine needles will be very acidic (pH 4.5–5.5), while a covering of maple leaves will be nearly neutral (pH 6.5). Below this natural mulch is a layer of pure, rich leafmold. It has a spongy texture and a dark, almost black color. This layer may be just a thin sprinkling of material, or it can be up to several inches thick. The store of nutrients it contains is very great and they are constantly being leached into the soil below at a very slow rate. It can have a pH range from very acidic to near neutral, although of all the layers of soil found in any given spot, it will be the most acidic.

Beneath the leafmold layer is the topsoil. It retains moisture well and yet is well-drained, allowing air to penetrate to plant roots. It can easily be identified by its slightly lighter color and by the presence of mineral matter that is usually alkaline in nature. These minerals percolate up from the subsoil, making the topsoil less acidic than the leaf mold layer. Below the topsoil is the subsoil. It is much lighter in color and contains more mineral matter than humus. It can have a chemical reaction ranging from slightly acid to strongly alkaline. Beneath the subsoil is solid rock or impenetrable clay hardpan.

We want a soil that can duplicate the characteristics of a woodland environment while supporting a wide range of plants. Synthesized woodland soil must be well drained, yet hold tremendous amounts of moisture; it must provide an enormous amount of humus material and the proper soil acidity. It should duplicate faithfully the natural conditions that woodland plants have adapted to.

Consequently, mix your soil in layers that will closely conform to those in nature, while keeping a pH range of 4.5 to 5.5. This is one of the few times that I recommend the use of chemical fertilizers. They are extremely acidic and help maintain the proper pH level of the soil. They may also be used to quickly adjust a pH problem that arises in midseason. Begin by mixing together equal parts of superphosphate, ammonium sulphate, and powdered sulfur and set the mixture aside.*

Fill a large container such as a half whiskey barrel with two to four inches (depending on the height of the container) of drainage material. Mix together 2 parts top soil, 2 parts peat moss and 1¼ parts vermiculite (don't substitute perlite, it doesn't retain moisture as well) and add a ¼ cup of cottonseed meal for every gallon of mix. Fill your container to within ten inches of the rim. Dust the soil with a light coating (⅛ inch) of the superphosphate mixture and scratch it well. You've now completed your bottom layer of soil.

The next layer should consist of 2 parts peat moss, 1 part top soil, and 1 part vermiculite. Again add a ¼ cup of cottonseed meal per gallon of mix. You may substitute all or part of the peat moss with well-rotted leafmold compost or humus. Coffee grounds, which are acidic, may also be included, as well as sawdust or bark chips, but remember to add a little blood meal when using these. If it is possible, also add a handful of natural woodland soil to the mixture. This will introduce the tiny bacteria and fungi that can survive and flourish in such acidic conditions and which woodland plants find so beneficial.

Fill your containers to within four inches of the top and again add the superphosphate mixture and cultivate lightly. On top of this, place a one-inch layer of organic material. Well-rotted leafmold or humus is preferable, although some peat moss may be substituted. Don't add too much peat though, it tends to shed water when dried out.

You are now ready to add your layer of mulch material. If you have gathered some natural ground litter, so much the better, but any good

---

*Growing Woodland Plants,* Clarence & Eleanor G. Birdseye (New York: Dover, 1972).

mulching material will do. If you don't like the appearance of leaves, you can always cover them with pine bark chips or cocoa bean hulls, which also make wonderful mulches on their own. This layer is most important and should be left in place year-round.

Water well and allow the soil to mellow for two weeks, then take a pH reading. Make sure to take samples from both the first topsoil layer as well as the second, taking care not to touch them with your hands. To adjust a soil mixture that is too alkaline, dissolve ½ cup of superphosphate into a gallon of water. If your soil is too acidic, you can adjust by using a solution of ½ cup lime dissolved into a gallon of water. If only a minor adjustment is needed, dilute the solution with more water before application. Water the container thoroughly and allow the soil to rest for a day before retesting. Remember to begin slowly; within a few days you should reach the proper level to begin planting. Improper soil acidity is the most common reason for failure and is easily avoided. It is wise to take pH readings often, about once a month during the first year, thereafter about once every three months. Make sure you test your source of water as well and avoid using concrete containers, as these tend to be alkaline.

## Year-Round Protection

Woodland plants have adapted themselves to the natural protection of a year-round mulch. You run the risk of damaging your plants if you don't provide this covering.

A leaf cover of oak, beech, hemlock, or pine is ideal if you can provide it. Not as beneficial are maple, willow, or poplar leaves, as these are near neutral and mat down tightly, trapping out air. If you can't provide leaves, you may use any good mulching material. In the spring, remove the winter mulch and lightly cultivate. Add a one-inch layer of leafmold, compost, or humus and then renew the mulch. From time to time during the growing season, be sure to remove the mulch and cultivate again, adding more organic material.

Although wild flowers are tough when it comes to disease and insects, their delicate leaves and flowers will bruise easily under an elemental onslaught. Be sure to provide some form of sheltered location or protection from strong winds.

## Fertilizers and Plant Nutrition

Woodland plants are wildlings and require very little in the way of fertilizers. They gather their food from the organic matter present in the soil.

A light dusting with the superphosphate mixture in the spring is beneficial, as is a midsummer dressing of a quarter inch of well-rotted manure under the ground litter. The inclusion of cottonseed meal scratched into the soil will also provide a natural source of nitrogen. The trick is not to overdo it. If woodland plants are fertilized too heavily, they will produce too much foliage and too few flowers. If enough organic material is provided, fertilizers will not be necessary.

## Insects and Diseases

In general, most wild flowers are not bothered by insects, but they are also not used to the conditions of a domestic garden. Occasionally they may be attacked by insects or fungus blights. Although most remedies used for normal domestic plants are quite safe when used on wild flowers, some, such as petroleum-based products, may be too strong and damage your plants, especially ferns. If you are in doubt about the product you are using, place a little of the insecticide on a leaf and wait a few days to see if there is any reaction. Most fungicides found on the market are acceptable. Powdered sulphur is also a good treatment and has the added advantage of a low pH factor. When washed into the soil it will not raise your pH reading to dangerously high levels.

Air pollution is another problem encountered in an urban environment. Try not to confuse it with damage from insects. Little is known about the effects of air pollution on wildlings, and some species may not survive it. You can ask for more information from the nursery where you purchase your plants.

## Increasing Your Collection

Almost all mail order firms have a few woodland plants to choose from, but for a wider selection contact reputable firms that specialize in wild flowers. Try to choose firms that grow their own rather than gather them from the wild. You will be getting specimens with good healthy root systems, which are accustomed to domestic situations. You may also be sure that the plants you will be receiving have not been illegally gathered, no matter how rare.

Your plants may also be increased by propagation. Many wild flowers, when given the proper conditions, multiply rapidly. Propagation is by the same methods as any plant and includes division, cuttings, layering, and seeds. In order to succeed, care must be taken to give them the same cultural requirements that they would need as mature specimens. Cuttings should be rooted in a mixture of peat and vermiculite, adjusted as described earlier to produce the proper pH range.

Seeds may be purchased from most wild flower garden catalogs or wild flower nurseries, or they may be gathered directly from the wild. When purchasing seeds from a nursery find out as much information as you can to ensure successful germination. Do not hesitate to ask the nursery about the necessary conditions to ensure success.

## Propagating Plants from Seed

When planting seeds, use a sterile mixture of half peat and half vermiculite as you would for your other plants. Seeds are buried three times their thickness, and, like their parent plants, must have the proper soil pH in order to germinate and flourish. You can adjust the pH as much as you need to by the methods prescribed earlier in this chapter. The type of special treatment seeds of various species need in order to germinate can be determined largely by their period of flower. Plants that flower and release their seeds in the spring generally need warm temperatures to germinate, while those that flower and release their seeds in the fall generally need cool temperatures or a period of freezing to break dormancy.

When collecting seeds from the wild, place them in envelopes marked with the species, the date, and the location of collection. Test the pH of the soil immediately around the parent plant (both a surface reading and one several inches deeper). Also note the depth and nature of the ground litter and the types of trees present. Note the amount of light coming through the tree cover, and if it receives morning or afternoon sun. Is it on a north slope or south? Can you imagine the amount of light it receives in other seasons? These are all clues to the conditions individual species need for survival. If you have a 35mm SLR camera, bring it along and use it to tell the amount of light a plant is receiving. Set the ASA to 10 and the shutter speed at 1/100th of a second. Place a white card next to the plant and set your camera's F-stop to get the correct exposure. The chart below will tell you the amount of light the plant is receiving. Make sure that the white card fills the visual frame of the camera, and that you do not cast a shadow on the white card. You can then find the best location for the plant in your garden by duplicating the same procedure.

F 3.5 = 400 footcandles
F 4.5 = 500 "
F 5.6 = 750 "
F 8 = 1000 "
F 11 = 2000 "
F 16 = 6400 "

Dig up a handful of soil and take it with you. After the seeds germinate and it is time to transfer the seedlings to individual pots, they will stand a greater chance of adjusting to domestic conditions if some of the original soil is mixed in.

## Collecting Plants from the Wild

Many states have laws that are meant to protect rare plants from total destruction by prohibiting their removal from natural surroundings. But there are situations in which gathering them may be done freely and with a clear conscience. In areas that are to be drained, flooded, cleared, or otherwise destroyed, you will actually be preserving these rare plants by gathering as many as you need. As they multiply under optimum conditions, many can be reintroduced to areas in which their populations have dwindled to a dangerously low level. In fact, the cultivation of native wild flowers can do much to increase our supply of rare plants. As when gathering seeds, take extensive notes on the conditions present around the plant. You will find that the presence of certain trees will indicate the most likely places to find particular plants and will help you return extra plants to areas that hold the greatest chance for their success. A white pine forest provides such dense year-round shade that almost nothing will grow. The soil is strongly acidic (about pH 4–5) and covered with a thick mat of decaying pine needles. An oak forest provides full sun in the early part of spring. As the weather warms, the trees leaf out, providing shade ranging from dense to light, with some areas still receiving full sun. It contains a well-aerated ground cover of leaves that breaks down to form a humus-rich soil, slightly less acid than pine (pH 5–5.5). A mixed tree forest made up of primarily hemlock, pine, oak, and beech contains conditions similar to an oak forest. It generally has a thin layer of humus-rich soil with a pH range of 5–6. Other plants will require the same pH requirements as blueberry, huckleberry, cranberry, azalea, laurel, rhododendron, spruce, fir, and chestnut, although many of these differ concerning other cultural requirements. A maple forest indicates a soil that is only slightly acid to neutral (pH 6–7). The trees generally leaf out earlier in the spring with fairly dense shade in the summer. Other plants that indicate a near-neutral soil area are the cedar, basswood, poplar, elm, willow, dogwood, ash, hickory, butternut, walnut, cherry, aspen, birch, and tulip tree.

When gathering plants, try not to disturb them too much. Take a generous rootball and some extra soil for repotting. Also take some of the natural ground litter, for you can always cover it with bark chips. Take pH readings of both the surface and subsurface soil and rate the trees present.

Wild flowers and ferns may be gathered anytime with sufficient care, but some periods are better than others. Early-blooming plants generally finish their aboveground growth by the end of July. Plan on moving these after they flower, certainly by June. May and June flowering plants usually finish their aboveground growth by October and should be transplanted at the end of August when nights are cooler. Late-blooming plants can be transplanted just before the first frost in the fall, or in the early spring as they begin to emerge.

## Ferns for a Wild Flower Garden

Ferns are perhaps nature's most successful experiments, and the most ancient plant form. Primitive in their structure and possessing a long, complicated reproductive cycle, ferns have existed for four hundred million years while modern man dates back a mere seventy thousand.

The physical form of a fern is a leftover vestige from this earlier age before plants had begun to develop true leaves, flowers, and seeds. Instead, ferns developed two different types of fronds—sterile fronds for the manufacture of food and fertile fronds that bear spores. These latter develop after the plant matures and can be distinguished from sterile fronds by the fruit dots or sori that are located on the underside. Each sori is actually made up of many tiny spore capsules that are grouped together. When immature, they are green, changing to dark brown or black when mature. They then break open, releasing thousands of tiny spores from each plant to make their way to a suitable spot to begin life. This alone is a formidable feat. In order to germinate, they need the right conditions of light, moisture, temperature, and soil, which must be maintained over several months. Out of the thousands of spores released, only one or two may make it to maturity. When a spore finally encounters all the correct conditions for growth, it cracks open, spilling out a mass of individual cells that quickly organize and multiply to form a small, green, scale-like structure known as a *prothallium.* This is the very first stage of a fern, and one that few people ever see. It is a remarkable structure and recalls the age of dinosaurs when most plant reproduction was sexual. The prothallium roots itself to the ground, while its moist, dark underside develops two distinct areas, one for the production of eggs, the other for the production of spermatozoa. The spermatozoa wiggle toward the eggs, eventually fertilizing them. Two to six months later, if the proper climatic conditions of constant moisture and subdued light are maintained, the first primitive fronds are formed, and within a year or two the plant takes on its more identifiable form.

# Culture

Ferns are ideal for busy people in that once you get them going they are inexpensive to maintain and require very little care. They prefer a shady location and will thrive where there is little light for anything else. Ferns are sensitive to fertilizers, only needing a top dressing of leafmold or peat moss each spring and a winter cover of leaves or straw each autumn. Any soil is suitable as long as it contains a high percentage of organic matter. They are not especially bothered by insects or disease.

What they do need is plenty of moisture and protection from drying winds. Although there are some species that prefer somewhat drier conditions, most prefer to have their roots kept constantly moist. Some will even tolerate full sun if given enough moisture. When beginning a fern garden for the first time, choose species that prefer slightly drier conditions.

Ferns may be propagated by division, runners, or by growing them from spores. This last requires a great deal of patience and attention, but if you feel adventurous, the method is outlined below.

# *Propagating Ferns from Spores*

Shake a fertile frond over a white piece of paper. If spores are released, they will cover the paper with dark speckles. Gather as many as you can and set the paper aside in a safe place while you prepare your planting medium.

Prepare a soil mix of one part leafmold and one part vermiculite or builder's sand. Sift these together to get a fine-grained medium and adjust the pH according to the directions given earlier in this chapter. Place the dampened soil in a Pyrex baking dish and fill to within an inch of the top. Press down the surface to form a smooth, even plane and set the dish, uncovered, in a warm oven (225°–250°F.) for a period of two hours to sterilize. Remember to place the glass cover in as well. Let it cool before removing. If the soil has completely dried out, redampen it with a small amount of boiled water that has been covered and allowed to cool. Add just enough to moisten but not drench the mix and allow the planting medium to cool to room temperature. Sprinkle the spores over the surface and do not cover: They need light to germinate. Place a transparent lid on the dish and place in a cool, shaded spot. Check from time to time to make sure the soil is moist. If you need to, moisten with sterilized water only, added to one corner of the dish in small amounts. In this way you will not disturb the growing spores.

Within a few weeks, the surface should turn green. If everything has been sterilized properly, these should be the prothallia. Within a few months, the first fronds should develop and the plants can be potted up individually. Use a mixture of one part leafmold and one part vermiculite and keep covered with cellophane. Bottom water, and never allow them to dry out until they are well on their way.

## Plant Labels

You may find that plant labels are helpful. Many plants die down to avoid the heat of the summer. If labeled, these plants will run less of a chance of being damaged by surface cultivation. Colorful shade-loving annuals may be planted in between them to give summer color. Check with your nurseryman about what to plant. In the fall, these annuals may be left in place to become part of the winter mulch.

This chapter has discussed the reasons behind success and failure with wild flowers. They are not necessarily an undertaking for the novice gardener although having little experience does not doom you to certain failure. You need a flexible approach and an open mind to experimentation. There are many acceptable methods in gardening to accomplish the same thing. Never try only one approach. Do not be discouraged by initial failure.

The plants listed below were chosen for their beauty, popularity, and because their cultural requirements are easiest to provide. These plants can be found growing in the wild throughout much of the eastern United States. (A glossary of terms used in this chapter can be found in the Appendix on page 365.)

## Recommended Plants

*Mountain aster (Aster acuminatis).* There are many varieties of aster native to North America that are suitable subjects for a wild flower garden, but the mountain aster is one of the nicest with its light purple, daisy-like flowers that measure one inch to one and one-half inches across. The plants reach a height of three feet and bear their blooms above pointed oval leaves in clusters. They bloom in July and continue through October, giving good late season color. The plants are easy to grow and require a slightly moist soil and a pH range of 5 to 6. The plants prefer light to medium shade and propagation is by root division.

*Bloodroot (Sanguinaria canadensis).* When the stem is broken, this plant oozes a red sap, hence its name. It is one of our most beautiful native wild flowers. After it emerges, the leaves completely envelop the flower bud, which rises on a separate stem. When almost completely mature, the flower bud is suddenly revealed and is borne on a stem six to eight inches high. Unfortunately, the flower is short-lived. The leaves continue to mature, growing to a height of twelve to fourteen inches. These are deeply lobed and roundish in appearance. Bloodroot makes an excellent garden subject when given a rich soil with a pH of 6 to 7. It likes a slightly moist soil and semishaded location. Propagation is by root division.

*American bluebell (Campanula americana).* The blue-violet star-shaped flowers are borne in the leaf axils along a six-foot stalk. The flowers, measuring one inch across, bloom from June to August. This plant prefers medium shade and soil with a pH of 6–7. It can be grown with no special care and propagation is from seed.

*Virginia bluebell, Virginia cowslip (Mertensia virginica).* Purple, pink, and blue flowers shaped like long, slender bells are grouped on the ends of erect, twelve- to twenty-four-inch branched stems in April and May. Leaves are oval and measure two to five inches long. Plants are propagated by seed, or by division of the perennial rootstock. Once this plant flowers, the foliage disappears. This plant prefers moist conditions in a semishaded location and a pH between 6–7. It is best transplanted just after flowering.

*American columbine (Aquilegia canadensis).* These beautiful scarlet, spurred flowers nod in the wind above foliage that resembles the maidenhair fern. The plant grows thirteen to eighteen inches tall and prefers dry soil in partial shade or full sun. It blooms in May and June. It prefers a pH of 6 to 7 but will tolerate a range of 5.0 to 7.5. It requires little care and spreads easily by seed.

*Delphinium exaltatum.* Spikes of lavender and blue flowers rise from a perrenial rootstock to a height of between two and six feet when this plant blooms. The flowers measure three-quarters of an inch across individually and appear in July and August. These plants prefer a rich, slightly acid soil with a pH of 6–7. It is a wonderfully easy plant to grow for midsummer color, preferring semishade. Propagation is by seed or division.

*Wild geranium (Geranium maculatum).* This plant is a close relative of the garden species, with rose-purple flowers that measure one to one-and-one-half inches across. It begins to flower in late April and continues until July. It likes rich, damp soil and partial shade. It is easy to cultivate and is not bothered by pests. It has a wide pH tolerance, from 4.5 to 7.0.

*Hepatica (Hepatica americana).* Fuzzy buds and stems push their way through to a height of four to six inches. These buds soon turn to white, pink, or purple blooms sometimes as early as March. The three-lobed leaves appear after the plant has flowered. Hepaticas prefer dry, humus-rich, acid soil with a pH of 4.5 to 6.0. A light winter cover is desirable but should be removed by late March or early April. They sometimes suffer from blight and insect attack. Propagation is by seed or division in the fall.

*Trumpet honeysuckle (Lonicera sempervivens).* This wild honeysuckle has paired oval leaves and bright flowers of scarlet or orange that appear in July and August. The flowers are born in clusters at the axils of upper leaves. These are followed by red berries. The vines prefer moist, cool locations in the shade and an acid soil (pH 5–6). Propagation is by seeds, layering, or softwood cuttings.

*Large yellow lady slipper (Cypripedium parviflorum pubescens).* With its wide pH tolerance (between pH 5–7), the large yellow lady slipper is fairly easy to grow. It is very long-lived and is found over a wide area of eastern North America. It prefers a soil rich in leafmold, the same as its cousins. The stalk bears one yellow and brown bloom. The leaves are plaited, broad, and oval, alternating on the stem. It should not be confused with the small yellow lady slipper (*Cypripedium parciflorum*), which is much more difficult to grow. The large yellow lady slipper is stocked by most wild flower dealers.

Lady slippers are widely sold by wild flower specialists and cannot be propagated by the amateur from seed. You can increase your supply by dividing the fleshy roots that form buds every year. This should take place just prior to the disappearance of the leaves. When planting, care must be taken not to set the crown too deep. Lady slippers are also subject to fungus blight and insect damage.

In the spring they need a light dressing of manure and a level table-spoon each of ammonium sulphate and 20 percent superphosphate. Fertilize the plants again in July to give the new buds a good start.

*Showy orchis (Orchis spectabilis).* This beautiful orchid is not as well known as the yellow and pink lady slippers. It bears a spike of from three to ten white and purple flowers atop a stalk that rises from two glossy leaves three to six inches long. The plant stands from six to twelve inches high and has short, thick roots. It is one of the earliest orchids to bloom, beginning in late April and persisting through June. It enjoys rich, moist leafmold with a pH of 5.5 to 6.5, and may increase by root buds. It must be protected from insects and disease.

*Common shooting star (Dodecatheon media).* This is one of the many species of shooting stars. They are all characterized by a flower stalk that rises from a rosette of basal leaves and is topped by several dart-shaped flowers, which are held loosely, giving the appearance of flight. This particular species has pink and white blooms. The perennial root stock is quite heavy and can be divided if more plants are desired. It does best in semi-shade, in well-drained soil that is not too rich, with a pH of 4.5 to 6. It is not particularly bothered by pests or disease and may be propagated by seed.

*Purple trillium, wakerobin (Trillium erectum).* Blooms appear from late May to July, depending on different local conditions. They vary in color from deep magenta to pink. The plants range in height from eight to sixteen inches and are rather easy to cultivate. They do well in rich leafmold with a pH of 4.5 to 6.0, in full or moderate shade. The fruit matures in the autumn and the seeds must be planted then and allowed to winter over. They may also be propagated by root division. A word of caution—don't plant these too close to where you like to sit as the blooms have a bad smell.

*White trillium (Trillium grandiflorum).* This beautiful plant resembles the purple trillium, except the leaves are light green, and the flowers large, white, and odorless. It begins to bloom in May or June, and the flowers last a month, becoming rosy hued as they mature. It prefers partial shade and humus-rich soil with a pH of 6 to 7. It is the easiest of the trilliums to cultivate, and is often found among common domestic garden plants. Propagation is by seed or root division. Seeds must winter over in order to germinate.

*Violet.* There are several dozen species that are grown in gardens and it is difficult to tell one from the other. Most prefer humus-rich soil and lots of moisture and a pH of 6. Different varieties prefer different amounts of shade, ranging from light to heavy. They all flower in the spring between April and June. There is no doubt that you can find one or two of these popular plants for your garden.

## Selected Ferns for a Woodland Garden

*Christmas fern (Polystichum acrostichoides).* A mass of fronds rise from a stout creeping root stock to a height of twelve to thirty inches. The fronds are long and narrow, once-pinnate, and evergreen, with the fertile fronds rising above the sterile ones.

This fern will grow in almost any humus-rich soil in good shade. It has a pH range from strongly acid to neutral and is not bothered by insects or disease. Propagation is by division.

*Cinnamon fern (Osmunda cinnamomea).* The cinnamon fern is one of our largest, most beautiful native ferns. It can reach a height of six feet and is found growing widely in eastern North America. Unfortunately it becomes quite unattractive in autumn and should be cut back. Each spring, fiddleheads emerge, covered with a dense white fuzz that turns brown and drops off. The dense mat-like root stock gives rise to several groups of fronds, which are formed in vase-like patterns. The fertile fronds appear first in the spring, growing from the outside of the crown, and are erect and thick-stemmed. As these mature, the upper portion of each frond becomes covered with fruit dots that change from bright green to dark brown. As these stalks wither they take on the appearance of cinnamon stalks, thus the name. The sterile fronds grow from the inside of the crown, curving outward, enclosing the cinnamon stalks in a vase-like pattern. Give this fern a large container and light to moderate shade. It prefers constant moisture and an acid soil with a pH range from 4 to 6.5.

*Common wood fern (Dryopteris intermedia)*. This species is evergreen with long, narrow, lacy fronds that reach a height of sixteen to thirty inches. Frond stems are covered with light brown scales that usually have darker centers, and the fruit dots are small and located near midrib of the pinnules. It grows from a center crown, which extends well above the ground. Cultivation is easy as long as ample moisture is provided—this fern likes its feet wet. It also prefers a humus-rich soil with a pH range of 4.5 to 7.5, and a shady location.

*Ebony spleenwort (Asplenium platyneuron)*. This fern is unusual in that its sterile and fertile fronds are completely different from each other in every possible way. The sterile evergreen fronds are only two to six inches long and prostrate. The fertile fronds are 24 inches long and erect with a lustrous dark brown stem. The sori are long and narrow, forming a herringbone pattern on the back of the pinnae. Both types of fronds are once-pinnate and grow from a spreading root stock. It prefers a moist, fast-draining soil with a pH range of 4.0 to 7.5, and light shade. It is found widely in the eastern and midwestern states.

*Hay-scented fern (Dennstaedtia punctilobula)*. This wonderful fern exudes a wax with the scent of new mown hay. What a lovely change for a city garden! It has light green, twice-pinnate fronds with brown stems, which reach a height of eighteen to thirty-six inches. It prefers a dry soil with a pH of 4.5 to 6.0 and full sun or partial shade. It spreads quickly from an extensive root stock and must be contained.

*Lady fern (Athyrium Filix-femina)*. This fern has many varieties that differ widely from each other in appearance and culture. The fronds are twice-pinnate with deeply toothed pinnules. The stems can vary in color from light green to reddish or wine colored. The fronds rise in dense tufts from a heavy root stock that is often only half buried. Depending on the variety, these plants prefer full sun or partial shade, although most prefer moist soil and a pH range of 4.5 to 6.5. They become unattractive in autumn and should be cut back. Protect from drying winds.

*Leather wood fern, marginal wood fern (Dryopteris marginalis).* A beautiful evergreen fern characterized by leathery oval fronds that taper to a point. It is twice-pinnate with blue-black sori found at the very edges of the pinnae, or leaflets. The stems are covered with light brown scales and rise from a creeping root stock to form a vase-shaped circle.

The leather wood fern prefers nearly pure leafmold and shady locations. It occurs throughout most of the eastern United States in soils that range from strongly acid to slightly alkaline. It can be propagated by both division and spores, and has few insect or microbial enemies.

*New York fern, tapering fern (Thelypteris noveboracensis).* This is a lower-growing fern, reaching a height of only eight to twenty-four inches, with yellow-green, ovate fronds. The fertile fronds (sporophylls) are not produced until summer and are somewhat longer and narrower than the sterile ones. It has a creeping root stock and spreads rapidly, crowding out other plants if not contained. The New York fern is suitable for drier culture, although it also does well in moist situations. It prefers a shady location, and an acid soil with a pH range of 4 to 6.0.

*Ostrich fern (Matteucia pensylvanica).* The ostrich fern is by far our most beautiful and spectacular native fern. It produces fronds that range in height from two to eight feet tall, in even clusters, from a dense creeping root stock. Give it full sun or partial shade and wet, porous soil with a pH range of 5.0 to 7.5. This is a northern plant, and is not found south of Virginia and Iowa.

*Wild Flowers*

| PLANT | TYPE | HEIGHT | RANGE | pH RANGE | BLOOM PERIOD | COLOR |
|---|---|---|---|---|---|---|
| Mountain aster (*Aster acuminatis*) | P | 3' | Labrador to Ontario, south to Georgia and Tennessee | 5–6 | July-October | Whitish to light purple |
| Bloodroot (*Sanguinaria canadensis*) | P | 12–14" | Nova Scotia to Manitoba, south to Florida, Alabama, Arkansas, Nebraska | 6–7 | March-April | White, pink |
| American bluebell (*Campanula americana*) | A,B | 6' | Eastern North America | 6–7 | June-August | Blue violet |
| Virginia bluebell, Virginia cowslip (*Mertensia virginica*) | P | 12–24" | Ontario to Minnesota, south to South Carolina and Kansas | 6–7 | April-May | Purple, pink, blue |

| PLANT | TYPE | HEIGHT | RANGE | PH RANGE | BLOOM PERIOD | COLOR |
|---|---|---|---|---|---|---|
| American columbine (Aquilegia canadensis) | P | 12–18" | Nova Scotia to Florida and Texas | 5.0–7.5 | May-June | Scarlet, white, yellow |
| Delphinium exaltatum | P | 2–6' | Pennsylvania to Minnesota, south to Alabama, Nebraska | 6–7 | July-August | Lavender, blue |
| Spotted or wild geranium (Geranium maculatum) | P | 20" | Maine to Georgia | 4.5–7.0 | April-July | Rose-purple |
| Hepatica (Hepatica Americana) | P | 6–8" | North—Nova Scotia to Alaska, south to Florida, east to Minnesota | 4.5–6 | March | White, pink, purple |
| Trumpet or coral honeysuckle (Lonicera sempervivens) | PV | | Newfoundland to British Columbia, south to Maryland, Colorado, California | 5–6 | July-August | Scarlet and orange |

| | | Height | Range | pH | Blooming | Color |
|---|---|---|---|---|---|---|
| Large yellow ladyslipper (*Cypripedium parviflorum pubescens*) | P | | Nova Scotia to Ontario, south to Alabama, Minnesota, Nebraska | 5–7 | June | Yellow |
| Showy orchis (*Orchis spectabilis*) | P | 6–12" | New Brunswick and Ontario, south to Georgia, Kentucky, Minnesota, and North Dakota | 5.5–6.5 | April–May | Purple, white |
| Shooting star (*Dodecatheon media*) | P | 12" | Manitoba to Pennsylvania and Texas | 4.5–6 | Late spring | Rose, white |
| Purple trillium, red trillium (*Trillium erectum*) | P | 8–16" | Nova Scotia and Ontario, south to North Carolina and Tennessee | 4.5–6.0 | May–July | Purplish-red to pink |
| White trillium (*Trillium grandiflorum*) | P | 8–16" | Quebec and Ontario, south to North Carolina, Missouri and Minnesota | 6–7 | May–July | White, changing to rose hued |
| Violet | P | 6–8" | Depends on species | 6 | April–June | Violet, white |

# ⊷ 18 ⊶

# Water and Bog Gardens

ONE OF THE MOST UNLIKELY and exotic choices for a garden design is the inclusion of dark pools, porcelain tubs, or rustic barrels filled with tropical water lilies and fantailed fish. Water gardens seem impractical to construct and too difficult to maintain on a rooftop or terrace, but this is not necessarily the case and the wide variety of plants that grow in water and bog gardens seldom seen outside their natural environment are some of the most beautiful in the plant kingdom.

Water gardens have a long and ancient history. Elaborate pools of flowers and fish are pictured on the tombs of pharaohs, while spectacular fountains and waterfalls graced the royal gardens of Chinese dynasties. The idea of using water as a focal point in a garden is not merely aesthetic, it's practical. Gardens are places of tranquility and relaxation; adding the soothing trickle of water or the hypnotic effect of a reflecting pool can be the ideal feature of a garden design.

The addition of water to your garden design can be as simple as placing a single whiskey barrel in an empty corner, or as elaborate as constructing a tile pool with waterfalls. What you need to consider is how much space you have and the structural soundness of the building beneath you. Water is heavy and can place a great deal of stress on the building below. Even so, a small pool should be possible in almost any situation.

Virtually any container that holds water can be used to create a water garden. The creativity that goes into choosing pool containers can't be overemphasized, especially since smaller, transportable containers are the

*Fig. 57   A water lily in bloom*

most practical for urban terraces and roof gardens. A good example of an innovative choice is the old bathtub with lion feet that was going to be carted away to the junk yard. It is sturdy, will stand up to the elements well, can be transported by two or three people, and is large enough to support three or four water poppies, some eel grass, a water hyacinth, a bed of sagittaria and a half dozen goldfish. With a little enamel paint (both inside and out) it could become the unusual and stunning focal point of your garden. Other containers that can be used include a plastic wading pool, whiskey barrel, horse trough, or antique crock. In addition, a wide range of fiberglass or durable plastic pools can be purchased from garden centers. The advantage of fiberglass is its durability, lightness, and flexibility. Many fiberglass pools are prefabricated and come in a large range of sizes and shapes, from small containers about two feet in diameter, to large, free-form tubs. The containers can be surrounded by containers of plants or left free standing against a wall or patio. Pools generally come in aqua or black, with black fitting into the natural landscape better as well as giving the illusion of greater depth. Any container used for such gardening should be at least twelve inches deep.

Choose a location that is predominately sunny, but if you plan to include fish in your pool, try to situate it where it will receive some shade in the afternoon. Most aquatic plants will need four or five hours of sun, but on a hot day the water temperature can become too warm for fish to handle. Also place it where it will not be surrounded by overhanging trees so you won't have to constantly clean out falling leaves and twigs.

The next consideration when setting up a pool is plumbing. A perfect ecological balance is extremely difficult to obtain and some form of filtering system is needed. Some gardeners may also wish to include a fountain. Modern aquatic equipment is so simple to install that beginners can create sophisticated effects easily and quickly. Modern pipe fittings make plumbing a minimal task of connecting hookups. The length of the pipes that connect the pump to the filter or fountain must be taken into consideration when choosing a proper pump. A pump that is capable of a water output of 600 gallons per hour will be considerably reduced if a longer pipe is used. There are many different electric pumps and automatic fountains sold through catalog houses and garden centers. Basically they fall into two groups: surface pumps and submersible pumps. Surface pumps must be housed outside the pool in a waterproof housing. Submersible pumps are placed in the pool itself, close to but below the water level. Installation of surface pumps is easy but more time consuming and more complicated than submersibles. They operate by drawing water from the pool through a polyethylene pipe and convey the water to a waterfall, fountain, or back to the pool through a second pipe. Powerful surface pumps can work several waterfalls or fountains simultaneously.

Electric submersible pumps are very easy to install and require little planning or maintenance. One length of polyethylene pipe is necessary to pump water to the fountain or waterfall, which must be located close to the pump. It is important to fit all pumps and pipes with efficient strainers in order to prevent clogging and mechanical damage. Before frosty weather the pumps should be lifted and drained.

Lighting is another consideration that can be incredibly sophisticated or simple, depending on desired effects. Pools may be lighted by hanging or mounting ground level lights, or they may be lighted by submarine fixtures that require underground circuits. You'll want to consider color and intensity of light as well as area and focus. For terrace and container gardens, versatility is an outright necessity.

One last thing to consider is what to do with the pool in the winter. Many water plants and fish will survive winters providing their pools do not freeze solid. Containers that are deep enough to be used year-round (more than eighteen inches) need to be insulated from the cold. The pool can be covered with a piece of plywood and a foot of heavy mulch. Pine needles and straw make the best insulators. Cover the mulch layer with chicken wire or a sheet of heavy plastic or canvas, weighted down with bricks or logs in order to keep the mulch from blowing away. A small hole should be allowed for air exchange into the pool. One of the best ways to insulate aboveground pools is by surrounding them with other containers of plants. The remaining odd spaces should be filled with bags of loosely packed soil. Once filled, the bags can be planted with bushy shrubs, creepers, or other flowers. Not only will this insulation protect the pool in winter, but it will keep the roots of water plants from becoming too hot in summer. A small heater may also be used during winter to keep pools from freezing completely, but they require maintenance, occasional checking, and efficient electric hookups. The smallest containers for water gardens should be emptied and stored for the winter to protect them from harsh weather.

Once you have selected and placed your pools, the next step is to decide what to put in them. There are three basic types of aquatic plants: those with root systems embedded in the bottom of the pool that send long stems to the surface and bear clusters of leaves and flowers (water lilies are the best example of this kind of plant); those with dangling root systems that float on the water (water hyacinth and water lettuce fall into this group); and oxygenators, or plants that are totally submerged, giving off fresh supplies of oxygen to the water (eel grass and *Hygrophila*). Any pool that is large enough to hold more than a single plant or two should be balanced with a combination of the three plants (especially if fish and scavengers are used in the pools to control algae and mosquitoes).

The most common way to grow water plants is in individual pots or trays placed in the pool container. This method not only makes pool cleaning easier, it allows for much more efficient plant control. You can add new plants or remove old ones without disturbing the rest. It is best to use plastic pots or trays, since clay pots will become water-bound, giving off a thin, muddy film. Containers are filled with a rich soil mix made up of 2 parts topsoil and 1 part cow manure. To this add a generous handful of bone meal and a slow acting balanced fertilizer (10–10–10). Subsequent feedings can be made easily by adding fertilizers in tablet or granular form. Tablets can be pushed into the center of the root clump, while amounts of granular fertilizer (one ounce portions are good) should be wrapped in cheesecloth and pushed down the sides of the container. I would avoid the use of greensand entirely, since it was formed from marine deposits and probably has a high salt content that could be detrimental to fresh-water plants and fish.

Once the plant is placed in the soil, the surface should be covered with a half inch of fine sand (not beach sand) or small pebbles to keep the soil from muddying the water. An alternate method is to place a sheet of burlap in the container before filling, then draw the ends up around the base of the plant and secure with a string. Water the plants thoroughly until they are quite saturated and place them in the pool. The pool should then be filled very slowly so as not to disturb the soil in the containers, for escaping air pockets in the soil can uproot the plants.

Like other types of plants, water plants are sometimes attacked by insects. Aphids are the most common insects that damage water lilies, and they are easily washed off the leaves with a hose. If you have fish in your pool, chances are the aphids will quickly disappear. More serious pests are the larvae of delta moths. The larvae will quickly eat the lily pads into shreds and must be controlled as soon as they are spotted. Affected leaves should be removed immediately. Dipel sprays contain a bacteria that kills the larvae and can be used without harming fish or snails. (When using any insecticides around a pool be sure that they are safe for fish and water plants, since most are not.)

# Fish, Scavengers, and Natural Balance

One of the most interesting aspects of water gardening is the creation of a miniature ecosystem whose success depends on a delicate balance of nature. In a balanced pool, the carbon dioxide in the water is absorbed by the water plants (mainly the oxygenating plants), which in turn release oxygen back in the water. The fish in the pool breathe the oxygen and expel carbon dioxide, which in turn is used by the plants. The various plants compete for sunlight, preventing the development of algae. Scavengers such as snails, mussels, and clams eat the small amounts of algae that manage to grow in the water. Finally, the fish eagerly feed on insect larvae, keeping the mosquito problem around your pool to a minimum.

The real trick of balancing a pool is providing it with just enough snails to eat the algae, but not enough that they begin feeding on the desired plants. It includes finding just the right number of oxygenates to keep the water pure and healthy for fish, but not enough that they compete with the water lilies and other flowering plants for nutrients and sunlight. Balancing is a simple concept to understand, but it is not so easily achieved in a pool.

The best way to achieve a balance is through careful trial and error. Often, water gardening catalogs will suggest how many scavengers, oxygenates, and fish are necessary for a healthy pool. Start from their formula and keep a close eye on your pool's progress. If the water tends to become cloudy, you'll know to add more scavengers to keep the algae population down.

There are countless varieties of goldfish that live comfortably in water temperatures ranging from 50 to 80° F. Comets, calicos, fantails, shubunkins, koi, and veiltails are especially good for outdoor use, and most will survive through the winter if the pool is deep enough. The Japanese koi is incredibly beautiful and available in a wide variety of colors. They have been bred for tameness and enjoy eating out of your hand and receiving a nice pat on their backs.

When water temperatures reach the low 30s, goldfish don't require food because their metabolism becomes incredibly slow. They live easily under ice and feed on the leaves of oxygenating plants. The rest of the year, their diets should be supplemented with a high protein fish food. Be careful not to overstock the pool. A good rule is to allow one gallon of water for every one inch of fish.

Introduce the fish to the pond from April through July and handle them as little as possible. Like all animals, fish are attacked by parasites and disease—two problems that are particularly difficult to fight. Don't ignore diseased or sluggish-looking fish; remove them immediately from the pool. Sometimes a fifteen-minute salt bath can be effective in helping fish that suffer from fungus diseases, and oftentimes live food such as *Daphnia* or worms help to keep fish healthy.

Though the addition of fish to a garden seems like an added responsibility, they are really a small burden and can make the difference between a clear, shimmering pool and a murky, unbalanced environment. But more, they can be a touch of exotic, active life submerged in your tranquil garden pools.

# *Water Lilies*

Probably the best known of all aquatic plants, water lilies are so beautiful that they might be a sole justification for beginning a water garden. They produce brilliantly colored and sweetly scented blooms that, if contrasted against the surface of a black reflecting pool or a tall row of border plants, can be quite breathtaking. Part of the genus *Nymphaea,* they fall into two broad catagories: hardy herbaceous perennials such as those native to North America, and less hardy, tropical varieties that can be planted as annuals in all but the warmest climates. Water lilies grow from rhizomes that, depending on the particular species, are planted at various depths in the soil.

In the late nineteenth century, a Frenchman named Letour Marliae produced several hybrid varieties of water lilies, ranging greatly in size, color, and shape. Some of the varieties are described as having autumn tones because they change color as they mature, opening as yellow and turning rich bronze.

Different species of water lilies require different depths of water. Some require pools that are one to three feet deep, while others need only three to ten inches of water. Most water lilies that are suitable for planting in deeper pools can be grown in shallower containers, provided they are started as younger plants. But the shallower varieties will not grow in deep water. (Remember that the depths given are measured from the surface of the soil the water lily is planted in and not the depth of the pool.) Some varieties and their required water depths are listed below:

*Shallow Pools (3 to 10 inches)*

Candida (white with yellow centers)
Conquerer (rose and crimson blooms)
Aurora (buff yellow)

Froebelii (bright red)
Pygmaealtelvola (yellow)
Laydekeri lilacina (pink)
Laydekeri rosea (rose pink)
Gonnere (white)

## Medium Pools (10 to 24 inches)

Escarboucle (crimson flowers)
Marliacea alba (white)
Sunrise (yellow)
Rose arey (pink)

## Deep Pools (15 inches to 3 feet)

Charles de Meurville (pink or wine red)
Gladstoniana (white)
Colonel Welch (yellow)
Masanjello (rose pink)

Hardy water lilies open in the early morning and close in the late afternoon. A single plant may produce as many as five blossoms at a time, and the flowers generally last for about four days. Colors range from white and pink to salmon, rose, crimson, orange, deep red, and sunny yellow. Through the middle part of the summer, new buds are ready to open as old flowers fade. Most hardy water lilies float on the water surface. They have thick, pad-shaped leaves, which are tough and leathery.

Plants are bought from nurseries or shipped through catalog houses, and they arrive with bare roots and leaves, oftentimes ready to bud. They should be unpacked and planted immediately. The best time of the year to do this is in the spring or early fall. Plants that arrive through the mail will need about three weeks to establish themselves, but careful planting will allow flowers to bloom within a month of setting it in the pool.

Like other perennials, hardy water lilies should be divided every two or three years. Plants should be repotted in new soil, and divisions should be planted in separate pots. You will notice several "eyes" or new growing tips on the rhizome which can be broken off and propagated in small pots. The cuttings will develop into blooming-sized plants during the summer. In New York it's best to divide water lilies in the early spring.

If your pool freezes solid in the winter, then it will be necessary to remove the hardy lilies and store them in a cool location. The plants should be covered with plastic or burlap, and they *must be kept moist* throughout the winter.

Water gardeners quickly discover that tropical water lilies are the most spectacular of plants. Not only do they produce terrific amounts of flowers, but they bloom well above the water line. In addition, unlike most of the hardy hybrids, tropical lilies give off lovely, sweet scents. Their blooms open both during the day or night (depending on variety) and range in color from blue and purple to yellow, red, orange, and pink. In warmer areas of the United States—particularly Florida and southern California—tropical water lilies bloom until Christmas. Night blooming varieties are a treat for people who spend a lot of time around the pool during the evening hours. They bloom at sunset and last until noon the next day, but since they grow so tall they are only suited for deep pools.

Tropical varieties are bought and planted in exactly the same way as their perennial cousins, with the following exceptions. They cannot be planted until water temperatures consistently exceed 65°F. during the day. They will not survive freezing temperatures. In the north it is best to treat them as annuals, discarding them at the end of the season. Most nurseries and catalog houses will not ship tropical lilies until it is safe to plant them. The other difference between hardy and tropical water lilies is that the tropical lilies grow from a tuber rather than a rhizome. Tubers are hollow and therefore easily broken or bent. Make sure the roots are spread out in the pot with the tuber planted in the center. Since tropicals are treated like annuals, they can be fed later into the growing season than the hardy species. As fall approaches, they should be fed every five or six weeks.

Water lilies make wonderful cut flowers and should be used all summer as floating centerpieces on tables or fresh accents throughout the house. Make sure you cut the newest flowers, which are characterized by their erect stamens. The blossoms will last better if they are floated in a bowl of water, and they will open and close as if they were still on the plant. If you want to keep the flowers from closing at night, drop some wax on the base of each petal.

## *Other Aquatic Plants*

Besides the several types of water lilies, there are an abundant number of aquatic plants to consider for shallow or transportable pools. Most of them grow in rich topsoils, though a few float on the water and dangle their roots. They are often cared for in the same manner as water lilies, with a few of tropical varieties able to survive indoors through the winter as houseplants. In general, they need plenty of light and frequent feedings. The following is a list of a few aquatic plants that do well in small pools.

*Acorus Calamus* (variegated sweet flag). This is a lovely foliage plant with sword-like leaves one-and-one-half to three feet in height, and similar to that of iris. The foliage is striped green and white, making a lovely contrast to other plants. It does well in shallow water and is winter hardy.

*Cyperus alternifolius* (umbrella plant). A tropical plant that is characterized by a long stem, it is topped with a rosette of leaves that radiate like the spokes of a wheel. This particular species grows two-and-one-half feet tall. Other members of this genus include *C. haspen,* the dwarf umbrella palm; and *C. Papyrus,* the Egyptian papyrus, which grows eight to ten feet tall. All members of this genus should be grown in shallow water and wintered over indoors.

*Eichhornia* (water hyacinth). This is a free-floating plant that is especially dazzling in a garden. Its violet spiked flowers have yellow eyes, and some of the more exotic species are lavender or purple with peacock eyes. The thick trailing roots are especially good for spawning goldfish. Water hyacinths are extremely difficult to get because they cannot be shipped interstate. Florida, Texas, and other states prohibit their importation and sale.

*Hydrocleys nymphoides* (water poppy). This is a tropical plant similar to the water lily, with small, pad-shaped leaves and three-petaled, yellow flowers, which open and close daily. Water poppies are excellent for small tubs and can be overwintered indoors in an aquarium. They should be planted in rich soil and fed once a month during the flowering season.

*Beardless iris.* The plants of this genus are all close relatives of the tall, bearded iris we are all familiar with, and are just as lovely. Included in this group is the popular Japanese iris, *I. Kaempferi.* These plants are really bog plants growing along the water's edge. Set their containers just below the surface of the water and plant as you would any rhizomatous iris. While dormant during the winter, they prefer to be kept on the dry side. Lift them from the pools but give them some protection. *I. Kaempferi* blooms in July bearing large, heavily veined, pancake-like blooms in shades of violet, blue, and white. They have neat sword-like foliage and grow to a height of three to four feet. They are hardy as far north as southern New York and will adapt to the coastal areas of New England and the Pacific Northwest. Their biggest threat is alkaline soil and alkaline water.

Other iris species for water gardens include *I. Pseudacorus,* the water flag or yellow flag iris that blooms in May and June bearing bright orange yellow flowers on 2 to 3 foot stems; *I. laevigata,* with its brilliant blue flowers borne on two-foot stems at intervals from June to September; and *I. versicolor,* the blue North American water flag, which blooms in May and June.

*Nelumbo* (lotus) This is one of the most unusual and striking water plants. The beautiful bowl-shaped flowers measure ten to twelve inches across and are produced in shades of cream, white, pink, and rose. The blooms may be single or double. The leaves are fan-shaped, measuring two feet in diameter and are held above the water. The genus is made up of two species, the Chinese lotus, *N. nucifera,* which is sometimes erroneously called the Egyptian lotus, and the American lotus, *N. lutea.* Most lotus varieties are tender although there are some that will survive as far north as zone 7. They need a water temperature of 60–65°F. and a rich soil mix. They grow from tubers that are quite large and easily damaged. They should be planted two inches below the soil surface in a five-inch container. The surface of the soil should be no more than eight inches below the surface of the water.

*Nymphoides.* Also called the fairy water lily, water snowflake, or floating heart, the leaves of this plant resemble those of water lilies but are much smaller, making this plant a good choice for a smaller garden. It also bears lovely white or yellow star-shaped flowers. Many are heavily fringed giving them an unusual appearance. Some species are hardy while others are tender. Often a single leaf will detach itself and float away forming a new plant. Depending on the species, they will require a water depth of from two to more than six inches measured from the surface of the soil to the surface of the water.

*Pistia stratiotes* (water lettuce or shell flower). This is a lovely foliage plant that forms a leafy rosette. It floats on the surface of the water and does particularly well in pools that have fountains.

*Pontederia cordata* (pickerel, pickerel weed). This bears spikes of lovely blue flowers reminiscent of hyacinths. The large green leaves are heart-shaped and the plant stands two feet tall. Plant it in two to six inches of water.

*Sagittaria.* This is a genus of twenty aquatic and moisture-loving plants with arrow-shaped leaves. They flourish in water that is six inches deep or more. Most are hardy but a few are tropical. Not only are they decorative, but they have valuable oxygenating capabilities as a result of the small underwater leaves that are much narrower than those that float on or are held above the water. The plant grows from a roundish tuber and some were eaten by Indians. Most notable of the group is *S. sagittifolia,* with its dark green leaves and clusters of white flowers. Place it in a container beneath six inches of water.

*Imperial taro.* A lovely plant with large leaves, this resembles caladium. The leaves are marked with dark brown and black on green. It is not hardy but can be wintered over if kept wet and placed in a cool location. Place the container just under the surface of the water.

*Thalia* (water canna). This is another flowering bog plant. Actually a perennial herb, its sharp, spear-shaped leaves are complemented by deep purple flowers atop long, arching stems that reach three to four feet. Position the container at six inches below the water's surface. Unlike the canna grown in the gardens, this plant is hardy.

## Oxygenating Plants

The most recognizable varieties of oxygenators for most people are the different grasses and seaweeds found in every fishbowl or aquarium. *Oxygenators* is a collective term for aquatic plants that are completely submerged beneath the water surface. They come in a variety of textures and shapes, and are almost always a shade of deep or bright green. Some are fern-like, some have long, ribbon-like leaves, and others have bushy, needle-like leaves or bunches of long flat blades.

Though most oxygenators are not readily visible or even attractive, they are an essential part of a water garden. Not only do they liberate oxygen for fish and scavengers, they absorb water impurities and help prevent the growth of algae. They are an ideal supplementary feed for fish, as well as a necessary camouflage for baby fishes. Finally, they require the most minimal care and survive easily year-round.

Oxygenators should be planted in small boxes or five-inch pots. A single pot will accommodate three or four plants. They should be kept in containers separate from lilies or other flowering plants because they will compete for nutrients needed to produce blooms. Cover the top layer of soil with about an inch of gravel to prevent muddying the water. Plant at least one bunch per square foot of surface area.

The following oxygenating plants thrive easily in pools: *Anacharis, Cabomba, Vallisneria,* milfoil, *Sagittaria sinensis,* green *Hygrophila,* red *Hygrophila,* jungle *Vallisneria,* moneywort, and *Ludwigia.* Most are relatively inexpensive and can be bought either individually or by the dozen. Many mail order houses sell packages of several varieties grouped together at special prices.

## Plants and Suppliers for Water Gardens

Paradise Gardens,
14 May Street
Whitman, MA 02382

Slocum Water Gardens
1101 Cypress Gardens Road
Winter Haven, FL 33880

Three Springs Fisheries
Lily Pond, MD 21717

William Tricker Inc.
Box 398, Dept. J-2
Saddle River, NJ 07458

Van Ness Water Gardens
Rt. #1, Box F,
Upland, CA 91806

# ❦ 19 ❦

# Hydroponics

HYDROPONICS IS A METHOD OF GROWING PLANTS without using soil. Derived from the Latin for "water work," hydroponic gardening has been practiced for more than three hundred years and has seen little change since German methods were developed in the late nineteenth century. It is based on a simple premise: If the amount of nutrients and water a plant receives can be carefully controlled, premium flowers, vegetables, and fruit will result. Hydroponic plants are placed in a soilless medium such as gravel or perlite. Then a specially prepared nutrient solution is pumped into the medium several times a day and drained into a holding tank for recycling. This process provides all the food and moisture needs of plants in the hydroponic garden.

If it sounds to you like gardening in a laboratory—a calculated, generic way of growing plants—you are right. Some gardeners are simply not attracted to hydroponic gardening, just as some cooks would never microwave a roast. But there are several advantages that hydroponics has to offer, particularly to the terrace or roof gardener who has limited space. First of all, the method allows the gardener to control practically every growing condition, ensuring good results. Hydroponically grown plants yield the largest and most abundant fruits, vegetables, and flowers one could imagine and are amazingly pest and disease free. Second, any plant that can be grown in soil can be grown in a hydroponic solution, except cactus, orchids, or other plants that require very arid conditions. Third,

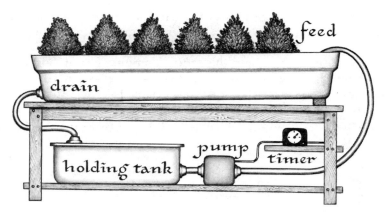

*Fig. 58   Automated hydroponic system*

hydroponics is perhaps the most economical way of growing plants, since all unused water and nutrients are reused. Finally, once the system is set up and the nutrient solution is carefully balanced, there is much less work to perform because the soil does not constantly have to be cultivated and the plants do not require frequent care.

Plants grown in soil can only directly utilize 5 percent of the nutrients they take in. The other 95 percent must be converted into a usable form. Hydroponic cultures provide 100 percent of the necessary nutrients in a usable form. Since the nutrients are diluted in solution, they will not harm roots. Since you are bringing nutrients to the roots rather than forcing the roots to grow out in search of nutrients, much less growing space is needed. A 10′ × 12′ growing space allows enough room to raise vegetables for an entire year. There is no need to revitalize soil or rotate crops from year to year since there is no soil to be worn out. Because the water and nutrients are used over and over, only 3 percent of the total water used in traditional gardens is needed (a factor that has made hydroponics essential to Israel and other water-scarce areas).

With an automated system, the only work that plants require is pruning and pinching new growth or training plants to grow along a trellis. Very few weeds ever crop up unless open growing flats are used. Occasionally, the nutrient solution must be checked for proper pH balance, but about twenty minutes a day will easily care for a 10′ × 12′ growing area— considerably less time than a conventional container culture.

In addition, hydroponics is becoming very popular for terraces and rooftops because the equipment is light, large amounts of dirt are no longer needed (eliminating the problem of carting the dirt up several flights of stairs), the stress placed on balconies or building structures is considerably reduced, and the inconvenience of watering plants is removed.

Hydroponics is also intriguing because it discounts several major conditions of conventional gardening. The growing medium is unimportant nutritionally—its only function is to anchor the plants; the plants can be placed very close together; and the natural amount of rainfall is unimportant. All these interesting and relatively easy changes in method make hydroponics a very attractive idea—especially for the future. The National Aeronautics and Space Administration (NASA) believes that hydroponics may be the most promising method of providing food for space travel.

# *Equipment*

The amount of equipment needed for a hydroponic garden is minimal, even for more elaborate systems. Basically, a garden requires growing trays, a holding tank, nutrient solution, water, and the growing medium, as well as some plastic tubing or pipes. More complex systems can be rigged to include pumps and timers to make the system even more care-free. You could even go away for a long weekend without making arrangements of any kind for the care of your garden.

There are several hydroponic systems on the market that are easily used and almost foolproof. Though the initial investment may seem high, the serious "hydroponeer" will find it well worth the money and time to find a good system. Growing trays may take many forms, but the best have flat bottoms and are made of fiberglass or plastic. Trays with ridges in the bottoms will disrupt drainage. Plastic wash basins, laundry baskets, and cat litter boxes all make suitable trays as long as they are more than seven inches deep. Metal trays are not recommended, since they corrode and can change the chemical makeup of the nutrient solution, adding toxins to the water.

The holding tank must be large enough to contain all the necessary solution to make each feeding complete. To provide for one tray measuring 3' × 12' × 8", the tank must hold seventy gallons of water. All pipes or tubes that connect the holding tank to the growing trays should be plastic or nonreactive rubber hosing. Connectors and fasteners should be bronze, brass, or plastic so that they will not corrode.

There are several types of growing mediums to choose from, but all have the same function. First, they should be heavy enough to securely anchor the plant. Three-eighths-inch gravel is probably the best growing medium, since it provides lots of support as well as good aeration for the roots. Gravel also is easy to handle, clean, and can be changed with minimal damage to plants if necessary. Perlite is second best to use as a growing medium, but it reflects light that can actually burn plant foliage. It will also blow in windy conditions and will not provide as much support for the plants. Perlite can be topped with an inch layer of gravel if desired. Sand and vermiculite are not suggested as growing mediums since both retain water for long periods of time. Whatever medium you choose, it must allow for the passage of air to the roots, and it should be light enough that plants can be pulled easily out of the medium without leaving roots behind (dead roots will rot and increase chances for disease), and it should be sterile and chemically stable, so as not to alter the chemical makeup of the nutrient solution.

A gravity-draining system is the simplest and most practical hydroponic system to set up. In this system, a large tray or several trays are set up so that one side is raised higher than the other. A drainage hole and hose lead from the low end to the holding tank. Plants are watered with the nutrient solution and the holding tank collects the runoff. A piece of screening should be placed over the drainage hole in each growing tray to prevent the growing medium from clogging the hose. An old bathtub with gravel spread six inches deep makes an ideal hydroponic system.

## *The Nutrient Solution*

There are several companies that manufacture nutrient mixtures for hydroponic cultures, and it is important to choose carefully since the outcome depends almost completely on quality and correctness of what the plants are fed. The nutrient concentrate must contain all the elements plants need for good growth. Some nutrients are naturally present in your water supply, while others will be lacking. In any case, they must be balanced to the correct proportions, so water analysis is essential. To have your water analyzed, contact your county agent or water supply company. They'll be able to tell you exactly what minerals and their varying amounts are contained in your water. A commercial agriculture or soil laboratory will be able to analyze your water as well. Take the analyses to a supplier of hydroponic equipment and ask which solution is best for your water. Nutrient solutions are sold in concentrate form, and the supplier will tell you the proper dilution to use.

The acidity or alkalinity of your water is also very important, and must be checked and carefully controlled. Acidity and alkalinity can change quickly and frequently in large water supplies, so do a pH test every four days. A pH of 6.5 is ideal, though a safe range falls between 6.0 and 7.0. The easiest way to test pH uses nitrazene tape dipped into the water and compared to a color chart. Water that is too acid can be neutralized with lime, and water that is too alkaline can be neutralized with a few drops of sulfuric acid.

Every time the solution is pumped through the growing trays and drained into the holding tank, some of the solution will be absorbed by the plants. Combined with evaporation, transpiration, and the moisture retained by the growing medium, you will notice that your solution level will drop little by little. For this reason it is important to mark the "full" level with a piece of tape on the outside of the holding tank. When the solution in the holding tank drops below 90 percent of the full capacity, you will need to add water. If too much water is allowed to evaporate from the nutrient solution, the chemicals become too concentrated and will damage the plants. The added water will not affect the nutritional value of the solution for about one week, but once water is added two or three times, the solution will become continually weaker and will need to be replaced. In the spring, less water will be lost than in the summer, when water must be added daily.

## Operating the Garden

The objective of hydroponic gardening is to grow a large number of premium vegetables and flowers in a very small space. To do this, the system allows the gardener to keep the growing medium damp at all times without suffocating the roots. The plants get plenty of oxygen at all times, and are fed directly usable nutrients through the growing part of the day.

Once you have set up growing trays, filled them with a suitable medium, tested your water, and mixed an appropriate solution, you will want to test your system to make sure it works properly. A good way to do this is by mixing chlorine bleach and water into the holding tank and then pouring it through the growing trays. This will not only allow you to make sure the system drains properly, but it will sterilize the growing medium, practically eliminating the chance of disease to your plants. After the chlorine solution drains into the holding tank, discard it and replace with clear water. Run the water through the trays a few times a day for about a week, changing the water periodically. This will rinse all the remaining bleach out of the growing medium.

Seeds should be started directly in the growing medium for three reasons. First, nursery-started seedlings are difficult to transplant into the soiless trays because all dirt must be washed from the roots. Soil that remains around the roots not only blocks the root openings, denying them oxygen, but also retains too much moisture and causes root rot. Second, starting the plants in the growing medium is the only way of ensuring there will be no soil-borne insects or diseases in the trays to affect the plants. Third, the process of transplanting from soil to gravel mediums is a great shock for the young plants, and may cause them to die because the roots must be thoroughly washed of all soil before they can be placed in the growing trays. The new plants will also have to adjust from taking nutrients from the soil and converting them, to taking nutrients directly from a solution.

Some large catalog houses sell seeds that are especially bred for soiless mediums, and these are the best to use. Most professional garden centers that sell hydroponic equipment will be able to advise you on the proper seeds to use. Generally, the seeds can be placed about a half inch below the surface of the growing medium and started with a quarter-strength nutrient solution until the seedlings are an inch or two tall. The strength of the solution can then be increased to half for a week or two, and increased to full as the seedlings reach three or four inches in height. Seeds should be spaced as close as one or two inches apart, since the roots will not be competing for soil nutrition.

The most popular method of feeding plants is to flood the growing medium twice a day—morning and late afternoon. It's important to feed plants during daylight hours only. The reason lies in the natural plant cycle of converting food into energy during the day (photosynthesis) and taking in oxygen at night. If the roots are not allowed to take in enough oxygen during the night, they will eventually suffocate.

There are many vegetables and flowers that are good subjects for hydroponic systems, including cucumbers, beans, peas, and other vine plants that do not have large root systems. Bush varieties of squash, melon, tomato, and eggplant are also excellent. Show varieties of gladiolus, tulips, and African marigolds will produce exceptional flowers for arrangements, and leafy varieties of vegetables including lettuce, Swiss chard, and mustard greens thrive in hydroponic systems. Pineapple, strawberries, and other difficult fruits can also be grown successfully in hydroponic gardens.

## *Maintenance*

Maintaining a hydroponic system is as routine and easy as taking care of any container garden. In fact, it is probably less time consuming. Aside from regularly checking the pH balance of the solution and the nutrient concentrate strength, the system should be flushed out about once a month. This is easily done by replacing the nutrient solution with water and running it for a day or two. Flushing out the system washes away any salt build-up in the growing trays and also lets you begin each month with a freshly mixed nutrient solution in the holding tank. The spent solution can be used to water your houseplants and other plants growing in soil mediums.

In addition to flushing out the system, the entire growing unit should be taken apart and thoroughly cleaned each year. The system should be sterilized with bleach and the old growing medium should be replaced. Filters and hosing should be flushed out and checked for corrosion or leaks. A mild, all-purpose fungicide such as captan will eliminate any fungus that gets in your system.

Any plants that develop diseases should be pulled up whole immediately, so as not to infect other plants. If the plant has developed a fungus, a mild dose of captan will effectively kill the fungus without harming other plants. But one thing is important to remember: Once a plant develops a disease, there is very little that can be done to save it. The best remedy is prevention—and that means eliminating disease before it starts.

The following list includes suppliers of hydroponic equipment and organizations that have more information on hydroponic methods of gardening:

Acorn Horticultural Equipment
1812 Laguna Street
Santa Barbara, CA 93101

Aqua Gro, Inc.,
Box 827
Powell, WY 82435

Dr. Chatalier's Plant Food Co.
Box 20375
St. Petersburg, FL 33742

Ferro Greenhouse Systems
2 Binnacle
Mount Harmony, MD 20836

Grow Master Hydroponics
McKee Road, Box E

Collegedale, TN 37315

H.H.H. Horticultural
68 Brooktree Road
Hightstown, NJ 08520

Hydroponics Society of America
P.O. Box 516
Brentwood, CA 94513

Hydro Gardens, Inc.
Box 9707
Colorado Springs, CO 80932

Hydroponics Corporation of America
745 Fifth Ave.
New York, NY 10022

Modular Hydroponic Gardens
Box 812
Fountain Valley, CA 92708

# ≈ 20 ≈
# Japanese Gardens

PROBABLY NO OTHER FORM OF GARDENING EXPRESSES THE IDEAS OF SERENITY, peace, and elegance as well as the Japanese garden does. Japanese gardens are simply the result of artistic and philosophic concepts that have evolved through time, dating back more than one thousand years. If the hallmark of Western gardens is to provide food for the table, the Japanese garden provides food for thought. Though it is lacking in vegetables and fruit trees, the careful observer will find an abundance of spiritual nourishment, as well as an articulate expression of aesthetics and the relationships of nature.

The most important influence in the development of Japanese gardening comes from Zen Buddhism—which is not only the predominant religion in Japan, but the elemental philosophy of the people. It influences nearly every cultural, traditional facet of Japanese life, from decorating a house to manufacturing an automobile. Evolved by a sect of Buddhist monks, Zen is a way of achieving enlightenment through meditation by relying on direct intuition. Like physicists who study the smallest particles of atoms to discover the order of the universe, Zen Buddhists contemplate the relationships of plants, earth, and physical objects to learn the secrets of nature. Consequently, their gardens became places of prayer, meditation, and beauty. These priests not only influenced the appearance and design of the garden, but also dictated a "way of gardening."

The philosopher Kenko stated the aesthetic ideal of Japanese gardening when he said, "In everything, no matter what it may be, uniformity is undesirable. Leaving something incomplete makes it interesting, and gives one the feeling that there is room for growth." For the Japanese, symmetry is an uninteresting (and unchallenging) design concept. This is one reason why formal Japanese gardens do not remotely resemble formal Western gardens. Instead of long reflecting pools and rows of flowers flanked by hedges that are intricate mazes, the Japanese garden uses plants, objects, and stones to depict symbolic scenes of nature. Large stones represent an island or mountain. Bamboo trees and pebbles are arranged to become a flowing river. Trees are not always grown tall and straight, but bend and twist to suggest wind or wilderness. Whereas the Western garden is designed to *conquer* nature, the Eastern garden tries to reveal some truth about it. The approach is always toward simple rather than complicated images, evoking mystery, peace, and comfort.

If the colors of the Japanese garden are less striking and brilliant than the traditional Western flower garden, the Japanese design places a premium on subtlety as well as texture. Moderate shades of green and brown, along with soft grays, prove interesting because they are always placed at an angle, providing the viewer with an endless combination of changing images depending upon his vantage point. Complemented by carefully selected objects such as lanterns and wash basins, the design is intended to set off visual stimulation, helping the viewer to meditate and reach enlightenment. This primary objective makes the Japanese garden a private place for consolation and personal discovery, which is perhaps the function of any garden.

Though it is probably impractical and undesirable for the average terrace or roof gardener to create a complete, formal Japanese garden, any gardener may wish to include some of the concepts of this very old and beautiful art. At most, it may lead you to create a symbolic corner of rushing pebbles and twisting trees—at the least it poses a set of provocative aesthetics to consider before formulating any design.

# Design

Because Japan is a tiny mass of islands dominated by rugged terrain and largely uninhabitable land, it is not surprising that the gardens are designed with a fine eye for compactness and with an acute awareness of spatial relationships. Lack of space is probably the pivotal common problem that Japanese garden designers and roof or terrace gardeners have to deal with. The Japanese discovered (as overpopulated city dwellers did) that a well-designed garden provides soothing relief from the rigors of daily life.

Three basic types of design evolved: the Sansui or "garden of movement"; the Karesanasui or "garden of contemplation"; and the Sakkei or "garden of borrowed scenery." Each is laid out to give the viewer a different type of experience.

The Sansui garden is designed to give the viewer a variety of moving images, created through the effects of waterfalls, streams, and ponds. Similar to the Western water garden (see Chapter 18), the Sansui presents bonsai trees and winding stream banks, with islands and stone bridges. For the Japanese, the Sansui is a hopeful garden, because the rushing water represents cleansing and long life. It is the most elaborate—if not most beautiful—Japanese design, but is least suitable for a roof or terrace. Still, it is possible to incorporate a waterfall or pool as a focal point of a design, and the roof gardener with extra money and space may want to incorporate Sansui techniques to give his garden a unique stamp.

The Karesanasui or garden of contemplation is less complicated, but certainly as dramatic. Its design gives the viewer many different experiences of motion, while relying completely on stationary scenes. The moving images comprise raked pebbles, stones, and bonsai trees that create dynamic "lakes," "waterfalls," and "streams." The gravel and rocks are laid out to create ripples and waves, while vertical stones form cliffs or riverbends. Colorful grasses or sharply twisted trees, as well as moss, are placed carefully to complete the illusion. Karesanasui gardens are the most symbolic gardens, and could even be likened to stage scenery—they create illusions for the viewer to contemplate.

The Sakkei garden is the most practical aesthetic garden design, because it incorporates a particular view that is actually outside the garden. This garden may or may not incorporate water or symbolic images, but its main feature always centers on "borrowed scenery." A view of a river, a bay, a city park or even particularly striking buildings is used, with the garden actually functioning like the frame of a picture window. Bamboo trees, large rocks, and water basins are used to frame the borrowed scenery in a way that appears different depending upon the viewers' particular vantage point. The garden is used to actually enhance the scenery behind it. Of the three different garden types, the Sakkei is by far most useful to terrace and roof gardeners.

Whatever design influences you, remember that the components of the garden are placed not in terms of a pleasing symmetry, but according to the way each object links together—the rocks to the trees to the water to the pebbles. Japanese design is *an internal way of approaching the composition of a garden,* rather than an external approach to creating a pleasing picture. The whole design is created step by step, starting from a single plant or shrub or physical object.

A concrete way of beginning to formulate a garden design is by dividing your space into a grid. Since the garden is made for *viewing* rather than *entering,* there should be no one vista, but several areas that serve as vantage points. On a small roof or terrace, it is quite possible to have as many as three viewing spots, if you are clever about setting up your space.

Once you have decided the natural vantage points, block them out on the grid. Remember that the strongest point in the garden will be the four points that outline the central block of the grid. One of these corners is the best place to put the focal point of the garden, and the other three points should be left open. Remember that if too much of the center space is used, it will dominate the garden, dwarfing everything else. Other components can then be blocked into the grid. Each component should be set at an angle, so that it forms a series of triangular relationships with all the other garden components, allowing for constantly changing views. Objects can also be placed to form curves or bowl-shaped images instead of triangles. For instance, two round water kettles can be placed next to each other at different heights to create an hour-glass shape. However you place your garden components, remember that the design should always tend toward simple images rather than elaborate ones. Finally, leave a little mystery; don't make the garden totally visible from one point.

# Garden Components

In Japanese gardens, bridges, walls, screens, and fences are as important as the selection of plants. The following section briefly describes the various components that are used in a Japanese design, as well as their traditional significance and usefulness to the terrace and roof gardener.

## Bridges

Bridges are an important aspect in Japanese gardening because they connect and link different areas of the garden. They need not be elaborate or expensive, and can be made simply from a few aged planks or a couple of railroad ties. Aside from offering dramatic structure within the garden, bridges direct the eye to various images and provide natural vantage points for the observer. They can cross running streams, reflecting pools, or raked pebble ponds.

## Fences, Walls, and Screens

These three components divide, connect, and surround the garden all at the same time. They are also one of the best components to create sight lines for the viewer. Bamboo screens can create paths or backdrops for unusual plants. They can also hide unwanted elements such as views of buildings or walls. Placed in an interesting arrangement, screens add mystery and contour to a garden. Fences and walls can be created out of rocks and shrubs, or by using bamboo poles wrapped in interestingly colored grasses. Every roof or terrace gardener is confronted with one unalterable boundary around the garden—the wall or fence that defines your space. Japanese designs offer a variety of interesting ways to camouflage or use this boundary to enhance or focus your garden.

# Islands

It is redundant to point out that islands are an integral part of the Japanese garden design. Whether or not water is actually present, it is the feeling of serenity that comes from water that is important to create. Large, jutting rocks, bonsai trees placed in appropriate containers, flat tree stumps make up the many objects that can be used to create an island effect in your garden.

# Ornaments

Three basic types of ornaments are used in the Japanese garden: the lantern, the water bowl, and the ornamental pagoda. Originally, lanterns were the objects that added light to the garden, but now they are primarily ornamental. They are available in electric varieties or traditional varieties that burn tallow candles.

Water bowls were introduced for washing—an activity that came before or after meditation. If they are not so functional in a Western garden, they provide an element of water and can be decorated with orange blossoms or water lilies. The ancient technique of Sozu employed water to create sound—functionally designed to scare away animals. Water trickles into a short bamboo tube that is balanced on two sticks. As the tube fills it tips and empties its contents into a stream or bowl of water, and then rights itself to be filled again. The base of the bamboo strikes a rock as it comes back into position.

The most ornamental object to include in a design is the miniature pagoda—a stone tower that resembles a shrine. These monuments were symbolic of Buddha's grave and were almost always placed in the central point of the garden. All of these ornaments should be carefully placed in relation to plants, rocks, or dividers, and must be considered with the original design—not as an afterthought.

Ponds, waterfalls, and streams also function as ornaments. Ponds usually come in two patterns—heart shapes or figure eights. Both patterns provide enchanting views, highlighting in particular the change of seasons. Raked "ponds" of gravel or pebbles must be carefully designed to mirror nature. An illusion is only effective if it captures the viewer, and the edges of these "ponds" must be raked upward to form higher ground. Plants that decorate the border of the "water" ought to be those found naturally at a pond's edge. Stones, bamboo, and bridges can be added to complete the illusion.

# Rocks

Rocks have always been a central part of the garden design because they represent an element that is intrinsically natural and cannot be changed. They speak for the massive elements of nature that dwarf the significance of man.

Rocks used in garden designs generally come in four basic shapes: tall and thick, large and squat, flat, and vertical arching. A variety of sizes and shapes is the best combination, forming mountains, islands, paths, bridges, and water basins. It is possible to have rocks even on an old roof by using feather rock. These are lightweight, usually porous rocks that appear to be quite massive. Feather-weight rocks should be used only for ornamentation, however—not as stepping stones.

# *Bonsai*

Bonsai has come to be a kind of generic Japanese expression without any real meaning, but in fact its definition is very precise. "To plant in shallow container" is not only the literal translation of the word, but an accurate description of the process. Of course every plant or tree planted in a shallow container is not a bonsai, but limiting a plant's root space is one of the first steps in creating bonsai.

The term also implies that the plant's appearance is carefully shaped and formed rather than grown naturally. By using various techniques, bonsai trees may be miniature forests not more than a few feet tall or they may be twisted to form a living sculpture. The basic idea is to use wire, bamboo poles, and frames to mold the shrubs or trees into a desired shape. Common bonsai forms include pines, yews, or Japanese holly that are grown in the shape of a twisting S.

The operation is simple but time consuming—taking more than a year to develop a single curve. First, the roots are trimmed and the tree is positioned in its container. If there is a tap root, it is cut off and the roots are spread out to radiate around the trunk. The root crown of the tree should be placed off-center in the container. It is set on a mound of soil so that it tilts to one side. Next, soil is worked around the rest of the roots. To add stability, copper wires are passed through the drainage holes of the container and tied around the roots to secure the plant. They should not be fastened too tightly or they will damage the plant.

Begin to trim the branches to take on the desired form. Always work with the natural form of the tree, remembering that asymmetry is the desired effect. Trees that put out two branches across from each other will usually have one of the branches removed. The remaining branches should radiate around the trunk.

Trees and shrubs that are still young and pliable can be wrapped with copper wire and molded into shape. The wire forms a sort of frame or cast. Eventually, the branches will naturally grow in the shape of the frame.

Shrubs that are pruned should be treated according to the nature of the plant. Boxwoods, azaleas, and yews are popular trees to mold into smooth mounds. The lower branches of shrubs can be removed to expose an interesting trunk or branch structure.

# *Plants*

It may seem inappropriate to discuss plants as the last part of a garden, but in the context of the Japanese garden, it is futile even to consider them before one has an understanding of the aesthetic concepts that create a garden. Like the apprentice who studies every detail of a trade for years before he performs any of its duties, the Japanese gardener must have a detailed knowledge of all the components that make up a garden, or its plants will reveal no truths about nature.

The soft earthy greens, browns, and grays that dominate garden colors are occasionally offset with splashes of brilliant hues—perhaps a flowering cherry or a clump of irises. Shrubs and trees in the garden are both evergreen and deciduous, so that the change of seasons plays its impact on the variety of images a garden offers.

Plants are generally chosen to create as natural a setting as possible. Large, brightly colored plants are most often inappropriate for a Japanese garden—they disrupt the simple beauty and are more distracting than attractive. Instead of using a colored border, the Japanese use a single flowering plant to highlight a fence or division.

Contrast is very important when choosing plants, especially in determining which shrubs and trees will be included in the design. The idea that "more is less" certainly seems to apply when choosing plants for your design, though the number of common Western houseplants that can easily be fitted into a Japanese-style garden is surprising.

The following list summarizes a few of the best plants to consider for a Japanese garden. It's important to remember that these pages only begin to introduce the subtleties and complexities of Japanese gardens, but they do offer a cheerful invitation to the gardener who is swept away by the mysteries and aesthetics of the East.

*Trees*

| | |
|---|---|
| Maple | Malus |
| Birch | Pinus |
| Crataegus | Prunus |
| Ilex | Thuja |

*Small Shrubs*

Buxus
Callicarpa
Cytisus austriacus
Daphne
Ferns
Hypericum
Juniperus
Potentilla
Spiraea

*Medium-Sized Shrubs*

Aucuba
Azaleas
Corylopsis
Cotinus
Cotoneaster
Mahonia
Nandina domestica

*Tall Shrubs*

Berberis
Camellia
Elaeagnus
Pittosporum
Rhododendrons
Salix purpurea
Viburnum

# Appendix

## Glossary (for Chapter 17)

**acuminate** Tapering to a point.

**bacterium** (plural—bacteria) A microscopic, unicellular, nongreen vegetable organism.

**compound** Used here to describe a leaf or frond naturally cut into several separate parts.

**crozier** An uncoiling frond.

**fiddlehead** A very young crozier that looks like the neck of a violin.

**fruit dots** Circular spots that are in reality a grouping of tiny capsules bearing spores and located on the underside of ferns' fronds. When immature, they are green and change to dark brown or black.

**indusium** The covering of a fruit dot.

**leafscale** A small rudimentary or specialized leaf, frequently without green coloring.

**ovate** A term used to describe a plant part that is narrow at the base, considerably wider in the middle, and pointed at the tip.

**pinna** (plural—pinnae) The primary division of a compound frond originating from the main stem; a leaflet.

**pinnate** A term describing the form of a compound fern frond that is feather-like.

> **once-pinnate** A compound frond with only primary divisions that emanate from the main stem.

> **twice-pinnate** A compound frond whose primary divisions emanating from the main stem are also divided, forming secondary divisions.

**pinnule** Small leaflets that are formed along the pinnae.

**prothallium** (plural—*prothallia*) The small green scale-like growth that is formed by a spore. The sexual stage in the life cycle of a fern.

**sorus** (plural—sori) Proper name for a fruit dot.

**sporophyll** A fertile frond bearing fruit dots.

# Index

Borage, 299, 300
Borax, 45, 56, 62, 94
Bordeaux mixture, 102, 119, 120, 125, 127
Borders, curved, 9
Borers, 112, 289
Boron, 44, 45, 49, 56, 62
Boston ivy *(Parthenocissus)*, 100, 161
Botanical tulips, 260–262
Botrytis, 102, 124
Bottom heat, for seed germination, 152
*Bougainvillea*, 217
Bouquet tulips *(Tulipa biflora)*, 260
*Bouvardia*, 162
Boxwood *(Buxus spp.)*, 160, 162, 163, 191–193, 363, 364
   *Buxus sempervirens*, 217
*Brachycome*, 29
Braconid wasp, 108
Breeder tulips, 241, 258
Bridges, in Japanese gardens, 360
Broad-leaved evergreens, 195, 197–198
   propagation of, 144, 146
Broad-spectrum insecticides, 92, 95, 96
Broccoli, 62, 281
*Brodiaea*, 252, 264
Broken tulips, 241
Broom *(Cytisus)*, 219
*Browallia*, 171, 270, 277
Brown rot, 102, 120
*Brunnera* (Siberian bugloss), 225
Brussels sprouts, 281
BT *(Bacillus thuringiensis)*, 85–86, 111–113, 115, 118
Buckwheat hulls, 67, 68, 69, 72
Budget for roof garden, 4, 5
Bud union, 148, 184–185, 200, 202
Builder's sand, 137, 138
Building codes, 3
Bulbous iris, 243, 244–245
Bulbs, 22, 42, 57, 61, 134, 231–265
Burnet, 300, 301, 303
Burning bush *(Kochia)*, 273
Burns, *Aloe vera* for, 302
Bush beans, 29, 286, 294, 296
'Bush Champion' cucumber, 289
Bush peas, 30
Bush squash, 30
'Butterboy' squash, 290
'Butterbush' squash, 290
'Buttercrunch' lettuce, 287
Butterfly gladiolus, 248
Buttermilk, 94, 115

*Buxus spp.* (boxwood), 160, 162, 163, 191–193, 363, 364
   *sempervirens*, 217
Bybloemen tulips, 241, 259

Cabbage, 29, 170, 280, 281, 294–296
   fungicide for, 103
   nutritional deficiency, 61
Cabbage loopers, 92, 93, 109
*Cabomba*, 348
Cacti, 29, 309, 311
Cactus-flowered dahlias, 246
*Caesalpinia Gilliesii*, 218
*Caladium*, 252, 264
*Calandrinia*, 29
Calcium, 35, 43–44, 45, 48, 62
Calcium hydroxide (quicklime), 35
Calcium nitrate, 54, 57–58
Calcium phosphate, 42
*Calendula*, 170, 172
California, Southern, plants for, 218
Calla lily *(Zantedeschia)*, 255, 265
*Callicarpa*, 364
*Calliopsis*, 29
*Callistephus*, 29, 270, 277
*Calluna vulgaris* (heather), 218
Callus formation, 140, 144
*Calycanthus floridus* (Carolina allspice), 217
*Camassia*, 253, 264
Camellia blight, 68
*Camellia japonica*, 140, 146, 161, 195, 217, 218, 364
Camera, light requirements determined by, 325
*Campanula spp.*, 29, 160, 161, 170, 277
   *americana*, 330, 335, 337
   *carpatica* (Carpathian bellflower), 225
   *medium*, 270
   *persicifolia* (peachleaf bellflower), 225
'Canape' pepper, 285
Candida water lily, 343
Candidum hybrid lilies, 250, 262, 263, 265
Candlestick tulip *(Tulipa Celsiana)*, 260
Candytuft *(Iberis)*, 39, 161, 170
Cankers, 88
Cankerworms, 112
*Canna*, 29, 253, 264
Cantaloupes, 290, 296
Canterbury bells *(Campanula medium)*, 270
Cape primrose *(Streptocarpus)*, 315

388 · *Index*